JEFFREY BENSON was born in London in 1937 and spent most of his working life in the wine trade whilst studying all the wine examinations. As a buyer he travelled extensively, searching out new, innovative markets.

He is the co-author of *Sauternes* and *St Emilion Pomerol* (Sotheby Publications), and *The Right Wine with the Right Food*, *The Definitive Cocktail Book* (Elliot Right Way Publications), and is also a major contributor to the *Global Encyclopaedia of Wine*.

One More for the Road is a personal record of his world travels. The author now lives in London and enjoys teaching and playing jazz saxophone.

ONE MORE FOR
THE ROAD
A Life in Wine, Food and Travel

ONE MORE FOR THE ROAD

A Life in Wine, Food and Travel

Jeffrey Benson

ATHENA PRESS
LONDON

To my wife, Clare
for all her patience and understanding
during my endless time away from home.

To Stuart Walton
whose help in editing my diaries was invaluable.

To all my generous hosts
for their kind hospitality during my visits.

Foreword

Enormous changes have swept through the international wine business since the 1970s. This has been a period in which a consumer boom in wine appreciation in the West has been accompanied by growing interest in wine in countries where there is a strongly developed tourist industry, but no indigenous wine production. These diaries chart the emergence of that new global wine culture, from the point of view of one who has worked in the UK trade for more than thirty years, and who now finds himself acting as roving wine consultant to parts of the map previously quite untouched by wine connoisseurship.

Jeffrey Benson's work involves him in tasting and choosing wines for the restaurant wine lists in a geographically diverse range of hotels and resorts, as well as initiating staff and guests on site into the fascinating and expanding world of contemporary wine. He also mobilises formidable technical skills in blending wines, creating styles that will prove suitable for a number of different outlets, including the retail trade (not a service most buying consultants are equipped to provide), and sharing with us his thoughts on what characteristics combine to produce a good wine.

As well as being the diaries of a wine expert, however, these are also the memoirs of a hugely entertaining, often acerbically witty, encounter with the modern tourist industry. The author uses his business experience to impart to us an insider's view of the hospitality industry, clocking up the Air Miles, eating and drinking heroically on behalf of the rest of us, having chance encounters in bars and street markets with a vividly colourful cast of supporting characters. Anybody who imagines that such a job can only be the cushiest of numbers will soon be disabused, as we find ourselves crammed into inadequate airplane seats, arriving battered and thirsty in executive lounges where a real drink is unobtainable, engaging in delicate negotiations with immigration officers, braving the challenging sanitation in a Bulgarian village, or else simply sitting alone and abandoned in a hotel bar in Cyprus waiting – as though for Godot – for a rendezvous with somebody who may or may not take our intrepid author to dinner…

The book will be divided geographically, with some of the destinations being visited several times over the years. Each section will open with a short introduction, in which the author sets the scene for that particular country or city, discusses how the wine and hospitality industries have developed during the years covered by these journals, and offers some general, non-wine observations on each place as a tourist destination. The introductions will be followed by the diaries of the various visits made, presented chronologically.

Contents

India and Dubai	*1989–2001*	13
North America and Canada	*1991–2002*	79
France	*1994–2001*	157
Sri Lanka, Maldives, India	*1999–2002*	199
Africa and Seychelles	*1993–2002*	229
The Caribbean	*1994*	289
Italy	*1995–2002*	305
USA, Japan, Thailand	*2002*	317
Far East	*2003*	347
Australia		
(via Singapore and Hong Kong)	*1992*	371
Europe	*1977–2003*	383
Dubai, India, Maldives	*2002*	413

India and Dubai
1989–2001

14–22 January 1989

14.1.89. We arrive at Heathrow Terminal 3 in time to have lunch before our Air India flight to Bombay, where we are to visit the Indage Wine Group, producers of a high-quality sparkling wine, Omar Khayyam, for whom I act as consultant in the UK. There are four of us: a specialist importer of Indian wine and food; Tom Stevenson, a wine writer specialising in sparkling wines; a wine buyer for a large group of retail wine stores, and myself. It isn't the most agreeable of journeys – the plane is extremely stuffy and the food awful, the final straw being that they run out of quarter-bottles of champagne – but our spirits are lifted on arrival. Although it is 7.30 a.m., two executives from Indage, Pai and Gopal, have come to meet us, solicitously hanging garlands about our necks.

We are taken to the Taj Mahal Hotel, which is absolutely superb, flanked by a statue of Sivaji, the Hindu nationalist hero, and overlooking the harbour and the Gateway of India, itself built in 1927 on the edge of the Bunder Pire in the old part of town. Although it is early morning, the temperature is already in excess of 90°F, and after a quick shower, we are off again on a two-hour drive to the beach at Akasa. We pass through market towns and shanty towns, and the squalor everywhere in evidence is appalling. On the way, we stop for refreshments, a glass of hadi (sugar cane juice) by the roadside, but the journey is by no means all plain sailing. Our first car turns out to have a puncture, an infirmity hard enough to ignore in itself, but when the passenger door falls off too, it becomes apparent that we may well not get to Akasa in one piece. No sooner have we hit the road again in a second car than this one breaks down. Perhaps we were not meant to get there after all.

But get there we do, arriving in time for lunch at another fine hotel, The Resort, situated right on the beach with its own swimming pool. Lunch is a buffet of various meat dishes, including pork vindaloo (which is not hot, as in the UK, but a

Goan speciality made with coconut vinegar) and chicken kastoori, accompanied by the locally brewed Haywards beer, after which we can't resist the prospect of a cooling swim beneath the palm trees. The taxi back to Bombay takes a pretty efficient hour and a half, and I sink into a deep two-hour sleep on our return.

We rendezvous at 7 p.m. for an aperitif of dark rum and soda, made with the excellent local, Old Monk. A 20-minute drive takes us to the Copper Chimney Restaurant, where Mr and Mrs Chougule, the owners of Indage, host dinner for fifteen. The beer with which we accompany it turns out to be another locally brewed lager – London Pilsner, which enjoys a 60% share of the Bombay market alone; but we also try Kalyani Black Label, a West Bengal brew of some distinction. The restaurant is very busy, with a nice, fairly informal atmosphere, and the cooking is fantastic – particularly the whole pomfret, a lemon sole-like fish of exceptional flavour. More Old Monk and soda makes a good partner for the food, as does the Marquis de Pompadour, a slightly sweeter sparkling wine produced by Château Indage for the domestic market.

Arriving back at the Taj at around 11.30, we decide to round off a convivial opening day in fine style with a nightcap (Lanson Black Label champagne) in the rooftop bar. But mindful of the fact that I have to be up again at 5 a.m., I am tucked up and spark out by midnight.

15.1.89. I had asked for a wake-up call, but seemingly somebody must have forgotten about it, for here I am awakening at 5.45 to a concerned call from Gopal. It turns out the hotel has not fallen short in its duties. They have indeed called me, not once but twice, but I have evidently slept through the phone both times. Ah well… Fortunately, I have had the foresight to pack, and am down in reception, showered and ready to leave in six minutes flat. We are driven in an inevitable mad rush to the station, where we only just make the 6 a.m. train to Pune (formerly known as Poona).

Bombay station is a sight not to be missed, a seething mass of people struggling to get to work by climbing on any part of the train, inside and out, leaving behind numerous bodies either

Street scene, Bombay

asleep or possibly dead under blankets on the station platform.

We travel First Class in a compartment with blacked-out windows, although I stand on the observation platform for a while and get a wonderful view of the sunrise. It allows me to reflect on my general impressions of Bombay after Day One. The squalor and poverty are beyond all comprehension. People living in mud huts in shanty towns may count themselves fortunate, as the remaining poor simply starve on the streets. As there is no compulsory birth registration, it is not possible to notify relatives when they die, and die they do every day. The average wage of a police officer is about £40 a month (at the current rate of 27 rupees to the pound). The number of beggars is frightening. Taking a walk outside the hotel as far as the Gateway of India, I find myself accosted at least half a dozen times by women with babies. Pai explains that easily 90% of them are non-genuine cases, the babies having been sold to pimps who disfigure them at birth, and then allocate them to various beggars, who are allowed to retain only 10% of the receivables.

Motorists drive completely on their hooters. Indeed, it is considered polite to hoot. On the backs of most vehicles is a sign that reads 'HORN OK PLEASE'.

Having travelled through some truly stunning scenery, the train arrives at Pune at 9.30 a.m. in a very busy station bustling with people. The town is much cleaner than Bombay, and the people generally better-dressed, mainly in white – a tradition that dates back to the days of the Raj. The Indian Army was based here, as the climate is cooler than Bombay. A small minibus then takes us on to the Château Indage Winery we are visiting, a journey of approximately two hours through small shanty settlements to the little neat village of Narayangaon.

We are greeted at the winery by the managing director, Mr Chitterle, and his oenologist, who turns out also to be the foremost viticultural expert in India. After drinks, we are treated to a buffet lunch of pan-fried pomfret, dhal, various salads and rice, accompanied by their 1988 Ugni Blanc, a fine dry white wine.

After lunch, three of us go and look around the village, which is situated about five minutes away from the winery. It's fruit and vegetable market day, an amazing display. The village comprises one main street, approached through an archway, with dozens of tiny shops offering everything from a haircut, shave and ear picking, to bangles, shirts and saris.

Following a short rest, we rendezvous again at 5.30 for a visit to the winery, which was set up in 1980 in collaboration with Champagne Piper-Heidsieck, with vineyards planted with imported vines such as Chardonnay, Ugni Blanc and Pinot Noir. It's fully equipped with the latest imported French stainless steel fermentation tanks and computer-controlled equipment, all very impressive. As with European vineyards, they have a similar problem in dispersing the birds, who eat the grapes prior to harvest; but whereas in Europe they have mini-cannons that fire blank cartridges at regular intervals to frighten them off, here they use a more interesting and novel technique. As labour is cheap, they employ local men from the nearby village to go through the vineyards brandishing gaucho-style bullwhips, cracking them as they go about on 24-hour shifts.

After tasting our way through the range of their well-made wines, we meet again in the courtyard for drinks at 8 p.m. The weather here is much less humid than in Bombay. It's seemingly more of a dry heat, cooling down noticeably towards evening, so that I have to put on a sweater. (The daytime temperature had been up in the 80s Fahrenheit!) Supper, served at 10.30, consists of fried chicken, dhal, mixed vegetables, naan bread and rice.

Accommodation at the winery is very basic, to say the least. I'm sharing a room with two of our guests but, having been starved of sleep for the last 36 hours, I sleep like a log until 6.30 a.m.

16.1.89. Having awoken early, I have time for a run before breakfasting on scrambled eggs, toast, fruit and coffee at 9. Half an hour later, we depart by road for Kolhapur, taking a route through Pune. The journey takes a sobering nine and a half hours, but fortunately our comfortable minibus has been fully stocked with sandwiches, whisky, gin, rum, beer and mixers. Just past Pune, we stop at a snake farm, where I have my picture taken with a cobra draped around my neck. Tom Stevenson, who has a deep-seated fear of snakes, refuses to go anywhere near them, as they are not in secure pens; but after much convincing by the snake-keeper, he allows a seemingly friendly python to be placed around his neck, with the instructions to hold the snake by the neck and tail. Just as we take his photograph, Tom suffers another attack of nerves that leads him to squeeze the python's neck a little too hard, resulting in it throwing up all over him, all of which is picturesquely captured on film.

Later in the day, we pause again at a local village market, where I buy some beautiful handmade bangles. We are travelling south through the Western Ghats, and the scenery is once again superb. At another stop, a tin shed with a fascia saying 'Suraj Hotel' fascinates me. Four cubicles that I thought were for dining turn out to house bare wooden slatted benches supporting twenty sleeping people.

At 7.30 p.m., we arrive at the Shalini Palace Hotel in Kolhapur, having completed the last 15 minutes of the journey in one of the local open taxis (or tuk tuks). More like a three-wheeled motorcycle with a hood, this makes for a pretty hair-raising experience. The hotel, which was built in 1934, is owned by the Indage chairman, Mr Chougule, and is a beautifully restored and converted former Maharajah's palace. I am in room 307, a vast and luxurious place with a communal balcony that runs around the entire first (top) floor. It is in complete and welcome contrast to last night, and I am soon busy with the camera.

We rendezvous at 8.30 for an endless stream of Old Monk rum and sodas. The eating timetable here appears to be roughly similar to that in Spain, and we have yet to dine any earlier than 10.30. The food is all regional specialities, and surprisingly mildly spiced, quite unlike English versions of Indian cooking. Indeed, all the food we have had so far has been totally different to anything found in the UK, and quite superb, the delicate and judicious use of spices serving to complement the main ingredients rather than overwhelm them. It is strongly advised that one avoids water and ice cubes (unless they are from bottled water), as well as salads, fruit, ice cream and any food from unrecognised hotels or restaurants; but for me, it's been so far, so good. We retire at just turned midnight, following a hugely interesting and exciting, if tiring, day.

17.1.89. I awake at 7.30 a.m. and catch the most amazing sunrise from my balcony. Going for a walk by the lake, I come upon Gajalaxmi, a female elephant housed in a small open temple. You hand her a two-rupee note, which she takes in her trunk and passes to the keeper; then you bow your head, and she places her trunk very gently upon your head to receive her blessing. The Hindus, who worship the elephant god, Gamesha, process around the elephant 21 times intoning prayers, but for such a venerated creature, she seems amazingly friendly and approachable, and is quite content to be stroked at great length. I return to the hotel for breakfast at 8.30: fresh orange juice, scrambled eggs on toast (written on the menu as 'scream bled eggs'), and coffee.

At 9.30, we embark on a sightseeing tour, taking in first the New Palace (built in 1874), and then the eleventh-century Panhala Fort in the village of Panhala, 2,500ft above sea level, before returning to the hotel for a 1.30 lunch. We are offered a superb range of dishes, from Afghan chicken cooked in a sauce of yoghurt blended with delicately balanced spices, to mutton rogan josh in a deliciously rich meaty gravy. The locals suggest that I accompany this by nibbling on a green chilli. This was an experience I shall never forget, as it turned out to be the hottest type of chilli produced, and removed my ability to speak for over an hour. The local firewater is called 'toddy', and is made from palm sap collected before sunrise and instantly distilled. It must evidently be drunk within six hours. Too late today, but I hope to try it tomorrow in Goa.

After lunch, we go shopping in Kolhapur's town centre, where there are many small businesses of one sort or another, travelling by rickshaw taxi. In bare feet, we visit the main temple, and then go to the Street of a Thousand Cobblers to buy sandals. We take tea at Mr Chougule's country house, which is very expansive and full of classical old Indian furniture. For the first time, I am bitten by mosquitoes, and it is a relief to be under the shower on our return to the hotel.

We meet at 8 for drinks in the bar, prior to a specially arranged dinner, which turns out to be a thali, a Southern Indian speciality, an assortment of small dishes in the fashion of Greek meze, all quite delicious and ranging from local vegetarian to classical meat dishes. The temperature today has been in the 80s again, but it has been a more restful day, and much needed at that. We are told there will be a 5.15 a.m. alarm call tomorrow, to begin the six-hour minibus drive southwards to Goa.

18.1.89. The alarm call comes at 5 a.m. and we breakfast at 5.30 – scrambled eggs on toast, orange juice and coffee once again. We begin the journey to Goa at 6.15. En route, we stop at a village called Sawantwadi, which specialises in artefacts of hand-carved wood, and where I buy three elephants and two merry-go-rounds. There is one more short stop, at which we refresh ourselves with sugar cane and coconut juices, and then settle down for the long onward drive to Goa.

Arriving at the Goan border (which ceased to exist in 1916), we pay the expected 50-rupee bribe that allows us to circumvent any paperwork, and make the Taj Holiday Village resort by 2.30. The change in terrain and vegetation is remarkable, having gone from arid and barren to the greenness and lushness of Goa, where all is rivers, palms and coconut trees. The hotel village complex is stunning, consisting of individual cottages dotted around a pool area, many overlooking the sea. (Note for future visits: the best-sited cottage is No. 61.) A lovely balmy breeze helps to ensure perfect climatic balance.

Lunch by the pool is grilled tuna; this region has a strongly fish-based cuisine. I go for a swim in the pool, which features a sunken bar, and then for a bathe in the Arabian Sea, followed by an hour's sleep in a hammock. On awaking again, I pay a visit to the Sports Centre for a workout in the gym, a sauna, and then a massage that includes one's head being soaked in olive oil. Then it's back to my cottage for a well-needed shower, and into my whites.

We rendezvous at the pool bar for aperitifs at 7.30, where I try feni, a local spirit made in varieties from either cashews, palm or apples. All the versions taste quite unusual, particularly, the cashew. Apparently, the best producer is somebody called

Madame Rosa. The locals drink them mixed with bitter lemon or lime. We have a buffet dinner consisting mainly of Goan specialities in the beach restaurant, with a band playing in the open air. The main influence in the cooking is of course Portuguese, with the focus on a fine range of fish, including lobsters and shellfish. This really is an idyllic place, with so much to absorb, a complete culture shock after the poverty of Bombay. After dinner, we repair for a drink to the nearby five-star Agua Fort Hotel, and are in bed by midnight.

19.1.89. After a 7 a.m. wake-up call, we breakfast in the beach restaurant on a buffet of regional specialities – delicious potato pancakes, eggs, dhal and fish.

At 8, we leave on a trip into the centre of Goa. The capital is Panjim (or *Panaji*, 'land that does not get flooded'), which takes around an hour to reach, with a ferry crossing along the way. There used to be a bridge, but it recently completely collapsed into the Mandovi River, with a large number of fatalities, and was the subject of a supposed investigation. This apparently revealed that, as the contractor had had to hand out so many bribes, he'd had to cut down on the cement-to-sand ratio. Nothing further was heard.

Panjim is a sprawling town on the coastline dotted with cafés, bars and tacky gift shops, but with an excellent market in the town centre. A five-kilometre drive takes us to Dona Paula, a delightful beach resort with lovely views of Marmago harbour and the Zuari River estuary. Here I buy a much needed local straw hat. We are back at the hotel by 12.30, and I have a swim and a palm feni sour, and then a superb lunch of barbecued lobster, followed by a couple of hours' rest by the pool.

At the bar later on, I try a cocktail called Palmeiro, a mixture of cashew and palm feni with gin, brandy and various fruit juices – interesting, to say the least. I have a six o'clock meeting with Gopal, and then shower at 7.

I am beginning to feel slightly queasy. It might be a result of the very rich masala sauce that was served with the very large, very rich lobster at lunch. Meeting again in the bar at 8, I try a couple of Old Monk rum and sodas to try to ward off any impending ailment, but the feeling doesn't pass. Two others are feeling similarly unsettled (not surprisingly, since we all had the same lunch), and I briefly consider not joining the party for dinner. However, not wishing to seem churlish, I go along and we arrive at O'Coqueiro Restaurant in Alto Porvorim, four kilometres out of Panjim, at 9. Another two exceedingly large rums and I start to feel better again at last, and am able to enjoy a light supper of stir-fried chilli beef and vegetable noodles.

The restaurant is locally famous for having been the place where the serial killer Charles Sobrad was finally caught. It is pleasantly decorated, and has a large covered terrace with palms and ferns, ceiling fans and large bamboo armchairs – a very congenial atmosphere. Sadly, the food was stone cold, but we have a good, jovial evening nonetheless.

Arriving back at the Taj village at midnight, we have a final nightcap by the pool, and are in bed by 1 a.m.

20.1.89. Awaking at 7.45 a.m., not surprisingly slightly hung over, I take a light breakfast and then repair to the health club for the full treatment – a head and full body massage, manicure and pedicure. After a short swim, I pack my case. We leave the hotel at 11.30 for Goa airport and a 50-minute flight to Bombay.

There, we check into the Centaur Hotel on Juhu beach, where I immediately go for a swim in the pool. The sea here, we are told, is to be avoided like the plague, as it is full of raw sewage. I go shopping downtown and buy three new outfits, which like all the clothes in India represent extremely good value, then back to the hotel for a shower and change. Later at 7 I meet the others in the bar, together with all the Chateau Indage staff. We eat at the hotel, which currently has a Sri Lankan festival running, tasting every dish available from a menu that takes in cutlis, patties, badhapu malu, thambapu kadala, thakkali isso, malu hodhi, kukul mus thakkali, bola curry, uru mus miris badun, kadju, ala badun and indi appa. After that series of mouthfuls, washed down with copious quantities of London Pilsner, I get to bed at 11.30.

21.1.89. The alarm call comes at 3.30 a.m. A bus takes us to the airport at 4, and we are frustrated to find that not only can we not upgrade our tickets but we can't even secure the seats we were allocated (the row with legroom on a 747 is row 18). We try to contact Michael Mascarenhas, the commercial manager of Air India, but he isn't available. The flight takes off at 7.30 a.m. local time, half an hour late. The service and overall quality on Economy flights with Air India is disgraceful. There is a complete lack of facilities, not to mention in-flight drinks. We set our watches back five hours, and arrive at Heathrow, Terminal 3, at 11.20 a.m.

To summarise: this has been an excellent and most fascinating trip. I am left with the tantalising feeling that India is a charismatic country that will require many more visits even to begin to understand it. As it happens, my education will resume later this very year.

30 October–4 November 1989

30.10.89. I arrive at Heathrow Terminal 3 at 2.30 p.m., where my travel agent has arranged for me to meet an Air India representative. Time goes by, and nobody shows up, so I check myself in at 4.30, and it seems I have already been upgraded to Business Class. This entitles me to visit the Maharajah Lounge, where free drinks, canapés, newspapers and TV are provided. I avail myself of a couple of whiskies, sample their smoked salmon and read for a while – a very civilised way of waiting for the flight to be called. Eventually we are summoned to gate 27 to board flight AI 20 to Bombay.

We board the plane with no queuing, and I am given a superb seat (62K) on the upper deck by the emergency exit. We are plied with unlimited Piper-Heidsieck champagne and numerous gifts, and settle down for take-off at 6.25. Then comes an announcement from the captain: 'Is there a doctor on board?'

Believe it or not, there is. It seems an elderly Englishwoman has been taken ill, and the doctor decides in due course that she is too ill to travel. This results in a long delay, while all the luggage has to be removed in order to locate and remove hers. We eventually take off at 9 – two and a half hours late, and a bottle of champagne to the good.

Dinner is fairly good, chicken curry, dhal, vegetables, naan bread and rice, accompanied by even more champagne and a truly dreadful film, *The Accidental Tourist*, which puts me to sleep, but I have a fitful night, despite the comfortable seat.

31.10.89. I awake at 3.30 a.m. and have a light breakfast at 4 (actually 9.30 a.m. local time). We land at Bombay at 10.25, local time.

It is customary when visiting hosts in India to take a gift or two, and I have been detailed by Indage to bring six bottles of Johnnie Walker Black Label whisky and six Marks and Spencer button-down, short-sleeved striped shirts.

I wait half an hour for my luggage, only to find, when it emerges, that there is whisky pouring out of my suitcase. It appears the baggage handlers must have been flinging the suitcases onto the carousel. This leads to the acutely embarrassing experience of having to pass through the 'Nothing To Declare' channel leaving a trail of Johnnie Walker Black Label all over the floor, the aroma of which overpowers the whole customs hall. It is a relief, then, to be greeted by a member of Air India staff who has received a telex from London to look after my needs, and couldn't be more helpful in whisking me through customs without a word, and also arranging for me to be upgraded on my return flight.

I am then met by Indage's inseparable Gopal and Pai (whom I have started to refer to as the Bill and Ben of Bombay). They take me to my hotel, the Sheraton Searock, which is right on the ocean, and where I have a room with a superb view. As the temperature is already in the 90s, I decide to get changed but, on opening my suitcase, discover that not one but two bottles of whisky have been broken, soaking every article of clothing. However, my bell captain immediately summons the laundry maid, who spirits everything away and returns within two hours having boiled my suit, which has now shrunk to fit a twelve-year-old boy, and similarly reduced my shirts to the extent that they are all two sizes smaller. The suitcase itself has been baked in an oven, so that the underside is nicely caramelised. In fact, everything is ruined, and there is a very strong smell of whisky in my room.

A 35-km drive takes us to The Resort at Akasa Beach, a five-star hotel with pool and a homely restaurant, where at around 4 p.m. we have chicken jalfrezi, rice, dhal and the local beer. Once again, I must get used to the quasi-Spanish eating times: lunch between 3 and 4, dinner around 9 or 10.

The landscape is stunning, as the monsoons have just finished and so the foliage is lush and green. It is also the final day of the week-long New Year festival.

We return to the hotel, where I have an hour's sleep and a shower before meeting the others at 8.30 for dinner. As I am ready early, I venture out shopping to replace most of my clothes, my purchases including a made-to-measure suit for about £20, which will be delivered to my hotel by the morning. A strong wind is getting up. The festival is still going on though, with fireworks and crackers being let off in the streets, and many small stalls selling hot food. Some of it looks tempting, but I am sure to be hospitalised if I were to be unwise enough to sample their wares. I have it on good authority that a number of the street food sellers use diesel oil for their cooking.

Back at the hotel, we have drinks in the bar – Olde Adventurer XXX rum, which turns out to be very good with lime and soda (no ice, of course). Then it's off to the restaurant, which is called Sheetal Samudra-Juhu, and where I am greeted from beneath the table by a spectacularly large cockroach. Notwithstanding that, it is a first-class seafood restaurant, the motto of which is Khane-ka-maza ('The Pleasure of Eating').

The starters are special Singapore lobster, served portioned in a medium-hot black bean sauce, jumbo prawns in Indian-style Szechuan sauce, and superbly fresh tandoori prawns with onions in a green mint sauce. Following those, we proceed to roomali roti, lamb maharajah, chicken with black dhal, and murgh malai masala. An interesting digestif is supari – husks left over from the preparation of the garam masala. It is all washed down with copious quantities of Old Monk rum and soda.

I finally retire at 12.30 a.m.

1.11.89. My alarm call comes at 7 a.m. Breakfast consists intriguingly of an Indian tomato omelette with bacon, sausage and Indian-style baked beans, followed by toast and coffee.

I am collected at 8, and driven to my first appointment, an 8.30 meeting with Rajiv Agarwal of the advertising and PR agency Nehus, which handles all Indage's wine promotional activities. We discuss aspects of the new packaging, cartons and labels, for Omar Khayyam, as well as considering new PR initiatives for the export market.

At 10.30, I have an extremely productive meeting with Dr Mhaski of the State Trading Corporation, and its general manager, Mr Shivaram. They give me a very detailed two-hour presentation on how to arrange financial marketing support for the export programme. My third appointment, at 12.45, is with

Ranjit Mansukhani of Hindustan Breweries, to discuss the viability of importing Bombay Pilsner, a fine 5% lager, into the UK. It's quite a fruitful exchange, and I shall be visiting the brewery tomorrow.

At 2 p.m., we have lunch at the Copper Chimney – tandoori chicken, kebabs, yoghurt with potatoes and curd, roomali roti and dhal.

My fourth appointment of the day, at 3.30, is with the new managing director of Indage. He is the chairman's eyes and ears, and frankly quite an unnecessarily difficult man, and so my charm has to be turned on to the maximum.

After a short meeting with Gopal and Pai, I return to the hotel at 6, going straight for a dip in the pool to cool off. The weather is extremely hot and humid. Thank goodness all the places I have visited so far have had air conditioning, a fact that contrasts glaringly with the extreme degree of poverty that one sees while driving through the city.

I am collected at 7.30 to be taken to a special banquet at the Oberoi Towers Hotel, whose Kandahar Restaurant is very highly rated, and correspondingly expensive. Drinks await us – far too much Omar Khayyam, in fact – followed by chicken kebab cooked in the tandoor, enormous tandoori prawns, rogan gosht, mixed vegetables with tomato, and rice with more chicken. All this superb food has been prepared especially for us by their very talented chef, Vineet Bahtia, in this new restaurant that aims to provide authentic Indian cuisine, even to the extent of not offering any cutlery. You eat everything with your right hand: quite an experience! It is all accompanied by even more Omar Khayyam.

The restaurant is in the latest extension to the Oberoi Towers, which is the most amazing five-star hotel, built around a hollowed-out centre with huge marble pillars. It has two superb bars with live music and no fewer than ten restaurants. Later I meet the general manager and the food and beverage manager, and am asked if I would give a wine talk to their staff on Saturday.

I return, exhausted, to the hotel at 12.45, but am woken at 3 a.m. by the stupid housekeeper, who persistently rings my bell to explain that she has forgotten to replenish the water jug. I tell her in no uncertain terms where to pour it, and then have great difficulty getting back to sleep, not least because I have a nasty bite on my neck.

2.11.89. I awake at 7 a.m., pack and then go down to a breakfast of scrambled eggs masala (which contains lots of chillies), tomatoes, onions and bacon. The eggs are so hot, I need a large soda water immediately afterwards!

I am collected at 8.45 to embark on a seven-hour drive to the Indage Winery. We stop at the Hindustan Brewery en route for further discussions with the head brewer, concluding with a tour of the fairly large, impressive facility, and leaving at noon. The drive continues along possibly the worst roads I have ever seen, full of giant potholes, not helped by endless punctures. I now realise why all Indian cars seem to carry at least four tyres, which are all as bald as the ones on the car.

We stop for lunch at a new resort complex called El Taj at Khandale on the Bombay to Pune road, where we have excellent tandoori chicken, chicken masala roti and dhal, all eaten of course with our fingers, and accompanied by the local Haywards beer.

The journey continues through the stunning scenery of the Western Ghats Mountains, during which we see the sixteenth-century carvings in the Karla caves, and then through many small villages, before arriving at Narayangaon and the winery. We are fulsomely greeted by the chief administrator, a great character who is an ex-Indian Army captain, complete with uniform, curled moustache and swagger stick, together with the winemaker and his team. After a quick change in the guest cottages, we are ushered into the garden for drinks – a special old rum – and a fine barbecue of chicken and lamb biryani.

We retire at 11. The accommodation is, to say the least, primitive. There are no sheets on the bed. There is a lizard in my suitcase, and my bites are disturbing me.

3.11.89. We are taken on a drive through breathtaking scenery to a small fishing village, where we buy fish for lunch. The inhabitants here all live in home-made tents, and do their fishing with the aid of circular, coracle-type wicker baskets, lined with what can only

En route from Bombay to Pune

Fishing (man-made lake) north of winery, India

be described as black plastic bin-liners. When I ask to take some photographs, the local women all change their clothes and wash their children's hair, while the men put on fresh shirts.

Then it's off to the winery for an 11 a.m. breakfast of omelette and coffee, and then an updated visit to the newly constructed cellar and a full tasting. The sparkling wine typically consists of 30–40% Chardonnay, 50–65% Ugni Blanc and 5–10% Pinot Noir, while the still wines are blended from 95% Ugni Blanc and 5% Chardonnay, and treated with oak chips. There is also some Indian brandy, bottled at 70% alcohol, the product of a private distillation.

Lunch is the fish we bought that morning, coated in spices and served with okra, chapatis, etc. As it is the captain's birthday, his wife and daughter produce a celebration cake.

We leave at 4 p.m. for the arduous seven-hour journey back to Bombay along exceedingly bumpy roads, and during the journey I start to feel slightly unwell. I arrive at the hotel distinctly ill with an upset stomach and fever, and have a very bad night.

4.11.89. I awake feeling very ill. Sick and feverish, I take more pills to no avail, and manage somehow to go to the office at 10.30. After a short meeting with Pai and Gopal, it is suggested they take me to see their private doctor who lives in the suburbs. After a torturous 30-minute drive, we arrive at a block of seedy-looking apartments, where I have to climb four floors, by which time I feel I want to die. Having interrupted the doctor's lunch, I am ushered into his bedroom. Bidding me sit on the edge of his unmade bed, he places his stethoscope to my navel and promptly announces I have Bombay Flu.

I suggest in no uncertain terms that I think it might be something more like dysentery. 'Oh no,' he insists, 'it is Bombay Flu,' and then proceeds to open a wooden box and extract a plastic cassette-tape holder, which contains a syringe and a phial of liquid. Having received my injection, we make a quick stop to exchange some previously purchased clothes, which although were labelled large would actually be the perfect fit for a small child, and then it's back to the hotel for a rest. I'm still running a high fever and feel very sick.

Gopal wakes me at 3 p.m., as I have promised to give a wine lecture and tutored tasting to the staff at the Oberoi Hotel. I am now feeling on top of the world, raring to go and flying high. I conduct a three-hour training session and wine tasting, but back at the hotel at 7.30, I start to feel extremely ill again. I ask Gopal what the doctor has given me to make me feel so good. Quite casually, he informs me that it was a straight morphine injection. My reaction to this is not of the politest, and I go straight back to bed. The high fever, sickness and diarrhoea continue all night.

At 3.30 a.m., with all the strength left at my command, I manage to get up and pack, to be taken back to the airport at 5, where I am promptly sick in the loo of the executive lounge, although I haven't eaten for 24 hours. The 9½-hour flight is an ordeal. I have a very bad stomach and am constantly in the loo, feeling permanently sick. Despite that, I am able to sleep most of the way (thank God for Business Class). Sadly, a great trip has been spoiled by what I suspect is gastro-enteritis, accompanied by high fever.

It later transpired that my ailment was Shigella Sonnei, a notifiable disease, which I then proceeded to pass on to the whole family. Further inquiries revealed that the culprit was the fish, which, although freshly caught, came from a man-made lake into which raw sewage is discharged.

Notwithstanding this salutary experience, I was to return to India again the following spring, this time in the company of Clare, my wife.

28 February–16 March 1990

28.2.90. Clare and I arrive at Heathrow, Terminal 3, by taxi at 1.30 p.m. We check into Business Class and, after a little duty-free shopping, recline in the Maharajah Lounge for complimentary drinks until our flight is called at 3.30. We are rather relieved to get away from the utterly inappropriate TV broadcast going on in the lounge on the subject of 'How to die and what to do'. We enjoy a fairly comfortable flight with the now familiar unlimited champagne.

We make our stopover in Delhi at 5.15 a.m. local time, but then a thick fog descends, and we get stuck on the runway until 10.30. As a result, we only arrive in Bombay at noon, which means we have spent a rather trying 12½ hours on the plane.

My old friends Bill and Ben (Gopal and Pai) are here to meet us, and we are taken to the Sheraton Searock Hotel, where room 1639, overlooking the Arabian Sea, awaits us. After a quick shower and change, we have a buffet lunch at the hotel, and then I accompany G and P to their offices, while Clare goes sightseeing and shopping with Ranjit, one of Indage's sales executives.

Back at the hotel, I shower again, and then meet everyone in the bar at 8.30. We are taken to dinner at a restaurant previously called Invitation 365, but which has now curiously changed its name to Today's Appointment, situated on Juhu Beach. An excellent dinner consists of tiger prawns masala, lobster in some sort of spicy sauce, raja gosht, roomali roti, tandoori chicken, and of course copious quantities of rum and soda. We get back to the hotel at midnight.

1.3.90. A 6 a.m. alarm call starts the day, and then Ranjit and his charming wife, Sharmila, collect us from the hotel to drive us to Dadar station, from where we embark on a one-hour first-class rail journey to nondescript Neral, on the Bombay to Pune line. There, we transfer to a tiny narrow-gauge toy train, which takes a further two hours to travel a further 13 miles up to the Matheran hill station, 800 metres up, where we are staying at a resort called Brightlands. This comprises an extremely primitive collection of huts, surrounded by woodlands occupied by a large family of monkeys. Matheran covers an area of 20 square kilometres, and is the only hill resort where no motor vehicles are allowed.

After a well-deserved Kingfisher beer, we enjoy a lunch of mutton and chicken soup, chicken tandoori, baked chicken and lamb dhansak, with chocolate mousse to finish. Then at 3.30, we venture on a pony trek around the hill station points, visiting Echo and Luisa Points, before the day culminates in an incredible sunset at Porcupine Point. We are on the very top of the mountain range, and the views from these points are stunning.

Arriving back at the hotel at 7.30, we are confronted by an army of giant ants in our bathroom. A boy is detailed to rid us of them, while another is despatched to the local village to purchase a much needed bottle of rum.

Dinner on the makeshift terrace at 9 is tomato soup, chicken korma, mutton with crisps and green moong dhal, with more rum and soda. We get to bed at around 10.30, but the bathroom is still alive with enormous ants. The houseboy arrives and sweeps them away again, but they reappear within two minutes. We must have killed hundreds. Our room is as primitive as can be imagined, the bed a hard board with a thin horsehair mattress, and the pillow rock hard. Notwithstanding these testing conditions, tiredness overcomes us and we sink into an eight-hour sleep, only to be awoken by the gentle tones of one of the house boys throwing up outside our bedroom window.

Our indelible memory of the day is of the boy selling ices at Porcupine Point at sunset, calling out his wares: 'Lice Cream! Lice Cream!'

2.3.90. After a substantial 9 a.m. breakfast of keema (minced lamb) with potatoes and chillies, and scrambled eggs on toast, we take another glorious pony trek around the southern points – two hours of breathtaking views. We return to the hotel at midday for a well-earned Kingfisher beer, and then head off for the station, a very young lad carrying our bags on his head. It turns out we have just missed the train to Neral.

We'll have to take a taxi instead, but as cars are not allowed in Matheran, we must hire a rickshaw to the taxi stand. Thus we are pulled and pushed along by two young boys on a journey that takes half an hour. The taxi journey to Bombay then takes another four hours along dreadful roads, with endless punctures along the way.

What a cheering sight the Sheraton Searock is once again. We are checked into room 1521, and immediately go for a swim in the lovely pool. After showering, we meet Gopal, Pai and Ranjit Mansoukhani from the Hindustan Brewery, at 7 for drinks in the bar.

Dinner is at the Shertal Samundra Restaurant, an excellent, highly recommendable place. We enjoy butterflied tiger prawns in Szechuan sauce, lobster in soya sauce and garlic, mutton rara masala, hajarvi pab masala (a chicken dish cooked in the tandoor and served in sauce), and makhani dhal, returning to the hotel by midnight.

3.3.90. At 8.30 a.m., we go up to the eighteenth floor to have breakfast in the executive lounge – caviare, croissants and coffee. Ominously enough, I have a slightly upset stomach. Out for a morning walk, we note how amazingly many of the old grand houses are in state of total disrepair. Pai later explained that inter-familial disputes account for a lot of it. It seems a great pity.

A car collects us at 10.15 to take us to Bombay Airport to greet our party of guests who have arrived from London. We arrive at 11, and are all greeted with sandalwood garlands, no less. We are driven to the Oberoi Towers where, after checking in, we are given a buffet lunch at 1 p.m. with a choice of Indian, Polynesian or Western cooking, or a cold buffet. I have a 3 p.m. appointment with Mr Chougule, while the rest of the party go by boat to the Elephanta Caves ten kilometres away, and see the impressive seventh-century cave temples.

I return to the hotel at 6 p.m., and then we rendezvous in the bar at 7.45. Dinner will be at the Jewel of India, a highly renowned restaurant at which it is evidently very difficult to get a table. The food is in fact appalling, and the service extremely slow. Dry tandoori chicken and various other nondescript dishes are hardly what we were expecting. After this disappointing experience, we are back at the hotel by midnight.

(The party consists of the general manager of a well respected country house hotel, a buyer from the Sunday Times Wine Club, the chief executive of City Centre restaurants, two journalists. The managing director of Adnams wine merchants. The wine buyer of a large wine wholesaler, and ourselves.)

4.3.90. The day begins with a 4 a.m. alarm call – yuk! We catch the 6 a.m. train to Pune and arrive at 9.30. Clare is sick at the railway station, and the day is not about to get any easier. We are now driven in an antiquated minibus to the Chateau Indage Winery, arriving at 1 p.m. It seems that Clare and I are not staying in the hospitality rooms at the winery, but in the local government apartments nearby.

We meet the new winemaker, Yves Pouzet, who has been working for Moët et Chandon in Brazil for the last two years, and at 1.30, embark on a full wine tasting.

Lunch is served in the winery gardens: pork masala with dhal, vegetables and rice, etc. I eat very little, as I am extremely tired. I go back to the apartment for a two-hour sleep while the others continue their winery tour, returning at 7.30 for drinks, but find myself declining dinner, which is most unlike me.

Our accommodation is a complex of suites, built in 1977 for visiting government officials who were here to check on the progress of construction work on the new dams. The rooms are very large, with mosquito nets over the beds, but the lavatories are not functioning, and I would imagine from the state of them have not been for a number of years. Clare is assigned a driver on call throughout the night to ferry her to the winery in case she needs the loo. It is all pretty basic and primitive. I sleep like a log (fully clothed, as there are no blankets or sheets) on an extremely hard bed, and awake at 7.30 a.m...

5.3.90... to find a sparrow in our room. I get up fully dressed and go for a stroll around the grounds. The whole place seems like some fantastical folly.

We are collected at 8.15 by Mr Suhas Bedekar, administrative manager of Indage, who will take us to the winery for a 9.30 breakfast of omelette and toast. Then we drive into Pune which was the residence of the government of Bombay during the rainy season, and which flourished under the British.

A trip around the old town, where many old buildings still remain, is absolutely fascinating. There is the Sassoon Hospital, designed by John Begg; the Roman Catholic cathedral dedicated to Saint Patrick; the Church of the Holy Name, with a lofty campanile modelled on the famous one in St Mark's Square, Venice; and the Deccan College, a rambling Gothic-style structure built of local grey stone. There are also many small alleys, market stalls and shops, all intensely alive and buzzing. Sadly, we discover there isn't enough time for the arranged lunch (which should have been at an Indo-Chinese restaurant). Instead we have to make do with an omelette sandwich at Pune airport at 3.30.

We check in at 4 for a 4.30 flight to Goa on an 18-seater aeroplane, only to be told that they had overbooked and there were not enough seats available. This is quickly rectified by Gopal, who produces a bribe sufficiently large to have other passengers magically removed from the plane. It's an hour-long flight enlivened by superb views.

On arrival, the Goan agent of Indage, accompanied by his wife and daughter, greets us with garlands of fresh flowers. Sadly the rooms at the Oberoi are still under repair, and we are diverted for one night to the Cicade de Goa hotel on Dona Paula Point, which is one hour's drive from the airport. It was used in the film *Bangkok Hilton*, starring Denholm Elliott and Nicole Kidman. The scenery is once again spellbinding, with fringes of palms spreading out along the coastline.

At 7 p.m., we are checked into room 311 overlooking the sea and a swimming pool – a lovely view. Although it is a good enough hotel, I fear it's the kind of place much used in the high season by tour operators.

We rendezvous in the bar at 8, and have dinner in the open-air restaurant overlooking the ocean. On the menu are stir-fried chillied beef, vegetable curry, dhal and so on, presented buffet-fashion, and with the added diversion of Goanese dancers and a good live group. One of the team even sang a number. We retire at 11.30, and go to sleep to the sound of waves lapping on the shore. Ho-hum.

6.3.90. After waking at 7 a.m., we take breakfast in the open-air restaurant – scrambled eggs, hash browns, grilled tomatoes and toast – and then rendezvous in reception at 9 to change hotels. Unfortunately, this hotel has the problem of being situated opposite the harbour, from where oil discharged from the ships drifts across on to the beach. Bidding goodbye to all that, we check in at the Oberoi at 10. This is more like it: an excellent five-star hotel, although the layout is not as good as the Taj Village. We are upgraded to suite 301, which boasts superb views from its balcony. We immediately unpack and change, and then go for a swim in the Indian Ocean.

A buffet lunch at 1.30 offers Goanese chicken, vegetable curry and naan bread, and then I sleep by the pool for a couple of hours, prior to another swim. (The temperature is now 90°+.) An excellent massage at 5 p.m. turns out to be just what the doctor ordered.

We rendezvous for drinks at 7, and get through a fair amount of Old Monk rum and soda. A superb evening ensues, during which we are entertained for three hours by dancers in astonishing Kathakali make-up. There is a barbecue by the pool and lots more to drink – all in all a great evening, ending with bed at 12.30.

7.3.90. Breakfast at 8.30 a.m. is as yesterday: omelette, bacon, hash browns and grilled tomatoes. At 9, a coach picks us up to take us on a tour of Goa. We look in on the excavation and restoration work that is in progress at the ruins of Santa Monica, and then at the Basilica of Bom Jesus, Goa's most popular and famous church. Built between 1594 and 1604. To the right of the altar is the Basilica's big attraction – the silver Casu enshrining the Mummified remains of St Frances Xavier, Goa's patron saint. The beach and the market stalls selling their trinkets.

Lunch is at 12.30 at the Hotel Mandovi's Rosonico Restaurant, a museum piece straight out of the days of the Raj. A three-piece white-gloved band (violin, guitar and drums) plays, lending the proceedings a real Palm Court feeling. The food is prawn curry

Chef at Hotel Mandovi's Rosonico Restaurant, Goa

with rice, dry fish fillet, cafreal fish in a green masala sauce with mixed vegetables), mutton xacuti (in a coconut masala sauce), mutton vindaloo, stuffed shinanyo (mussels), and sukka sumkta (small dried shrimps). As well as being the oldest (established in 1952), Rosonico also has the reputation of being the best restaurant in Goa, and I can't help but agree. It is all absolutely superb, including the best vindaloo I have ever tasted. The chef's name is Cardadu Alphonso: he modestly signs my diary.

After lunch, we take a tour of the beaches and the lighthouse, from where we have amazing views of the surroundings, then go down to Calangute beach and a snoop round the local bazaars, where I buy a hash pipe (empty, of course). Following that, we go to Mapusa above the Mundovi River, a hot, bustling town where there isn't much to see. We do some shopping, buying Goan coconut vinegar and bottles of Madame Rosa's renowned feni.

Then it's on to the Rondal Beach Hotel at Baga beach for a swim and change. Dinner – an excellent buffet table groaning with Goan specialities – was organised by the Indage agent for Goa, Mr Virani. I suddenly notice a movement by the side of the table and spot an enormous black rat scurrying past. As I have a complete aversion to these rodents, I let out a scream and jump on my chair, which turns out to be of the folding type, and sends me crashing backwards on to the ground. Everyone thought I had had a heart attack. Amazingly though, I am unhurt – other than an ugly bruise that appears on my shin!

We return to our hotel at 1.30.

8.3.90. I awake at 7.45 a.m. and breakfast on scrambled eggs on toast, bacon, hash browns and tomatoes, before going for a massage at 9. A very gentle day indeed: swimming and sunbathing until 12.30, and then we take a coach to the airport.

Our plane is delayed by half an hour, and we take off at 3.05, having had no lunch. Then it's a rushed trip back to the hotel for the wine tasting at 6.30. A press reception follows from 7.30 till 8 in the Sunset Suite. I give various interviews to the press, followed by a sumptuous buffet supper, and am in bed by midnight, having said farewell to our guests, as Clare and I are leaving to go south early tomorrow.

9.3.90. We are alarm-called at 5, and then taken by taxi to the Santa Cruz airport. The driver charges an exorbitant 150 rupees (£6). After a cup of coffee, we check in for the Indian Airways flight to Bangalore. We are half an hour late taking off, and arrive at 10. A bus takes us to the superbly luxurious traditional 20-acre West End Hotel, the oldest hotel in Bangalore, where we check in to room 1212.

Bangalore, capital of Karnataka State, is a much cleaner city, with wider streets, beautiful parks, long tree-lined avenues, flowers and shrubs, and seemingly much less poverty than Bombay. We take a cab to M.G. Road and go shopping, buying sandalwood and rosewood carvings at the Kaveri Arts and Crafts emporium, and gorgeous silk at the Janardhana Silk House.

Lunch is at 1 p.m. at the Princes Restaurant, 9 Brigade Road: keema mutter and aloo, a clumsy chicken jalfrezi, very dark tadkawali dhal, onion culcha, plain culcha and Kingfisher beer. This restaurant specialises in Hindustani cuisine, and offers a good view of the bustling streets below its first-floor windows.

As we leave the restaurant at 2, it starts to rain heavily. We take a 20-rupee cab back to the hotel and sleep until 4.

After the rain eases off, we book a city tour in order to explore Bangalore and visit the Government Museum, one of the oldest museums in India (established 1866), Tipu Sultan's palace, the Lal Bagh botanical gardens, Cubbon Park with its 'Fairy Fountain', the Bull Temple, the palatial Post Office, the magnificent solid granite Vidhana Souda, housing the Secretariat and Legislature, and the High Court. The itinerary includes two rides in a motorised rickshaw.

Back at the hotel, we meet in the Paradise Bar at 7 for drinks, after which we set out for the Windsor Manor Hotel, where Titoo da Dhaba (a Punjabi food festival) is the main attraction. The table is booked for 8. It is all beautifully laid out by the pool. No sooner have I ordered an Old Monk and soda than it starts to rain again, and we have to move indoors to the Coffee Shop. I order masaledaar jingha (prawns in masala sauce, that were overcooked and contained too much garlic); bateer masaledaar (quails in masala sauce, dried out and tasteless); gurde kapoore (kidneys, which were of fair quality, in the same sauce as the quails); meat raarha (lamb in a sauce, a dish that bore an uncomfortable resemblance to an unsubtle osso buco and contained way too much raw garlic); makke diroti (cornflour roti); and the normal methi roti. The bill came to 800 rupees (about £30). I feel constrained to fill in a report form, pointing out that if they are going to stage food festivals, they should do their homework first. The hotel is part of the Wellcome group.

We are back at our own hotel by 11.30.

10.3.90. The alarm call comes at 6.30 a.m. and we breakfast in the room: mango juice, fresh hot rolls, coffee and tea. We hire a car with a driver for the day to take us to Mysore, leaving at 7. It's a 2½ hour drive.

Mysore, with its seventeen palaces, derives its name from *Mahishasura*, the demon who wreaked havoc among the people of this area. Like Bangalore, the city is at fairly high altitude (770 metres), giving it a pleasant climate throughout the year.

There, we visit Daria Daulat Bagh, Tipu Sultan's elegant summer palace, built in the Indo-Islamic style in 1784, and constructed mainly of wood. The interior is beautifully painted in black, red and gold, with numerous murals depicting battle scenes. We then work our way 13 kilometres out of town, and up the 1072 metres of Chamundi hill to visit the twelfth-century Sri Chamundeswari temple, built in the southern Dravidian style, where we pay 20 rupees to have red dust smeared on our foreheads. Within there is an interesting pillar depicting Ganesh, Nandi and Shiva's trident, facing towards the solid-gold Chamunda figure. We then stop for a beer at the Rajenda Villas Hotel, which is perched high on a hill overlooking the whole of the city. It's all terribly run-down, rather a shame. A third of the way down Chamundi Hill is the huge Nandi Bull monolith, the third largest (4.9 metres high) in India, and then the Lalitha Mahal palace, which is now a five-star hotel run by the government – a truly superb establishment.

We drive into town, stopping for a little light shopping at the Kaveri emporium, and then visit the Zoological Gardens, one kilometre east of the city, which are – apart from Hyderabad – reputedly the best in India. We see the magnificent white tiger, the Indian and African elephants, leopards and lion cubs. It's quite a sizeable zoo, as they go, but many of the pits and cages are deserted.

Lunch is at the Vishala Restaurant in the Dasaprakash Paradise Hotel. We pay 20 rupees for a vegetable thali, seven assorted vegetable dishes and rice, accompanied by chapatis and poppadums, plus a speciality only served at the weekends: bisibele huli anna (a rice dish cooked in stock with vegetables, very good). Somehow I don't think I could live on vegetable thali alone, though, albeit at 75p a head.

We head back to the car at 2.30, and visit the Maharajah's palace in the town centre, Mysore's main attraction. Built over a period of fifteen years (1897–1912) after the old wooden palace was razed by fire, it is an imposing structure, a gleaming profusion of domes, turrets, archways and colonnades. The interior is full of treasures: the Durbar Hall, with its jewel-studded throne, mosaic marble floors, crystal furniture, hammered silver doors and a stained glass domed ceiling. It's quite stunning, and not to be missed.

Leaving Mysore at 4.30, we are back at the hotel at 7, where we pack. Final drinks on the terrace by the pool are followed by dinner in their speciality Thai restaurant in the open air. It is designed to look like a Thai village, and the food is quite good but contains rather too much MSG. We are amused to see a white man arriving at the hotel dressed in duffel coat, balaclava and scarf, in temperatures of 92°F.

We retire at 10.30.

11.3.90. Up at 6.45 a.m. for a cooked breakfast, after which we take a taxi to the airport, meaning to catch a 9.25 plane to Cochin, but the flight has been rescheduled to 2.15 p.m. So another taxi (a very old one, that is only just still running) takes us back to the hotel. We check back into the same room and sit by the pool, enjoying a swim and a delicious lunch of tandoori chicken pieces rolled into a roomali roti with vegetable curry, accompanied by Kingfisher beer.

At 12.30, a taxi takes us once more to the airport, arriving at 1 for the Cochin flight. The organisation, quality of service and cleanliness at Bangalore are a compliment to India – certainly compared to what we have seen at Bombay. The West End Hotel has been particularly impressive.

The flight eventually takes off at 2.30, arriving at Cochin at 3.15. It's extremely hot and humid, but fortunately there is at least a nice breeze. We share a cab to the excellent Hotel Malabar with a Mexican, who is married to an Indian lady and now living in Florida. The hotel is situated right on the edge of the peninsula of Wilmington Island, quite an amazing site. We are given room 116, which affords wonderful views of the sea and fishing boats. Cochin is situated in one of Kerala's most beautiful regions – a lagoon of islands and peninsulas separated by the backwaters of the Arabian Sea.

Clare goes off for a swim, and I take the ferry to Fort Cochin, where Vasco da Gama set up Portugal's first Indian trading station. He died there in 1524 and is buried in the church of Saint Francis, the only Portuguese building still standing. The heat and humidity are terrific. I walk to the tip where the boats are bringing in their catch, and then take the 5.20 ferry back to the hotel. Coincidentally, it turns out that some cousins of Clare are in the room next to ours and we arrange to meet them for dinner at the Ceylon Bake House after drinks in the hotel bar, which is desperately lacking in atmosphere. A cab takes us to Ernakulam to look round the shopping area, and then we meet outside the restaurant at 8.15. It looks and smells like a derelict shanty shack – too risky, we decide – and so we take a rickshaw to the Sealord Hotel, which has a pretty good Chinese restaurant on the roof. The ferry gets us back to the hotel at 10.30.

We have decided that Cochin generally is altogether quite grubby and sordid, and has the makings of a ghost town.

12.3.90. We awake at 7 a.m. to an amazing view from our bedroom window of the rice boats punting by. We breakfast at 8 on scrambled eggs, bacon, tomatoes, potatoes, pancakes and toast.

At 9, we embark on a tour of Fort Cochin, visiting St Francis' church and the church of Santa Cruz. Built in 1557, the latter is a Roman Catholic church noted for its brilliantly coloured interior paintwork. We then go to the northern tip of Fort Cochin to see the huge Chinese fishing nets. After a look round the Mattancherry Palace, built by the Portuguese around 1555 and presented to Rajah Veera Kerala Varma as a goodwill token, we visit Jewtown and the 1568 synagogue, (destroyed by the Portuguese in 1662, rebuilt by the Dutch in 1664) one of the oldest in the world, with its Delft tiles, beautifully crafted brass pulpit, and wonderful Belgian crystal chandeliers. It has only twenty-seven remaining members, but sadly the 80-year-old beadle was too unwell to see us.

Back at the hotel at 11.30, we take a well-earned swim and drink. The temperature is in the nineties, making things very sticky. After a buffet lunch, we have a nap in the gardens.

Checking in at Cochin Airport, we take a 2 p.m. flight to Madras. Arriving an hour later, we are driven in a bus from the airport (probably the oldest vehicle I have ever seen – and certainly no suspension!) to the Hotel Taj Coromandel. It's 4.30 and Madras is overpoweringly hot, in the middle to upper nineties, with very high humidity. We have a superb room on the seventh floor (721) with views over the city.

We shower and change and, after a tour of the hotel, meet for drinks in the bar and then a fine dinner in the hotel's Mysore Restaurant, murgh tikka lababdar (chicken tikka with tomato, cream and butter), achar gosht (Hyderabad lamb), dahi palak (spinach puréed with yoghurt), dhal kabila (lentils, tomato, ginger and coriander), and tomato pulao. It is all set against a backdrop of Bhanata Natyam, hypnotic dancing and music. We are in bed by 10.30.

13.3.90. Breakfast at 8.a.m. includes omelettes and bacon, etc. and the local South Indian coffee – wow!

A car is booked for 9 to take us for a tour of the city and some shopping. Madras, capital of Tamil Nadu, differs from the three larger Indian capitals (Bombay, Delhi and Calcutta) in three major respects. First, it is the home of the ancient Dravidian civilisation. Next, it is unusually extensive, covering 80 square kilometres of parks, gardens and beaches. Lastly, it has managed to grow from rural village to modern metropolis in 350 years without losing its simple, small-town charm. It was also the first

English settlement in India. We visit Fort St George, rebuilt several times between 1642 and 1749; St Mary's church, built in 1680, the first Anglican church in India; the Fort and Government Museums; and the Marina Beach and Lighthouse, taking in the dazzling colour of the Armenian market along the way.

We try the Connemara Hotel for lunch, but the restaurant turns out only to be open in the evenings, and the Amaravathi Hotel, which doesn't serve alcohol but looks good anyway. So we repair to our own hotel for an excellent Chinese lunch of double-cooked Szechuan pork with spring onions, leeks and chillies, seafood chow mein and Singapore noodles – delightful!

In temperatures of 100+, we decide to rest and sleep by the pool until 5, and at 6 go for a total head and body massage, an experience not to be missed. Drinks in the bar at 7.45 are followed by dinner at 8.30 in the Mysore Restaurant once more where, after consultation during the afternoon, the chef Ralph Sunil has prepared a special feast for us. It is a classic southern Indian Tamil dinner served as a thali (none of these dishes is on the menu): ghee (to pour over the rice), rasam (pepper water), sambal, prawn chettinand (named after the province), tamil yera (prawns in a superbly delicate sauce), keera kootu (dhal with greens), vartha melaga curry (a mutton and pepper fry), kholi kolumbu (Madras chicken), vendakai pachadi (okra in yoghurt and coconut), semeya payasum (vermicelli), gulab jamun, thari (yoghurt), thari sadma (yoghurt and rice), and pooris (deep-fried flatbread). It is an outstanding meal, and we retire quite full and contented at 10.30.

14.3.90. We awake at 6.30 a.m. and breakfast at 8. A car takes us to Fisherman's Cove, which is a Taj Hotel right on the beach, 24 miles from Madras. The beaches here stretch untouched for at least 40 miles, and the hotel, which was an old Dutch fort, consists of a series of cottages situated right on the shore. (The best rooms are 7 and 9.) It is superbly remote, quite idyllic, and we spend the day swimming in the warm Bay of Bengal. Lunch is a mixed tandoori affair, with prawn masala, roti and rice.

Back at the hotel at 6, we pack for the journey to Bombay tomorrow. Drinks in the bar at 7.30 are followed by dinner in the

Peshwari Restaurant in the Chola Sheraton Hotel, which specialises in Frontier tandoori cuisine, and where we meet Mr Narendra Malhotra, the food and beverage manager, who has planned our menu. We eat an excellent tandoori pomfret, chicken in a curiously strong but delicious tomato paste, and yellow dhal, and get back to our hotel at 10.30.

15.3.90. After breakfasting at 8 a.m., we take a taxi to the airport at 9.45 for the 11.30 flight to Bombay. We arrive at 1.30 to find it crushingly hot and humid. Ranjit is there to meet us. We taxi to the Centaur Hotel at Juhu beach and are checked into room 5053.

Later on, I take a cab to the Indage office and have a conference with Mr Chougule until 5, when a car is sent to take me to the offices of Hindustani Breweries for a meeting with the owner, Mr Jain. The car back to the hotel has to inch its way through ridiculous traffic and I only make it back two hours later – nine o'clock! After a quick change, it's time for a Chinese dinner and then bed by 11.30. The sheets are damp, and there is a noisy TV in the room next door.

Next morning we are alarm-called at 4 a.m., and taken in a taxi to the airport. We are upgraded to Business Class on flight AI 101, and proceed to enjoy a serene breakfast in the executive lounge and a comfortable flight back to London.

This has been one amazing trip, my third to the subcontinent in just over a year. It was to be another nine years, though, before I was able to return.

25 February–7 March 1999

25.2.99. A minicab arrives to take myself and wine journalist Rose Murray-Brown to Heathrow Terminal 3. We'll fly Air India Business Class to Delhi. I am assigned a very good seat, 16J, which is upstairs on the Boeing 747–400. We have coffee in the Maharajah Lounge, following a superbly efficient instant check-in, neatly avoiding a two-hour queue. Estimated take-off is 8.45, but we actually leave the ground at around 9.30.

The in-flight breakfast consists of a cheese omelette, chicken sausages, a rice cake and coffee, after which I manage to grab a half-hour's sleep. Lunch, when it comes, is rather good: an aperitif of Veuve Clicquot champagne, asparagus soup, a chicken dish, murgh rogini, with spiced vegetables, pilau rice and a paratha, accompanied by more Clicquot. I while away the rest of the flight with a mixture of sleeping and reading, and we land at Delhi at 11.30 p.m. local time. After a 90-minute wait here, we make it to Bombay by 3.30 a.m., checking into the Oberoi Tower, room 3029, at 4.15. I sleep until 8 a.m.

26.2.99. The day begins with croissants and coffee on the 27th floor overlooking the Arabian Sea, as does my room. At 9.30, all the guests on the trip are collected for a city tour: Peter Jago, winemaker of Penfolds Australia, Nicholas Faith, a wine writer, Antoine Merlaut from Bordeaux, Michael Wilkolm from Germany, Eric Wente of California, the reigning Miss California, Rose Murray-Brown and myself. The sights take in Gandhi's house, which is now a museum and well worth a visit, the washing market full of clothes drying on the pavements, the Gateway to India opposite the Taj Mahal Hotel, the Victoria Rail Terminus and the Prince of Wales Museum, built in 1905 to commemorate George V's (then prince of Wales) first visit to India. A refreshing drink back at the hotel is a little china mug of draught Kingfisher (the new logo on the Kingfisher bottle announces that the beer is 'most thrilling chilled'), and then at

1.45 we go to lunch in the Kandahar Restaurant on the first floor of the hotel.

The cooking here is superb, without a doubt the finest Indian cuisine I have tasted. My main dish is murgh rasampatti, chicken in a fiery tomato and chilli sauce, served with black lentils and plain rice. The bill comes to 734.50 rupees, ie. about £10. At the end, we are served a plate of chopped up, silver-coated dates.

I meet Arun Shah and Sham Chougule, Indage's managing director and chairman respectively, at 2.30. They have arranged an interview for me with a journalist from the *Indian Times*, which lasts no less than two hours, following which – back in my room – I fall into an hour's fitful sleep.

After showering at around 6, I go to meet Sham Chougule and the rest of the party again. At 7.30, there is to be a large reception in the Roof Garden of the Oberoi Tower. This turns out to be a magnificent occasion with a buffet, live band and unlimited sparkling and still wines. The invitees are a pretty sparkling bunch too: I am introduced to the Vice-President of Oberoi, the Mauritian Consul, the First Secretary from the British Embassy, and many other dignitaries. Miss California, another of the guests on our trip, gives us a song. At 9.30, the Millennium pink champagne is launched in magnums to the accompaniment of a machine sending out soap bubbles. The wine is excellent, having spent eight months on its lees.

I am photographed by the *Indian Times* to accompany my interview, which is to be published on Sunday, after which I am interviewed live on Indian TV, tasting and discussing the wine. I finally get to bed at 11.45, very tired.

27.2.99. I awake at 8 a.m. and go to breakfast in the Palm Restaurant – scrambled eggs on toast with bacon and baked beans. It seems there is a slight alteration to a later stage of the itinerary. March 2nd is a religious festival, which means that no appointments can be made for then, so I'll be travelling to Delhi that day rather than the 3rd.

I have a meeting at the hotel at 9.30 with Ranjit Mansoukhani of Hindustan Breweries, producers of Bombay Pilsner. We take a Club soda in the Oberoi's Belvedere Club, which is a very exclusive members-only club. The meeting includes Mr Jain Jnr, the brewery owner's son, who has just arrived back from the USA with an MBA from Harvard University. He is very genned up and keen to export their products; only time will tell if it will ever happen.

After packing, I am taken to the Press Clubhouse at the Bombay Sports Club, a very old-colonial sort of place. A superb buffet is laid on. Here I chat with Antoine Merlaut, the Bordeaux proprietor whose properties include Châteaux Cos d'Estournel, Gruaud-Larose, Haut-Bages-Libéral and Chasse-Spleen, as well as the negociant house of Ginestet. He is very interested in exporting his wines for distribution in India.

We then embark on a 4½-hour car journey to Sahara City, a brand-new, still unfinished resort complex set in 5000 acres halfway between Pune and Bombay. When completed, it will be an entire city with hospital, school, timeshare cottages, a pool, hotel with restaurant, golf course and so on. The whole place is designed to look like a Portuguese golf resort. At the moment, it is lacking many facilities, including telephones. I share one of the cottages with Peter Jago, a great character. The evening is taken up with a buffet and drinks (including fine Black Dog whisky) and some Indian dancing. I am in bed at 11.30.

28.2.99. After a 6 a.m. call, I breakfast in the Round Tower Restaurant on scrambled eggs, bacon and baked beans.

A 3½-hour drive brings us to the winery, where the first ever Indian wine festival is being held on the lawns around the winery and vineyards. There are 250 guests and what a splendid show, reminiscent of an Ascot garden party! I am asked to plant a Chardonnay vine with my name on the metal stake, and then there are more interviews to be done, and pictures for the local newspapers. After that, and a little light grape-treading, we tour the winery before embarking on a superb buffet lunch.

Laid out on a group of trestle tables are: tandoori paneer tikka, vegetable kebabs, chicken hariyali, chingari kebab, maral fish, prawns, mutton chops and kaleji gurde kheri (excellent chicken and vegetables cooked in a large open wok). Separate main course tables hold kadai vegetables, palak paneer, dhal makhani, sukka gosht kalimiri, chicken masala and pum ki gosht biryani.

We leave at 4.15 and get back to Sahara City at about 7.30. A quick shower, and then a pre-dinner drink of San Miguel beer, now brewed locally under licence. Sham Chougule hosts a dinner for sixteen of us. In addition to the various Indian wines, Peter Jago has provided bottles of the 1992 Grange and 1993 St Henri, while Eric Wente from California has brought his Cabernet Sauvignon and Merlot. A quantity of Black Dog whisky and soda is also taken, and Miss California sings for us once again, this time with a local guitarist. I am in bed at 11.30.

1.3.99. I go to breakfast at 8.30 for scrambled eggs on toast, sausages, baked beans and coffee, after which we all assemble for a group photo.

Leaving Sahara City at 10.15, I am driven to the Aqua Club, a health and fitness centre at Borivali, to the east of the centre of Bombay (or rather 'Mumbai – green and clean', as a road sign has it). The journey takes four hours. I check into room 6, which has a large balcony overlooking the pool and water slides, and get the distinct feeling that I am the only one here. There are many ante-rooms with encouraging signs on the doors: 'Aerobics', 'Yoga', 'Gym', etc. It's all very smart, members only, and yet the outside wall backs on to a shanty town.

I bid goodbye to the others and head for the restaurant, and a large Kingfisher. I lunch on mutton gosht, naan bread, rice and dhal (not good), and then sleep until 5 p.m. It turns out the masseur is on holiday, sadly, and the club appears to have no facility to make STD long-distance calls. Perhaps I should have availed myself of the offer seen on a poster: 'Mobile Phone – use for 10 minutes, 2 minutes free. Phone an old flame!' Tomorrow, March 2nd, is a holy festival and holiday, in the course of which everybody is expected to get drunk in the streets and pour paint and coloured liquid over each other.

At 7.30, I come down to the bar and have a couple of Old Monk rums with lime juice and soda. When I go into the restaurant, I am seated alone at a table for 10. I order chicken tikka to start, which is very good and spicy, and then chicken kadai, plain rice, dhal and two naan, accompanied by Kingfisher beer.

On the whole, though, the food is poor and the accommodation mediocre.

2.3.99. Having slept well, I awake at 7.30 for coffee and toast, and then a car arrives for me at 8. The driver, Vinod Kumar Yadau, is superb, hired from a local taxi company, and takes me all around old Bombay, the red-light district through Falkland Road, to which very, very few tourists would dare to go (the girls are still displayed in cages stacked two high), and the real slum areas, where the poverty is quite unacceptable – awesome and eye-opening. We eventually arrive at the Indage office at 10.45.

After a meeting with Sham Chougule on the subject of increasing exports of his wines to the UK, we repair to his house on the beachfront. From the outside, this looks like a building-site (to discourage burglars, apparently), but inside is a kind of marble palace, quite luxurious, with a very large balcony overlooking the Arabian Sea. Both of his wives have come to lunch, as has his youngest son, Ranjit, and his lovely wife, Rina. We have prawns, lamb, vegetable curry curiously served on a toasted English muffin, and curried eggs, accompanied by San Miguel Lager and Chantilli, a very well-made Cabernet Sauvignon from Indage that could easily be mistaken for a Bordeaux at a blind tasting.

Leaving at 1.40, I am taken on a 50-minute drive to the international airport. I'll be taking flight AI 302 to Delhi at 3.40, in Business Class, seat 58K. The flight is actually bound for Tokyo, via Delhi and Bangkok. After coffee in the Executive Lounge, we board, and I have a lovely, large, old-fashioned Club Class seat by the window with nobody next to me. Ice-cold towels are provided – a great idea – as is club soda, for the flight is strictly dry within Indian airspace. Flying time is one hour and 35 minutes, and we land at Delhi at 5.20, where I am met by another Ranjit, the Indage executive who looks after the northern part of the country.

The city is less hot and humid than Bombay, and we drive to the Habitat Centre (nothing to do with the Terence Conran store of the same name). It's another club-type complex, built like a prison. Room 502 looks quite good, but there is no air conditioning and the plumbing doesn't work. To add to my woes,

I have developed painful haemorrhoids and have been bitten all over my back.

To soothe away some of my tribulation, I go up to the sixth-floor bar, which is fashioned like an English pub, and order up a large Old Monk with lime and soda. The waiters are got up in tartan aprons. I decide I don't like this place.

Ranjit arrives at 7.15. I tell him I would like to be moved to another hotel for tomorrow night. He leaves to go and organise something, and I proceed to the Delhi O Delhi Restaurant in the complex next to the bar. This, like the inward flight, curiously turns out to be dry. I order a club soda and the menu of the month, which is a Hyderabadi meal consisting of dum ka murgh (chicken), gosht korma (lamb), shikampur (a sort of curd cake), khatti dhal, mirchi ka saalam (a chilli-hot dish), kakche gosht ki biryani (a rice dish) and gile firdaus, all served thali-fashion with silver dishes attached to a central silver plate. The bill is 220 rupees (about £3.75), but the food is appalling, tepid and badly cooked, lacking flavour, very disappointing.

I return to the bar for a nightcap, only to find it now packed solid. It is obviously a snob-value members' club. What a joke! I have a large McDowell's premium Indian whiskey and soda, and end a difficult day by retiring at 10 p.m.

3.3.99. I awake at 7.45 a.m., having slept well despite the lack of air conditioning. Breakfast is a potato and onion cake with spicy vegetables, mango juice, scrambled eggs on toast, and coffee. I check out at 10.30, as I shall be moved to the well situated Imperial Hotel in Janpath. On repacking, I discover that a bottle of country spirit, the local firewater flavoured with various herbs, which I bought in one of the villages, has broken in my case, disgorging its contents over clothes, shoes and travel books, imbuing everything with a most attractive aroma.

Lunch at 1.30 is in the Park Baluchi Restaurant, which is set in a deer park and has been voted the best restaurant in Delhi. Both location and food are indeed superb. After two 65cl bottles of Royal Challenger lager at 8.75% ABV, we eat achar gosht korma (mutton chunks in a sauce flavoured with pickle), zafrani mughlai chicken (cooked in authentic mughlai fashion with a saffron

Street scene, Delhi

Beard seller outside the Ref Ford, Delhi.

sauce), roomali roti, and zeree (rice cooked plain and then fried).

I am then taken on a sightseeing trip around Delhi. The highlights take in the Red Fort (Lal Qila), this huge red sandstone fort over overlooking the River Yamuna, built by Shah Jahan (1638–1648) as his personal residence. The battlements are 2.4 km long and 18.5 m high with two massive gates: Delhi Gate to the south and Lahore Gate to the west. Rastrapati Bhavan, the official residence of India's Prime Minister. It is a wonderful example of Lutyens' architecture. Jama Masjid. This is India's largest mosque completed in 1658. Qutb Minar. This is Delhi's most famous landmark, a soaring red sandstone tower, built in AD 1199 to mark the Moslem defeat of the last Hindu king. Emperor Humayan's Tomb. This is the first example of Moghul architecture, built in 1556 by Bega Begum, the widow of the second Moghul emperor Humayan and Chandi chowk – Delhi's main street, where I look in Ghatewala, the famous sweet shop. 'We teach you the good English,' proclaims a sign outside a school, 'and have photostate (sic) machine.'

Eventually, it's time to check in to the Imperial, which is quite stunning. One of the oldest buildings in the city, it has been renovated to five-star standard, retaining all the original marble. Room 103 is very large and smart, albeit with a lousy view. I have three Old Monk rums with lime and soda in the bar, which is all oak and leather.

Dinner at 9 is in the hotel restaurant, The Spice Trail. The decor is superb, similar to London's Blue Elephant, and indeed the menu is 50% Thai and 50% Indian. I order lamb appam (listed as 'Irach stew'), which is lamb with potatoes cooked in coconut milk, which turns out to be of very poor quality, tasteless chunks of meat and potatoes positively swimming in the coconut milk. And so to bed.

4.3.99. I pass a fitful night, taking some Imodium as a precaution only. A quick coffee at 6 a.m. and then I pay the bill – £150, very expensive, but this is a great hotel (apart from the restaurant). £20 of it is accounted for by a very short phone call to London. My driver is waiting outside at 6.30. He drives us very fast to Agra, which we make in three hours, passing through many primitive villages along the way: Faridabad, Kah Gaon, Sikri, Palwal, Mathura and Camely. Fleeting impressions, as we fly by, of dancing bears, performing monkeys and snake charmers. Just outside Agra, we stop at the beautiful Sikundra Temple for a quick visit, and to collect our guide, as the driver speaks no English.

In Agra itself, we take a full tour of the wonderful Agra Fort. Built in 1565 this enormous red turreted fortress contains over 500 stone buildings within its double wall. Inside is the superb Sheesh Mahal (Mirror Palace) built by Shah Jahan as a Turkish bath.

Taj Mahal, one of the seven wonders of the world, created by Shah Jahan to immortalise the memory of his wife, Mumtaz Mahal, who tragically died in 1631 giving birth to her fourteenth child. This monument took 20,000 workmen labouring day and night 22 years to complete which is awesome in every way, this remarkable piece of marble architecture, quite hypnotic in its overall effect upon the eye.

We arrive at the Clarks Hotel at 12.15, where I have a cold Kingfisher in the fifth-floor bar. Lunch is at a place strangely called 'The Only Restaurant', quite near the hotel. With two bottles of Royal Challenger, I eat gosht dopiaza (mutton cooked in a rich tomato and onion sauce), two naan breads, yellow dhal and plain rice. Also on the menu is 'assorted vegetables cooked in a rich tongue – a real gourmet delight'. No thank you. The bill comes to 380 rupees, about £6.

At around 1.45, I embark on a tour of old Agra, visiting the marble works where they do all the inlay. A gorgeous table is under construction, expected to take a year to complete at a cost of £10,000. Then it's on the Precious Stone Shop where I buy necklaces of beautiful local star-stones for Clare and my daughter, Holly, and thence to a spot of carpet-weaving.

Returning to the hotel at around 3, I sleep until 4.30, and upon awaking, am very, very sick indeed. Cross fingers, I'm getting rid of it all before the bacteria really get into my system. I suspect the dhal was the culprit but who knows? After this, I sleep for another half hour and awake feeling much better. At 6, I go for a full head and body massage for 450 rupees, and then pay another

250 rupees to see the hotel astrologer, who tells me I have conditions of the heart, ear and shoulder, but predicts I shall make it to the age of 75.

At 7.45, I am able to enjoy a large Indian whiskey and soda in the ground-floor bar. The hotel is like a strange hybrid of five-star and Best Western styles. Suddenly, a UK coach party arrives, a swarming mass of Sharons, Kevs and Traceys, quite unreal. They must be on a typical Golden Triangle five-star tour. After the rigours of the day, I decide not to eat, and go to bed at 10 p.m.

5.3.99. I awake and shower at 6.30 a.m. and can't quite manage breakfast, although I do generally feel much better. The driver arrives at 7, after I've checked out.

We drive to Fatehpur Sikri, a ghost city of the Moghuls built in the sixteenth century by Emperor Akbar as a grateful tribute to the celebrated saint, Shaikh Salim Chishti, but abandoned after fourteen years. There are magnificent carved stone temples and a palace, and a guided tour at 50 rupees. I buy two beautifully carved elephants and a set of hand-carved chess pieces. At 11, we stop at the Maglam Inn for a glass of Legend beer, and then on to Jaipur.

On the road to Jaipur, we pass the Ghana Bird Sanctuary, the Keuladeo National Park and Bahrator. At the border with Rajasthan is a police checkpoint, where a completely unnecessary 400-rupee 'passenger tax' must be paid. At Chukaward, we pass a run-over dog being greedily devoured by crows, and then a little further along the route, a sign advertising a 'Resort with rooms under nature' (i.e. with no roofs). Mahuna is a market town with an old fort, Sikendra a stonemasons' town and Dausa a shantytown with an 'English wine shop'. We make Jaipur at 12.45 – known as 'the Pink City' because of the rosy colour of the buildings. The picturesque capital of Rajasthan, it is the largest of the Rajputs' fortified cities.

I check into the three-star Maharani Palace Hotel, and am given room 208, which isn't too bad. I book a city tour for 2, and then go up to the first-floor (dry) restaurant for lunch, where I am the only diner. The buffet is vegetarian, so instead I order à la carte, mass ka achar with two roti. This is mutton chunks in a thick, fiery sauce, good local cuisine known as Merwar.

The city tour takes me to the old town, where there are visits to the Palace of the Winds, Kali Temple, Shish Mahal, the Sun and Moon Gates, and the Jantar Mantar observatory. Built in 1728 and renovated in 1901, it has a strange collection of surreal, Yellowstone sculptures, each having a specific astronomical function. Lastly I visit the immense City Palace for a guided tour of this magnificent establishment, most of the rooms which are still intact from the seventeenth century are full of mirrors and coloured inlaid stones. Dropped off back at the hotel, I am unexpectedly confronted by the driver with a bill for 8,390 rupees at a rate now of 75 to the pound I felt that was extremely good value.

I book in for a massage at 6 in the rooftop gym. In a very small, dark room, I am told to remove all my clothes. The treatment is excellent, but I do draw the line when he starts to administer a scrotal massage.

A tuk tuk auto-scooter takes me to the magnificent Taj Ramblagh Palace Hotel. A puppet show is taking place on the lawn. Over an Old Monk rum in the Polo Bar, I meet a German working in Bombay for Fiat Finance. I introduce him to the delights of Old Monk, lime and soda, of which we have numerous examples, and he then promptly disappears, having paid for all the drinks.

After that, I take a taxi to the highly recommended Nirds Restaurant in the MI Road in Jaipur. This too is dry and mainly full of Europeans, serving a disappointing menu of fairly commercial food. I order bhuna chicken in a rich sauce that is similar to the one with my lunchtime mutton (125 rupees), an onion naan (32 rps), jeera rice (55 rps) and a soda water (20 rps). The total, with tax, is 246.30 rps, about £3.50.

Then it's back by auto-scooter (50 rps) to the hotel, and bed at 10 p.m.

6.3.99. Awakening at 7 a.m., I shower and pack. The breakfast buffet is mainly Indian dishes, with mango juice, scrambled eggs on toast and coffee. I book a tour with elephant ride to the Ambra Palace, a spectacular location high on a hill overlooking the Moata Lake.

This turns out to be a fantastic experience. The elephant slowly and ponderously mounts the very steep hill to the eleventh century fort, a precarious twenty-minute ascent. One could almost get travel sickness but it is worth the journey. I sit on the front of the elephant's head for a photo, a pretty scary endeavour as one tries to keep one's balance.

Memorable signs seen in Jaipur include: 'Dr Gupta, dentist. We pull teeth. No pain'; 'English Medium', which turns out to indicate a prep school; and best of all, this condom advertising line, 'Twice as durable and no loss of shape'!

At 10.45, we stop at the Oberoi Trident Hotel for a Kingfisher beer by the pool, a very smart, small hotel but not a patch on the Taj Ramblagh Palace. Then it's back to the hotel at 11.30 for a further Kingfisher, and a noon cab to take me to lunch. The barman recommends a typical Rajasthani Restaurant in Chokhi Dhani, Tonk Road, Jaipur, an ethnic village resort. Sadly, the Rajasthani kitchen is only open in the evenings, so I speak to the chef in the main Indian Restaurant and decide to leave the menu to him.

I begin with a glass of Golden Peacock lager, made by Mount Shivalik Industries, Guntivehror district, Alwar, Rajasthan. The menu is strange, vegetarian, comprising bigan bhuta, a pulped vegetable that looks and tastes like tomato but isn't, cooked with garlic, interesting, and pitiradi, a sort of curry sauce to go with the aloo paratha. Mr Gautam is the chef. At least he tried. Other restaurants of note: Chanakya and the Kalinga.

Leaving at 1.45, I arrive in good time (2 p.m.) for the 2.55 flight to Delhi, only to be told it has been delayed by at least six hours. It seems the delay has been caused by this flight not having enough booked passengers to make it viable to fly, even though I was told I was on standby. The flight from Jaipur to Delhi takes all of 30 minutes. What joy to be stuck at Jaipur airport. We eventually leave at 9.

I arrive at the Imperial Hotel at 10, have three large Black Dog whiskies with soda but no dinner, and go to bed at 11.30.

7.3.99. I have booked an alarm call for 4 a.m. and luckily wake up at precisely that time – luckily for the call itself doesn't come.

Checking out, I find the room rate was 200 US dollars a night. Well, the rooms may be good, but the restaurant is lousy and the bar staff surly.

A taxi to the airport costs 300 rupees. I check in at the Executive Class desk (no queue) and go for coffee in the Maharajah Lounge. I am in seat 16J on flight AI 111, leaving at 7.15. (Make a note for future travel: the best seats in Business Class are 15B or 15J, rows 14 and 18 the worst.)

We eventually take off at 8.30, and I consume a delicious bottle of Piper-Heidsieck. I arrive at Heathrow, Terminal 3, at 12.30, where I am met by Clare and my son, Toby.

This has been another fascinating and enjoyable trip. Within the year, I shall be back for the Wine Festival.

More for my collection of noteworthy signs: 'Swastika Motor Company specialising only in repairs to German cars'; 'Coustumes For Sale'; 'Armpit Shaving'; 'Computer Eye Testing' (outside a small dirty shack in old Delhi). But there is nothing to beat 'Doctor Shagwaller – amputations and replacement limbs while you wait'.

Wine Festival II
27–30 January 2000

27.1.00. A cab arrives to take me to Heathrow Terminal 3, from where a group of us will take the 9.45 Air India flight to Bombay via Delhi. I have arranged upgrades with Capt. Behari at the airline's offices. Guests on the trip to the second Indage Wine Festival are the wine journalists Oz Clarke, Joanna Simon, Tim Atkin, Richard Neill and Rosemary George. We check in at 6.30, only to find the flight has been delayed five hours and that Business Class is full.

We are given vouchers worth £4.50 for spending on breakfast at Garfunkel's, so we regale ourselves with egg, bacon, sausage, tomato, mushrooms and a potato cake, with coffee. They also give us a ticket for the Business Class lounge, but we must wait until we get to the departure gate to find out whether upgrades are possible. The whole situation threatens to become an unmitigated nightmare, but fortunately in the end we are all upgraded.

I'm in seat 10B next to Rosemary George on a very old 747–400. Piper-Heidsieck is served, and then a lamb curry. I read and sleep a little, and we arrive in Delhi after seven hours. There is a one-hour stopover, and we eventually land in Bombay at 5.30 a.m. local time.

28.1.00. We are met at the airport and delivered to the eco-friendly five-star Orchid Hotel near the domestic air terminal. There is an impressive lobby with a fountain in the centre, and lifts that operate in full view of the atrium. I'm in room 219, where I collapse into bed exhausted.

I go down to breakfast at 9, and have an omelette, bacon, tomatoes and baked beans, with coffee, after that a coach tour of Bombay has been laid on. We take in the Gateway of India, St Thomas's cathedral, dating from 1718, the 80-metre-high Rajabai clock tower, the superb Indo-Gothic Victoria railway terminus, and then go along Marine Drive to the lively Chowpatty beach with its collection of street-vendors and fakirs. Later, we meet up with two of the Indage directors at the colonial-style Gymkhana Club for lunch, which includes a lamb dish, a rich tandoori fish dish, and naan made of buckwheat, accompanied by Kingfisher beers.

In the afternoon, more tours are arranged, taking in the Gandhi Museum, the Prince of Wales Museum, and Crawford Market. It's an hour's drive through horrendous traffic back to the hotel.

After showering, I go to the Merlin bar and have some of my favourite Old Monk rum, with fresh lime and soda. At 7.30, a coach collects us to take us into town. Dinner is at the Khyber Restaurant, which has superb décor and amazing food, a very wide choice of both starters and main courses. All in all, it's a very successful evening, hosted by Manesh, a new young employee of Indage. The hour's drive back afterwards takes us through some of the magical sights of Bombay, and I make it to bed at 11.45, absolutely exhausted. It has, after all, been a very long day.

29.1.00. An alarm call wakes me at 7 a.m., although I could easily have slept for at least another two hours. I have a breakfast of omelette, bacon, garlicky tomatoes and baked beans, with watermelon juice and coffee.

The coach arrives at 8 to take us to the Bombay domestic air terminal for a flight to Pune. Indage has chartered a complete Indian Airlines 737 150-seater. It arrives in Pune at 10.30, where three coaches are filled up with guests attending the wine festival, which takes place at the Indage winery in Narayangaon, south-east of Pune.

As the coaches are full Rosemary George, Joanna Simon and I take a cab to the winery, a drive of two hours. There, we are greeted by a band of drummers and ancient trumpets, not to mention a glass of their Joie, a Cuve Close sparkler. We join the procession to the winery, accompanied all the while by cacophonously loud music, for what seems to be something like last time the equivalent of an Ascot garden party. An excellent buffet of various Indian dishes and barbecues has been prepared on the lawns in front of the winery, served by white-gloved

Indage Vineyard, Narayangaon, India

waiters, while different wine producers, such as California's Eric Wente and Peter Mertes from Germany, have stalls offering tastings. This is followed by a grape-stomping competition, to the accompaniment of a live band. The weather is very hot, but there is a welcome cool breeze.

After a flight back to Bombay, we take a cab back to the hotel, where I shower and have a much needed rum in the Merlin bar, prior to dinner. Another buffet of fine Indian delicacies has been set out. I drink a slightly oxidised Grover's Clairette Blanc, a poorly made demi-sec rosé and a very good Cabernet Sauvignon, in the company of Richard Neill, Oz Clarke and Tim Atkin.

I get to bed at 11.45.

30.1.00. I am awoken by a 5.30 a.m. alarm call and, after drinking some watermelon juice and coffee, get into one of the two courtesy cars that arrive to take us to the international airport. The computer only has upgrades recorded for three of us, necessitating an almighty fuss, after which three more upgrades magically appear, delivered by hand to the Business Class lounge.

After a coffee, we board flight AI 125 for London, leaving at 9.10. I'm in seat 16K. Piper-Heidsieck champagne is served in vast quantities, before a breakfast of murgh bharte ka omelette, tulsi anardana machchi, vegetable rösti and grilled tomato. I sleep for a while, and then more Piper is poured. Lunch is stir-fried black pepper chicken in oyster sauce, vegetables in soy sauce and fried rice, after which I watch *Grey Owl* with Pierce Brosnan. Our arrival time at Heathrow is estimated at 1.45 p.m. local time. It's a nine-hour flight.

The wine festival has made for an interesting trip, but one that has been sadly too short. As it turns out, I was to be back again in India in August that year.

20–25 August 2000

20.8.00. A cab arrives at 6.30 a.m. to take me to Heathrow, Terminal 3, where I check in at 7. There is a very long queue for Economy, but I have no problem in upgrading to Business Class, seat 16J (the request is already in the computer, courtesy of Air India).

In the Maharajah Lounge, I have coffee and croissants, before boarding flight AI 102 to Bombay at 9.45. We take off at 10.05. I'm seated upstairs on the 747. There is no champagne, only Henkell Trocken, a semi-sweet German sparkling wine – even in First Class, apparently – an absolute disgrace. I fill out the appropriate complaint form.

Brunch is an omelette with herbs, chicken sausages and hash browns, with fruit and coffee. I read and sleep. The time will be 5½ hours ahead. Dinner consists of a very good chicken curry, with rice, chapatis and poppadums, which I precede with a couple of large Johnnie Walker Black Labels, and accompany with an acceptable 1996 Bouchard Père Bourgogne Chardonnay.

We arrive at 11.30 p.m., local time. The officials at the airport are beginning to know me by now and I am waved straight through VIP passport control, and to a car that takes me to the Ambassador Hotel, room 607. After a snack and nightcap, I am in bed at 1.30 a.m.

21.8.00. I breakfast at 9 on scrambled eggs and bacon with mango juice and coffee.

(In the light of day, I decide it would be a good idea to move rooms. The enamel in the bath and wash-basin has begun to give up the ghost, and there is a dank and damp atmosphere that I certainly won't be able to stand for five days at my time of life, not even for a discounted $50 a night. I am moved to room 403, which has evidently been recently refurbished. This is absolutely perfect, and I am delighted to find that there is no change in the room rate.)

I arrive at 10 at the new Indage offices at 33B Sir Pochkhanwala Road, Worli, prepared for a day-long meeting, broken only by –

believe it or not – a tomato sandwich at 2.30. It rains all day, which causes great problems for those living on the streets. Still, after all my visits, the poverty – and, moreover, the general acceptance of it – are difficult for me to tolerate, and yet the second-generation rich are swanning about in flashy sports cars and frequenting trendy restaurants and cigar bars, spending unmentionable sums on Dom Pérignon and Roederer Cristal champagne. The wholesale shift to Western ways seems inevitable. It's all very sad.

I have my first meeting with the Ranjit Chougule, the Indage managing director. The idea is to set up a joint venture company, Chateau Indage Vintners Ltd, between myself and Indage, to import foreign wines for distribution to the hotel and restaurant trade in the main cities of India. We eventually agree contract terms, which are sent to the solicitors, the aim being that the final documents will be drawn up and ready for signature before I leave on Friday 25th. Having had prior meetings with certain wineries around the world, we finally agree which agencies we will be representing in India. These will be Laurent-Perrier (Champagne), Louis Latour (Burgundy), Ginestet (Bordeaux), Hardy's (Australia), Santa Carolina (Chile), Peter Mertes (Germany), and Berberana (Spain) – all in all, quite a nice start.

Leaving the office eventually at 7.30, I go to dinner at a fashionable new Franco-Italian Restaurant, Indigo, serving indifferent and expensive food. It's full of the young set, who find it fashionable to eat anything other than Indian cuisine. After a couple of large Old Monk rum, lime and sodas, I drink a glass of Sauvignon Blanc made by the Sula winery (it's oxidised and dreadful) and a glass of their Chenin Blanc (which is only just acceptable). The starter is layers of pasta with roasted vegetables, and the main course chicken cooked in the tandoor with a French-style reduced sauce and croquette potatoes. What a shame there isn't one Indian dish on the menu. The place is packed with trendies.

Back at the hotel at 10.30, I have a large Monk and soda in the bar, where a live performer sings 'My Way' to an out-of-tune piano. I am in bed by 11.

22.8.00. Once again, it rains all day. I am awoken by an alarm call at 7, and have a 7.30 breakfast of omelette with onions and tomatoes, bacon, toast, sweet lime juice and coffee.

A car collects me at 8 to go to the office, and I spend the morning working on the proposed new list and costings, as the duty rates on imported wines are extremely high, in excess of 100%. At 1.30, we go for lunch at the Bombay Brasserie. We are regaled with a very large, and superb, buffet spread, from which I try two different kinds of chicken dish, one dry in a sort of yoghurt, the other in a sauce of chillies, onions and tomato, accompanied by rice, potatoes, a butter naan and a San Miguel larger.

Afterwards, I go on to the Oberoi Hotels head office to meet the vice-president, and discuss our new venture, about which he is very enthusiastic. Back at the office, I work on the computer list until 5, and then on the conversion to rupee prices. Leaving the office at 9, I find it's still pelting down with rain. Well, it is the monsoon season, I suppose.

At my hotel, I go to dinner in the revolving restaurant, the Pearl of the Orient, on the 12th floor, which takes 90 minutes to make a full revolution. The food is an interesting new Indo-Chinese amalgam; I begin with a couple of Old Monk rums with lime and soda. I order prawn dumpling in garlic and chilli paste, a Shanghai dish, and then Hunanese crispy chilli lamb, Cantonese chicken, and Cantonese fried rice with char siu. The food here is excellent, and all the portions very large.

23.8.00. Waking to an alarm call at 7.45, I discover that it is still raining naturally. I breakfast on sweet lime juice and coffee only, as I still feel full from last night.

A car picks me up at 8.30, and I work solidly all day, eating no lunch and seeing no daylight, until 7.30 p.m. Eventually, the wine list is finished.

Back at the hotel at 8, I go for drinks in the 14th floor bar, which boasts a great view, and also serves barbecue food and snacks. The rain has stopped, and suddenly, it's a very pleasant evening. At 9, I have dinner in the hotel's Indian restaurant, where the menu reflects the recent changes in Indian culinary culture among the wealthier sections of the population. It is made up of 50% French flambé dishes. I choose rogan gosht with two naan breads, which is quite good, and accompany it with a 60cl bottle of Kingfisher beer. The pianist plays Frank Sinatra tunes on an instrument that is hilariously out of tune. A great change is imminent in this country. You heard it here first!

I get to bed at 10 at the end of a very taxing couple of days' work.

24.8.00. An alarm call rouses me at 8.15, and fifteen minutes later I am setting about a breakfast of scrambled eggs, bacon and baked beans, with sweet lime juice and coffee.

At 9, a car takes me to the office, where the final touches are put to the list. Lunch at the Mela Restaurant just down the road from the hotel is an excellent buffet affair with three different types of chicken dish and various barbecued items of fish, meat and chicken. There are also rice, roti and butter naan.

Later, I have a meeting with Sham Chougule, the chairman of Indage, at which we sign the joint venture deal. We mark the moment with a glass of Omar Khayyam, and at 9, I return to the hotel. The torrential rain has at last stopped.

I pack and book a 3 a.m. alarm call for my 6.30 flight. I go for a final drink in the 14th floor bar. The floor is awash and there's a strong wind, but it's a pleasant enough evening on which to view the fabulous view. I have an Old Monk rum and soda, and then go down to the Pearl of the Orient, and sample various dishes from three different Chinese regions, all of which are very good.

25.8.00. My alarm call comes through at 4 a.m., an hour late, and I take a fast taxi to the airport for the 6.30 flight. I am upgraded to Business Class and this time it's a good journey, but with no champagne – again! We arrive at around 9.30 a.m. local time.

15–25 February 2001

15.2.01. A cab arrives at 6.15 a.m. to take me to Heathrow, Terminal 3, where I check in for the Air India First Class flight AI 112, seat 1A, to Delhi. I have coffee and croissants in the Maharajah Lounge, and learn that the flight has been delayed by an hour to 9.40. Foggy conditions look likely to cause further delays, so I have a couple of large Bloody Marys. We are finally boarded at Gate 2 at 11.05, and eventually take off at 12.30.

The journey will be a very civilised one in the First Class nose of the 747 and, once on board, I drink a couple of glasses of Marquis de Pompadour, Indage's domestic sparkling wine, and then sleep for an hour and a half. Prior to lunch, Piper-Heidsieck champagne is served, and the food – chicken tikka and lamb chops – is very good. I watch a stupid film about a dog show championship, accompanying it with a brace of Johnnie Walker Black Labels with soda.

Dinner, which is served at 11.30 p.m. local time, begins with Piper again, followed by caviare with vodka and all the trimmings, a fine Indian chicken dish with rice, vegetables and chapati, accompanied by good 1996 Bouchard Père Bourgogne Pinot Noir Vieilles Vignes, and then a cheese selection of Camembert, Cheddar and Roquefort.

We arrive in Delhi at 1.45 a.m. local time (8.45 p.m., according to me). A driver collects me at the airport and delivers me to the five star Nikko Hotel at 3. I go straight to bed, and pass a very bad night.

16.2.01. An alarm call wakes me at 8.30 a.m. from a short, fitful night's sleep. I shower and then take juice and coffee only for breakfast. I meet briefly with Bali, newly appointed sales director of Indage, and then leave for the office at 9.15.

There, I meet with Gagan, sales executive of the Delhi office, and visit a local company that owns a convenient bonded warehouse, which can be used to store our wines for distribution in and around Delhi. After a snack lunch in the office, I visit a number of Taj and Sheraton five-star hotels, all of which are keen to start business with us, and then return to the hotel at 6.

In the evening, I confine myself to the excellent Old Monk rum with soda, and feast on some small chicken snacks, meeting up with friends of Bali.

I am in bed at 10, quite shattered.

17.2.01. Awakening at 8.45 after a good sleep, I have a breakfast of poached eggs, bacon and toast at 9.30.

My first meeting of the day is at the Park Hotel, the second at the Nikko, and the third at the Imperial, a superb hotel, where I also have a lunch of biryani and Kingfisher beer. In the afternoon, I'm at the Intercontinental and then the Radisson, before returning to my own hotel.

After a couple of large Old Monk rums, I have dinner in the hotel with Bali: lamb, dhal and naan bread. I get to bed at 11.

18.2.01. The day begins with a 7.30 breakfast, and work on the Delhi wine lists, after which I drive to the superb Baluchi Restaurant in the deer park for lunch with Rukn Luthra, a new appointee of the Gallo winery in California. The food is excellent, chicken balls stuffed with minced pork, a tandoori dish and pork, with dhal.

Back at the hotel, I read by the pool, and at 5, am treated to a massage by a Japanese sumo wrestler with the face and breathing difficulties of a pug.

Drinks in the bar later precede a great dinner of chicken and lamb at a new restaurant, a very popular and busy place along the road from our hotel. After a nightcap at the hotel, I'm in bed at 12.

19.2.01. After breakfasting at 9, I take my first meeting with Mr Salle, the new food and beverage manager at the Oberoi. More meetings take place over lunch with representatives of the Turquoise Cottage, Obsession and Geoffrey's restaurants, who are all ready to proceed.

We are then driven to the airport, where we board the 8 p.m.

flight to Bangalore, arriving at 10.30. A car picks us up and takes us to the Antrim Hotel, a fairly tacky place, where I have a nightcap before retiring at 12.

20.2.01. Having benefited from a good night's sleep, I awake at 8, and have a mango-type juice and coffee for breakfast. I then meet with George, sales manager of Indage's Bangalore office. It turns out there are no bonded warehouses in Bangalore, and only one in Mangalore. I arrange to meet with their distributor at 4 to discuss an application for our own bond licence.

My further hotel appointments are with the Taj, the Oberoi, the magnificent West End, the Windsor, the Park and the Meridien. Lunch at the Taj is a mediocre Chinese buffet, followed by a further meeting with a local government official, who will hopefully grant our application for a bonded warehouse licence.

I'm back at the airport at 7 for the 8 p.m. flight to Bombay, eventually arriving at the Ambassador Hotel, room 403, at 11.

21.2.01. I breakfast lightly at 8 a.m. on juice and coffee, and then at 9.15, I conduct an in-depth training session with all the Indage sales staff on the new wines about to be imported for distribution to all the Indian hotels. The session is videotaped. I then take meetings with the directors of the Ambassador and Oberoi hotels, and then go to a superb lunch in the Kandahar Restaurant at the Oberoi, consisting of chicken in a bright yellow sauce, lamb in a dry gravy, butter naan and ice cream made from milk. This is without doubt my favourite restaurant in Bombay.

Further meetings with the Taj, Indigo and Marine Plaza ensue, followed by dinner in the Pearl of the Orient revolving restaurant at the hotel – dim sum and a lamb and chilli dish, accompanied by Kingfisher beer.

I awake at 5 a.m. with an upset stomach.

22.2.01. Beginning the day with juice and coffee at 9, I make the one-hour drive to the Sun n Sand Hotel to meet the owner, Mr Arora, and then travel on to the newly opened seven-star Regent Hotel to see Mr Harry, the food and beverage manager. We have an excellent lunch in their Chinese restaurant overlooking the ocean.

In the afternoon, I make a full 90-minute presentation to 15 staff at the Sheraton ITC, a new hotel near the airport. I return to the Ambassador, shower and change, and then at 8.30, attend a party for Sham Chougule's eldest son Vikrant's wedding in the roof garden of the Jewel of India Restaurant. There is a superb buffet offering dishes from all the regions of India, complemented by a full bar.

Feeling very tired, I make it back to bed at 12.

23.2.01. I take juice and coffee in my room at 8.30, and then at 10, I have the first of the day's meetings, with Mr Lam of the Taj Mahal, followed by another at 11.45 with the Palm Grove. An excellent lunch accompanies my meeting at the Orchid, and the afternoon and early evening proceed as follows: 3.30, the Meridien; 5, the Leela; 6.15, the Holiday Inn/Club; 8, the Sheraton ITC.

Dinner is at a Peshwari Restaurant at the Sheraton with the food and beverage manager, and comprises tandoori shinga, prawns with yoghurt and red chillies, murgh makhani, tandoori chicken with tomatoes and onions, black dhal and a roomali roti – all magnificent. He insisted that we all get through a fair quantity of Old Smuggler rum, malt whiskies and so forth.

24.2.01. Once again, the day is taken up with meetings: with Arvinder at 10, the Taj President at 12, the Khyber Restaurant at 1.30, and Vikrant Chougule's Athena Club at 2.30, after which, between 4.30 and 9, I conduct a full wine training session for their staff.

Dinner is a fusion food stir-fry at the Athena, which is a sumptuously decorated club and disco.

I am back at 12.

25.2.01. Waking to my alarm call at 6 a.m., I pack and am collected half an hour later to go to the airport. I check in for the Air India First Class flight AI 125 at 9.10, seat 1A. (I prefer 2B or 3B, as they are aisle seats.) After coffee in the Maharajah Lounge, we board and I sleep for an hour. Upon waking, I am served Veuve Clicquot champagne with caviare, and then lamb and chicken curries, and a paratha with 1990 Château Giscours, followed by cheese with port. I sleep for another three hours, and we arrive at 1.35 a.m. local time. There is no car to collect me, although one was reserved, and I have to find a black cab to take me home.

Once again, India has provided me with another successful, if extremely tiring, trip.

Dubai and India
9–12 October 2001

9.10.01. A chauffeured car, courtesy of Emirates Airlines, arrives at 6.15 a.m. to take me to Gatwick, North Terminal, where I check in for the First Class flight EK 008 to Mumbai, via Dubai, seat 2J. Security, a month after the World Trade Centre attacks, is very tight; there are police with machine guns and automatic rifles patrolling the airport, and we are only allowed one item of hand luggage. My ticket allows me use of the Delta Lounge, which is very comfortable, and I have coffee and croissants in there.

The flight is due to leave at 10, and we board at 9.30. I have the First Class cabin to myself, and am served Duval-Leroy champagne as soon as I am installed. We take off at 10.10, and Dom Pérignon 1993 is poured, with some warm toasted nuts to accompany. Lunch is served at noon, by which time I must have consumed at least a bottle of the DP, along with caviare and all the trimmings. I pass on the soup and salad, and have chicken with rice, and then lamb chops in a lovely crust on tomato sauce, with Scottish Cheddar to finish. The wines are a youthful 1994 Château Montrose, and Taylor's 1994 LBV port. I read and sleep for a couple of hours, and then tea is served.

We land in Dubai at 8 p.m. local time (three hours ahead of GMT). In the First Class lounge, I have a couple of Johnnie Walker Black Labels with soda, and then at 10 we board flight EK 500 to Mumbai, taking off at 10.30. Once again, I'm in seat 2J, but there are now three people in First Class. It will be a 2½-hour journey.

The superb Lanson Noble Cuvée 1989 is served, and then a meal comprising mixed smoked fish and yoghurt, and chicken balti with rice, accompanied by 1992 Château Soutard, an awful wine. I switch to an Australian Cabernet Sauvignon for relief, and Taylor's 1995 LBV is served with the cheese. I sleep for an hour, and we arrive in Mumbai at 4 a.m. local time.

10.10.01. I take a taxi to the Ambassador Hotel, and try to sleep for a couple of hours, before an alarm call wakes me at 7.45 a.m. I drink a black coffee and some bottled water, and then the driver from Indage Group collects me at 8.30.

I have a meeting with Ranjit Chougule, to discuss the possibility of collaborating with African and Eastern wine importers, in Dubai, and we then go to a buffet lunch at the Bombay Brasserie, which takes in a meeting with our newly appointed sales manager, Sylvain Fetzman, whose father is the winemaker at Louis Latour in Burgundy. The food is very good, a chicken dish, rice, tandoori items, and so on.

At 5, I have a lift to the airport for the 7 p.m. flight back to Dubai, on which I'm again booked in First Class, seat 2B. Lanson Noble Cuvée 1989 is served once more, and there's a fine chicken curry with rice. After lots more champagne, we arrive in Dubai at 8 p.m. local time. A chauffeur is on hand to take me to the Emirates Tower Hotel, where I'm put in a brand new room, 1911.

I have a Famous Grouse whisky and soda in the bar on the 51st floor. It's an altogether magnificent hotel, with amazing views over Dubai. I fall into bed at 11, extremely tired.

11.10.01. I am awoken by the alarm call at 7 a.m., having slept very well. Breakfast is poached eggs on toast with bacon, mango juice and coffee.

A car from African and Eastern collects me at 8 for a full morning's meetings with sales director, Jason Dixon, and Kevin Bullock, the managing director. The company is the largest distributor of imported wines and spirits in Dubai, and is interested in extending its operation to India. We are discussing the possibility of joining forces.

Afterwards, we drive to their huge bonded warehouse in the duty-free town of Jebal Ali, on the outskirts of Dubai. It's a sizzling 38°C outside.

We have a very impressive buffet lunch at the Royal Mirage Hotel, a lovely place on the beach, and then return to the office for meetings until 6. The meetings have been very productive. After a visit to one of their retail shops, we go back to the hotel, where I have a pre-dinner large Famous Grouse in the 51st floor bar.

At 8.15, I am collected to be taken to dinner at Gordon

Ramsey's new restaurant at the Hilton Creek Hotel. We get through a very pretentious eight-course *menu dégustation*, as follows: gazpacho with balsamic vinegar; a three-tiered foie gras dish; lobster tart; venison in dark chocolate sauce; cheeses; poached pear; Bailey's bread-and-butter pudding with Bailey's ice cream; coffee and chocolates. With these, we drink Joseph Perrier champagne, a good Brown Brothers Australian Sauvignon Blanc, an excellent McWilliams Australian Merlot and a Tokaji 5 puttonyös. At one point, with great affectation, the sommelier decides to produce, at our expense, a white wine served in a hideous Riedel decanter, for us to identify blind. I normally find this type of game under these circumstances quite offensive, but nonetheless correctly guess the wine to be a Meursault of at least ten years old. (It was in fact 1988.)

I round things off with a J&B whisky, and we make it back to the hotel at 1 a.m. It has been another tiring day.

12.10.01. The alarm call wakes me at 7 a.m., and I eat a hearty breakfast of poached eggs, bacon, sausages and mushrooms.

At 8, my friends at African and Eastern have arranged an adventure for me, and so I set off on a trip into the desert, a terrifying four-wheel drive over the dunes at the hands of some crazy young Arab driver, who almost overturns the vehicle no fewer than three times. During the course of the trip, I go falconing, and ride a camel into the desert. My goodness, camels are bad-tempered creatures, foul-smelling and continually spitting at you.

Back at the hotel at 11, I shower and change and then check out. The Emirates' chauffeured-limousine arrives at 12.30 to take me to the airport. My flight leaves at 2.15. I check into First Class, seat 2J, but before boarding, I have four out of my six bottles of Indian wine samples confiscated. At 1, I go and sit in the First Class lounge and have a Bloody Mary. We board at 1.45, and once again, as the First Class cabin is deserted, I have the attentions of the staff to myself. They supply me with copious quantities of 1993 Dom Pérignon and mounds of caviare, followed by a trolley of delicious hot dishes.

This has been a good trip, but of too short a duration to justify the long flights.

North America and Canada
1991–2002

San Francisco
20–26 September 1991

20.9.91. Arriving at Gatwick, South Terminal, at 7 a.m., I check in for American Airlines flight AA 2737, and am upgraded to Business Class. I am greeted by special services representative Val Cushing, and am escorted to the Admiral's Lounge for coffee. Talk about VIP treatment! She personally escorted me to the aircraft, waving aside the queue, and to seat 8B, apologising the while that First Class was full, otherwise she would have seated me there. It is a superb airline with first-rate service and lovely big comfortable seats.

As there is a seven-hour backward time difference, dinner is served at noon UK time. Pommery Cuvée Louise 1985 champagne is followed by fillet steak served on proper china plates. Two films are shown, as this is a very long flight. We stop at Fort Worth, Dallas, for two hours to unload and check the baggage in again. This is effectively 9 p.m. UK time, so we have been travelling ten hours. While at Fort Worth, I visit the Admiral's Club VIP lounge for a bourbon and soda, and then check in again to flight AA 71 to San Francisco. The plane is full, and I am very lucky to get a last-minute upgrade.

This will be a three-hour flight with a further two-hour time difference, so we are now eight hours behind the UK. We arrive at San Francisco at what my body thinks is 2.30 a.m., but which is actually 6.30 p.m. local time.

Nora Comée, who, although she hails from San Francisco, works in London representing various California wine producers for whom we are the UK agents, collects me and drives me to the Orchard Hotel, 562 Sutter Street. It's quite small but clean and comfortable, and good value at $80 a night. I'm feeling surprisingly fit and not too jet-lagged. We meet at 7.30 for a drink, and then go for an extended walk, to Union Square and then to the Hyatt Regency Hotel, in the Embarcadero Centre where the amazing hollowed-out 17-storey atrium has a revolving 360-

degree rooftop bar called the Equinox. Here I am poured a thunderously strong Wild Turkey 101 bourbon.

We then take a cab to the Juet Lee, one of the best Cantonese restaurants at 1300 Stockton Street, on the corner of Broadway. It's a very basic place but the food is great: clams in black bean sauce, barbecue pork chow mein, beef with ginger and onion, and rice with shrimp and peas, accompanied by Budweiser lager. I cab back to the Orchard at 11 p.m., now quite shattered. Sleep is difficult though. I awake at 3 a.m., then again at 6 and again at 8.30.

21.9.91. I breakfast at 9 a.m. on two eggs over easy, bacon, hash browns, fruit, toast and coffee. My goodness, they certainly do serve substantial breakfasts. The morning is spent at Fisherman's Wharf, with its variety of street performers, restaurants and shops; the Anchorage, a two-level shopping centre; the Cannery, previously the Del Monte Fruit Company's peach packing plant in 1909, refurbished in the 1960s now houses the museum of the city of San Francisco as well as over fifty shops and restaurants on three levels; and Ghirardelli Square, a renovated chocolate factory dating from 1893 is a now beautiful landscaped centre with new elegant shops, restaurants and the famous Ghirardelli chocolate factory. From there I take the Red and White ferry across to Alcatraz Island, which was in the 1770s known as *Isla de los alcatraces*, or Island of Pelicans. The island served as a military fortification in 1859, and during the Spanish-American War. In 1934 it later became famous as a maximum-security Federal Prison for Mafia criminals and high-risk convicts until 1963, and it was opened to the public in 1973. There I take the guided tour on tape, excellent and highly recommended.

Afterwards, I drive to Union Street and lunch at Perry's. This consists of enormous portions of potato skins with crispy bacon covered in cheese, with a hamburger, and Michelob and Coors on draught to drink. Following some more sightseeing by car, I return to the hotel at 4.30 to sleep.

Later, I meet with Jim and Stephanie Faber of the Foppiano Winery based in Sonoma County. We go to the Redwood Room at the hotel for drinks, and then to the Zum Zum Room in

Haight Ashbury, which is the last of the hippie bars. Still decorated like a Persian brothel, it is only open between 6 and 9 p.m. and only serves Vodka Martinis. The owner has retained his ponytail and bandana. Nora asks for a glass of wine and is promptly told to leave in no uncertain terms. We then go to dinner at Zuno Café, 1658 Market Street; anchovies with Parmesan are followed by a main course of red snapper. We drink two Chardonnays and some Iron Horse fizz, and finish with a half-bottle of Laurel Glen botrytised wine. The evening is rounded off at the Cypress Club, 500 Jackson Street the latest place to be seen, a new venue with offbeat wild decor, where I polish off a quantity of Wild Turkey.

I am in bed at 1 a.m.

22.9.91. I awake at 6 from another fitful night's sleep, watch TV and doze again until about 8.30. Breakfast at 9 is scrambled eggs with toast, Canadian bacon and hash browns. Nora has gone off to see her sister, and so the intrepid me is to be on his own for the day.

I stroll down to Market Street and then take a two-dollar cable car ride to Fisherman's Wharf. At Pier 39, I buy a ticket for a 75-minute narrated cruise around San Francisco Bay on the Blue and Gold Ferry. The trip takes in Alcatraz Island, Oakland Bay Bridge and the famous Golden Gate Bridge built in 1937, it is the world's second largest single-span bridge, a memorable experience. Back on dry land, I take a look around the Pier 39, the Wharf's working hub, which sells the local fishing fleets' catch. A particular delicacy is cracked crab, and it's delicious with sourdough bread bought from the nearby French bakery. The general atmosphere feels just like London's Covent Garden. The Pier is also home to a colony of over 600 sea lions, which adds to the lively atmosphere with a corporate bark that sounds like dogs with laryngitis. I partake of a couple of locally brewed Anchor steam beers in a bar overlooking the Bay. After that, I decide it's about time for lunch, and walk up to Bobby Rubino's, 245 Jefferson, for the largest plate of spare ribs and onion rings I have ever seen and some cold draught Budweiser.

After lunch, I take a guided bus tour around most of the city.

It drops me off at Union Square and I go shopping in Macy's and other stores, buying presents for the family along the way, before going back to the hotel at 5.30.

Later I meet Nora for drinks at Top of the Mark at the Mark Hopkins Hotel, the 360-degree view from which is superb. We go to a recommended Italian Restaurant nearby called Vanessi's, 1177 California Street, for dinner. It's located in the basement of an apartment block – very dark and very indifferent food.

I'm back in bed by 11.30.

23.9.91. After a light breakfast at 8, I am driven to the Sonoma County district for a visit to the Foppiano Winery, arriving at 10.15. Jim Faber takes me through the vineyards, around the winery and thence to an extensive tasting. This is followed by a meeting with the two Louis Foppianos (junior and senior). Louis Foppiano Snr is a wonderful character, standing well over six feet tall, very muscular and not looking anything like his 75 years. His son relates a great story about him. When his father was younger, he was involved in an accident in which a tractor slipped backwards and trapped him underneath. Somehow he managed to lift it off himself single-handed, and crawled out – sustaining, as he said, 'only a couple of broken legs'. We then have a salad lunch at Tre Scalini in Healdsburg, the nearest town. On the way back, we stop at Sausalito for a drink by the ocean, to see the fog rolling in.

Nora is off to dinner with her mother, and so I go to the famous watering hole, Lefty O'Doul's bar, 333 Geary Street, named after its founder the former famous baseball player. There are three televisions showing a baseball match, and so I ask the man sitting next to me to explain the rules of the game. As he starts, the rest of the bar joins in, contradicting and talking across each other the whole time, with the result that I am even more confused when I leave than when I arrived. I return to the hotel at 10.30.

24.9.91. Breakfast is at 8, and then I am driven to Sonoma once more, this time for a visit to Chateau St Jean. They have highly impressive premises in a superb location, and Bob Jackson, the winemaker, conducts me on the winery tour and through a full tasting. I must say their wines are extremely good.

Lunch is at the Kenwood Restaurant at Kenwood, and a fine one it is too – crab cakes, followed by rabbit. After this, I meet with Pat Roney, the president of Chateau St Jean.

I am driven back into town, go for a drink and dinner at Stars, 150 Redwood Alley, the newest trendy restaurant and bar run by Jeremiah Towers. I order a Wild Turkey 101 with soda. When the drink arrives, it appears to contain almost a quarter-bottle of bourbon. I have to ask for an empty glass to make two drinks from the one. Dinner is typical West Coast fusion, salmon with Asian spices (overrated), after which I proceed for a nightcap to the Balbao Café, 3199 Fillmore Street, feeling – it has to be said – quite tipsy. I am in bed by 11.30.

25.9.91. I spend the day sightseeing through the Financial District where old style banking halls from the early twentieth century stand alongside the glass and steel skyscrapers, Chinatown, visiting Kong Chow Temple, Old St Mary church, Tin How Temple, and wandering through narrow alleys full of traditional shops and restaurants, and North Beach, with its café orientated atmosphere which has long appealed to bohemians and Lombard Street banked at a natural incline of 27° twisting back on itself eight times, it is known as 'the crookedest street in the world', then do some serious shopping at Macy's – what a great store!

Pat Roney of Chateau St Jean invites us to dinner at another newish restaurant, Lascaux, 250 Sutter, a rather good French brasserie with great live jazz music.

We are then taken to the Sol y Luna, a busy Spanish bar with music and dancers, great fun and very trendy, where we drink a bottle of Chateau St Jean sparkling wine, and repair to the hotel at 11.30.

26.9.91. After breakfasting at 8, I am driven to the airport and checked into First Class. Once again, I am shown to my seat ahead of the queue. We have a 3½-hour flight from San Francisco to Forth Worth, Dallas, where there is a quick change for the onward flight to the UK. I am now in Business Class, seat 11B.

Both food and service are excellent again. We take off at 5.30 p.m., and should land at Gatwick – all being well – at 9.30 a.m. local time.

San Francisco
10–17 October 1992

10.10.92. I arrive at Heathrow, Terminal 3, at 11.30 a.m. for the United Airlines flight UA 931 direct to San Francisco, checking into Business Class, and then take myself off to their Red Carpet Lounge for gin and tonics. It turns out the flight is delayed; it's due to leave at 2, but we are told it will now be 3.20. We board at 2.30. I am in seat 16H, which is one of the window seats with maximum legroom. Perrier-Jouët champagne is served immediately, and kept permanently topped up. During the 10½-hour flight, we are to be entertained with *Batman Returns*, not to mention beef fillet and more champagne (this time Veuve Clicquot). I take two naps, one of three hours, the other of a single hour, but am happily awake for the overflight of the Salt Lakes, a superb view.

We arrive at 5.40 p.m. local time, and I am taken to the Grand Hyatt Hotel, Union Square, where I check into suite 219/220. My first drink is taken in the bar on the 36th floor, a well-deserved Wild Turkey 101 Bourbon.

There's a Chinese celebration going on as I walk through the pagoda gates on Grant Avenue through the crowded streets of Chinatown, housing over 10,000 Chinese in a 20-block radius, then along Columbus Avenue to the corner of Green, where I eat a delicious pizza at Calzone's, followed by a nightcap in a local bar, and return to the hotel at 11, quite shattered.

11.10.92. I awake at first at 4 a.m., and then doze until about 8. Leaving the hotel, I take the cable car to Fisherman's Wharf to have breakfast at Chick's Place on Pier 39 with unsurpassed views of the Golden Gate Bridge. Portions are inevitably huge: three eggs, bacon, hash browns, muffins, etc.

I check out of the hotel at 12.30, and meet up with Nora Comée, who represents a number of wineries in California, including one owned and run by Andrew Quady. Quady started adult life as a chemist in Los Angeles making fireworks, but had always had a passion for vintage port and a desire to recreate as near as possible the same style of wine in California. One day, whilst experimenting with a new type of firework, he blew himself up, losing most of his hair, eyebrows and lashes, which left him looking like a mad professor. It was then he decided to sell up, move and buy a property that would enable him to start his vinous adventures. He selected a house and land near Madera in the middle of Death Valley, and proceeded to plant original port grapes, such as Touriga Nacional, Bastardo and the like. The initial results were encouraging, but demand was poor. One day a nearby fruit farmer asked Andy what he could do with a large overcrop of Orange Muscat grapes. Andy processed them as he would with his port style, by fortifying the wine with grape brandy prior to the completion of the fermentation. The results were stunning, and so he designed an avant-garde label, calling the wine 'Essencia'. It became an instant success, and he subsequently extended it to include an equally successful Black Muscat wine called Elysium, claiming it was the only wine that could be drunk with chocolate. His ongoing attempts with the port style resulted in a superb wine, which couldn't be called port, as that is a protected name; and so – thinking laterally – he called it Starboard, producing a non-vintage called Batch 88, as well as a vintage.

The journey to Quady's house and winery takes four hours travelling south-west in very hot conditions. The temperature is now well into the nineties. We stop for lunch on the way at a Mexican Restaurant, La Morenita, where the food is so hot it requires numerous foul-tasting Mexican beers to put out the fire.

Arriving at Quady's at 5.30, I am invited to go for a swim in their pool, a welcome prospect. Andy is cooking dinner, and regales us with a seafood spread including mussels, crab, salmon and so on, accompanied by numerous wines. Andy then informs us that he only has one spare bedroom, which Nora and I will have to share. Now, I am neither shy nor prudish, but the prospect of sharing a room with a gorgeous 25-year-old married Barbie doll is going to be interesting. Fortunately, it's a large room with two double beds. We retire in shifts at 10.30, and I am kept awake all night by the worst snoring imaginable. From now on, she is to be known as Nora the Snorer.

12.10.92. After breakfasting at 8 a.m., Andy gives us a full tour of the winery, followed by a tasting that keeps us occupied until around 1. We have a Mexican lunch in Madera again. The food is not only like a volcano erupting in my mouth, muting my vocal cords in the process, but the quality is appalling. I am beginning to think that perhaps Mexican food is not for me.

Leaving at 2.30, I am driven to Sonoma, where we arrive at the Vintners Inn at 4350 Barnes Road, Santa Rosa, around 6.30. This is an excellent hotel, plumb in the middle of the vineyards. I have a large tastefully furnished room on the first floor with a ravishing view over the vines.

We go into Santa Rosa for dinner at Fan's, 620 Fifth Street, where the Euro-Pacific food is first rate, superb fish and steaks, and a good Ravenswood Zinfandel. I'm in bed at 10.30.

13.10.92. Following an 8.30 breakfast, I am driven to Chateau St Jean. This is a superb winery in the most beautiful setting, easily the most up to date I have seen in California, now owned by Suntory of Japan, who have invested heavily in modern equipment and new oak barrels. I have a full day's programme, and an extensive tasting with Don Kelly, their export director. Their single vineyard wines are excellent, as is their botrytis-affected dessert wine. The visit is only interrupted by lunch at Café Citti, a good pasta restaurant.

In the evening, we spend a very pleasant time at a barbecue at the house of Nora's sister and brother-in-law, Elizabeth and John. Her parents, who are cattle ranchers, are there too, and provide the most enormous and delicious steaks I have ever seen let alone eaten.

14.10.92. I go to the Foppiano Winery in Sonoma at 9.30 for a full tasting. They have an extensive range of good, if commercial, white and red wines, including a stunning Petite Sirah Reserve. Afterwards, we have a sandwich lunch al fresco at Louis Jnr's home.

Dinner is with Louis Foppiano Jnr and Jim Faber, his export director, at California Thai in the Brickyard Centre, 522 Seventh Street, Santa Rosa – very good food. I end the day with a bourbon nightcap at the hotel.

15.10.92. Off to Carneros Creek Winery in the Napa Valley for a full tasting and tour of the vineyard with the owner, Francis Mahoney. This boutique winery specialises in Pinot Noir, his Signature Reserve being the finest example of California Pinot I have yet to taste. We take lunch at the Old Sonoma Creamery, 400 First Street, East Sonoma. This consists of an enormous and delicious 'Kraut dog'!

Later I am driven for dinner at Chateau St Jean with Mike Kenton and Don Kelly, two of their directors, Louis Foppiano, Jim Faber and Francis Mahoney. Their chef, Anne Seeley produced a superb meal.

> 1982 Grande Cuvée, Méthode Traditionelle
> 1991 Fumé Blanc, La Petite Étoile Vineyards
> Scallop Bisque
> 1990 Chardonnay, Robert Young Vineyards
> Autumn Salad with a Walnut Vinaigrette
> 1988 Cabernet Sauvignon, Sonoma County
> Beef Filet with Gorgonzola Sauce, Potato Dumplings
> Winter Squash with Curry Butter
> 1989 Johannisberg Riesling, Hoot Owl Creek Vineyards, Special
>   Late Harvest
> Apricot Soufflé with Hazelnut Butter Cookies.

Jim Faber has brought a particularly memorable bottle, Fox Mountain Cabernet Sauvignon 1981, from a small vineyard owned by the Foppiano family. We have nightcaps at a nearby bar in Kenwood, and I am in bed at 10.30.

16.10.92. After breakfasting at 8.30, I check out of the Vintners Inn and am driven back to San Francisco and the Grand Hyatt Hotel, Union Square.

I spend some time shopping, and then have a pasta lunch at Nordstroms Champagne Bar. I while away the afternoon with a long walk through Chinatown, centred around Portsmouth Square, where the first Chinese immigrants settled in the 1850s, In 1846, Captain John Montgomery raised the American flag in Portsmouth Square to claim California as part of the United States. The 1906 earthquake and fire destroyed the entire district, which the Chinese quickly rebuilt. It is also worth seeing Old St Mary's Church, California's first cathedral built by Chinese labourers. I then take a cab to Pier 39, which is always buzzing with street entertainers and the like.

Back at the hotel at 5.30, I go for drinks in the Regency Club on the 36th floor. Jim Faber arrives to meet me at 7.30, and we go to Haight-Ashbury district, which during the 1960s gained worldwide attention as the centre of the counter culture, free love and anti-war movements, it is still reminiscent of the 'hippie' period, stopping for drinks at Harry's Bar. We eventually rendezvous with his wife Stephanie at 9 at La Folie, 2316 Polk Street, for a fine two-star French dinner. I am back at the hotel at 12.30.

17.10.92. After a 9.30 breakfast, I leave for the airport at 10.30, where I am upgraded to Business Class for the journey home.

Memo to self: I need to go on a serious diet before my next trip.

San Francisco
18–25 September 1993

18.9.93. Having arrived at Heathrow, Terminal 3, at 11.45 a.m., I check in for United Airlines flight UA 933, and am upgraded to Connoisseur Class. I take coffee and drinks in the Red Carpet Lounge before boarding at 1.45. I'm in seat 9E. We leave at 2.20.

The flight begins with Louis Roederer champagne, served with warm mixed nuts, the hostess always enquiring if they were toasted well enough for me. Canapés before lunch are smoked salmon, caviare and Parma ham. The first course is a salad dressed in raspberry vinaigrette, and that's followed by fillet steak in honey sauce with asparagus and rösti, served with a 1988 Heitz Cabernet Sauvignon. Quality is excellent throughout. At 5.25, we are suddenly treated to breathtaking views over Greenland. Then I sleep for a couple of hours and am awakened with coffee.

We arrive at Seattle Airport at 4 p.m. local time (i.e. midnight on my body clock). I am transferred with my luggage to another terminal, but get stuck on the way in one of the unmanned trains, alone, and have to be embarrassingly rescued by an engineer. I am upgraded on the next portion of the journey to seat 2C, departing at 5.30. After bourbon and sodas in the Red Carpet Club, we board at 5.10. It's a small plane with a mere four Business Class seats. We're given Cajun prawns and more bourbon and soda, and I sleep for another hour. We land in San Francisco at 7.30.

Nora Comée is here to collect me, but disaster strikes. It turns out United have misplaced my luggage. Eventually, it's tracked down, and is found to be still sitting at Seattle Airport, where it will now stay until tomorrow. I'm taken to the Hotel Triton, 342 Grant Avenue, a supposed four-star hotel right on the edge of Chinatown, Room 603 is rather dank and dark - more what I'd expect in a two-star place, really.

We go to the rather staid Westin, St Francis Hotel, 335 Powell Street, for drinks, then a cab to the popular Washington Square

Bar and Grill, 1707 Powell Street, for dinner. Cajun red snapper is accompanied by Acacia Vineyards 1992 Chardonnay, which is still too young, but nonetheless a well-made wine. I finally make it to bed at 11.30, completely shattered.

19.9.93. I wake up at 3 a.m., then at 5.30, then at 6.45. When I finally get up, it's difficult to manage without my luggage. I walk through Chinatown on a lovely morning, buy some replacement items and then take coffee outside the hotel at 10.

At 11.30, I take the ferry to the wealthy resort of Sausalito, which means 'the little grove of willows', sipping a beer at an al fresco bar while waiting for the boat. The eight-mile crossing takes half an hour. Once there in this Mediterranean-style hamlet, I go for brunch at the Casa Madrona on a fifth-floor patio and terrace. It's a self-service buffet of excellent foods: oysters, smoked salmon, bacon omelette, bacon and green salad, accompanied by Iron Horse Chardonnay 1991. The return ferry takes me back at 3.15, and from the landing, I walk back to the hotel to find a message waiting for me. I'm to meet Jim and Stephanie Faber from Foppiano Vineyards in the lobby at 5.30.

After drinks we leave for One Market Restaurant, 1 Market Street, a large, new, bustling restaurant, where I enjoy a fine dinner. Smoked salmon with fried onion rings is followed by pheasant, matched with Drouhin Pinot Noir 1990 and Silverado Cabernet Sauvignon 1989. Afterwards, we repair to the Moose Bar for a Red Tap beer, and then back to the hotel at 11, by which time – thankfully – my luggage has arrived.

20.9.93. I awake at 2 a.m., then again at 4, and then again at 6. I dress and pack, having been told I am being moved to a suite; perhaps the message got through regarding the state of my room. A light breakfast is two eggs (over easy), bacon, toast, grapefruit juice and espresso coffee.

I'm meeting Andy Quady at noon. He takes me to the oldest Italian restaurant in the city where I eat anchovies, calamari and pasta, and try a couple of Zinfandels – Sonoma-Cutrer 1990 and Ridge 1990 – both superb. It's 4 by the time we leave, after which I head for Macy's and an afternoon of serious shopping.

At 7.30, I go for drinks, and then dinner at a recommended Mexican Restaurant, Salud, 500 Van Ness. It features regional food from all parts of Mexico, and has indifferent food but a lively atmosphere. I'm back at the hotel by 11.

21.9.93. Leaving the hotel at 7.30 a.m., I'm driven to Carneros Creek Winery in the Napa Valley for a tasting of the new vintages in cask. Their Signature Reserve Pinot Noir will clearly be a stunning wine in a few years time.

Lunch is at 2 at a local restaurant in the tiny village of Napa, fresh pasta with shrimps and garlic. The drive back to the city takes us through the Haight and Castro districts. Castro, the centre of San Francisco's gay community is particularly colourful with its beautifully restored Victorian houses. Then we go to the beach area. I realise San Francisco is much larger than I had always thought. We arrive back at the hotel at 5.30.

After some light shopping in Nordstrom's, I take a cab to Fisherman's Wharf, and a drink at Castagnola's, which fronts on to the Wharf itself. Then I have another at Tarantino's, a great first-floor bar overlooking the harbour. At 9, I arrive at Bobby Rubino's for a gargantuan dinner of ribs, described on the menu 'for the hearty appetite' with onion rings and all the trimmings, with plenty more Budweiser draught beer, a superb repast. I'm back in bed by 11.

22.9.93. The day begins with a 7.30 start and a drive to Foppiano Winery in Sonoma for an all-day meeting and full tasting of the new and current vintages, which lasts through until 6.30 p.m. The day is punctuated by lunch at Samba Java in Healdsburg.

In the evening, I join Nora for dinner at her sister's, and then it's a 60-mile drive back into the city, and bed at 11.30.

23.9.93. After breakfasting at 7 a.m. on scrambled eggs and bacon, we leave at 7.30 for Chateau St Jean. I have a full tasting of the new and current vintages with Don Kelly and Michael Kenyon, the sales and export directors respectively. We then take a superb lunch in their dining room prepared by Chef de Cuisine, Matthew Gipson:

1995 Grande Cuvée sparkling wine

1991 Fumé Blanc, La Petite Étoile

Smoked Chicken and Baked Brie on Toastettes, salad with Balsamic Vinaigrette.

Fresh Broiled Sea Bass, Julienne of Carrots, Zucchini and Bell Peppers. It is probably the best sea bass I have ever eaten, accompanied by truly memorable Robert Young Reserve Chardonnay 1990.

Apple Poppy Seed Layer Cake with Late Harvest Butter Cream Frosting

1989 Johannisberg Riesling, Alexander Valley Special Select Late Harvest

After a look-in at the impressive Sonoma Wine Center, which only opened in December 1992, it's back to the hotel.

I embark on yet another shopping expedition to Macy's, and stop off for a beer at the wonderful Lefty O'Doul's bar, just off Union Square. This really is one of the great watering holes of the world, with lantern-jawed barmen who seem to have been there forever. I ask one of them why they never smile. Back comes the reply: ''Cos we got nuttin' to smile about, bub.' Well, there's no answer to that. Back at the hotel, I pack up, as I'm moving rooms once more since it has been discovered that the plumbing is faulty.

In the evening, we have a brilliant dinner at China Moon Café, 639 Post Street, where the chef / proprietor Barbara Tropp produces stunning food, the high points of which are Buddha buns stuffed with hoisin-flavoured pork blended with wok-seared yellow onions, Szechwan-style bay string beans with minced shrimps, browned noodle cake topped with juicy beef strips, ruby chard, asparagus tips and wild mushrooms, in a spicy orange sauce. It's accompanied by the fine locally brewed Anchor steam beer. I make an early return to the hotel at 9.30.

24.9.93. I shall spend the final full day on my own. Leaving the hotel at 9.30 a.m., I drive to Santa Cruz, Monterey and Carmel, along the well known 17-mile drive. The weather is superb, all the better to enjoy some magnificent scenery. I stop for a mediocre hamburger and Budweiser beer at the Pebble Beach Golf Club.

A further 150-mile journey on Highway 1 takes me along the Big Sur with its stunning views of the Pacific Ocean. Arriving back at the hotel at 4.45, I find I'm now in room 519, a nice corner room.

At 5, I go down to meet Jim Faber, Louis Foppiano Jnr, his wife Cynthia, and Nora Comée. They take me to Candlestick Park for a baseball game – the 49ers versus San Diego. It's a magnificent, very infectious atmosphere, replete with hot dogs, peanuts and Coors beer, and the game itself is electric, finishing with a home run win for the 49ers. I still find the rules most confusing.

I'm back at the hotel by 11.30.

25.9.93. Once packed, I am driven to the airport at 10.30 a.m., where I check in for flight UA 930 direct to London. I am upgraded to Club, seat 13C, and once more enjoy the hospitality of the Red Carpet Lounge. We depart at 2 p.m. for a very pleasant flight home, with fine food and champagne, and the usual well-drilled service from the staff of United Airlines.

Vancouver
19–26 February 1994

19.2.94. I arrive at Heathrow, Terminal 3, at 12.30 p.m., check in for the United Airlines flight to Seattle, and am upgraded to Business Class, seat 6B upstairs. Following a gin and tonic in the Red Carpet Lounge, we board, and the flight leaves at 2.15. Veuve Clicquot champagne is served with superb canapés, and then a delicious filet mignon with well-balanced Conn Creek Cabernet Sauvignon 1988. I take a little port with the cheese, and the dessert is a chocolate pudding. A bourbon and soda rounds it all off.

The first film is *For Love or Money*, but the views are not to be missed either – incredible vistas as we pass over Greenland and Baffin Island, snow, barren mountains, the end of the world. Another film comes on, *The Age of Innocence*, and then tea is served, with sandwiches and scones. We land in Seattle at 3.15 p.m. local time.

I manage to secure an upgrade for the onward flight to Vancouver, but am told there may be a problem with doing so on the return journey. There's a three-hour wait for the connecting flight, so I have a few beers in the bar, and try to fathom out the crazy internal train system at Seattle Airport, which was obviously designed by a madman having a nightmare.

The onward flight is only twenty minutes, and there are only eight Business Class seats. On arrival, I taxi to the Meridien Hotel, 845 Burrard Street, where I am given room 1510, an excellent mini-suite. It's 10 p.m. (or 5 a.m., as my system understands it), and after a quick bourbon and soda in the busy bar, I collapse into bed at 10.30, quite exhausted.

20.2.94. I awake at 5.30, and find myself watching *Demolition Man* on cable TV. At 8.30, I have a full Canadian breakfast, including two poached eggs, bacon, hash browns, toast, etc.

Venturing out, I walk in the rain to see the sights of Gastown.

The oldest part of the city, this quaint area stretches east from Canada Place to Maple Tree Square along Vancouver harbour. Gastown is notable for its distinctive late Victorian architecture, and for some superbly appointed stores and restaurants. A steam-operated clock, the only one of its kind in the world, chimes at the corner of Water and Cambie streets. A statue of the city's founding father, Gassy Jack Deighton, stands in Maple Tree Square. Then to Robson Street with its elegant stretch of stores. I then take a cab to Granville Island, with its collection of jauntily renovated wharehouses. It is a warren of theatres, artists' studios and craft shops and home to the Granville Island Brewery. Its thriving public market is known for its fresh seafood and produce. Here I meet up with Christine Colletta of the British Columbia Wine Institute. We drive east to Penticton, stopping off on the way for a club sandwich at a place called Hope. The journey takes us through some stunning mountainous scenery towards the beautiful lakes of the Okanagan Valley, a truly outstanding location. Rumour has it that it's inhabited by a creature known as Ogopogo, the Canadian equivalent of the Loch Ness Monster. I'll be staying three nights at the Penticton Lakeside Resort Hotel in a great second-floor suite, 243, with views over the whole lake.

Later, we meet Harry McWatters of Sumac Ridge Winery for drinks in the bar, and then go to dinner at Theo's, a local Greek restaurant. Sadly, the food is awful. We are back at the hotel by 10.

21.2.94. After a full breakfast at 8, we leave at 9 for a visit to Brights Wines established in Ontario in 1874. They also have a winery in Oliver at the southern end of the Okanagan Valley opened in 1981. Brights is owned by Vincor, the largest wine group in Canada, which also owns Inniskillin in Ontario and Cartier in British Columbia – clearly a very acquisitive company. The installation is quite large, with modern equipment and a laboratory, and there is a good range of wines, from VQA (Vintners Quality Alliance) to locally labelled 'Chablis' and 'Burgundy' in three-litre bottles. We do a full tasting, including 1993 tank samples. The winemaker is Frank Sudernaic, and is producing some very well-made wines, not forgetting a superb Icewine.

Over a hamburger lunch, I meet the lawyer-owner of Okanagan Vineyards, who uses over 95% non-Canadian grapes to produce four-litre bag-in-box wines for the domestic market... interesting!

After lunch, we make a visit to Gehringer Brothers Estate Winery, established in 1985. The brothers, Walter and Gordon, produce mainly German-style wines in hock-shaped bottles. These are well made, including a noteworthy Pinot Auxerrois blend with 7 grams of residual sugar. Following this, we look in at Domaine Combret, owned by Robert and his son, Olivier Combret, originally from Provence. Here they have built a brand new winery and have a seemingly open chequebook. They have purchased a fourteen-acre vineyard of 15-year-old vines. The young son trained at Montpellier, and has a perfectionist urge to produce fine wines in the French idiom, currently focusing on Chardonnay and dry Riesling. A bright future beckons.

Back at the hotel, we have an aperitif before heading off to a local Tex-Mex restaurant for a gargantuan portion of spare ribs. I am in bed by 10. Weather-wise, it has not been a particularly inspiring day. It has rained unceasingly and been very cold. Maybe better tomorrow?

22.2.94. And indeed the sun is shining, offering sumptuous views across the lake during my 8 a.m. breakfast.

At 9, I leave for Sumac Ridge with the owner, Harry McWatters. Established in 1980 in Summerland, it is the largest winery/vineyard operation in British Columbia, and the first producer of méthode traditionelle sparkling wine. Harry takes me for a full tour and extensive tasting. Lunch at Fisherman's Cove consists of enormous portions of fish and chips, accompanied by a pint of Spring Brewery pale ale. The brewery is owned by the father of Eric von Krosigk, winemaker at the Summerhill Winery.

After lunch, we visit Sandra and Tilman Hainle of Hainle Vineyards, established in 1987 in Peachland; their organic wines are excellent. A self-evidently dedicated couple, their eighteen-acre property has fine views over the lake.

In the evening, we go back to Harry's house for dinner chez lui, and I am in bed at 10.30.

23.2.94. After coffee in my room at 7 a.m., I pack for the one-hour drive to Kelowna. Here, I check into the Grand Okanagan, a fabulous hotel with yet more stunning views over the lake. I'm in room 601, or at least I am eventually, after some initial trouble getting the key to work in the door.

We begin with a visit to the seventy-five-acre Quails' Gate Winery, established in 1990. The wines here are lovely, and a credit to the single-minded dedication of the owner, Ben Stewart. After this, I make what is my second visit to Mission Hill Winery established in 1966, owned by Anthony von Mandel, who also owns Mark Anthony Wines, a well-known wine wholesaler in Vancouver. John Simes is the winemaker, a New Zealander who was previously at the Montana Winery in Marlborough; his portfolio here spans the range from the good to the frankly commercial. Then it's off to Calona Winery. Established in 1932, this is Okanagan's oldest winery, a very big commercial operation with no vineyards and rather indifferent, often blended, wines made by one Howard Soon.

In the evening, I take a quick shower and then we leave for the Eldorada Hotel for a dinner in my honour hosted by the local growers. Many local wines, of course, to accompany a huge portion of stuffed chicken. I then make a speech outlining the pros and cons of exporting wines to the UK. I am back at the hotel at 11.45.

24.2.94. Following an 8 a.m. breakfast, I have a meeting with Christine Colletta. Then at 10, we drive to meet Stephen Cipes at the Summerhill Winery, established in 1992 with 38 acres. He is a crazy Jewish New Yorker making sparkling Riesling in a pyramid, a structure in the grounds of the property in which the wines are left to mature for six months. His house sits at the top of a hill, looking majestically down over the lake. Eric von Krosigk is his winemaker. They are interesting wines, and come in pyramidal black bottles.

From Summerhill, our next port of call is the 31-acre vineyard, Cedar Creek Estate Winery, owned by a millionaire gold mine proprietor, Ross Fitzpatrick, since 1986. Ann Sperling is the winemaker here, and has made a particularly fine 1993

Merlot. After a sandwich lunch with Icewine, we arrive at the 25-acre estate of St Hubertus Vineyards, established in 1992 by Leo Gebert. The winery is named after their family lodge in Switzerland. Their slightly sweet, Germanic-style wines are rather indifferent.

Dinner is at an out-of-town ranch-style pub with Christine Colletta, Brenda, her secretary, and Eric von Krosigk – nachos, burgers and so forth. It is still bitterly cold. I'm in bed by 11.

25.2.94. I descend at 8 for a full breakfast, and find that it's snowing heavily. I work in my hotel room, and then meet Mike Warren, an Englishman working for the British Columbia Agricultural Board. Christine joins us for a buffet lunch in the hotel at noon.

After lunch, we drive to Vernon in the northernmost part of the wine-growing region, at the 50th parallel, where we visit George and Trudy Heiss of Gray Monk Vineyards for a full tasting. Like many others, they too enjoy fine views over the lake, and their wines are good, the installations fully up to date.

Later, we drive to the Vernon Lodge Hotel for drinks and a dinner hosted by the Tourist Association. I am once again called upon to speak. The buffet, an expansive range of local food and wines, is very good, and I am introduced to the Minister of Tourism, with whom I have an extremely interesting conversation. I am driven back to my hotel at 11.

26.2.94. After packing, I take an 8 a.m. breakfast and then check out. A cab brings me to Kelowna Airport, and I arrive just in time to catch the 9.30 flight instead of the scheduled noon. It's a 75-minute journey in a twin-engined plane, with British Columbia Airlines.

At Vancouver, I encounter idiotic delays trying to check in for the onward flight to the USA. Just as well I caught an earlier flight as the whole check-in procedure takes an hour and a half. Fortunately I'm upgraded for the entire journey to London. The short flight to Seattle is scheduled to leave at 2.40. We arrive at 4.30, and I have a cheeseburger and beer at the airport, before checking in to the Red Carpet Club for complimentary bourbon and soda, and a comfortable 6.25 flight to London.

22–26 March 1994

22.3.94. I'm flying Air India, flight AI 85, to Toronto for £200 return, and on checking in at Heathrow, Terminal 3, I am upgraded to Executive Class, seat 59J, which is upstairs on the Boeing 747. Heading for the Maharajah Lounge for a complimentary drink or two, I find I am the only white patron in there.

After an hour's delay, I am told my seat allocation has been changed to 4C. This turns out to be in First Class, the normal scheduled fare for which would have been £2,650! What you get is a luxuriously big seat, which reclines to horizontal, with six feet of legroom. I am plied with caviare and Veuve Clicquot champagne. When the food arrives, it is served from a trolley on china plates. The film, as luck would have it, is *Mrs Doubtfire*, which I saw last week on a previous flight.

I sleep for a couple of hours. The flying time is 7½ hours, and local time is five hours behind the UK, so we arrive at 5 p.m. I pick up a Hertz hire car and embark on a 90-minute drive to the little Peyton Place-style village of Niagara-on-the-Lake, where I am staying at the Prince of Wales Hotel, room 172, for $40 a night. I take a Crown Royal rye whiskey and soda in the bar at 8, and reflect on what a difference there is in the level of hospitality to that afforded me last month in British Columbia. There has been nobody to meet me at the airport, I've had to hire my own car, pay for my own hotel, and find my own way to the Wines of Canada Ontario offices tomorrow. Something about 'chalk and cheese' springs to mind.

23.3.94. I awake at 4.30 a.m. to various phone calls, watch some TV news and shower. Breakfast at 7.30 is scrambled eggs, bacon, sausages, apple juice and coffee. I leave at 8 for the offices of the Ontario Wine Council, a 45-minute journey.

There, I meet with Peter Gamble and Bill Hussman until 11, discussing the proposed export programme After this, I take off on another 3½ hour drive to the Pelee Island Winery in the extreme south-west of the province, passing on the way a road sign indicating 90 miles to Paris and 120 miles to London. I also unfortunately see a fatal accident near Livingstone.

At 3.30, I meet Walter Schmoranz, the manager of the winery, a very good man who has some attractive wines. His is the only Winery on the island. We go through a full tasting – he makes a good range of whites and a pair of reds – and I leave at around 5.30. I only make it back to the hotel at 9, feeling as though I have done too much driving already, but I am glad I made the effort.

The hotel is a confusing maze of corridors, and with my sense of direction, I am slightly surprised that I manage to find my room at all. At 9.30, I go to the bar and start on a comparative tasting of rye whiskey. It being totally out of season, there is only one other person in the bar, a short and moderately attractive, very well-endowed lady having an early supper. She suddenly breaks into song in quite a loud voice, and when she finishes, I applaud. Encouraged thus, she then moves to my table, explaining that she is a training to be singer and dancer, and lives in Buffalo just over the bridge border to the USA. To make ends meet, she works as a nude dancer in a lap dancing club called Private Eyes, just nearby under the QE2 Bridge, and rejoices in the name of Maria Elena 'La Fire'. She writes her voicemail number down for me. Frankly the last type I expected to encounter in the middle of nowhere, she is rather brassy, a typical blonde no-brainer, giggly and dumpy, five feet tall. She says she is into mysticism, herbs and 'vibes', and that her ambition is to become an opera singer. The dancing is merely to fill in until she receives her due recognition. Well well well. She leaves for work at 10.30.

The odd thing is that I drive past this address every day on my way back to the hotel and have never seen it; I might try and pop in tomorrow.

I suddenly realise I have had no supper. Notwithstanding that, I have one more rye and then go to bed at 11.

24.3.94. I awake at 6 with a slight hangover, make some phone calls and then breakfast at 8 on scrambled eggs and bacon, apple juice and coffee.

My first appointment is at the Reiff Winery, where the evidence of big investment is paying off in the form of some good wines made by the owner, a nice chap called Klaus Reiff. At 11.30, I arrive at Hillebrand, a sizeable operation owned by Underberg. These too are impressive wines; I have a sandwich and soup lunch with them at 1.

At 2.30, I visit Inniskillin, an old-established Winery with good product, and then drive up to Niagara Falls. It's out of season of course, which is just as well (it must be a nightmare in the summer). Most of the waterfall is frozen, and I pay $4.50 to visit the underground viewing room behind the falls. I try a local beer, Trapper, made by the Niagara Falls Brewery, a malty-tasting brew, somewhat lacking in fizz.

The drive back to the hotel takes me along the shore of Lake Ontario, where there are some enviably lovely houses. I decide to visit Private Eyes for a quick drink on the way back to the hotel. It turns out to be an enormous barn tucked away underneath the QE2 Bridge, open from 10 a.m. to 2 a.m., seven days a week.

As I enter, the most amazing sights greet my eyes. Firstly, there are two full-size boxing rings with girls stripping to very loud music. The ringside seats are taken up by local farm lads, who continually jump into the ring, and lie on their backs with rolled dollar bills in their mouths, which are promptly removed by the girls using various parts of their bodies. Secondly, there are two twelve-foot cinema screens showing the hardest of pornography, and then there are the proverbial screened-off lap dancing parlours. The interesting thing is that there is no entrance fee, and drinks at the bar are served at normal prices. Alas, there is no sign of Madame Maria Elena La Fire, and after a couple of Molson beers, I leave in a trance.

I arrive back at the hotel at 7.30 and go down to the bar, and then eat dinner alone in the restaurant at 8. The amuse-gueule is a slice of salmon terrine in wholegrain mustard sauce, a dry and tasteless offering. My first course of veal prosciutto with roasted peppers is raw and salty, and the peppers are not roasted at all. With that, I drink a searingly acidic Stoney Ridge Chardonnay. The main course is pork fillet with noodles and soy, which is quite tasty but served in a ridiculously huge portion, and with which I try Konzelman Gamay Noir, a cooked and hollow-tasting red, prickling with CO_2.

I go up to bed at 10.30, feeling very, very tired.

25.3.94. I awake at seven after a good night's sleep and make various phone calls, including one to Christine Colletta from Wines of Canada in Vancouver. Having forgotten that Vancouver is three hours behind, I have called her at not much later than 4 a.m. I expect my popularity there has now taken a dive.

The first appointment today is with Alan Schmidt at Vineland Estates. He is a young, committed winemaker, whose vineyard is established on the Bench escarpment, producing very good wines. At 11.30, I go to meet Len Pennechetti at Cave Springs Cellars, a big investment with superb, extensive underground cellars in the historic old town of Jordan. He is a good man, and very dedicated to the VQA system. His wines are made by Angela Pava, and very good too. They also have their own restaurant with an excellent chef, where we have a lunch of large mussels, followed by quail, accompanied by stunning Cave Spring Dry Riesling.

At 3, I arrive at the Henry of Pelham Winery to meet Paul Speck. This is a large, family-owned investment with extensive vineyard holdings, 95% of which produce VQA wines. The wines are exceptional – probably the best in Ontario – and he is a great chap. I leave at 6.30.

Back at the hotel, I am asked to change rooms to 101, which is a little smaller. I ask why, as the hotel is virtually empty, but no one has a sensible answer. I decide it hardly matters for one more night. At 8, I repair to the bar for three large Adams rye and sodas and a club sandwich. It has been a very tiring day. Unlike in British Columbia, I have to do a full export-marketing proposal at each Winery. Peter Gamble, the chief executive of the Wines of Canada VQA programme in Ontario, has been of no help whatsoever. I'm intensely looking forward to going home, feeling that I have done more than my fair share of travelling just lately. Loneliness and homesickness are getting to me.

26.3.94. Waking at six, I work until nine on my tasting notes report of all the wines I have tasted on this trip, and then take breakfast. I then have a meeting with Don Kennedy of Brights Winery. He is a brash salesman type with fists the size of ham hocks, only really interested in volumes of low-priced, blended wine made from non-Canadian grapes. A couple of hours later, he gives me his home number, in case I want to keep in touch without telling anyone. I wonder why?

I pack and check out of the hotel, and then drive to Chateau des Charmes, which produces some fine wines. They have built a superb new Winery and tasting rooms in the style of a French château, as well as a state-of-the-art wine laboratory.

Driving on from there, I head for Toronto and a meeting at the Four Seasons Hotel with Donald Ziraldo, managing director of Inniskillin Winery, a great extrovert character, and Peter Gamble. Following this, at 7.15, I head off for the airport, checking in at 8. I am extremely lucky to be upgraded to a Business Class seat on the upper level. Before leaving, I enjoy a well-earned Molson ice beer in the bar.

30 September–14 October 1994

30.9.94. I arrive at Heathrow, Terminal 2, at 2 p.m. ready to check in for Canadian Airlines flight CA87 Business Class to Toronto, on which I have reserved seat 4G. In the Service Air lounge, I have a couple of drinks, and we board the 767 at 4 o'clock. Scheduled take-off is 4.20.

Business Class turns out not to be a patch on that in other airlines. There is no champagne before take-off, only twenty seats and no First Class. Bricout Champagne is eventually served, and there is a salad and a main dish of beef with potatoes in mustard sauce. We drink Henry of Pelham Canadian Vidal 1993 and a very good 1993 Châteauneuf-du-Pape, Domaine Julliet, which is actually still too young. Cheese is Double Gloucester, served with Cockburns LBV port. After eating, I have a rye and soda, and then sleep for three hours.

We arrive in Toronto at 6.30 p.m. local time, only to find no Alamo car hire desk at the airport. Apparently they don't operate in Canada, even though I have been given a prepaid voucher and confirmation number – very strange. Instead, I hire a Toyota from Hilden, and then drive the two hours to the Prince of Wales Hotel at Niagara-on-the-Lake. I have been given superior room 303 on the third floor, and go straight to bed, as it's now 10.30 local time.

1.10.94. I pass a fitful night, but feel fine in the morning. After taking an 8.30 shower, I go at 9 to a breakfast of scrambled eggs, bacon, French toast, fresh orange juice and coffee. It's pouring with rain and quite cold.

At 11, I have a meeting with the export manager for selected Canadian wineries who wish to export to the UK. We then depart for a full tasting at Cave Spring Winery in Jordan. Lunch follows at their own restaurant, 'Twenty', in the company of Peter Gamble, who is in charge of the VQA programme, Angelo Pavan, the winemaker, and Len Pennechetti, the proprietor of Cave Spring Winery. We drink a local micro beer, and eat smoked fish with salad, followed by roast quail on rice; an excellent lunch. The wines served are Cave Spring Riesling 1990, the Chardonnay 1990 and their Late Harvest wine from the same vintage, all showing very well.

The afternoon, from 2 until 6.30, is taken up with a growers' seminar, after which we all have drinks at Private Eyes, which is as unreal as when I first visited it in March of this year. Later on, I have drinks at the hotel, where a jazz band plays, and am in bed by 12.

2.10.94. I drink a wake-up coffee at 6.45 a.m., and then we depart for Pelee Island, Leamington. It will be a four-hour drive, during which we stop for breakfast at Burger King, just outside Hamilton. The waitress asks me, 'Are you senior?'

'What?'

'Pardon me,' she demurs, 'but are you over?'

'What?' is all I can reply. 'Over what?'

'Over 60? If so, you are entitled to 10% discount.'

The entire exchange is rounded off with 'Have a nice day!'

I arrive at the Pelee Island Winery at 11. The weather is beautiful today, crisp but with blue skies. Our host Walter Schmoranz conducts a tour and tasting, and then we have lunch in the Goose Goose, a local restaurant – salad and fried chicken.

Afterwards, we take a speedboat for three-quarters of an hour across the bay to Pelee Island itself, which is lovely. We make a tour, visiting pheasant farms, as well as the winery and vineyards. At the winery, there is a film followed by a full tasting of their wines, which are aimed at the commercial end of the market.

I leave at 6.30 for the long drive back, and contrive to lose myself, going miles out of my way through Dundas, eventually making it back to the hotel at 10.30, absolutely shattered. There's just time for a couple of large rye and sodas and some spare ribs, before falling into bed at 11.15.

3.10.94. Awakening at 7.15, I pack for the onward journey to Vancouver. I have a breakfast meeting with Hillebrand Winery at 9, while some visiting wine journalists and buyers from the UK go to Niagara Falls.

Having packed the car, we set off for Stonechurch Vineyards for a tasting, tour and barbecue lunch with Rick and Fran Hunse. Again, the wines are aimed at the commercial retail end of the market. After this, I leave at 1.15 for Cave Spring Winery, and I am interviewed for a video Len Pennechetti is producing about Canadian wines.

I depart there for Toronto Airport at 2.30, from where I take a Business Class flight for Vancouver and then on to Kelowna, due off at 5 p.m. Bloody Marys in the Club Lounge precede a five-hour flight in seat 3A. Good Thai food is served during the flight.

Reaching Vancouver at 6.40 local time, I then have a one-hour wait for the Canadian regional flight CP 1282 to Kelowna, leaving at 7.40. This is an hour-long flight on a small, cramped plane, on which I am charged $4 for a rye and soda.

Kelowna is three hours ahead, and I arrive at midnight local time. A taxi ride ($90) takes me to the Coast Lakeside resort at Penticton, where I am assigned room 334. Looking out across the lake I am convinced I catch a glimpse of the elusive Ogopogo, but then I am exceptionally tired. Not surprisingly, I sleep like a log.

4.10.94. I am collected at 8.30 a.m. and driven, along with four other judges, to the Summerhill Research Station. There, over the course of the next few days, from 9 until 5 p.m., we shall taste over 80 Canadian wines a day, with just a short break for lunch. It proves very demanding having to award medals to some of these wines, tasted blind, and it's very tiring on the palate.

At 5.30, we return to the hotel, and Jane Mavety from Blue Mountain Vineyards later collects me for a visit to her Winery in Okanagan Falls, established in 1992 on 50 acres. After a full tour and tasting it really confirms what fantastic wines they make.

I return to the hotel at 9, and have dinner with the other judges, followed by more drinks in the bar. I retire at 11.30.

5.10.94. I am collected at 8.30 for what will turn out to be another exhausting day, tasting over 80 wines, with a short lunch break, and then more. To make matters more gruelling, the tasting room has no windows. We are evaluating Rieslings, Gewürztraminers, Pinot Gris, Bacchus, etc.

Back at the hotel at 6, I am interviewed on television, and am later picked up and taken to a dinner of smoked salmon, beef and lamb at the recommended Young's Brasserie. Once more returned to the hotel, I have an early nightcap at 9, before falling into bed at 9.30, extremely tired.

6.10.94. The morning is then spent once again at the Summerhill Research Station, tasting Late Harvests, Icewines and port-style wines.

I'm back at the hotel once more at 4, and am collected at 4.45 to go to Quails' Gate Winery for an open-air wine and food event in period costume (which detail yours truly eschews). Dinner for 150 people is served in a marquee. The whole evening is great fun, and I eventually get back to the hotel at 11.30.

7.10.94. After an 8 a.m. breakfast, I drive and check into the Grand Hotel in Kelowna then on to a 10.30 visit to Gray Monk Winery, and a tasting of their well-made wines. It's a gloriously hot, sunny day, and the tasting is followed by lunch on their terrace, comprising Thai stir-fried chicken, lobster, smoked salmon and salad, all superb.

In the afternoon, we proceed to Cedar Creek Winery for an alfresco tasting of their well-balanced wines, and then to Summerhill Winery, the one that makes only sparkling wines from the Riesling grape. A proportion of the wines are laid to rest for six months in the famous pyramid, this apparently adding another dimension to the flavour and quality of the wine. The sceptic that I am, I ask for a tasting of pyramid-cellared against non-pyramid-cellared, and the results are duly amazing. The pyramid-cellared wines have far more finesse and depth of flavour. Stephen Cipes, the owner, explains that this dates back to an early religion, and takes me into the pitch-black pyramid, asking me to stretch out my arms, close my eyes and feel the vibrations flow through my body. I must confess to experiencing pins and needles in my fingertips – all very strange.

I return, shower and change for the Wine Masters' dinner, for which the drill turns out to be semi-formal dress. I have only packed a sports jacket, and end up borrowing a blazer from one of the winemakers.

At 6.30, 250 people rendezvous in readiness for a seven-course dinner at which I shall have to talk about the future of West Coast Canadian wines for the export market, and then comment on the wines we are drinking with dinner. I must say that out of the twenty-odd different wines served, only three are disappointing.

I am gratefully in bed at 11.30.

8.10.94. I take breakfast at 8 a.m., and then go to an 8.30 export meeting and seminar with the growers in the Conference Center at Summerhill. At 11.30, we go for a visit, tour, tasting and lunch at Sumac Ridge Winery, which is a great success.

Shopping in the mall at Penticton makes for a pleasant afternoon, and on my return to the resort at 6.30, I shower and change for the medal awards in the evening. A huge tasting has been arranged in the Conference Centre, followed by the awards ceremony being the result of the three-day blind tasting. After the medals have all been handed out, it seems that a few growers are disappointed that their wines have not been selected.

We go to dinner at Theo's Greek Restaurant, and then on to a party at the hotel hosted by Harry McWatters of Sumac Ridge. I am in bed at 11.30.

9.10.94. Following a 9.30 breakfast, I pack and check out, and the day starts with a visit to Mission Hill Winery, with a full tasting of their latest superb VQA wines made by John Simes from New Zealand. This is followed by a full buffet lunch in their marquee. A visit and tasting to Quails' Gate Winery is scheduled for the afternoon. Again the wines are superb and well made, in particular a botrytis-affected Late Harvest Optima. I then head off to Kelowna airport at 4 to check in for the 45-minute flight to Vancouver.

There, I transfer to the 8 p.m. flight to San Francisco, which will take four hours. I use my points to get an upgrade, but it turns out to have been barely worth the bother. They are essentially the same seats as Economy, except that there are two where there would normally be three, and the food is little short of disgraceful.

I arrive in San Francisco at midnight, where I hire a car from

Alamo (note: never again!). The terminal is seven miles from the airport, and I have left my suitcase behind at the car hire desk.

Once in the city, I check into the Monticello Inn on Market Street, a dreadful room with noise continuing through the night. I get to bed at 1 a.m.

10.10.94. Arising at 9.30, I take a coffee, and then organise a move to a suite to get out of this room, but the suite itself is still quite small and tacky.

At least the weather is nice. I walk about, do some shopping in Macy's, and then have a much needed beer in Lefty O'Doul's bar near Union Square, where the locals again attempt (in vain, I may say) to explain the rules of baseball to me.

I meet Nora Comée for lunch at the Fog City Diner 1300 Battery Street, a superb place, where I have a great hamburger with onions, fries, etc. In the afternoon, I go shopping for a tennis racquet for my wife, Clare, which turns out to be a hilarious episode. As I do not play tennis, I have a note of the make and size required. The assistant is most helpful and produces an unstrung racquet (I have since learnt that this is how they are sold). I innocently wonder how one could play with this as the ball would surely go straight through it. The assistant replies without batting an eyelid that he will put strings in it for me if I tell him what type I would like... A phone call home soon puts the matter to rights. I then return to the hotel for a two-hour sleep.

Later, I meet up with Jim and Stephanie Faber in the hotel bar, and we go to Plump Jack's for dinner. This is a new, very good place much in vogue. I choose mushrooms with Parmesan, and then a pasta dish with aubergine and garlic, pairing the food with Chapelette Chardonnay and then the Calera Viognier. I end the day with a nightcap back at the hotel, and get into bed at 12.30, watching the wonderful jazz singer, Anita O'Day, on the TV.

11.10.94. I breakfast at 7.30 on coffee only, and then embark on the drive to Sonoma to visit Chateau St Jean. There, I have a meeting with the directors and winemaker, followed by a full tasting of their excellent wines. We have a superb lunch prepared by their chef, Lois Weinstein:

1985 Grande Cuvée, Méthode Traditionelle

1992 Chardonnay, Robert Young Vineyards

Steamed Clams with a Julienne of Vegetables in Tomato Herb Brodo

1990 Cabernet Sauvignon, Cinq Cépages

Roast Duck Breast with Cranberry Sauce, Fruited Wild Rice, Green Beans

1989 Johannisberg Riesling, Russian River Valley Special Late Harvest

Champagne Honeydew Melon Sorbet with Amaretto Butter Cookies

Later, we drive around the Napa Valley with its rolling hillsides, in the heart of the Californian Wine Industry supporting almost 30 Wineries, some dating back to the nineteenth century, then back to the hotel. After drinks with Andy Quady, we go to dinner at the Boulevard, 1 Mission Street, another new and very good venue housed in the Audiffred building, built in 1889. I eat pork wrapped in ham on a bed of wine-soaked rice, prepared by the highly acclaimed chef, Nancy Dales, accompanied by a delicious bottle of 1977 Ridge Zinfandel, eventually reaching my own bed at about 11.30.

12.10.94. I'm up at 6.30 in time to get to an 8.30 breakfast meeting with Francis Mahoney, owner of Carneros Creek. We take a tour of the vineyard and cellars, and taste the new 1994 Pinot Noir, which is showing good signs of fruit and extract.

Then we continue to Piper Sonoma for a tasting of their delicious sparkling wines and a sandwich lunch. In the afternoon, there is a tasting with Louis Foppiano Jnr, with dinner later at his home, during which he shows four vintages of the Petite Sirah – 1988, '86, '84 and '81 – all showing extremely well. Returning to the hotel, I am in bed by midnight.

13.10.94. After an 8.30 breakfast, I go shopping at Ghirardelli for some of their superb chocolate, and then drive up to Clos du Val Winery in Napa Valley. There, I met the director Bernard Portet, followed by a lunch of spare ribs at the Rutherford Grill. Then we have a full tasting of their excellent wines, going back to 1984.

I continue on to Dry Creek Vineyards, arriving at 5, where I undertake a tasting and tour in the company of the winemaker. The wines here are not showing well.

Returning to the hotel at 7.30, I have pre-dinner drinks, and then eat in the restaurant of the Monticello Inn. There is very good Thai-style lamb, among other things.

I am in bed at 11.30.

14.10.94. The day begins at 6.30 with packing, which is extremely difficult, as I seem to have bought too many gifts. I just manage to get the suitcase closed, and must cross fingers that the zip will hold out.

At 10.30, I drive to the airport for a two-hour flight to Vancouver. An airbus takes us into the city, and I do some sightseeing and have drinks at the magnificent Pan Pacific Hotel, 300 Canasa Place, with its five soaring white Teflon sails reminiscent of a giant vessel. Returning to the airport by bus, I check in for the flight to London via Calgary.

It's a ten-hour journey to Heathrow, Terminal 2, and I'm in Business Class, seat 3B. I arrive totally exhausted at 2.30 p.m. local time, on the afternoon of Saturday 15th.

21 September–7 October 1995

21.9.95. At Heathrow, I check in for the 1.30 p.m. Air Canada Executive First Class flight AC 897 to Vancouver, a Boeing 747 on which I am allocated seat 3K. I am processed immediately upon arrival, the fast-track system being admirably smooth. Going shopping, I buy a much needed pair of comfortable loafers from Bally, and then repair to the Air Canada Lounge at 12.30 for a gin and tonic.

The flight is on time, and the First-Class cabin is superb, with enormous seats and plenty of legroom. We are served Mumm champagne with smoked salmon and other bits, followed by beef medallions, and then cheese, with Château Giscours 1990, and Graham's LBV port. I then have a Crown Royal rye and soda when the film, *Batman Forever*, comes on, after which I sleep for around five hours. On awakening we are given smoked salmon sandwiches, and we arrive in Vancouver at 2.30 p.m. local time.

I experience some bother trying to obtain an onward air ticket for Kelowna. They seem to require me to go into the city to collect it, but I finally manage to convince them to issue it at the airport. In a bar there called Cheers, I have a couple of Granville Island beers and a well-made cheeseburger.

The flight to Kelowna is at 6.50 p.m. Once there, I hire a car from Hertz, and go to the Grand Okanagan Hotel, 1310 Water Street, where I check into suite 127 which has a wonderful view of the lake.

22.9.95. Having passed a fitful night, waking virtually every hour, I rise for an 8 a.m. breakfast of rye toast, honey, fresh apple juice and coffee in the company of export manager, Christine Colletta, export director of Wines of Canada.

At 9.30, as this is the start of the Okanagan Wine Festival, I go off for a seminar with the winegrowers at Quails' Gate Winery. Next up is a visit to Mission Hill Winery, with a tasting and tour of the vineyard and cellars, followed by a working lunch with

John Simes, who is now making some excellent wines there, although they are in short supply.

The afternoon is then taken up with a trade tasting of the growers' wines at the Coast Capri Hotel, 1171 Harvey Avenue, from 2.30 until 6. After a short break for drinks, it's back to the tasting, from 7 through till 9.30, by which time I have comprehensively tasted and noted over 100 British Columbian wines. Dinner is at the Chinese Laundry Restaurant in downtown Kelowna, where the portions are enormous, and we witness an incredible fire nearby. It turns out it may have been arson.

I am in bed at 11.

23.9.95. I breakfast lightly at 8 a.m. on toast, apple juice and coffee, and then go to see Ben Stewart, the owner of Quails' Gate Winery, at 9 for a full tasting. There, I have a very interesting conversation about vine growing and winemaking in British Columbia with Jeff Martin, the new oenologist, who was previously at McWilliams in Australia.

Lunch is at a place called Earl's by the lake. I have a Rhino beer plus another local brand, and we eat gargantuan portions of ribs and chicken. The main event of the afternoon is the Calona Great Grape Stomp at 3.30. I am back at the hotel at 4.30 for a much needed sleep.

In the evening, we go to McCulloughs for drinks at 8, and decide to stay on for dinner, a beef stir-fry accompanied by local microbrewery beers. I'm back at the hotel by 10.30, quite shattered, but doomed to spend another interrupted night of waking every hour.

24.9.95. I go down to the buffet for breakfast at 7.30 a.m. and help myself to scrambled eggs, bacon and sausage, with toast, apple juice and coffee.

The day begins with a visit to Harry McWatters at Sumac Ridge. Arriving at 9, we undertake a full tasting of his well-made 1994 wines, the Merlot Reserve in particular standing out. It's very hot, and by 10 the sun is blazing, 29°C. I decide to skip the buffet lunch, and instead we drive on to Le Conte Winery to see Eric von Krosigk. A tasting of his '94s is less than inspiring. The

Winery is very run-down, and has just been purchased by Harry McWatters, so one can expect to see much better wine in the future.

Afterwards, we head on to Blue Mountain Winery, where Jane and Ian Mavety make the finest wines in the Okanagan Valley, a Chardonnay, a Pinot Blanc, a stunning Pinot Noir and a fizz. They are arguably the Romanée-Conti of British Columbia. We then drive the two hours to Gray Monk, the most northern Winery in British Columbia at Parallel 50, stopping en route for a beer and snack at the little town of Winfield. We undertake a full tasting at Gray Monk, including their excellent Pinot Gris, and then drive to Kelowna, where the day is rounded off with a roast beef dinner in the company of Alison and Jack Akers of Calona Winery, at which an unusual red hybrid, Chancellor 1991, is served.

I am back at the hotel at 1 a.m., and at last I have a good night's sleep.

25.9.95. Breakfast at 8 consists of poached eggs and bacon, after which the day starts with a meeting and full tasting at Cedar Creek Winery. This is followed by the same at Summerhill nearby. Lunch at noon is a multi-ethnic affair of sushi and lasagne, served with their Brut Rosé, and pyramid-aged Chardonnay Brut. After this, we are off for another full tasting at Calona Winery at 2.30.

Back at the hotel, we have drinks, and then take a stroll around the marina. At 8.30 in the evening, following drinks at Earl's, where they serve a mean Crown Royal Rye whiskey, we have dinner next door at Mekong, a Vietnamese Restaurant – sizzling beef and noodles, with the excellent Kokanee beer.

I am in bed at 10.30.

26.9.95. At 8.30, I have coffee and check out of the hotel. The bill comes to £800. Driving to Kelowna Airport, I check in for the 50-minute flight to Vancouver. It's overcast and raining, but for all that, the weather over the last five days has been superb. The plane is a twin-engine 30-seater Dash, and we arrive at our destination at 11.15.

Here, I have lunch in the Island seafood restaurant at the airport. Strangely for a seafood restaurant, the set lunch is pasta with pork sausages, accompanied by Granville Island lager. I'm checked through Immigration and, using my points, await an upgrade for my onward flight to the USA. It turns out there are only eight seats in Business Class, so an upgrade isn't possible.

Flight UA 1697 departs at 3.25, and I am in seat 60. I have a Jack Daniels and soda and settle into the 2½-hour journey. We arrive at 6. I hire a Ford Mustang from Hertz, and drive to the Grand Hyatt Hotel on Union Square, where I am given suite 2006/7. In the rooftop bar on the 36th floor, I drink a Wild Turkey Rare and soda.

My daughter Danielle (who was living in San Francisco at the time) arrives at 8, and we go to dinner at Ernie's 847 Montgomery Street, with Andy and Laurel Quady. It's a wonderful old French restaurant. The main course is guinea-hen, served with Mantzas Chardonnay 1993, and the superb 1993 Nalle Zinfandel.

I am back at the hotel at 12.30.

27.9.95. At 8.45 a.m., I collect Danielle from her house in Berkeley, and we drive into the Napa Valley to meet Francis Mahoney at Carneros Creek. We taste some brand new 1995 Chardonnay and 1994 Pinot Noirs, which are all very good, particularly his Signature Reserve Pinot Noir. We then press on to Clos du Val, and have lunch at the Napa Valley Grill in Yountville, a fine venue. I eat a garlicky pasta dish and we drink the excellent Clos du Val 1993 Reserve Cabernet Sauvignon. Then it's back to the winery for an extensive tasting back to 1983. My word, they do make superb wines.

We are back in the city at 7 for some shopping at Macy's. After that, I do a quick change and have drinks at the hotel. I meet Danielle's friend, Lynette, a super girl. We all go to Hawthorne Lane Restaurant, 22 Hawthorne Street, for dinner. We begin with 1994 Stag's Leap Chimney Rock Merlot rosé with prawns in soy, which is followed by lamb served with an amazing 1977 Stag's Leap Merlot. It's a very 'in' place, packed, but makes for a fun and enjoyable evening.

I am back at midnight.

28.9.95. I collect Danielle at 9 a.m., and we drive to Foppiano Vineyards in Sonoma County. The tasting of their 1993 and '94 white wines is frankly not very good. We eat a picnic lunch of chicken and pasta salad with their brilliant 1993 Petite Sirah Reserve.

Leaving at 2, we take a two-hour drive to Esparto, near Sacramento, where we visit the magnificent state-of-the-art R. H. Phillips Winery, which covers 5,000 acres and used to be a sheep farm. Their experimental XP Viognier and Syrah are superb.

We leave there eventually at 7, and arrive back in the city for dinner at Harry Denton's Restaurant at 9. This is another 'in' place, full and buzzing, and after starting with a bourbon, I dine on crab cakes and then a pot roast, accompanied by 1994 Clos du Bois Chardonnay and 1990 Mataro (Mourvèdre), which includes 5% Zinfandel and 5% Alicante Bouschet in the blend, bottled at 13.6% ABV.

I am back at the hotel at 11.30, and reflect that it's great to see Danielle so happy.

29.9.95. Awakening at 5 a.m. to an alarm call, I drive to the airport and check in for Air Canada Executive First Class flight AC 758 to Toronto. This time, conditions are an absolute disgrace. We are crammed in three seats to a row with no legroom, and I'm in 3F, a window seat. Breakfast consists of eggs with peppers and raw sausage. At least the film, *Congo*, is very good: it's a four-hour flight. There is a three-hour time difference, meaning we arrive in Toronto at 3.25 p.m. local time.

I hire a Ford Cougar from Hertz, and drive through traffic jams to the Niagara Falls. The Foxhead Skyline Hotel overlooks the Falls, and offers a dramatic view, but for all that it's a tacky place at £100 a night, plus 13% local tax.

After drinks in the rooftop bar I drive to Jordan for dinner at the Twenty Restaurant at Cave Springs Winery. The food is superb, taking in various starters, an absurdly big sausage and chicken.

I am back by midnight.

30.9.95. I take a full buffet breakfast in the penthouse, which affords amazing views of the Niagara Falls which attracts 12 million visitors a year. The hotel seems to be full of Japanese, all of whom seem to be devoid of any table manners.

To start the day, I drive to Cave Spring Winery for a seminar with all the East Coast growers to discuss the development of their wines in the UK market. For lunch, we are back at Restaurant Twenty with Angelo Pavan, the winemaker of Cave Spring, and then there are more meetings, and a tasting and vineyard tour.

Back at the hotel at 6, I go for a drive around the Falls, and find the route full of tourists. I get out and take a walk up Clifton Hill (known as the street of fun), an appalling place with an ambience like the worst of Blackpool or Southend. Stopping for a drink in the Yanks bar, I am recommended to go to Casa d'Oro to eat, but it turns out to be fully booked, and I end up having what must be the worst meal ever (rib of beef and fries) at the Loveboat, a seafood and steakhouse place. On a happier note, I drink the 1993 Konzelman Pinot Noir, which is good, although it still has slight CO_2.

I am back at the hotel at 11.

1.10.95. After a full buffet breakfast at 7 a.m., I pack and check out. I then drive to the Prince of Wales Hotel at Niagara-on-the-Lake, one of North America's best preserved nineteenth century towns, where I drop off my suitcases and am allocated the Bell Cottage, a complete two-bedroomed home.

Driving on, I make the 3½-hour journey to Pelee Island. It's a lovely, warm, sunny day. Arriving at 11.45, I have a meeting with the winemaker, Walter Schmoranz, and then we go to lunch at the Harbour, overlooking Lake Erie, a stunning view. We eat wonderful Cajun prawns and garlic prawns, and three different kinds of fish – yellow perch, pickerel and whitefish – accompanying them with Pelee Island 1992 and 1994 Rieslings. Back at the winery, we undertake a full tasting.

Leaving at 8, I drive the 3½-hours back to the hotel, arriving at 11.20. After three large rye and sodas, I fall into bed, shattered, at 12.15.

2.10.95. I begin the day at 8 a.m. with a full buffet breakfast, and the morning is scheduled to continue at 11 with a tasting at Vinelands Winery, where we get through a very good selection. Lunch on the terrace is pasta and stir-fried beef, with Vinelands' winemaker Alan Schmidt. We go on to taste over 40 Ontario and British Columbia wines, of which Henry of Pelham is the best among the former, and Mission Hill among the latter.

Back at the hotel at 6, I have a much needed large rye and soda, and then at 7.45, I head into town on foot. I taste some local lagers – Angel and Connors – at the Angel Inn, a pseudo-pub. Afterwards, I have dinner at Fan's, the local Chinese restaurant; prawns, beef and pork, all very good, accompanied by Molson lager.

I am in bed at 10.30.

3.10.95. I awaken at 6.30 a.m. and use the time to write numerous letters. Leaving the hotel at 9.30, I go to Rief Estates for a cellar visit and tasting, and discover that they have some good wines. I then have a hamburger and lager lunch at the hotel.

At 3, I drop in at the Konzelman Winery, where most of the wines are thin and very Germanic in style, before driving on to Hernder Estates to see Cowboy Fred, the biggest grape grower in Ontario, who is now beginning to produce wine under his own label. What a character!

I'm back at the hotel at 7. Following drinks at Cave Spring Restaurant, referred to locally as being 'on the 20', I go to dinner with Alan Schmidt at Vinelands. We drink his 1980 Chardonnay, then the 1994 Cabernet Sauvignon with châteaubriand, and finish with a stunning 1993 Icewine. It's raining heavily. I am home by 11.30.

4.10.95. I start the day with coffee in my room at 8 a.m.

My first visit of the day is to Stonechurch Vineyards at 9.30, where I meet Rick Hunse and Glen Hunt for a tasting that takes in their well-balanced 1994 Chardonnay, a Morio-Muskat and a Gewürztraminer.

Afterwards, I drive to St Catherine's to see the Wine Council of Ontario for further discussions regarding the export programme. Following a snack lunch at 2.30, I head for Henry of Pelham, where I have a meeting and full tasting of their excellent 94s, a Chardonnay sur lie, Rieslings, a Cabernet Franc rosé, a Baco Noir, a Cabernet-Merlot, and a magnificent 1993 Icewine.

Later, I have a couple of local beers at the notorious Private Eyes which, although a lap dancing establishment, also doubles as a normal bar at normal prices, and is anyway quite a fun place. At 9, I have Chinese dinner at Fan's, near the hotel – barbecue pork and Singapore noodles.

I am in bed at 11.

5.10.95. Awakening at 7.30 a.m., I have fresh apple juice and coffee, and then drive to Grimsby to visit John Peller at Andres, the second largest Winery in Ontario. Arriving at 10, I am treated to a full tasting and meeting, before lunch at 1.30 in Rigatoni, a local Italian Restaurant, accompanied by a carafe of volatile red wine. Back at their offices, the meeting continues until 4, after which I visit Pillitteri Winery for a tasting and meeting with the winemaker and owner, Charlie Pillitteri. There could be potential for their 1996 and 97 wines, with a red and white available at $22 a case.

Returning to the hotel at 5.45, I pack, and then have drinks in the bar. I eat dinner here too at 8.30, quail followed by pork tenderloin, accompanied by the 1994 Inniskillin Chardonnay Reserve and the superb 1993 Stoney Ridge Merlot. Hurricane Opal is doing its worst, and there is incredible rain. I get to bed at 10.30.

6.10.95. I spend a dreadful night, as the rain and hurricane persist unceasingly. Arising at 8, I take a shower, and then breakfast on poached eggs and bacon with toast. After packing, I leave Niagara-on-the-Lake for Toronto.

A visit to Southbrook Farms on the way reacquaints me with the delightful proprietor, Bill Redelmeier, who produces a very good framboise dessert wine at 15% ABV. Lunch in the winery is corn on the cob, followed by roast lamb marinated in cassis, with pumpkin pie to finish. (It is Thanksgiving weekend, after all!)

I then drive through horrendous traffic back to Toronto and briefly take in some of the sites. Fort York, where Toronto was founded in 1793, Mackenzie House, given to William Lyon Mackenzie by his friends in 1859 in appreciation of his lifelong efforts to reform the Canadian political system. After that I travel via Bloor Street to the airport, a route that takes me through much more interesting ethnic districts.

Once arrived at 4.30, I check in for Air Canada Business First flight AC 856 to London. I'm given seat 1B. After drinks in the Club Lounge, the flight, a Boeing 747, leaves at 7.50. It's a good journey, during which I manage to get a much needed four hours' sleep, and arrive at 6.50 a.m. local time on Saturday 7th, completely exhausted.

30 September–5 October 1998

12.3.98. This trip came about as a result of my winning the 'Executive Traveller of the Year 1998' award, having been shortlisted with three other finalists. An award ceremony and dinner took place at the London Transport Museum in Covent Garden, with the trip following later that year.

30.9.98. A chauffeur-driven car collects us at 12.30 to take us to Gatwick, South Terminal. We're flying Business First Continental Airlines to Newark. Their Business First class is equivalent to everybody else's First – huge seats, and only 24 of them.

In the Business Class lounge, I have a Jack Daniels and soda, while my wife Clare has a Bloody Mary. Our flight is a 3 p.m. departure.

Somewhat unfathomably, they elect to serve Spanish cava before take-off and then Ruinart champagne thereafter, a silly mistake. We have two glasses of the latter with toasted nuts, attention to detail from the air hostess extending to an enquiry as to whether the nuts were toasted to my satisfaction; this courtesy is often presented and gratefully accepted. Dinner begins with jumbo prawns and salad, served with an excellent 1996 Puligny-Montrachet, En Pimont. The main course is duck breast with roast potatoes and vegetables, with a choice of 1995 Leroy Bourgogne rouge (passable), 1995 Château La Tour-Pibran (thin), or 1995 Glass Mountain Merlot (acceptable). With the cheeses (Stilton, etc.), Fonseca's Bin 27 port is served. In sum, very good food, with some indifferent wines, save for the 'R' de Ruinart and the white burgundy.

After a short sleep, there are tea and scones at local time 4 p.m. (9 p.m. on our body clocks).

On arrival, I am stopped at Passport Control, because the authorities had not given me an exit stamp the last time I left the USA. This leads to me having to spend two hours in a secure room with illegal immigrants, some of whom are in handcuffs and chains. As I am sitting there, in an atmosphere putrid with the smell of body odour, an immigration officer who sits up high above the internees points to me and calls out, 'Mohammed Mohammed!'

Startled for the moment, I respond with, 'You must be joking,' to which he replies, 'I never joke, bud, it's the guy behind you.'

Eventually I am interviewed, and having seen from the stamps in my passport that I have travelled to numerous countries during my alleged overstay in the USA, an apology is reluctantly issued, along with a promise to make a correction entry in the computer. At last I'm free to go, collecting Clare, who has been wondering where the hell I had got to, and am glad to find the complimentary stretch limo still waiting.

It takes us to the Holiday Inn on Broadway and 32nd Street, where we find we have been upgraded to the penthouse suite (sic) on the 17th floor. I wonder what the other rooms are like if this is the penthouse suite.

We take a walk around Times Square, the centrepiece of New York's theatre district and certainly lives up to its reputation as the 'blazingest mile of street in the world'. It was originally called 'Longacre', the publisher of the *New York Times* in 1904 asked the city to change the name of the area before moving his offices there. We then stop and have bourbons at the Radisson Hotel and at the Playwright Tavern nearby, where they are currently half price, $9 for two doubles. Supper is well made hamburgers and home-brew beer at the Times Square Brewery.

In bed by 11 (4 a.m. to us). There will be lots to see. The weather is good, and there are seemingly not too many tourists.

1.10.98. We have breakfast at a diner next to the hotel – eggs over easy, bacon, plus everything else available… My goodness, the American breakfast is a true experience. Afterwards, we book a couple of day tickets for a bus tour, and then take a trip downtown through SoHo, which is an abbreviation for South of Houston Street. It is full of avant-garde galleries, shops and trendy restaurants, and has cast iron buildings which appealed to poor artists, who transformed the area into one of the city's hot spots;

Greenwich Village, once the city's Bohemian centre, famed for its restaurants, curio shops, bookshops, and nightclubs; and Wall Street, home of the New York Stock Exchange since 1903. This world-famous district at the southern tip of Manhattan is named for the wall erected in the mid 1600s by Dutch settlers as protection from the Indians and the British (who were growing increasingly hostile over Dutch mercantile success). The wall was torn down when the British colonised Manhattan in 1664. We then took a long walk viewing the shops along Madison Avenue where we lunch on very good pizza with bottled Budweiser.

Clare goes for some serious shopping at Bloomingdale's on Lexington Avenue, while I take the bus back to Greenwich Village, visiting the Cherry Lane theatre on Commerce Street, the oldest theatre in New York; The Village Gate, one of the most famous jazz clubs in the world, now sadly closed; then to Balducci's market, which offers an amazing array of fresh and international produce, ending at Washington Square Park at the foot of Fifth Avenue, where many artists gather and display their works in open-air shows during the spring and summer. I then take a cab to the Empire State Building. Built in 1932, this art deco building soars 1,454 feet into the sky. I take the lift to the 86th and then the 102nd floor, where the views are spectacular; then it's back to the hotel to change for dinner

An old friend and avid collector of old wines, Richard Steinberg, collects us at 8.15 to take us to dinner at the Gramercy Tavern. It's his 63rd birthday, and we are regaled with a *menu dégustation* comprising a warm oyster and caviare, sea-urchin, poached turbot, squab, filet mignon and two different puddings – superb food. The wines to accompany from his personal cellar are: 1935 Meursault Goutte d'Or, Dr Barolet, still fresh and lively; 1935 Vosne Romanée 1er cru, Dr Barolet, a stunning, old-fashioned Pinot showing no signs of age; a superb, rich, ripe 1945 Crozes-Hermitage; and the 1935 Smith Woodhouse vintage port, sheer perfection.

We are in bed by 11.30.

2.10.98. We awake to wonderful blue skies, and go up to Fifth Avenue for a bagels-and-coffee breakfast. After, we walk to

Second and 30th for our complimentary helicopter tour of Manhattan. This offers wonderful, suitably breathtaking views of the Statue of Liberty, 151 feet high on a 156-foot pedestal, presented to the US by France in 1884 to commemorate the two countries' alliance during the American Revolution. We see Ellis Island in New York harbour, the nation's main point of entry for millions of immigrants from 1892 to 1924. It is now a museum. We fly over the exotic art deco Chrysler Building, then Central Park, Columbia University, the George Washington Bridge and much more.

Afterwards, we put in a little light shopping at Macy's, and then go for drinks and lunch at P G King's opposite the Empire State Building, for barbecued pork rolls and draught Bud.

Clare then goes off for some more serious shopping at Bloomingdale's, while I go on an interesting walking tour of Chinatown, home to more than 150,000 residents. It is a tangle of narrow streets just west of Chatham Square and has been the centre of New York's Chinese community for more than 100 years. Chinese Restaurants and shops line the streets and vendors crowd the busy sidewalks

After changing for dinner, we go to meet another friend, John Holtz, his wife Susie, his mother-in-law, Nancy, and secretary, Joan Levene. We have a drink at Fresco's, 34 East 52nd Street, a trendy but good bar with an Italian restaurant. Clare and I leave at 7.30 and, as there are no cabs, we hire a stretch limo for $40 to take us to the World Trade Center.

There, we have dinner in the Windows on the World restaurant on the 107th floor. This is the highest building in the USA, and the third highest in the world (sadly later destroyed in the 9/11 attacks). We are given a lovely table for two. After a half-bottle of Veuve Clicquot, we have smoked salmon and caviare, followed by organic chicken with smoked bacon dumplings and a medley of mushrooms, accompanied by a good selection of California wines served by the glass, all wonderful. There is no bill, as $195 has been credited to the house in advance as part of the prize.

We take a cab back to the hotel at midnight.

3.10.98. The day begins with breakfast at Brook's Deli on Fifth Avenue. We then take a bus trip up to Harlem. Within the boundaries of the Hudson and Harlem rivers east to west, and 165th and 110th streets from north to south, this urban African-American community has many fascinating sights, including the Studio Museum, the Abyssinian Baptist Church, the African-American Wax Museum, the Cotton Club, famous for its soul food, and the lovely Apollo Theater, where amateur night is every Wednesday.

Next we visit the Rockefeller Center, which is a thriving commercial complex with offices, shops, hardens and entertainment areas where they were showing the magnificent Louis Vuitton vintage car collection. We have lunch at a local bar, superb ground sirloin with Hamber home-brew beers. Then we wander through the Plaza Hotel, and walk down Fifth Avenue, taking in Saks, Tiffany's, the Trump Tower, etc.

Next a stroll through the SoHo district again, which bears a slight resemblance to a more up to date Covent Garden, and then we walk slowly back to the hotel.

In the evening, we amble over to Molly Malone's bar for bourbons, and then take a cab to the theatre to see *Miss Saigon*, a great production. After more drinks at Rosie O'Grady's, we go to dinner at nearby Martini's. A mediocre pizza is accompanied by a good bottle of 1995 Palmers Long Island Cabernet Franc.

We take a cab back at midnight.

4.10.98. Richard Steinberg collects us at 9.30 to go to 'Friends on the Farm', a must for breakfast in the Gramercy district. A monster size omelette with fried onions, bacon and cheese is served in a skillet with a side order of potatoes and more onions, quite superb.

Two full-scale parades are taking place in New York today, a Polish and a Korean one. As we are in the Korean district, the roads have been blocked off to allow this amazing procession.

We take a cab to take a look around the Lower East Side area, but it starts to rain and so we turn round and watch the parades instead. At O'Reilly's pub, we have a couple of beers and snacks (fish sticks and onion rings). Miller Lite and Bud are both on tap, as is Miller Bitter.

Later, as part of the prize, we have a vast double super-stretch black limo to the airport, arriving at 4.30. We're booked on a Virgin 747 flight in Upper Class. In the Clubhouse, we avail ourselves of Georges Gardet champagne, with some super little snacks – pieces of pork, beef and chicken on toasts.

Our flight takes off at 6.30. There's champagne, and the centrepiece of the meal is lamb, served with pleasant 1995 Château La Croix from Pomerol. We have seats 7A and 7C right in the nose of the aircraft. I sleep through most of the flight, and we arrive back in the UK at 6.30 a.m. local time.

This has been a fantastic trip, made all the more enjoyable for being a prize.

California
13 July–4 August 2000

13.7.00. I take a 7.15 a.m. taxi to Heathrow Terminal 3, to catch the Virgin Atlantic flight VS 019 to San Francisco. On this trip, I am accompanied by Clare, our 18-year-old daughter, Holly and 17-year-old son Toby. I'm deposited in row 31 in the four-seat middle section. We take off at 11.15, which will be 3.15 a.m. in California. The seats, as I suspected, are so squashed together that I have to be consoled with a complimentary bottle of champagne, Georges Gardet NV. Dinner is roast beef, etc., quite good, and the film is *Pitch Black*. It's an 11-hour flight, during which I manage to consume rather a lot of Jack Daniels, which affords me six hours sleep, and then, after a service of various bits of indifferent food, we arrive in San Francisco at 2 p.m. local time.

Again, I am held up at Immigration over the question of the alleged time I overstayed in the USA on a previous visit, but unlike New York, where it took two hours to convince them of my bona fides, this time I am through in ten minutes. We take a cab to the Grand Hyatt Hotel on Union Square, where we are allocated suites 2419/2420, which command fantastic views over the square.

After a walk around Chinatown, we come back to the Hyatt Regency Club, where beers are served with free hot canapés on the 36th floor. Afterwards, we go out to RSG on Geary Street, a superb Chinese restaurant, for fabulous dishes of crab, beef and pork, only let down by a bottle of indifferent California Sauvignon Blanc.

I am in bed at 11.

14.7.00. Breakfast is free of charge in the Regency Club, which is a good way to start the day, and shopping at Macy's is an even better way to continue. I stop off for a beer at my favourite watering hole, Lefty O'Doul's, off Union Square, before meeting the others for lunch at the Fog City Diner on Battery Street. I order a seafood platter, including crab cakes, onion rings and truffle fries, and we drink a good bottle of Clos du Bois Chardonnay.

After lunch, we walk along the waterfront to Piers 39 and 41, and then take the $2 cable car back to Union Square for more shopping.

At 6, we repair to the Regency Club for drinks, and I avail myself of a large Jack Daniels. (It's a self-pouring system.) Dinner is at Hunan Home's Chinese restaurant at 622 Jackson Street. Beginning with a couple of large Korean beers, we then eat barbecued pork, prawns with asparagus in black bean sauce, mu shu, pancakes stuffed with chicken and vegetables, Mongolian beef and rice. All this proves very tiring, and we turn in at 10.30.

15.7.00. I awake at 6.45 a.m., and after drinking some coffee, we book a city tour, with a company called Tour de Force, for 8.15 a.m.. We then have breakfast in the Regency Club.

The city tour proves to be excellent. They are a new company using a seven-seater converted luxury car, although this trip is just the four of us. We are chauffeured all over the city, to the Barbary Coast, Telegraph Hill and Coit Tower, Pier 39, Ghirardelli Square, North Beach, Chinatown, The Financial District, Nob Hill, Union Square, the Civic Center, Alamo Square, Mission, Castro, Twin Peaks, Haight-Ashbury, Golden Gate Park and over the bridge, Cliff House, Lincoln Park, Sea Cliff, the Presidio, the Palace of Fine Arts, Union Street, Russian Hill and down the incredible winding Lombard Street, before being dropped off at Haight-Ashbury. The weather is overcast and windy, quite cold, but otherwise it is a truly memorable morning.

We eat an indifferent Tex-Mex lunch at Cha Cha Cha, 1801 Haight Street, with its wild interior décor, then take a cab back to Union Square for some shopping. I end up having to buy a sweatshirt, it's so cold. We book hotels en route for our trip on Tuesday.

Later, we meet some friends for drinks at the Westin St Francis, an old Victorian hotel, 335 Powell Street, and then go off to Tony Roma's on Ellis for ribs, an unexciting experience.

We are back at the hotel at 10.30.

16.7.00. Today's agenda begins with another trip, this time to Alcatraz, at 10.15. This, too, is an excellent tour, very professionally organised with headsets explaining the history of the prison and its inmates. Once again the weather is very poor. It's cold and overcast, with some rain.

We have lunch at Bobby Rubino's on the wharf – excellent spare ribs as always, the largest loaf of onion rings I have ever seen, fries and coleslaw, all very good – before strolling along the piers. A cab takes us back to the hotel, and as the weather is inclement, we rearrange to leave San Francisco a day earlier (i.e. tomorrow), booking the itinerary in advance.

After drinks in the Regency Club, we go to dinner at Bix, 56 Gold Street, a great place in the style of a 1920s speakeasy, with a jazz pianist. We dine on Bix's chicken hash and Silverado Napa Valley Chardonnay, returning to the hotel at 10.30.

17.7.00. Following an 8 a.m. breakfast, we check out. The room rate was $475 a night for the suite. We go to collect the car at Alamo on Bush Street, an Isuzu 4x4, but there is only one man running the check-in desk and we have to wait two hours to collect our car, yet again confirming that this is one hire company I shall never use again.

We take Highway 1, completed in 1937 after 18 years of construction, mostly by convict labour. Driving immediately south of San Francisco, this is home to farming communities preoccupied with proclaiming themselves 'PUMPKIN CAPITAL OF THE WORLD', the road twists tortuously along the magnificent coastline offering majestic scenery, passing the 2,200 acre Butano State Park covered in redwood trees, arriving in Santa Cruz, which has managed to hang on to its boardwalk and old-fashioned wooden roller coaster. There, we have lunch at the Ideal restaurant on the seafront in lovely sunny weather – mahimahi in tortillas with a couple of bottles of Coors beer.

In the afternoon, we drive through the scenic national parks and get to Monterey at 4, where we check into the Monterey Plaza Hotel and Spa, 400 Cannery Row. It's an excellent place, and I am given a wonderful room, 1423, with a balcony and views over the ocean. The weather continues sunny and warm, and we walk around town for a while, coming back eventually for a beer on the terrace. Then we walk to Fisherman's Wharf for dinner at Domenico's, which is superb. I have angel hair pasta with Dungeness crab, a Wild Turkey 101 bourbon with soda, and a bottle of over-oaked 1998 Boyer Chardonnay from Monterey County.

Back at the hotel, I have another Turkey 101 and soda at the terrace bar, and then get to bed at 10.45.

18.7.00. We rise at 7.30, and find the weather warm but overcast once more. Breakfast at 8.15 consists of poached eggs, bacon, smoked chicken and apple sausages and hash browns, with orange juice, coffee and brown toast.

I start the day with a visit to the aquarium. Featuring 6,500 species of marine life in more than 100 display tanks, including a towering three-storey giant kelp forest, huge sharks and sea otters, it is well worth a visit. Then we take the famous Seventeen Mile Drive, a loop around the peninsula where one enjoys the most magnificent coastal scenery, stopping off to take in Bird Rock which is home to sea lions and harbour seals, then on to Carmel by the Sea, famous for having Clint Eastwood as its mayor, which is overly twee and has no beach restaurants. Returning to Monterey's Fisherman's Wharf, we have lunch at Abalonetti, a seafood trattoria, but the swordfish with ratatouille is no better than average.

After a mediocre Swedish massage at 4 o'clock in the hotel spa with Ynez (and somewhat overpriced at $100), we have drinks in the room, and then go to Chart House Restaurant for excellent steaks. This is served with a 'Wine Flight', which is a great idea – a small glass each of four white and four red wines as tasting samples, served in a wooden tantalus, enabling one to choose appropriate wines to accompany the food.

We're back at the hotel at 10.30.

19.7.00. I'm woken by the alarm at 7 for checking out. After a 7.30 breakfast, we drive the seventeen-mile drive again along Highway 1, passing quickly through Carmel and then to the stretch of road known as Big Sur, with the most spectacular coastal views imaginable. This is a dangerous road for it skirts vertiginous cliffs with many of the sections unfenced. We then pass over Bixby Creek on the 320-foot single arch Bixby Bridge, climbing as high as 1,000 feet above the ocean. From there we go to Nepenthe, built on a promontory that Orson Wells bought for Rita Hayworth after their honeymoon in the 1940s. Since 1949 it has been run as a bar restaurant. At 10.30, we stop here for a Big Sur Light beer, and then drive on through the Julia Pfeiffer Burns State Park where California's only coastal waterfall - the stunning 50-foot McWay Falls – drops straight into the sea, and on to San Simeon where the Big Sur ends.

We stop en route for a fish lunch on the terrace of the Gorda Café in conditions that are sunny and hot but very windy, before driving on to Cambria, where we will be staying at the Moonstone Inn on Moonstone Drive by the ocean. This is exceedingly twee. We are in the bottom half of a house, done out like a bridal suite, with the kids in the motel part, room No. 8. The male owner is distinctly weird, and spends all day baking cookies. In due course, we are brought carafes of red and white wine in huge silver wine coolers, with cheese and grapes, in what only can be described as his sitting room. The whole place is built for left-handed people. We take ourselves off for a spot of whale-watching, but conditions are still very windy and sadly see nothing.

Venturing into town, which really consists of Main Street and Burton Drive, we pass restaurants with such names as 'The Sow's Ear' and 'Mustache Pete's'.

We stop for dinner at the Sea Chest Oyster Bar and Sea Food Restaurant, 6216 Moonstone Drive, a great location where we dine on oysters and sea bass, accompanied by a dull Cambria Chardonnay from Santa Barbara. Walking back to the hotel we spot a group of sea elephants, as though in compensation for missing the whales.

20.7.00. We breakfast in the room, and check out at 8.20.

At 10, we are booked in for a tour of Hearst Castle, set in 25,000 acres on a hill overlooking San Simeon. It still sets the standard for stylistic excess. This weekend getaway was built by the newspaper magnate, William Randolph Hurst, during the 1920s and 1930s and is a bizarre mixture of Italian, French, Moorish and Spanish architecture. The interiors are an eclectic blend of Gothic and Renaissance sculptures with Persian carpets, revealed in an absolutely fantastic two-hour tour. It's an astonishing folly with no expense spared in its building as is crammed with antiques and treasures.

We stop for lunch in Cayucos at the north end of Estero Bay where we see the remnants of Cass Landing - a rickety old pier, which the locals use as a great spot to dive off. From there we drive to the fishing town of Morro Bay, famous for its elephant seal colony, where we are staying at the excellent Morro Bay Inn. The hotel has fine views of Morro Rock, and a jacuzzi on the deck of each room. The best rooms are those numbered in the 400s.

After driving around town for a while, we have drinks in the bar, and then at 8, go to dinner at Hoppé's Back Pocket Bistro on Embacadero Street. We have good crab ravioli and 24oz steaks, accompanied by a delicious bottle of 1998 Edna Valley Chardonnay.

We are back at the hotel at 10.30.

21.7.00. The day begins with an 8.30 breakfast of poached eggs and bacon, with toast. It looks like a lovely sunny day. Checking out of the hotel at 9.30, we drive along the coast through San Luis Obisco and Pismo Beach, one of the few remaining places where it is still legal to drive on the beach, then on to Santa Barbara, which interestingly enough prior to a single film being made in Hollywood was the nominal capital of Southern California, by virtue of its Spanish mission located at 2201 Laguna Street. The 'Queen of the Missions', as it is called, sits halfway up the hill, overlooking the city. It is one of the 23 missions dotted along the spine of California that has managed to remain continuously active since the Franciscans introduced their brand of Western civilisation to the state some 250 years ago. Arriving around midday, we check in to the West Beach Inn, 306 West Cabrillo Boulevard. The patio suite we are assigned is very comfortable, with two bedrooms and a large sitting room.

We take a walk up to the pier, and have lunch at Longboards Grill – a huge portion of beef ribs, with local Santa Barbara beer on tap. Afterwards, we promenade up State Street with all its fine shops and Restaurants including one that features a 60-foot-long salad bar; opposite, there's a bar called Left at Alburquerque, offering 140 varieties of tequila. It is easier to take in the town from the tower of the Santa Barbara County Courthouse. A 1925 earthquake levelled the city and new regulations ensured reconstruction would be no more than three stories high. So the tower offers a spectacular view of Santa Barbara, which looks like a village showcase of the Californian-mission style of architecture. Its plethora of painted tiles and low-storeyed, white washed Spanish-Mediterranean buildings suggests a town from another time and civilisation, when in fact it has been mostly built in the final quarter of the last century. This really is a very attractive town, with a good beach, and we can be glad that the weather is fine.

We make our way to the top of Main Street to cash some money. Strangely, the banks here don't have foreign exchanges. We manage to do some light shopping, and then return to the hotel for a swim and a sauna.

In the evening, drinks on the patio precede dinner at Andria's Harborside restaurant, 336 West Cabrillo Blvd., starting with spring rolls and prawns, followed by huge portions of delicious crab cakes. A local Sauvignon Blanc turns out to be bland, but the Chardonnay is better. In the bar, a jazz pianist and bassist are playing. We are back by 11.

I am running out of money at a rate of knots, and my credit cards are almost up to their limits.

22.7.00. Another superb, sunny day begins with coffee on the patio at 8.15 a.m., following which we drive up to Sycamore Creek to see some relatives of Clare's, and have bagels and cream cheese with them. They have a superb house with the creek actually running through their garden. Then we drive on to Cold Creek Canyon for a beer at a wonderful old tavern that was the original watering hole of the gold prospectors, but which is now a weekend meeting place for Harley-Davidson owners.

Returning to Santa Barbara, we have lunch on the pier, beginning with a huge cocktail. We share a vast fish platter, and then go back to the hotel to swim.

At 8.30, we walk up State Street, and have dinner at Lock's at an outside table, accompanying Korean ribs with an over-oaked 1998 Santa Ynez Sauvignon Blanc. The town has a great atmosphere, very lively and buzzing at night. We return at midnight.

23.7.00. Checking out of the hotel at 9.30, we drive to Santa Monica through Ventura and Malibu, arriving at the quite excellent Shutters on the Beach Hotel, 1 Pico Boulevard, at noon. Our suite isn't ready, so we have lunch in the restaurant, turkey hash with local beer. As our room was on a late checkout arrangement, we are upgraded to the Presidential Suite, 302, which is altogether amazing, with a huge sitting room and bedroom and balconies all the way round – and so it should be, at $5,000 a night! I go for a swim in the hotel pool, and then take a walk along the pier. Built in 1916, it is the oldest pleasure pier on the west coast, quite touristy with its old-fashioned carousel.

In the evening, we go to dinner at the over-expensive Beach House, 100 West Channel Road, for ribs. We are back by 11.

24.7.00. We start the day with a drive to Bel Air, the district where many of the film stars' homes are, taking in Beverley Hills, Rodeo Drive, lined with very smart expensive shops, and Hollywood itself, which is a sleazier quarter than most visitors might imagine. We eat lunch at a local diner, and visit Mann's Chinese Theatre (known as Grauman's in the days when it hosted glitzy premieres), with its stars' walkway with 1,500 star names studded into the pavement.

Returning to the hotel at 3, we go for a walk along to Venice Beach, which is a fun place with outdoor entertainment, and lots of beach shops. In the evening, after drinks in our suite, we go out to the Buffalo Club, 1520 Olympic Blvd, for dinner. This is a very exclusive place, reflected in the fact that it's very difficult to find, looking misleadingly derelict from the outside. Within, though, is a very nice patio and garden, and we dine on lobster dumplings, chicken legs and steak, which are all rather indifferent, although Clare and Holly give excellent reviews to their lobster main course. It's inevitably very expensive, including an interesting bottle of 1996 Bonny Doon Vin Gris.

We are home at 10.

25.7.00. Breakfast at the hotel consists of eggs and bacon, strawberry and orange juice and coffee. We then drive to Universal Studios, the world's largest working film and television studio, and purchase a VIP ticket at $125 a head, but the tour is so brilliant, it's worth it. Starting at 10, we are taken on a trolley tour of the film sets of *ET*, *Backdraft*, *Jurassic Park* and *Back to the Future*, and then queue-jump at all the rides. After lunch at the Hollywood Cantina, a Mexican self-service restaurant with the rudest chef I have ever encountered, we spend the afternoon at Waterworld. It's been a breathtaking tour.

Back at the hotel at 6, we walk up to the Third Street Promenade, and have a dinner of ribs and Corona beer at George's Bistro. We are back by 11.

26.7.00. After a final coffee on our wonderful terrace at 8.15 a.m., we check out and head for La Jolla, taking the Highway 1 coast road through Long Beach, stopping for a snack lunch at Laguna Beach. We arrive and check into the Sea Lodge Hotel next to La Jolla Beach and Tennis Club, an establishment that is twinned with the Hurlingham Club in London. We have a lovely suite overlooking the ocean, and the weather, though slightly overcast, is still warm.

My eldest daughter, Danielle, and son-in-law Gareth, who live in San Diego, have arranged to meet us in the bar of the Marine Room restaurant at the Club at 7. We have drinks and an excellent dinner, enjoying the view over the ocean. They both look to be in great health.

I get to bed at 11.30.

27.7.00. Waking up to another warm day, we check out and drive up to Del Mar, where we check into the Les Artistes Hotel, a very Bohemian place in which every room is named after a famous artist. Ours is Gauguin. It's clean, but there is quite a difference in quality to the previous hotels; but then the price reflects that, at $168.

After dropping off our luggage, we lunch locally at El Paz on their terrace, accompanying fajitas with local micro-Brewery beers.

Later, we drive to Danielle and Gareth's place, a delightful house, dropping off Holly and Toby, who will be staying there. Dinner is at the Beach House Restaurant, 3263 Camino Drive. Upstairs, the Top of the House features seafood and steaks, which are mediocre – a pity, as the tables have a great ocean view.

28.7.00. Today, we head for Mexico, where we will be staying at the Isabel Mission Hotel. We eat a very commercial lunch of fajitas at Rosarita in humid conditions, and later have dinner with copious quantities of a range of tequilas sitting outside at a restaurant on the main street.

29.7.00. After breakfasting on scrambled eggs and bacon with hot sauce, we check out and drive 30 minutes to the Blow Hole, which is quite a spectacular site as the ocean seems to take a breath and then spews water high into the sky. We eat lunch at a local bistro, which will later give us all a sort of food poisoning.

Tonight will be spent at the Pyramid Resort timeshare at Chula Vista by the ocean. The place is being rented out by the night until it is sold. We eat a very good dinner in a nearby open-air restaurant overlooking the ocean – spare ribs with prodigious quantities of tequila.

30.7.00. We drive back to San Diego, but by now most of us are permanently on Imodium, and not in the mood for lunch or dinner.

31.7.00. Feeling much better now, our day is taken up with a tour around San Diego, a cultural city with many theatres and more than ninety museums. We started at old town, which dates back to 1820, when Spain sent Gaspar de Portola to establish the first European settlement in California, taking in the Old Drug Store museum, San Diego Union museum and Bazaar del Mundo, reminiscent of a Mexican marketplace, with shops, restaurants and nightly performances of flamenco dancing. Downtown San Diego, with its Victorian-style Gaslamp Quarter is the home of the nightlife in the city with many clubs and bars and restaurants, and no trip to San Diego would be complete without a visit to their world-famous zoo in Balbao Park with more than 4,00 rare and endangered animals. We are staying nearby in the superb Coronada Hotel, which is built entirely of wood.

In the evening, we take in a baseball game, the San Diego Padres versus the Philadelphia Phillies, and then have dinner at P F Chang's China Bistro, 4540 La Jolla Village Drive, where the portions are huge, and it's difficult to do justice to what seems to be very good food. An accident results in peanut sauce being spilled over everyone, but they offer to pay for the cleaning bill.

1.8.00. The morning is taken up with shopping in the outlet stores at Carlsbad, which more than a century ago attracted the rich and famous, as well as health-conscious people, to benefit from the water's acclaimed healing properties. We have a hamburger lunch at Ruby's Diner. After spending the afternoon on the beach, we have dinner at the Chart House Restaurant, 2588 South Highway 101, Cardiff; this is quite a large chain operating in California which consistently serves very good steaks.

2.8.00. We start the day by driving to Yos Isdres on the Mexican border, where I am pulled over, American-style, by the police for allegedly speeding. What ensues is reminiscent of a film scene, with my being asked to 'step outside the car and place your hands on the roof, sir'. As I have left my driving licence, insurance and passport in the hotel, I am instructed to accompany the officer to the police station. I eventually manage to appeal to her better judgment, and I am given a ticket and told to appear in court in three days' time. Even though I explain we are leaving for London the next day, she still issues the ticket and insists that everything has to be done by the book.

We then continue on our way for more shopping at the factory outlets. The K-Mart in particular is very cheap.

In the evening, we have a barbecue at Danielle and Gareth's place, before repairing to the very smart L'Auberge Del Mar Hotel for a nightcap.

3.8.00. At San Diego airport, we check in for the United Airlines flight to San Francisco at 10.37, arriving at 11.40. Here, we have the use of the Red Carpet Lounge before boarding the Virgin Atlantic flight VS 20 at 4.30. We are allotted bulkhead seats, which at least afford more legroom. The food is indifferent, and we are charged £15 for a bottle of the uninspiring Georges Gardet champagne, which takes an age to arrive. Other than that, the flight back to the UK is fairly good.

This has been another fascinating and exhausting trip, but one that has taken an extreme toll on my bank balance.

Miami and Fort Lauderdale
11–14 January 2001

A Visit to Gallo Wines Export Division

11.1.01. I take a cab at 8 a.m. to Clapham Junction station, and then the 8.10 train to Gatwick South Terminal, where I check in for the Virgin Atlantic Upper Class flight VS 005 to Miami, seat 2K. In the Virgin Clubhouse lounge, I have coffee and croissants. The flight is due to leave at 10.45, but actually takes off an hour later than that. I am upstairs in the first row. Surprisingly, there is no on-board bar, and no in-flight massage service available. Champagne is served, prior to a noodle salad with Thai curry and rice, accompanied by Marqués de Murrieta Reserva 1996. Having watched an indifferent film, *Sexy Beast* with Ben Kingsley, I sleep for two hours, and then coffee and sandwiches are served, which I accompany with a bourbon and soda.

Great views of the eastern coastline of the USA appear presently, and we land at 3.30 local time. Yet again, I am stopped at Immigration, but this time pass through without being detained for too long. I find the Hertz desk and the shuttle bus. My credit card is initially rejected, which causes great hassle, but eventually goes through, and I am compensated with an upgraded car far too big, in fact.

It then takes over 3½ hours for me to find the hotel on what should be a 45-minute drive, because I lose my way so many times. At one stage, I find myself in a none too salubrious part of town and stop to ask directions at a local minimart, where the owner sits behind a thick wire cage with an extremely large shotgun on his lap. He advises me in no uncertain terms that I should get out of this neighbourhood with the utmost haste. I then go to the wrong Marriott Hotel in Fort Lauderdale, but finally make it to the Courtyard Marriott. After all that, it's quite basic, like a Holiday Inn. I'm in room 231.

I drink Jim Beam and soda in the small, empty hotel bar, and then take a taxi to Bobby Rubino's, which is dark, cold and damp. The ribs I order are tepid, not a patch on their branch in San Francisco, and I drink an Ice House beer. I get to bed at 10.30 (3.30 a.m. London time).

12.1.01. Having spent a fitful night, even with the assistance of a sleeping pill, waking up four or five times, I eat a breakfast of two over easy eggs with bacon on rye toast, apple juice and coffee, and then leave at 9. I drive along the coast road, right down to South Beach, which is full of superb Art Deco buildings. Lunch is at Deux Fontaines on Ocean Drive, carpaccio of tuna and grilled grouper, accompanied by local beer and Kendall Jackson Chardonnay.

I take the drive back nice and slow. It's intensely sunny, 80°F, and on return I read by the pool for a while.

In the evening, I down a couple of Jim Beam and sodas in the bar, before cabbing at 7.45 to Rainbow Palace, 2787 Oakland Boulevard, a smart, highly rated, Chinese restaurant. Despite its reputation, there are no chopsticks (other than on request) and the receptionist appears to be the only Chinese member of staff. The waiters are all gay and over-attentive. I order two glasses of 1998 Alexander Valley Chardonnay at $9, a highly oaked but good wine, and partner them with a quartet of tough shrimp and lobster dumplings in a strong dressing of pepper, chilli and soy ($15), and a large portion of the chef's not hot but well-balanced spicy fried rice ($16), containing pork, shrimp and chicken. Basically, it's good fusion Chinese food, served to a backing of piped Italian opera.

My cab back at 10.30 costs an excessive $20.

13.1.01. I am awoken at 6.30 by the horrendous noise of the garbage being collected. An hour later, I have a breakfast of scrambled eggs, bacon and toast, and then meet with a member of the Gallo export department in the lobby at 8.30.

We drive to their offices and I am treated to a long and boring video of the history of the Gallo Corporation. They are interested in my joint venture in India and are considering opening an office in Delhi. Afterwards, we all go to lunch in a local steak and ale house. I eat a fillet steak marinated in soy, and drink Coors Light. They drink water.

Back at the hotel, we chat about the possibility of joining forces in India. Later, the hotel bus takes us to the Rainbow Palace again for a good dinner. From where the hotel is located, it is difficult to go anywhere without a 15–30 minute cab ride costing around $20, as we are plumb in the middle of the commercial district.

14.1.01. I breakfast at 8 a.m. on two over easy eggs on brown toast with crispy bacon, grape juice and coffee. After packing, I check out at 10, and stop at the Old Navy store in the Colony shopping mall and buy two pairs of jeans for $50. I drive the coast road to South Beach, with its art deco hotels and crammed claustaphobically full of holiday apartments, and stop for lunch at Colony on Ocean Blvd on very good pork fajoles with draught Budweiser.

I then take the car back to Hertz, and check in for the Virgin Atlantic Upper Class flight back to London. Once again, I'm upstairs, in seat 2K. The Upper Class check in is smart and separate from the rest, and I drink a Becks beer in the American lounge.

We take off at 6.30, and are served champagne and a cooked breakfast. I sleep until our arrival at Gatwick at 7 a.m. local time.

Hawaii via Los Angeles
24 May–1 June 2001

24.5.01. My daughter Joanna and I are travelling on an Air New Zealand Business Class flight to Los Angeles, departing at 16.25. On checking in, I discover that they have not reserved adjacent seats for us. We are in 9K and 11K, and I am forced to raise absolute hell.

In the so-called Red Carpet lounge, I have a gin and tonic but there is no food. We are at last informed that the seat allocations have been changed to 9J and 9K on the upper deck in Business Class. Once on the flight, we are served with a couple of small bottles of Deutz Marlborough Cuvée New Zealand sparkling wine. The flight, a 747–400, is full.

After take off the aperitif is Piper-Heidsieck champagne, and dinner consists of roasted peppers, very good lamb shank with mashed potato and cabbage, served with Wolf Blass 1998 Reserve Cabernet Sauvignon, and then cheese, with McWilliams botrytised Semillon. I sleep for three hours, read a little, then sleep for three hours more, and we arrive in Los Angeles at 6 p.m. local time (eight hours back). As usual, I am irritatingly stopped at Immigration.

A shuttle bus takes us to the Marriott Airport Hotel, where we are given rooms 4094 and 4096. I have a Maker's Mark bourbon and soda in the Sports Bar, and then dine on spare ribs with onion rings; not good at all.

I get to bed at 11.

25.5.01. After a fitful night's sleep, I am woken by an alarm call at 8 a.m. I eat a breakfast of fried eggs, sausage and bacon, toast, orange juice and coffee at 8.30, and then check out of the hotel. The rooms cost over $200 each for the one night.

A courtesy bus takes us back to the airport at 9.15, and we check in for the United Airlines flight to Kona, Hawaii, a 5½ journey. The plane is again full.

I drink a couple of quarter-bottles of Fortant Chardonnay with a fairly good meat and vegetable dish. In a competition to guess the time in mid-flight, I win second prize, a bottle of Bouvet sparkling wine. The film is *Chocolat*, which I quite enjoy, and we land in Hawaii at 3 p.m. (another three hours back, so we are now 11 hours back on UK time).

Daughter Danielle and son-in-law Gareth are on hand to meet us with luaus of flowers, and we hire a car from the dreaded Alamo, a Pontiac, to drive ourselves to our hotel, the Outrigger on Waikoloa Beach. I'm in room 6275, with a view over Lara Rock towards the ocean.

After unpacking and showering, we have drinks downstairs in the bar in quite a nice setting. Most hotels here are resorts in themselves. Then we drive to Gareth and Danielle's self-catering apartment overlooking the ocean.

Dinner is at Jameson's next door, at a table right by the water. The menu is ono fish in soy sauce with rice, which I accompany with two glasses of house Chardonnay. It's a 45-minute drive back to the hotel, and I'm in bed at 11.30.

26.5.01. I rise at 6.30 a.m., and breakfast at 7 on fruit, and scrambled eggs and bacon. We go for an adventure drive to the volcano, setting off north over the top of the island and down the east side to Hilo, an attractive old town, and then to the volcano, an 11-mile journey. We make a circuit of the crater rim, with lots of sightseeing stops, and then walk through the lava tunnel and the rainforest. By the time we have driven back to the hotel, it's 2 p.m.

I take a rest by the pool and sip at a much needed beer. At 5, I go for an excellent massage lasting 80 minutes, including a spot of faith healing. This was an amazing experience, as his hands seem to heat up to an almost unbearable level, removing all pain from my troublesome lower back.

After showering and changing, I meet Joanna in the bar at 7.30, and drink a couple of Wild Turkey 101 bourbons with sodas. We have dinner à deux on the terrace overlooking the pool and gardens – tuna and pork in a pastry conch-shell, and mahimahi in teriyaki sauce with noodles, both good. A fine bottle of 1999 Chateau St Jean Chardonnay accompanies. I am in bed at 11.30.

Live volcano erupting into the ocean, Hawaii

Hawaii

27.5.01. Sunday is the big day, and the reason we are here. Danielle is participating in the 'Iron Man' triathlon, hence my 5.30 alarm call. We drive to the peninsula near where she and Gareth are staying, arriving at 6.25. There are 850 contestants. For the first leg, they must swim 2½ miles in the ocean. Danielle is in the top half at this stage. Then there is a very quick change to the second leg, which is a 110 km bike ride, with us following in hot pursuit by car, stopping from time to time to cheer her on. She is still in the top 50% of the field. For the third leg, they must run a half-marathon of 15 miles. I clock her at the finishing line in 6 hours 46 minutes. She has finished in the top 60.

We celebrate with a couple of beers and a dreadful hot dog in a nearby hotel. Despite all her exertions, she looks great and we are all suitably proud of her.

Afterwards, we drive back to the hotel, where I swim and rest, and then have a couple of Wild Turkey 101s, and then a couple more. At 7, we drive to the Kona Inn Hotel, 40 minutes south, for more drinks with the greater part of the day's contestants. I try a glass of good Sauvignon Blanc in a bar by the ocean.

Dinner is at Lulu's, a lively bistro – huge portions of ribs with Lara Red beer. I play some pool, meet with one of the contestants and her husband, as well as her divorced mother who, by dint of extreme persistence, gets me to dance. What next? I ask myself.

We drive back at 11.

28.5.01. I breakfast with Joanna at 8 a.m. on fruit, scrambled eggs with rice and bacon, guava juice and coffee. It's a very hot day with clear blue skies, and I do nothing more than sit by the pool for a while. I try to swim, but it's too hot. Danielle and Gareth arrive at 12, and we go to the beach. Lunch is pastrami on rye with two Kona draught beers.

At 2.30, I have another 80-minute massage with Mr Magic Hands, then relax and read until 5. After a shower and a sleep, I meet Joanna, Gareth and Danielle for drinks at 6.30, and we have dinner in the hotel at 8. I opt for the same menu as on the first night, as it was so good, pairing it with an overly oaky 1999 Estancia Chardonnay.

I am in bed at 11.

29.5.01. Breakfast with Joanna at 8 consists of two poached eggs on rye toast with bacon and fried onions, a very large guava juice and coffee.

Danielle and Gareth arrive at 10.30, and we make the two-hour drive to Hilo via the waterfall and the airport, from where we take a helicopter tour of the volcano. This is an amazing sight, as it is still so active, with lava flowing out to the ocean. The trip lasts 50 minutes.

We then wander around the run-down town of Hilo, which is reminiscent of early Havana, before going for a late 3.30 lunch of good chicken fajita. Afterwards, we drive back to the hotel, and stroll over to the King's Mall shopping centre for a browse around.

Beginning the evening with drinks in the bar at 7.30, we are recommended to have dinner at Sam Choy's, which is off the airport road up in the hills. It proves almost impossible to find, situated as it is in the middle of an industrial estate. When we do finally get there, it turns out it doesn't open for dinner. It's pouring with rain. Rescuing the evening, we eat at a place called Huggo's, where I have a very good steak, accompanied by Beaulieu Vintners' fine 1999 Cabernet Sauvignon.

We get back to the hotel at 11.30.

30.5.01. For a change, we decide to have breakfast at the Hilton beach resort next door to our own hotel, at 8 a.m. Their hotel complex is like a mausoleum, with ghastly large Gothic arches, and a monorail and water buses to transport you around. Our breakfast by the pool consists of a three-egg omelette with ham and onions, guava juice and coffee.

Afterwards, we take the shuttle bus back to the Outrigger, and meet up with Danielle and Gareth at noon for hot dogs and Kona beer on tap. I do a little shopping in the King's Mall opposite.

Later, we drive back to the airport where, at 1 p.m., I deliver the car back to Alamo and then check in for the flight. There is no Business Class, but seats with extra legroom are available to 'holders of full paying air tickets'. I enquire with Customer Relations what this means, only to be told by the assistant that she doesn't understand it herself. The flight is United Airlines UA

128 from Kona to Los Angeles, and it's full. On board, they serve Sam Choy's meatloaf with mashed potato, and I drink two Jim Beams with soda at $4 each, as well as a quarter-bottle of Dourthe Bordeaux rouge, which latter is free as a consequence of Joanna finding an insect in her salad.

The journey takes 5½ hours, and we arrive at 11.30 p.m. local time (three hours ahead). A shuttle takes us to the Marriott Hotel at the airport, and I get to bed at 1 a.m.

31.5.01. I awake at 8 a.m., check out, store our luggage, and take a cab to Venice Beach for a breakfast of eggs and bacon. We stroll along the beach road, which is full of fortune-tellers and suchlike, all very hippie. Joanna has a henna tattoo put on her hand, and we continue on to Shutters on the Beach at Santa Monica, and have a beer by the pool overlooking the Presidential Suite, in which I stayed in July 2000.

A cab takes us back to the Marriott, from where we pick up the shuttle to the airport terminal. We check in for Air New Zealand Business Class flight NZ 002 to London, departing at 15.40. There is a very good VIP lounge, in which I have a vodka and V8.

We take off at 4.30 in seats 9J and 9K, and make sure that we drink lots of Piper-Heidsieck. The meal is lamb with mashed potatoes, followed by cheese. I sleep for much of the long flight, and we eventually land at Heathrow Terminal 3 at 10.15 a.m. local time.

This great trip was made all the more enjoyable by Danielle doing so well in the triathlon finals.

Boston
31 July–4 August 2002

31.7.02. We arrive at Heathrow Terminal 3 at noon for the
Continental Virgin Upper Class flight US 11 to Boston, seats 8A
and B. The futuristic Virgin Clubhouse lounge serves wonderful
Jacquart champagne and sushi.

On the flight, which is due to depart at 14.35, we are plied
with more Jacquart. We have booked a manicure service on board,
as well as a neck massage, and there is also a bar area with proper
stools – all the gimmicks, in other words, but only a very limited
menu.

Having taken off one hour late, we are served with Moët &
Chandon, prior to a salad and steak lunch, accompanied by a 1996
Château de Meursault, which is a quite deep and rich white
Burgundy, but with a fairly light finish. We land in Boston,
(home of fifty colleges and universities) seven hours later (five
hours behind UK time), and taxi to the Colonnade Hotel at 120
Huntington Avenue, situated in the trendy Back Bay area of
Boston. This is theoretically a four-star hotel, but has more the
appearance of a three-star, being in need of some renovation.

We are welcomed by a letter from one Tracey Taverna,
director of business travel, informing us that we have been given
an upgraded room, 813, only to find that there is a huge hole in
the bathroom basin. We are therefore moved again to 623, which
is no more than adequate (perhaps I have been spoiled by the
elevated quality of many of the hotels I have recently stayed in).

After unpacking, we go for a walk along Newbury Street,
which is a little like London's Kings Road, full of trendy shops
and bijou restaurants. Back at the hotel, we change and then head
down to the bar, which doubles as Brasserie Jo, a French style
bistro, for a much needed bourbon and soda. The temperature is
around 85°F.

Dinner will be at Jimmy's Harborside Restaurant, 242
Northern Avenue, on the waterfront adjacent to the World Trade

Center and Boston's Fish Pier, a huge place, and quite touristy. We dine on crab cakes, followed by scrod and chips. 'Scrod' is the term for any fresh fish of the day; I think mine was cod. A bottle of 2000 Chateau St Jean Fumé Blanc is well-balanced, with a good fruity finish. We make our way back to the hotel at 11.

1.8.02. Having passed a fitful night, I go for the full American breakfast at 8.30, consisting of two eggs over easy, with back bacon and hash browns, multigrain toast, fresh orange juice and coffee – $13.

After this fortifying start, we take a walk through the Prudential Center, this popular shopping mall has over 75 shops and restaurants including an incredible panoramic view of the city from the Skywalk Observatory. We then buy tickets for the city tour by 'duck' (Dukw), which is a wartime amphibious vehicle. The earliest one leaves at 10.30. By now, the sun is up and it's 32°C, and hot. Unfortunately, my seat is out in the open, causing me 90 minutes of torture. The tour, however, is excellent, progressing partly by road and partly by water, taking in Paul Revere's House, Chinatown, the theatre district, Downtown and the Waterfront, plus many more sights of Boston.

Returning to the hotel, I drink a necessary draught beer and then go for a swim in the rooftop pool. Our snack lunch is accompanied by the local well-made beer, Samuel Adams. In the late afternoon, we go shopping once more. The malls are very modern and immaculately maintained, and have all the stores one might need.

We have arranged to meet up with friends who live in Boston for dinner. At 8, we are collected and taken to a recently opened Peruvian Restaurant, at which all the dishes bear a marked visual similarity to those in the average Indian restaurant, and taste like it too. They are washed down with a couple of bottles of Ravenswood Zinfandel, a very good California red.

We make it back to the hotel by midnight.

2.8.02. After another fitful night, I rise at 7 a.m., and eat an excellent omelette filled with a huge quantity of bacon and onions.

Our day begins at 10 with a tour of the Berklee College of Music, rated as the finest college of contemporary music in the world. Toby has applied for a four-year Bachelor of Music degree course here, starting in September 2003. At 1.30, we go to a meeting with the 'international counsellor', who informs us that he has been accepted, which of course is the occasion for great celebrations.

Back at the hotel, we eat a light lunch of prawns and house salad. (When I ask the waitress what the 'house salad' is, her reply sounds – dryly enough – like 'bricks', but when I ask if it also includes windows and doors, she remains quite deadpan, offering no comment. It turns out she had said 'beets'.) The afternoon proceeds with a tour of the many second-hand record shops.

In the evening, after a couple of 7 o'clock bourbons in the hotel bar, we go to dinner at Bob the Chef's restaurant and jazz café, at 604 Columbus Avenue. It is a type of bistro, serving Southern soul food to a backing of soul music from a great blues/soul band, and has a very casual feel. The Cajun chicken wings are glorious, although the spare ribs are not that great, and there are French fries and corn to accompany, as well as a bottle of J Lohr Cabernet Sauvignon 2000, which is deep and fruity, and curiously quite sweet. All in all, it's a fun place, even though the food is no great shakes.

3.8.02. We breakfast at 9 on poached eggs, ham, fresh orange juice and coffee for $13.95, and then take a cab to Macy's for some serious shopping.

Lunch is dim sum at the Empire Garden, 690 Washington Street, in Boston's Chinatown, a huge restaurant that probably accommodates something like 800 people. It must at one time have been a ballroom or cinema, judging by its beautiful old ceilings and ornate frieze work. The dim sum, served from trolleys rolling endlessly past, are superb, offering an expansive range of prawn, pork, chicken, dumplings, etc., with Tsingtao beer to accompany.

Back at the hotel, we go for a swim in the rooftop pool, as the temperature has now hit 38°C.

We have been invited by the parents of a friend of Toby's to dinner at their house at 8.30. They live in Somerset Road in the Brookline district, which is a $20 cab ride away. We are regaled with an extremely good chicken curry with cauliflower and dhal, with which they serve 1998 Chateau Souverain Cabernet Sauvignon from California (well-balanced and mature, with good fruit and tannin), the excellent 1999 Ravenswood Zinfandel, and a 1999 Sauternes, Château Lafon, which is young and lacks botrytis.

We are back at the hotel at midnight.

4.8.02. Skipping breakfast, we check out at 9.30, and make an attempt to visit the top of the Prudential Building, but it turns out that ID cards are now required. Instead, we cab to Macy's for more retail therapy, and have a coffee opposite. We then take another taxi to Harvard Square in the Cambridge district. The streets of Cambridge run in seemingly arbitrary directions, along well-worn routes carved out according to long-forgotten, ox cart logic. Eventually the major thoroughfares converge at Harvard Square full of shops and restaurants. We then go to Harvard Yard to have a look around the university, founded in 1636 and set in twenty acres with very English-looking buildings.

At midday, we go to the House of Blues, at 96 Winthrop Street, Cambridge, for brunch. They run three sittings, at 10, 12 and 2, and the ambience is that of a Baptist church, complete with live gospel singers. You help yourself to as much as you want, from eggs, sausages, pasta, barbecued chicken, refried beans, roast beef, etc., accompanied by Sam Adams beer and fine Bloody Marys. Everybody sits side by side at very long trestle tables, singing and clapping along to the superb singers. What a great, fun place! The principal singer is introduced as Rufus L Jackson. When I comment that surely nobody could possess such a name for real, the lady next to me says, 'Oh yes, they can – he's my cousin.'

We leave at 2, and taxi back to the hotel to collect our luggage, before going on to the airport, where we check in for Virgin Upper Class flight VS 12. They share a lounge here with Northwest Airlines. The flight is due to take off at 19.25, but finally gets under way at 20.20. After a six-hour flight, we land at Heathrow at 7.05 a.m. on Monday 5th.

France
1994–2001

Loire
31 January–1 February 1994

1.2.94. After having spent the previous day at the Wine Fair in Angers, I check out of the Jeanne de Laval Hotel at Les Rosiers-sur-Loire some 30 km east of Angers at 9 a.m. The Restaurant with nine rooms has one Michelin star, but sadly is closed on Monday nights. I therefore had dinner last night with Christian Ripoche and Michel Dron of the wine company Rémy Pannier at a local restaurant – raw and smoked salmon, followed by saddle of lamb. The food was average, but the restaurant had good views over the Loire.

I drive the scenic route along the Loire to Saumur for coffee, and on to Azay-le-Rideau to visit the château, then to Chinon. The latter is a picturesque medieval town, capital of the Rabelais country surrounded by 3,200 acres of vineyards and featuring the Château de Chinon built by the Plantagenet King of England, Henry II, which is well worth a visit. It differs from the usual Loire châteaux as it is more like an English castle; in fact it is three castles, although only a shell remains. Then on to lunch at Au Plaisir Gourmand in Chinon, which has one Michelin star. I begin with a coupe of Vouvray pétillant with cheese puffs and caviare, and continue the drinking with a fruity 1992 Chinon blanc from Olga Raffault, and then a sturdy 1985 Chinon rouge, J-M Raffault.

With these, I eat a fricassée de grenouilles with confit onions, celeriac and carrots (the frogs' legs deboned, and providing an interesting combination with the vegetables in a very light cream sauce); coquilles St Jacques with chopped leeks, truffles and a truffle jus (a superb dish served with home-made bread); half a roast lobster with vegetable julienne in a light lobster butter sauce with chives, and then pigeon topped with foie gras wrapped in cabbage (an excellent main course with a classic demi-glazed sauce that nonetheless doesn't quite blend with the other flavours), served with celeriac purée (overcooked), haricots verts and a wafer-thin potato galette. I have come to the conclusion that I don't like the texture of hot foie gras; it reminds me of bean curd. Also, as I get older, I find I cannot take these very rich cream and butter sauces. I believe flavour can be created without recourse to dairy fats.

A cheese course consists of Reblochon, Fourme d'Ambert and Vacherin, served with home-made walnut bread. The Fourme, a cow's-milk blue cheese, is unripe, but the Vacherin turns out to be in perfect condition. Pudding was an indescribable creation consisting of crème anglaise squeezed between two pastry biscuits with exotic fruit, oranges, etc., and garnished with mint.

Au Plaisir Gourmand deserves its one rosette only. It is interesting that many one-rosette places seem to excel in the dessert department. This is a good restaurant with a lively atmosphere and surroundings, but it lacks the sprinkle of magic to lift it into the two-star category. A final serving of lemon sorbet, a very light version with high acidity, comes with honey biscuits, and well-made chocolates accompany the coffee.

Why is it that most of my best meals are taken on my own? *Quel dommage!*

After lunch I take a much needed walk through the town and in particular to the attractive Rue Voltaire with its wood-beamed houses almost touching each other head to head, as the street is so narrow. I decided to drive the scenic route back towards Nantes through Doue la Fontaine and Cholet, arriving at St-Sebastien-de-Loire where I spend the night and have dinner at the Manoir de la Comète, another one Michelin star establishment. The amuse-gueule is red mullet on balsamic toast, with which I drink a couple of glasses of champagne. For my first course, I have scallops, which come on a square glass plate on a bed of leaves in balsamic vinegar. This is followed by daurade (gilt-head bream) cooked in red wine, quite a salty dish. I partner these dishes with a glass of local Touraine white and two of Anjou red, and finish with an over-sweet Vieux Poire de Vallée de la Loire.

This is a very modern conversion of an old manoir, *très chic* and expensively done. I reserve judgment on the food, as I was insufficiently hungry before I arrived, but it is probably a little pretentious.

After a sumptuous breakfast I deliver my hire car to Nantes Airport for the short flight to London.

All in all, rather a pleasant way to spend a few days on the Loire.

Bordeaux, Gers, Dordogne
6–10 February 1994

6.2.94. I arrive in Bordeaux at 8.30 p.m. Once again, I have a temperature and sore throat; it is almost like I have a psychosomatic condition, resulting from too much air travel. Having hired a car, I check into the Hôtel Ste Catherine, 27 Rue Parlement, one that I like for its advantageous position in the centre of the old town. Later, feeling much better, I have a good curry locally at the Taj Mahal.

7.2.94. The day begins with a visit to Lebegue, the well-known négociants, with a full tasting of Bordeaux wines. We have buffet lunch at the owner Jacques de Connink's house in Fronsac, and a passable dinner at Ténarèze in the old town.

8.2.94. I drive south, through Sauternes and the beautiful Landes country to Armagnac. Visiting Domaine de Peberre, I meet their agent, Peter Eckersall. Their fine wines accompany a lunch of foie gras and palombe (dove) at Chez Simone opposite the church in Montréal.

In the afternoon, we visit two small growers, sadly making poor wines, and then drive west on to Villeneuve de Marsan, where we shall be staying at the three-star Hôtel Europe, which is very nice, ideal in fact.

At 8, we go to dinner at the two Michelin star restaurant, Francis Darroze, opposite the hotel, which turns out to be extremely disappointing. The menu consists of seafood ravioli, red mullet and ratatouille (with a coupe of champagne), very salty rack of lamb, and a chocolate and cream millefeuille. With these, we drink a delightful 1986 Château Reynon blanc sec and a magnificent 1982 Châteauneuf-du-Pape, Mont-Redon, rounding things off with a well-balanced 1975 Armagnac.

9.2.94. After breakfasting at 8.45, we drive eight kilometres north to the remote hamlet of Lacquy and to Château de Lacquy, a superb armagnac property, where we tour the cellars and have an extensive tasting in the chai of their vintages 1988, 1980, 1979 and so forth, continuing back to 1949. Lunch with the delightful family comprises of a delicious home-made pâté de foie gras, beef and a dessert soufflé, with which we drink an excellent Sauternes, 1976 Château Sigalas-Rabaud, a mature, soft 1985 Château La Lagune and a magnificent reserve Hors d'Age Armagnac.

After lunch, we drive to Tremolat, where we are staying at the one Michelin star Vieux Logis, a *Relais et Châteaux* establishment. Dinner is scrambled eggs and truffles, followed by duck parmentier (a kind of shepherd's pie), served with Bergerac white and red. My room is excellent, FF950. Dinner is FF500.

10.2.94. An early start to the day driving north towards the Dordogne with breakfast in Lalinde in the company of François Blachon, after which we drive to to the small village of Saussignac and visit his property, Château La Miadoux, a tiny but extremely impressive set-up. Their wines are excellent, rich and lusciously sweet, with good botrytis. Then we continue south on to Marmande and have a tasting of indifferent wines at the Coopérative de Beaupoy. A disappointing lunch is taken at the Lion d'Or in Marmande, following which we drive west back to Bordeaux for my 16.40 return flight to London.

Champagne
17–18 June 1994

17.6.94. Dinner at the superb Michelin three-star Restaurant Boyer in Reims is as follows:

A glass of delicious Laurent-Perrier Grand Siècle champagne accompanies an amuse-gueule of salmon in tomato coulis. The first course is foie gras five ways – smoked, raw, with cognac, cooked, and with a walnut oil jelly in the centre. With this dish, I drink the superb 1985 Alsace Tokay-Pinot Gris of Léon Beyer. Next up is smoked salmon au moment, a grilled piece of salmon served warm and smoked instantly, served with fine caviare potato cakes.

The next fish course is a panaché of three types (John Dory, red mullet and sea bass), sauced with truffles, raspberry vinegar and butter. This is followed by a small cup of reduced lobster tea, tasting much too high to my palate. 1982 Chateau Les Ormes de Pez in magnum accompanies the main course, which is veal in a reduced but delicate truffle jus containing tiny mushrooms. The claret is showing well, deep and brown in colour, with lovely ripeness and good fruit, just drying on the finish.

Dessert is chariot de chocolat, an absolutely ridiculous creation, so rich it was enough to send birthday candles through the head. I finish with a 1955 Vieux Marc de Calvados, which has a bunch of golden grapes in the bottle. Dinner has taken four and a half hours.

I'm staying at L'Assiette Champenois, in Tinqueux, quite a nice place, but it is worth avoiding the rooms at the end of the corridor, which only have very small windows.

18.6.94. Checking out at 10.30 a.m., I take a two-hour drive to Moulin de Mombreux at Lumbres for lunch. The weather is brilliant, and I set about a couple of glasses of Pol Roger champagne with a very fine dish of red mullet and sea bass in an Oriental sauce, with deep-fried vegetables, and then drink the sumptuous 1985 Henriot rosé champagne with the main course, stuffed rolled hare with noodles – quite delicious. I finish with a biscuit mousseux with chocolate and hazelnuts.

A most pleasant way to spend a weekend.

Marseilles, Cognac, Bordeaux
8–12 January 1995

8.1.95. I arrive at Gatwick North Terminal at 6.45 p.m. for the British Airways Business Class flight BA 3206 for Marseilles, departing at 8. I drink a whisky and soda in the Club Lounge and await the arrival of Thierry Caban, a well-respected wine négociant, who will be hosting the first leg of my trip.

I am in seat 4A. The plane takes off at 8.15, and we arrive at 10.30 local time. We take the navette to the overpriced Sofitel Airport Hotel, where I am assigned room 127. After a few drinks in the bar, I go to bed at 12.30.

9.1.95. I awake at 7 a.m., shower and pack. After breakfast at 8, we drive the scenic route north-west through Les Baux with its adjacent mediaeval deserted village to Chais Beaucarois. They have very large modern chais, and we are regaled with a long tasting of interesting vins de table and vins de pays, wines that are blended to one's own house style.

Lunch is at a local restaurant, and includes brochettes of lamb, beef and pork, with the local ham, and an acceptable Côtes du Rhône. After a tour of the warehouse and another extensive tasting of local wines we are driven back to Marseilles airport for me to catch the 8 p.m. internal flight to Bordeaux.

Once there, I hire a car and drive to the Hôtel La Normandie, arriving at 9.30. I'm given room 455. It's a fairly pleasant hotel, centrally located and certainly good value. I go out for a walk and have a Chinese dinner in a delightful part the old town, returning to retire at 11.30.

10.1.95. After an 8.30 breakfast, I drive to Lebegue, an old established wine merchant in Libourne. Here, we have an extensive tasting of Bordeaux reds, over 50 wines spanning the vintages from 1989 to 1994, quite a marathon.

For lunch, we go to Pierre de Duffau, the sales director's

house in Libourne, where we are fed on grilled monkfish, roast beef, cheese, and apple pie, accompanying it with a crisp 1992 Bordeaux Sauvignon, and an excellent 1988 Château Monbrun.

After lunch, I embark on the two-hour drive north to Cognac. I am staying at the Hôtel l'Echassier in Château-Bernard, a fairly modern and clean establishment.

Later, I have dinner with the directors of Louis Royer Cognac at the restaurant attached to the hotel. It's quite smart and the food is good: foie gras de canard, roebuck, and a chocolate soufflé. We drink a fresh-tasting white Côtes de Duras, followed by a quite superb 1989 Pomerol, Chateau La Conseillante, and of course, Louis Royer XO cognac.

I am in bed at 11.30.

11.1.95. Having eaten breakfast at 8, I have a most interesting mammoth tasting of Louis Royer cognacs from single regions, which lasts until lunchtime. We eat at 1.30 in their new dining room: salmon, carré d'agneau with six whole cloves of garlic and lentils, cheese and salad, and a sort of chocolate biscuit tart. With these, we drink the 1985 Château Lagrange, XO cognac, and a 5-puttonyös Tokaji Imperial.

I drive back to Bordeaux, dropping the hire car back at Hertz, and then taxi back to the Hôtel La Normandie, where I am now given room 115.

Later on, after drinks in the bar, I am collected by the export director of the well-respected négociants and château owners, Robert Guiraud, for an 8 o'clock dinner. This turns out to be at Restaurant Plaisirs d'Ausone, a very good find in the centre of the city at 10 Rue Ausone, with superb food brilliantly presented, deserving of a Michelin star. Sadly, after the excellent lunch I am not sufficiently hungry to do justice to the meal, and by the time I get back to the hotel (11 p.m.), I am very tired.

12.1.95. I am collected at 8 a.m. and we travel to the cellars of Robert Guiraud for a full tour, including a tasting of over 60 red and white Bordeaux wines, from the years 1990 to 1994. After 1990, these are a succession of poor vintages, with 1994 probably showing more potential than the others.

Lunch, at a small local restaurant near the cellars, comprises excellent snails en croûte, followed by magret de canard, accompanied by a very good 1990 Château Timberlay.

Afterwards, I am driven back to Bordeaux Airport, where I catch the 6 p.m. flight to Heathrow. From here, I have to take the coach to Gatwick to collect my car, eventually arriving home at 10.30.

I suspect it will take weeks to remove the tannin stains from my teeth.

Beaucaire/Les Baux
26–28 January 1995

26.1.95. I take an 11.15 flight from Gatwick North Terminal to Montpellier with a wine-buying colleague. We drink Billecart-Salmon on the BA flight, and arrive at 2.15 p.m. local time.

Hiring a car from Hertz, we drive the scenic route through Aigues-Mortes, a lovely old walled city, to Arles, with its magnificent amphitheatre dating back to the first century AD, where bullfights are still held, and then on to Les Baux de Provence. Here, we take a walk around the village, which is now divided into two parts: the inhabited village, with its steep streets, and the deserted village accessible only by foot, where the seventeenth-century castle is being tastefully restored. We check into Le Cabro d'Or, a *Relais et Châteaux* hotel owned by the three Michelin star L'Oustau de Baumanière, which sadly was closed for renovation; but Le Cabro d'Or has a Michelin star of its own. I'm assigned a splendid room on the ground floor, with a door leading out on to a patio.

I have a massage at 6.30, and then we go to dinner at 8. The *menu dégustation* is FF360, and is comprised of the following: terrine de gibier, cold foie gras, roast salmon with a red wine sauce, bourride of monkfish, grapefruit sorbet, carré d'agneau aux échalotes, a wonderful selection of cheese, and a caramelised apple tart with honey. We drink Perrier-Jouët champagne, Château Simone blanc 1991, and the superb 1990 Domaine de Trévallon rouge.

I am in bed at 11.

27.1.95. Breakfast at 9 includes some fine local honey, after which we drive to Beaucaire and to the chais of Beaucarois, for a tasting and to select some specific house wine blends. This is followed by lunch at Villeneuve-lès-Avignon, in a fine restaurant and hotel called Magnaneraie, 37 Rue Camp de Bataille. We have red mullet on rösti, and then rolled and stuffed guinea fowl, and a fine dessert of assorted mousses, accompanying them with a coupe of champagne, a local white wine, and a magnum of the delicious 1981 Domaine Mont-Redon Châteauneuf-du-Pape.

After lunch, we are taken on a guided tour of the ancient walled city of Avignon, city of the popes, taking in the famous Pont St Benezet, a bridge which spans the river by way of the island. Completed in 1190, it was for years the only crossing so far down the Rhone. The twenty-two arches have been reduced with the passage of time, by storm and floodwater, to four. On one of the piers stands the St Nicholas Chapel with two storeys, one Romanesque, one Gothic. Then to Les Palais des Papes, a great white, fourteenth-century stone palace covering over two acres; impressive from the outside and a maze of galleries, chambers and chapels inside. Avignon is a pretty place, and definitely worth a revisit. We fit in a quick stop at the Casino hypermarket owned by Chais Beaucarois, and then take the scenic route back to the hotel.

Dinner at 8 consists of smoked salmon and rack of lamb, both of which are superb. We drink half a bottle of 1991 Hermitage Mule Blanche, a half of 1988 Hermitage La Chapelle, a half of 1988 Côte-Rôtie les Jumelles, all in excellent condition, followed by Mont-Redon's Marc du Châteauneuf-du-Pape, and a local sweet liqueur called Frigoulet, which has a very aggressive nose.

I am gratefully in bed at 11.

28.1.95. After an 8.30 breakfast, we drive west to Montpellier via Nîmes, with its city arms 'a crocodile in chains'; this commemorates the defeat of Anthony of the Nile by the Emperor Augustus. Nîmes is larger than one expects, with a small district of older buildings, including the Maison Carrée. This temple, which has been known as the Square House since the sixteenth century, despite its obvious rectangular shape, was built in the first century; and we visit a roman amphitheatre dating from AD 500. Then we continue west to Lunel, famous for its vin doux naturel Muscat; another charmingly attractive town.

We arrive in Montpellier, with its fine university, and walk around the seventeenth century historic part of the old town, with its magnificent architecture and the dominating Château d'Eau du Peyrou.

Lunch is at Chez Maurice – duck rillettes, followed by a pavé steak and frites. We drink 1992 Domaine de Brougières, an oak-aged red of impressive pedigree.

After lunch, we drive back to the airport, arriving at 2.15 for the 2.50 flight to Gatwick.

Bordeaux Vinexpo
18–23 June 1995

18.6.95. I check in at Gatwick North Terminal at 5 p.m. for the British Airways flight 2336 to Bordeaux. The plane is full, and as usual the food is dreadful, virtually raw chicken and pasta salad, inedible. I compensate with two large whisky and sodas.

We arrive in Bordeaux at 8.15 local time, and quite by chance I run into Philippe Giraud, owner of Château Villemaurine in St Emilion, who drives me to La Réserve in Pessac for dinner. After a champagne aperitif, we drink a 1990 Rully, Louis Max, with smoked salmon, and then a delicious 1989 Château Coufran (which, strangely for a Médoc wine, is made from 100% Merlot) with noisettes of lamb. The restaurant has recently changed hands, having had at one time a Michelin star; the food is now no more than adequate.

I'm staying at the two-star Hôtel La Madeleine, Rue Georges Bonnac, where the rooms are incredibly small and singularly uncomfortable. I eventually get to sleep at midnight, but pass a fitful night, troubled by mosquitoes.

19.6.95. Awakening at 6.30, I discover it's a lovely day, sunny and very warm. I pay FF200 for a week's bus pass to Vinexpo (the largest wine exhibition in the world, held biennially in Bordeaux), but eventually end up going by cab as the bus goes via no fewer than four other hotels.

I arrive at the exhibition at 8.45 (the doors open at 9). In Club Mozart, I have a coffee and plan my itinerary, which of course involves visiting numerous producers on their stands, including some new Uruguayan and Peruvian wines (thin, flat and flabby specimens, mostly), and meeting a number of Canadian wine-growers from Ontario and British Columbia.

Returning to the hotel at 8 after a very tiring day, I soon head off for the nearby four-star Hôtel Burdigala for drinks with the

Canadians, and a dinner of steak frites at the Café Regent on the Place Gambetta, watching the locals parade by.

I am in bed at 11.30.

20.6.95. Having started the day with a coffee at 8, I call a cab to Vinexpo at 8.45. The day is taken up with many, many visits and tastings, and much negotiating. After lunch with Rémy Pannier from the Loire, there are more meetings and much more tasting, with the likes of Robert Giraud from Bordeaux, Jean-Claude Boisset from Burgundy, Georges Fourcroy, owner of Mandarine Napoléon liqueur from Belgium, John Brown from Brown Brothers in Australia, Jacques Vigouroux from the Rhône, and many others.

I return to the hotel at 6.30 exhausted, a bus arrives to collect me at 7 for a party and dinner at Château Cartillon in Moulis, which is owned and has been recently refurbished by Robert Giraud. There is a jazz band, and a superb dinner. The menu opens with *deux poissons*, served with 1993 Château Timberlay Cuvée Prestige, and continues with a lamb dish, which is partnered with the excellent 1982 Château Villemaurine in double magnums. We finish with the 1950 Château Cartillon, which is sadly now fading and showing its grey hairs.

I am back at the hotel by 2 a.m.

21.6.95. It's *fête de musique* day in Bordeaux. I arrive at Vinexpo at 9.35, and have a meeting with the president and export directors of Glen Ellen Winery from California. The day is fully occupied with meetings, in fact, including an interesting tasting with Aveleda from Portugal and some new Hungarian wines from Hungarovin.

I return to the hotel at 6.30, and from there take a taxi to the Conservatoire Nationale de la Plaisance, which is housed in the old wartime German submarine pens on the quais, restored and converted to large underground function rooms with yachts and powerboats on display. It's a great venue and there is a jazz band, with one of my old friends playing the tenor saxophone. I am there as a guest of the prestigious Rhône producer Vidal-Fleury, seated on a table for ten. We are regaled with a stunning buffet of oysters, lamb, spare ribs, saucissons, etc., accompanied by prodigious quantities of their delicious 1990 Côte-Rôtie.

I am back at the hotel by midnight.

22.6.95. After an 8.30 breakfast, I have a meeting and extensive tasting of Spanish wines with Berberana, followed by many other meetings and tastings, pausing in due course for a snack lunch of *saucissons*, ham and cheese.

I continue the day tasting new wines from Argentina, Vidal-Fleury and Domaine du Grand Tinel (their 1993 red Châteauneuf-du-Pape is light and thin, but the 1989 is superb). The day's business is rounded off by drinks with Jean-Claude Boisset from Burgundy and Victor Redondo, the chief executive of Berberana.

Back at the hotel at 7, I have further drinks with the chief executive Europe of Hardy's of Australia. We go to dinner in the attractive Vieux Bordeaux square, at a fish restaurant. Six Belon oysters are FF120, and are followed by a main course of red mullet. To partner them, we drink a 1990 Chablis from Louis Jadot and a 1991 Pouilly-Fuissé. Later, we have beers on the square, and I get back to the hotel at 2 a.m.

23.6.95. At 8 a.m., I call my daughter, Holly, to wish her a happy birthday, and at 9, turn up at Club Vinexpo. I have a meeting and full tasting at 9.30 with Carlos Muñoz of Concha y Toro in Chile. At 10.30, I meet with Bernard Chéreau, the owner of five excellent estates in Muscadet, whose wines were showing very well.

A Vinexpo car takes me to the airport for 1.30, where I find the BA flight 2335 to Gatwick will be delayed. We eventually take off at 3.10, and arrive at 3.30 local time.

This has been an exhausting but exhilarating trip, requiring immense stamina...

Bordeaux
19–21 October 1995

19.10.95. This buying trip to France begins with a 3.45 p.m. Air Inter flight from Gatwick South Terminal to Bordeaux. Despite the fact that the scheduled fare is £380, there are no spirits on the drinks trolley. It's a 90-minute flight, arriving at 6.15 local time. We have a beer at the airport while waiting for Régis Argaud, the export director of the prestigious négociants and château owners, Robert Giraud et Cie.

Once he arrives, we drive to the Hôtel Burdigala, I am allotted room 309 – FF 800 plus an extra FF 78 for breakfast.

After a gin and tonic in the bar, we drive at 7.30 to the excellent Plaisir d'Ausone restaurant, which now has a well-deserved Michelin star. With a first course of red mullet surrounded by herring and egg, minced olives, sun-dried tomatoes, potatoes, onions and bacon, we drink the Blason Timberlay blanc 1993, moving on to the Château Timberlay 1991 with a main course dish of beef cheek with assorted vegetables. Afterwards, we return to the hotel and I have a malt whisky, before getting to bed at 1 a.m.

20.10.95. After an 8 o'clock breakfast of orange juice, bacon and scrambled eggs, toast and coffee, we are collected at 8.45 to be driven to the offices of Robert Giraud. From there, we undertake a visit and tasting of over fifty wines at La Vignote, the Blason cellars, in the heart of the vineyards.

For lunch, we go a restaurant called Le Sarment, where the menu consists of a salad of smoked fish, pièce de boeuf, cheeses and a dessert selection. The 1993 Blason Timberlay blanc is served once more, as is the 1991 Château Timberlay, and then the excellent 1990 Château Villemaurine, the St Emilion grand cru classé which they also own, finishing with a mediocre Sauternes, 1988 Chateau Romer du Hayot.

A visit to Château Villemaurine follows, at which we taste the

1993 against the 1993 Clos Larcis, both showing well considering the poor vintage. We then continue with a visit to Château Timberlay, returning to the hotel at 5.30.

The evening kicks off with a champagne aperitif at 8, before we proceed to the Michelin one-starred Jean Ramet, 7, Place J. Jaures for dinner. The wines chosen to accompany tartare de poisson and a salmis of woodpigeon are Château Timberlay Prestige 1991 and Chateau Villemaurine 1986, both of which are superb. Leaving at 11.30, we make our way to La Borie jazz club, where Les Docteurs Jazz are appearing. I have brought my tenor saxophone mouthpiece with me and enjoy playing a couple of numbers with the band, one of whom was the rhythm guitarist with Django Rheinhard's 'Hot Club of France'. We drink a few beers, and I get to bed at 1 a.m.

21.10.95. Régis Argaud joins me for a 9 a.m. breakfast meeting, after which we drive to their Château Cartillon in Moulis. I am able to taste the new 1995s in tank, the Cabernet Sauvignon and then the Merlot. Both give evidence of a good future ahead.

We then make our way back to the airport, arriving at 12.45. Our 1.15 Air Inter flight IT 4488 has been delayed to 2.15. When we do finally get on, we are served with some of the worst food I've ever eaten on an airplane, and there are once again no spirits available.

We land at Gatwick at 3.45, and I am gratefully home at 4.45.

Champagne
9–10 November 1995

9.11.95. I leave for Paris on the 7.23 a.m. First Class Eurostar from Waterloo, a very professional, clean and well-organised service. It takes three hours direct to the Gare du Nord. There, I am collected by Thierry Caban, UK agents for Champagne Nicolas Feuillatte, and driven to Épernay, which takes about an hour and a half.

At 1.30, we go for lunch to Chez Pierrot, 16, Rue de la Fauvette. The amuse-gueule is frankfurters, served with the Feuillatte blanc de blancs NV. This is followed by pipérade, with their rosé, and then a very slightly curried lamb dish with rice. We finish with a very rich chocolate mousse, and espresso with equally rich truffles, only leaving the restaurant at 4.

From there, we take a tour of the Feuillatte cellars. It's a very large cooperative operation based at Chouilly, just outside Épernay. We conduct an extensive tasting of their champagne. One or two of the wines show a slightly oxidised character, but they are undoubtedly well made, particularly the 1986 and 1985 Palme d'Or.

I am staying at the Hostellerie La Briqueterie, a splendid *Relais et Châteaux* establishment among the vineyards at Vinay 6 km from Epernay. I'm in a spacious and well-appointed room called Lupin, 203.

After a quick change, we meet in the bar at around 8.30. In the very fine one Michelin star restaurant, we drink the 1985 Palme d'Or champagne, which is delicious, a 1992 Jaboulet Crozes-Hermitage, still quite young, a magnificent 1983 Jaboulet Cornas, and the 1986 Feuillatte, to accompany an amuse-bouche of goose liver mousse, smoked salmon and cucumber tagliatelle, noisettes of lamb in a very light but brilliant sauce, and a wonderful symphonie de desserts. Overfed and overtired, I make it to bed at midnight.

10.11.95. After breakfasting on croissants and coffee at 8.30, I am driven into Paris and have a couple of beers at the Gare du Nord, before boarding the 12.13 p.m. Eurostar back to Waterloo. The journey is a very smooth one.

I feel a long visit to the health farm might now be in order.

4–7 February 1996

4.2.96. I check in at Gatwick North Terminal at 1.30 p.m. for the flight to Nantes, which arrives at 5 p.m. local time. Hiring a Peugeot 605 from Hertz, I drive myself to the basic but comfortable Hôtel Mascotte, where I meet my old friend, Bernard Chéreau Jnr, proprietor of several prestigious châteaux in Muscadet, in the bar over Scotch and sodas.

Leaving the hotel at 8 p.m., I drive to their flagship property, Château de Chasseloir, for a dinner of oysters, grilled salmon, lamb *sur vigne*, cheese, and apple tart. Among the many wines, one that stands out is a 1990 Muscadet, Château du Coing, which goes into 100% new oak barrels each year – a startling innovation for this region, so much so that it was on national television.

Over dinner, Bernard relates a story: in each generation of the family, there has always been a son, always named Bernard, who, when he comes of age, always goes into the family wine business. Apparently when the current Bernard left school he nervously approached his father stating that he did not want to go into the wine business, but wanted to be a doctor. There ensued the most almighty family row, which eventually resulted in his father relenting, saying, 'If you wish to be a doctor, so be it.' So Bernard Jnr went off to medical school and duly qualified. Upon returning home, he was greeted by his father saying, 'You wanted to be a doctor and now you are. Having achieved that, you will *now* come into the family wine business', which he did.

We finish the evening with copious quantities of a delicious 60-year-old Marc de Melon, made from Muscadet grape pips, and totally illegal. I'm back at the hotel by 12.30.

5.2.96. Starting the day at 6 a.m. sharp, I drive to Saumur for an 8 o'clock meeting with the wine company Rémy Pannier, and an extensive tasting of their excellent Ackerman Laurence sparkling wine, together with a full range of their well-priced still wines. Leaving there at noon, I drive on to Beaune, arriving at around

6 p.m, having looked around the magnificent fifteenth century Hospice de Beaune, I check in to Hôtel Athanor, room 204, a nice old hotel with a good bar. Bernard Répolt, the extremely eccentric winemaker and general manager of Jaffelin and Bouchard Aîné, arrives at 6.30. We have drinks there, before driving in his S1 Rolls Royce to Vougeot. He has laid on Jaffelin 1993 Rully to drink on our journey in the car!

At around 8, we reach the home of Jean-Claude Boisset, the well-known Burgundy producer based in Vougeot. As an aperitif, we drink his Chardonnay Mousseux, a dry and well-balanced sparkler, and follow it with the 1993 Fixin blanc, which has a lovely buttery nose and firm fruit; then 1994 Rully blanc, a well-made wine, but still young and with a tight finish. The 1992 Santenay is soft fruity Pinot Noir with good depth of fruit. 1982 Clos Vougeot, which is fully mature, has an outstanding Pinot Noir berry fruit nose and flavour, and a long finish. We conclude with some fine very old Armagnac. Dinner is chicken in a white wine sauce, local cheese and fruit. Jean-Claude is a great person, full of energy and humour, and having spent a most enjoyable evening, I finally leave at 12.30.

6.2.96. I leave the hotel at 7, and drive south to a breakfast meeting with the ever charming Patrice Noyelle, export director of Mommessin, at the Novotel Mâcon Nord. I leave at 10, and continue my journey through horrendous snowstorms and icy roads to Lyon, and on to Rive-de-Gier, 39 km to the south of the city. Here, at Hostellerie La Renaissance, I have a very productive lunch meeting with Patrick Morel, head of Chais Beaucarois, the large southern wine producer I visited last year. The food – raw salmon with cucumber, lamb, and a cheese crêpe – is superb, and we drink champagne, a stunning 1992 Condrieu Vieilles Vignes, Guigal's 1988 Côte-Rôtie La Landonne, a most outstanding Rhône wine, very full, deep and rich, which will certainly outlive me, and an unusual 1982 Château Cotnari, Sélection des Grains Nobles, from Moldova, a rich and luscious dessert wine with good botrytis.

At 3.30, I head off south to Vias, a four-hour drive, where I have dinner with Pierre Besinet of Domaine du Bosq at Restaurant Les Saveurs Singulières in Sète. We have the wines from his other estate, Domaine de Pourthe, which produces very good Sauvignon and Chardonnay, and drink them with foie gras, and then a mixture of fish with mushrooms. We leave the restaurant at 10.30, and drive to Marseilles Airport, arriving at the overpriced Sofitel Hotel at 1.45 a.m.

7.2.96. My alarm wakes me at 4.30 a.m., as I have to be on the 6.30 flight to Gatwick. It has been a 2,000 km drive – all in all, quite a shattering itinerary.

Provence
23 August–2 September 1999

23.8.99. A taxi arrives at 4.30 p.m. to take us (myself, Clare, Holly and Toby) to Gatwick North Terminal, a journey that ends up taking an hour and a half. We're booked on the 7 o'clock BA flight to Marseilles, in bulkhead seats 11A–11D, and I have a couple of large whiskies and some smoked salmon on the plane. It's 10 p.m. local time when we arrive.

I pick up the car from Hertz Rental, a Renault Mégane, receiving instant service through their No 1 Club Gold. We are booked in overnight at the Primotel at the airport, and after a nightcap, I'm in bed at 11.

24.8.99. We check out at 7.45 a.m. The bill is FF390 per room, plus 6%. We drive to Marseilles in perfect weather, and breakfast on coffee and croissants at the Old Port, sitting at an outside table.

Driving slowly along minor roads, we make our way north to the wine growing region of Corbières, and stop for a glass of local wine at 11.30. An hour later, we roll up for lunch at Le Petit Pascal in Manosque. Sitting outside on the tree-lined pavement, we eat very good steak and chips with a pleasant bottle of Côtes du Lubéron rosé.

After lunch, we head across the Durance on to the pretty village of La Fuste, where we will be staying at the Michelin-starred Hostellerie de La Fuste. Checking in at 2, we are given superb rooms with balconies overlooking a vista of trees and shrubs – a true Provençal scene. I go for a swim and then take a nap in a hammock, followed by a beer next to the pool, and then a shower at 6, all very civilised.

The weather is luxurious, 30°C+, and at 7, we have drinks on the terrace, pastis, and champagne with an amuse-gueule of aubergine and tapenade. At 8 o'clock, at a lovely table set under the trees, we enjoy a fantastic dinner, the *menu dégustation* at FF750 for two. It begins with a warm mousseline, going on to a soup of haricots verts, and then lamb in two ways – firstly, as a navarin with an excellent sauce, more green beans, carrots, onions, etc., and then as the whole roast leg, with three types of mushrooms and garlic cream. The cheese selection includes Reblochon and Pont l'Evêque, along with four other local types, and the dessert is a sandwiched creation of chocolate and raspberry mousses. With the lamb, we drink a 1969 Chapoutier Hermitage at FF400, which shows very well.

By the end of it all, I am getting weary and decide to retire at 11.

25.8.99. After spending a fitful night – not surprisingly in view of the amount of food consumed last night – I awake at 8.45 to find the weather is once again glorious. I am writing this on the terrace overlooking vegetable gardens, olive trees, flowers and vines.

After breakfast on the terrace, we leave at 9.30 and drive through Esparron de Verdon by the Lake taking D and C roads all the way and drinking in the lovely Provençal countryside, the region of truffles and honey. We stop at Riez for an *assiette de charcuterie*, and then press on to Moustiers Ste-Marie, and La Bastide de Moustiers, south of the village which is owned by the well-known chef, Alain Ducasse, where we shall be staying for the next two nights.

The rooms are excellent, adjoining each other to form a suite, and we have a majestic Alpine view. I go swimming until 5.30, and then shower and change for dinner, which we'll have on the terrace, a truly wonderful setting. I preface it with a couple of glasses of their very good pastis, and then we embark on the table d'hôte menu, on which the only choice is at the main course stage.

Tomate farcie is excellent, the tomato stuffed with minced courgette, baby olives and tapenade. Next is artichoke cooked in the regional manner with bacon, and including all the edible parts of the vegetable. For the main course, I opt for pigeon roasted with ceps and truffles, another typical local dish, and then there is a full range of goat's cheese, with just one cow's milk specimen to make up the numbers. With the pigeon, we drink a wine from Palette, Château Simone 1996, which has a lovely, rich, ripe cherry nose and is young and tannic on the palate, with good depth and length.

I am in bed at 10.30.

26.8.99. We breakfast at 9 a.m. on fresh fruit salad, crème caramel, brioche, breads and croissants with a range of home-made jams and local honey, and coffee drunk from a huge bowl.

After driving to Moustiers, an old Romanesque village cut into the hillside, we head on via the Green Route through the Gorges de Verdon, which have amazing views, to Point Sublime, where we have lunch. Rabbit in mustard sauce with frites is accompanied by a 50cl bottle of Château de Pousset rosé from a local grower. Continuing on along the very pretty Green Route to the other side of the Gorges, we pass through the Balcon de la Mescla, and then to the lovely Lac de Ste-Croix, before returning to the hotel in a 30-minute cloudburst. Later, it starts raining again with a vengeance.

We have booked a table tonight at 8 at Les Santons, a one-star Michelin Restaurant in the Place Eglise, Moustiers. By now, the rain is coming down in torrents. I drink a pastis in the bar at 6, and we drive to the old village, arriving at the restaurant at 7.15. Sadly, because of the wet weather, we are not able to sit out on the terrace.

A couple of coupes of champagne are served with over-concentrated tapenade and very thin cheese straws. The first course, a 'minestrone' of langoustines with Parma ham, vegetables and cream, is very clumsy and salty, while the pièce de Charolais with garlic sauce and chips is an absolute disgrace, covered in rock salt and quite inedible, a terrible waste of good meat. There is a full range of cheeses, but one is only allowed to choose three (and they aren't in good condition anyway), and then café crème, and finally a congealed fig tart served with fromage blanc.

With these delights, we drink 1990 Château de Peyrassol, Cuvée Marie Estelle, an AC Côtes de Provence, which has a very deep colour, but is quite thin and hollow on the palate, with a short finish. Back at the hotel, I have a Vieux Marc de Bandol, planning my letter to the Michelin guide, and go to bed at 11.

27.8.99. After an 8.30 breakfast on the terrace, we check out. Our bill was £1,000. We drive south through the lovely old town of Aups, Tourtour with its museum containing dinosaur eggs, Lorgues with its fourteenth century fortified gateways, and

Vidauban through the vineyard areas of the Côtes de Provence, through Grimaud, with its eleventh century château and then to St. Tropez, with its legend: that Tropez (Torpes), a Christian centurion beheaded in his native Pisa by order of the Emperor Nero, was placed in a boat with his head beside him and cast adrift with a cock and a dog, who were meant to devour his remains, which however they left intact. The boat is supposed to have come ashore where St Tropez now stands. Today it is the playground of the rich and famous with many expensive yachts moored in the harbour. We have lunch at Les Mouscardins, a one-star Michelin restaurant by the port.

I have a much needed beer, and then order a bottle of the 1998 vintage of the local rosé, which accompanies pot gourmand – cod and potatoes cooked in a sealed pot, served with olive bread – ratatouille with a poached egg in olive oil (superb), and excellent sardines with roasted sweet garlic, onions, olives and roast potatoes. The cheese plate comprises Reblochon, Tomme de Pyrenées and a local blue, and we finish with crème brûlée and a selection of chocolate, raspberry and lemon sorbets. The prix-fixe is FF225, including wine.

In the afternoon, we drive along the coast to our hotel '83' on La Fossette Plage, where we are assigned a perfect room, 32, with a panoramic sea view. We wander down to the small, crowded beach and have a swim in the sea, and then take a trip to Le Lavandou, which turns out to be a horrid place, full of concrete buildings all alarmingly close to each other.

Dinner is at the brasserie on the beach in the small village of St Clair. After a pastis, we try the L'Estadon rosé produced by M. Baconis at Pierrefeu. It's a vin de pays du Var, quite thin and acidic, and with it I eat a pizza piola, topped with egg, ham and anchovies. I end the evening with a whisky on our balcony. It's been a lovely day.

28.8.99. We begin the day with a light breakfast in the La Fossette auberge. Friends of ours, Rosalie and Ian, who live in La Favière, come to meet us, and we drive north into the mountains above La Fossette to Sauvage, a superb auberge miles from anywhere, equipped with a pool and tennis courts.

Over beers and a bottle of the local rosé, we eat a lunch of sardines and pogre (a local fish), grilled over a wood fire, and then drive on to Bormes les Mimosas, strolling around the old streets in this pretty little town with its colourful profusion of mimosa, oleander, camomile and eucalyptus.

Back at our hotel, I take a well-earned swim, and then we have drinks and dinner on the hotel terrace. After a couple of glasses of pastis and a coupe, we drink a 1998 Domaine de Peigros rosé and the excellent 1996 Domaine de l'Olivet, a red Bandol, alongside tough côte de boeuf and frites, followed by Reblochon, Pont l'Evêque and a local blue cheese.

I get to bed at 11, just as it is starting to rain.

29.8.99. I am woken at 8 by a severe attack of cramp in the calves; perhaps the local rose is getting to me. The weather is still beautiful, if a little cooler, and we take breakfast on the hotel terrace.

Lunch is booked at the Pergola in Cavalaire-sur-Mer. After the concrete jungle drive through Cavaliere and La Raol, our drink on the beach turns out to be altogether more pleasant. The Pergola is given two knives-and-forks in the Michelin Guide, and is well situated, with tables set out under a vine-clad pergola, but sadly, it starts to rain again, causing everybody to rush inside.

The set lunch menu consists of melon balls with a glass of sweet Asti, Parma ham, a disappointing quail with polenta in an olive sauce and apple tart, with which we drink a passable non-vintage Côtes de Provence rosé from Les Maîtres Vignerons de St-Tropez.

The rain finally stops and we drive back to the hotel. I sleep in our room for an hour, and then we have drinks in the bar. We eat dinner in their own restaurant, an excellent grilled daurade with the local rosé.

I am in bed by 10.30.

30.8.99. Our alarm call wakes us at 7 a.m., and we pack and drive west along the coast to Giens to catch the 9 o'clock ferry for the 20-minute crossing to the Île de Porquerolles, the largest and most westerly of the Hyères islands, measuring 7 km long by 3 km wide. We are collected by the hotel bus and taken for a two-night stay at La Mas du Langoustier, a lovely, very secluded, one

Michelin starred hotel set in 40 acres of protected forest and parkland leading down to the sea. We are in rooms 841 and 842.

After a swim in the sea, we take a stroll to the old fortress, then back for lunch on the hotel terrace. A superb dish of grilled daurade in a lemon butter sauce is served with green salad and a rosé produced on the island at the Domaine de l'Île de Porquerolles. In the afternoon, we go back to the beach for some sunbathing and swimming.

At 7.30, we have drinks on the terrace, a couple of glasses of pastis, and are then led to a brilliant corner table for four in the open-air Gastronomique Restaurant. The *menu surprise* begins with a coupe of champagne, which we follow with a half-bottle of the light, dry 1998 island rosé and then a bottle of the 1997 island red, which turns out to be very good. These accompany duck pâté in a Beaumes-de-Venise jelly with almond toast, langoustine tails on crisp lettuce with tapenade, celery hearts and balsamic, daurade baked in pastry with spring onions, tomato and a lemon coulis, roast lobster lightly deep-fried in batter with spinach in balsamic, and a basket of garlic and tomato mayonnaise (a little too heavy on the garlic), poached beef in balsamic with an olive and potato mix, pistachio ice cream with avocado purée, a gâteau of strawberries, redcurrants and chocolate, fresh fruit salad with a sorbet of melon and tomato, mini rum babas and chocolate nuts.

It is a wonderful meal, and we only finish at 11.

31.8.99. For breakfast at 8.30, we have Parma ham with delicious home-made French bread, after which we take the hotel bus at 10 to Porquerolles village, a journey of 3.8 km. It's small and extremely crowded, receiving 10,000 visitors a day in the high season. We walk up to the Fort Ste-Agathe, built in 1532 by Francois1, which has great views of the islands.

It's now getting quite hot, and we stop for a couple of beers before taking the bus back to the hotel, for a lunch of grilled faux-filet and potatoes and a bottle of the local rosé. In the afternoon, I sleep under the pine trees.

After a pastis on the terrace, dinner begins with a coupe of Laurent-Perrier, with an appetiser of tapenade. The first course is daurade baked in pastry with a tomato coulis and lemon zest, followed by lamb fillet en croûte with couscous and onion coulis, concluding with cream cheese served with cold vegetables and olive oil. With the lamb, we drink a bottle of Domaine Gavoty, Côtes de Provence 1988, a very deep, rich and well-balanced wine. All in all, an excellent dinner.

I am in bed at 11.

1.9.99. Breakfast on the terrace takes place this morning with the opening of cards. It's my 62nd birthday, amazing I have survived another year.

We check out of the hotel at 9.30, paying a bill for £1,700 for two nights for the four of us. The hotel bus takes us into the village, and then we leave by the 10 a.m. ferry. Collecting the car, we drive slowly along the coast road through Toulon. France's second naval port is a most attractive old town with its colourful market in the Cours Lafayette. Then we move on to the pleasant resort of Bandol, where we have lunch at 12.30 at La Réserve, which is located right by the sea.

I drink a coupe of champagne on the pontoon, and we have lunch under the trees. Nine oysters served *bleu* and six grilled red mullet with green salad are accompanied by the excellent Château de Pibarnon rosé 1998. Later, we stop for a swim at La Ciotat, which is a dreadful place, very crowded, with only a small beach.

We arrive in Cassis, a small, bustling fishing port, at 5, and check into Le Jardin d'Emile, a six-room establishment that has a knife-and-fork in Michelin. The rooms are terrible, badly in need of redecoration (FF650 too), but at least they overlook the sea. We walk down to the port area, which is quite pretty if touristy, and have a couple of drinks.

In the evening, we have dinner in the garden. A version of pissaladière made with rascasse and onions on a pizza base is very good, and the main course of carré d'agneau with ravioli is almost as impressive. With them we drink a half-bottle of 1998 Domaine du Paternel rosé, and then a 1997 Domaine Tempier red, which is deeply flavoured and very fine, rounding things off with a Marc de Cassis.

2.9.99. Having spent a fitful night, I get up early and go for a walk. The weather is beautiful already at 8 a.m. In fact, apart from the one wet day, it has been superb throughout our stay.

We have breakfast in the garden at 8.30, and then check out and drive to Marseilles Airport, from where we should take the flight to London at 1.35, were it not delayed for an hour. This has been a great trip, even if very expensive; but then it was after all my birthday.

Brittany
4–7 May 2001

4.5.01. I pick up Clare at noon from the school where she is a teacher, and we drive to Gatwick North Terminal, leaving the car in the long-stay car park. We then have a dreadful lunch at Garfunkel's. We are flying on a 3 p.m. twin-engine BA flight to Nantes, and are given seats by the emergency exit, where there is extra legroom. It's a 90-minute flight. We drink a couple of quarter-bottles of Piper-Heidsieck, at £4 each, to go with a sandwich, the content of which remains a mystery.

We arrive at 5.30 local time, and hire a Renault Clio from Hertz to drive the 80 km north-west to Domaine de Rochevilaine, Billiers on the peninsula at La Pointe de Pen-Lan-Sud, getting there at 7.30. It's a *Relais et Châteaux* property overlooking the river, with a Michelin star, and we are given a superb suite, 38, at FF1,375, plus FF90 for breakfast.

The coupe of Besserat de Bellefon rosé we drink as an aperitif is sufficiently impressive to persuade us to order a bottle with dinner. An amuse-gueule begins proceedings, a mousseline of red pepper en gelée, following which we have a galette of foie gras with raspberry vinegar, John Dory en croûte (actually a breadcrumb coating), a cheese selection that includes Livarot, Epoisses, Reblochon and very fine Brique des Cévennes, and an assiette de desserts. This last is comprised of vanilla cream, chocolate mousse, brandy snaps filled with raspberries and strawberries, and petits fours. I finish with a very large measure of 1988 Martinique vintage rum. It all adds up to a good one-star Michelin meal. The hotel also incorporates a thermal baths, and the views are fantastic.

We get to bed at 11.

5.5.01. A lovely sunny day begins with orange juice and coffee in the suite, after which we take a walk around the old parts of the hotel and up to the lighthouse. A slow drive brings us to Belon, a small pretty port in the heart of the oyster beds, and at 12.30 we meet Bernard Chéreau there at the excellent restaurant, Chez Jacky, which overlooks the river.

Lunch opens with a dozen delicious Belon oysters each, followed by a whole grilled lobster per head, and we get through two bottles of Bernard's Château de Chasseloir Muscadet, the 1998 and the 1994, both stunning examples.

In the afternoon, we drive to the pretty town of Quimper, visit the fine thirteenth-century cathedral with its remarkable fifteenth-century stained glass and buy some of the famous hand-painted pottery produced from Breton clay and kaolin, followed by a stomach-settling pastis at an outside café nearby. We then drive to Le Pouldu, where we are staying in room 103 of the Hôtel Le Pouldu, with excellent views of the port and harbour, FF385 a night.

After a couple of glasses of pastis in the hotel bar, we eat a dinner of steak and chips, accompanied by a 1995 Côtes de Bourg, with a tot of eau-de-vie de cidre as a digestif. We are in bed by 11.

6.5.01. After spending a fitful night, I rise to a sunny day and breakfast at 9.30. The view from our bedroom window is truly beautiful.

We begin the day by driving around Pont Aven, famous as a favourite resort for painters and situated at the point of the River Aven. The Aven used to drive numerous mills; hence the saying: 'Pont Aven, a famous town; fourteen mills, fifteen houses'. Then on to Le Letty, a small hamlet by the Mer Blanche, Benodet with its pyramid lighthouse and Concarneau, with its lovely walled town area and France's third largest fishing port, before stopping at 1 o'clock for lunch at the Michelin-starred L'Agape in Ste-Marine, 5 kms west of Benodet. A couple of coupes of L'Aubry et Fils champagne precede an amuse-gueule of raw mackerel tart dressed in dill and balsamic, then langoustines with artichokes and orange zest, and lobster with asparagus and morels, before the main course of pigeon and duck liver wrapped in cabbage, with mousserons, roast potatoes and a truffle sauce. With the food, we drink Trimbach's rich, ripe and full 1990 Riesling Cuvée Emile, which is sadly slightly drying on the finish. The dessert selection includes pear poached in red wine, crème brûlée, raspberries en croûte and a sorbet. Coffee comes with petits fours, and we finish, at around 4 p.m., with a Fine de Bretagne.

In quite brisk but still sunny weather, we take a digestive walk through the Fousenant forest, whose village produces the best Breton cider, we then drive back to Pont Aven.

Back at the hotel at 6.30, we have a couple of glasses of pastis, and eat a light dinner there – avocado and prawns, followed by an *assiette* de *charcuterie*, accompanied by a bottle of 1995 Faugères.

We are in bed by 11.

7.5.01. Checking out of the hotel at 9 a.m., we make a slow journey through Port Louis, with its sixteenth century citadel, and follow the coastal route back to Nantes, arriving at 12.30.

Lunch is booked at L'Atlantique, a one Michelin starred Restaurant on top of the new Congress building. The menu, with my star-ratings for each course, is as follows: a glass of tomato gazpacho with mint jelly (★★); la chair d'araignes en millefeuille et ventre croustillante (★); a single fat langoustine cooked on a sizzler, with cucumber and a vinaigrette dressing (★★★); a slice of roasted turbot with mousserons (★★★); an assiette of milk-fed lamb done in various ways (★★★★); a cheese selection of St-Marcellin (★★), St-Feliciennes (★★) and Vieille Lille (★★★); and desserts that included a fromage blanc and strawberry creation. We finish with a selection of gourmandises with coffee. With the lunch, we drink a bottle of delicious Billecart-Salmon NV champagne and one of 1982 Chinon, Clos d'Olive; an excellent, full and rich Loire red; and round things off with an aged Martinique rum.

We then make our way to the airport for the 6 p.m. flight to Gatwick North. This has been a superb *weekend gourmand*.

Laurent-Perrier and Bordeaux Vinexpo
13–21 June 2001

13.6.01. I take a 10.30 a.m. cab to Waterloo station, and catch the 11.53 Eurostar to Paris Gare du Nord. The First Class carriages are very civilised, with Pannier champagne served throughout the three-hour journey. Lunch is a goats' cheese salad, followed by chicken and rice, and we arrive at 4 p.m. local time.

I meet with Ranjit Chougule, my joint-venture partner from Indage in India, where we are the sole agents for Champagne Laurent-Perrier, and we begin a wait of what turns out to be two hours for the Laurent-Perrier driver, Sigrid. There is heavy rain and appalling traffic, but notwithstanding the conditions, he drives like a bat out of hell to Reims, where we arrive at 8.15 at L'Apostrophe Restaurant.

All the world's Laurent-Perrier agents have been invited. Unlimited quantities of their delicious rosé are served in magnum, and there is a superb buffet celebrating regional cuisines from all over the world: stir-fries, dim sum, sushi, etc. Music is provided by a very good jazz quartet.

We leave at 11.30 to check into our hotel, the three-star La Champagne, a Best Western establishment in Epernay. I get to bed in my very small room at 12.30.

14.6.01. I awake at 6.30 a.m., shower, and eat two boiled eggs and ham, a roll, and orange juice and coffee, from the breakfast buffet. The coach leaves for Laurent-Perrier at 8.

A full day's conference on sales and marketing takes place, with all their international agents in attendance. We break for a buffet lunch on the lawn, with which are served magnums of the 1993 vintage. The conference finishes at 5.30, and we return to the hotel.

In the evening, we rendezvous at 7 for a smart soirée in the Laurent-Perrier cellars, with dancing. We have our first aperitif at Château Louvrois in the village of the same name, with unlimited amounts of Laurent-Perrier Grand Siècle being served, and a party of hunting-horn players to fanfare us into the grounds.

Dinner itself is in the cellars, with more Grand Siècle being served, as well as the 1990 vintage. The menu is lobster, salmon and lamb, the last accompanied by a perfect 1982 Château Talbot, with a finale of the stunning 1990 Grand Siècle Cuvée Alexandra rosé. We dance until 1 a.m. It's been a wonderful evening.

15.6.01. We make a 9 a.m. start for a tour of the Laurent-Perrier cellars, including a full tutored tasting by Alain, the winemaker. Lunch is at Brasserie Flo in Reims, crab and then chicken, accompanied by limitless quantities of Laurent-Perrier in jeroboam, followed by the rosé.

Afterwards, we take a coach to Paris, arriving at 7.15, and check into the four-star Villa Malliol, Avenue de Malakoff, in the 16th arrondissement, a very good place and useful to know of. At 7.30, another coach takes us to the Lido on the Champs-Élysées for dinner and an amazing floorshow, featuring breathtaking settings and costumes. The astonishing succession of acts includes a pair of gold-painted acrobats. With lobster and monkfish, we drink jeroboams of Laurent-Perrier, eventually returning to the hotel at 1 a.m.

It's been a brilliant finale to an equally rewarding visit.

16.6.01. I begin the day at 9 with a hearty breakfast of orange juice, scrambled eggs, bacon and sausages, with toast and coffee, and check out of the hotel at 11.15. Going for a very long walk around the centre of the city, I somehow manage to get lost. I take a cab back to the hotel, and am just in time for my reserved cab to Montparnasse Station, from where – after a beer – I catch the 12.15 train to Bordeaux.

It's a three-hour journey by TGV. There is only one buffet car with a half-hour queue, and they have no sandwiches left by the time I get to the counter. I buy some ham, cheese and fruit, and a coffee, for about £7.

We arrive at the Gare St Jean in Bordeaux in pouring rain. A private Vinexpo car takes me to the Hôtel Chantry on Rue Georges Bonnac, which I remember from last time under the name of Hôtel La Madeleine, a dreadful two-star place with no restaurant and no bar, and extremely small rooms without minibars.

After a rest, I head out for the Hôtel Burdigala, where I have a couple of Famous Grouses with Perrier. I then walk into the old town and go to dinner at the Taj Mahal on Rue Ste. Catherine, which seems to have changed hands, as the food turns out to be awful, and then stroll up the Place de la Comédie, which has a fair going on. I drink a whisky and water at Le Régent on the trendy Place Gambetta, and then return to my hotel, going to bed at 10.30.

17.6.01. An alarm call wakes me at 7 a.m., and after breakfasting on a croissant and coffee, I take the 8 o'clock courtesy coach to Vinexpo. At 9, in the so-called VIP Club Vinexpo lounge, I have an espresso. It's raining again.

I am just marking out my programme for the week when Ranjit arrives at 9.45, and we go to our first appointment, with Sutter Home of California, where we meet with Roger Trinchero, the owner, and Steve Searle, his export director, who has responsibility for India. We have a good meeting, and then after a first-course-only lunch at 1.30 (salad and toast spread with meat, with a glass of their Chardonnay), we go to our next meeting at 2 with Louis Latour, for whom we are the sole agents in India.

At 4, we have a meeting and extensive tasting with our Spanish agency, Berberana. Later, I drink a glass of champagne with Malcolm Davis, sales director of Champagne Duval-Leroy. It has been arranged for us to go to dinner with Graham Cranswick-Smith from Australia, but he isn't at his stand when we arrive. So, after a couple of glasses of champagne at Club Vinexpo, a chauffeured car takes us to the Place de la Comédie for dinner in an awful Chinese restaurant in the old town. I stop for a final nightcap at the Burdigala, but find myself questioning the barman as to the authenticity of the 'Famous Grouse whisky' he has served me. Reluctantly, he opens a fresh bottle, and this one turns out to be correct.

I am in bed by 11.

18.6.01. I am roused at 7 by the alarm call, and half an hour later, have a breakfast of juice, coffee and a croissant, before joining the 8 a.m. coach to Vinexpo. On the bus, I meet Tim Dennison, the export manager of Louis Royer cognac, whom I haven't seen for years, and we arrive at the fair at 9.10.

I have coffee in the Vinexpo lounge, and then Ranjit turns up at 9.50. Our first meeting and tasting is with Terry Beckham from Hardy's, our Australian agency. At 12.15, we have a full tasting with our Bordeaux agency, Ginestet, followed by lunch at a brasserie, sitting outside, as the weather has now turned warm and sunny.

At 2.30, I meet with our agents from Santa Carolina of Chile, and then wander around the exhibition, tasting here and there. Later, I meet up again with Ranjit in the Club lounge, where we have a glass of champagne, and then take the courtesy car to the Hotel Burdigala for more champagne.

For dinner, we go to the restaurant du Golf by taxi, where we are able to eat and drink copiously, courtesy of Duval-Leroy.

I get back to the hotel at 1.30 a.m.

19.6.01. The day begins as before, with a 7 a.m. alarm call and then the usual breakfast at 7.30.

At the fair, I have meetings with Laurent-Perrier and Girelli of Italy, who have asked us to represent them in India, and then grab a snack lunch at Club Vinexpo, before having a further meeting with Laurent-Perrier. The sales director from African and Eastern, a firm of wine merchants based in Dubai, comes over especially to meet us in the Club at 5 to discuss the possibility of a joint venture in India, after which we drink some champagne, and then take the car into town for another indifferent dinner at the Taj Mahal. The day ends with a nightcap at the Burdigala.

20.6.01. After the usual boring breakfast, I get a lift to Vinexpo at 7.20 with Tim Dennison of Louis Royer. I arrive at 9 and, after an espresso at the Club, I meet with Daniel Orsolini and Anne Bayliss of Thierrys wine agencies, who have arranged the following visits: Champagne Nicolas Feuillatte, Champagne Marie Stuart, Alain Thiénot, Vauchère Père, and then – after a smoked salmon lunch – Chais Beaucarois and Vinival.

I drink some champagne in the Club, and then walk to Lac Mercure for some more. It's extremely hot now. There, I run into Thierry Caban and some other friends, and we all go to dinner at L'Estaminet as guests of Grassi, who make very good wine and Armagnac. After a good meal and plenty of their vinous and spirituous products, I like to think of it as 'product familiarisation'. I make it to bed at 12.30.

21.6.01. After the usual breakfast, I pack and get a lift to Vinexpo with Tim Dennison. I have a final meeting with Laurent-Perrier, and then take the courtesy car to the airport. My flight to London is at 15.40.

This has been a thoroughly exhausting trip, where I find the energy level required is beyond me.

Sri Lanka, Maldives, India
1999–2002

14–25 April 1999

14.4.99. Clare and I leave on Air Lanka Business Class flight UL 504 from Heathrow Terminal 4 to Colombo, seats 5A and 5C. The plane departs at 9.30 p.m., the flight and food are both good, and we arrive the next day at 1.30 p.m. (the local time is five hours ahead of the UK).

15.4.99. Sri Lanka is a pearl-shaped 25,000 square mile island located off the southernmost tip of India and surrounded by the Indian Ocean harbouring over 1,000 species of fish. Marco Polo referred to it as 'the finest island of its size in the world'; in fact Sri Lanka's ancient civilisation stretches back over 2,500 years, predating Christianity.

Occupations in the past by the Dutch, Portuguese and the Arabs, have left Sri Lanka with a legacy of varied influence of cultures. Between 1915 and 1948 Ceylon became a British colony and became an independent nation in that year changing its name to Sri Lanka on May 22nd 1972.

An air-conditioned car meets us at the airport, and drives the hour's journey to the Galle Face Hotel, a superb, colonial-style edifice on the beach, it is one of the oldest hotels in the world, established in 1864, we are given suite 108/9, which boasts a wonderful view of the Indian Ocean. As this is the local New Year, the Galle Face has decided not to serve alcohol, which is a great pity, as the bar and restaurant offer such sumptuous views; so we go to the Oberoi Hotel nearby for a much needed Lion lager served in pint bottles and brewed by the Ceylon Brewery Ltd.

Taking a walk afterwards along the beach and into town, we find the conditions very humid (the temperature is in excess of 90°F).

We take a put-put taxi, a three-wheeler, for a tour around Colombo, which is the commercial capital of Sri Lanka. The Galle Face green, a mile long promenade, which borders the fort of Colombo on the south, is the largest open-air stretch in the city used by many who take a stroll against the backdrop of a beautiful sunset. Colombo Fort has much to offer shoppers, with the many old shops and new shopping malls, which specialise in gems, silks, curios, old stamps, excellent leather goods and ready-made garments. Colombo harbour gives one of the best views of Sri Lanka. The National Museum built in 1871 is a treasure trove of articles depicting Sri Lanka's historical past and present. We then went on to the President's House, the Clock/Lighthouse Tower, a Buddhist temple and various other local sights.

Back at the hotel, I have a beer from the fridge, which looks to be of c1920 vintage, and check on our onward flight to Male, only to find it has now been brought forward from 4.30 to 1 p.m., the third time it has been altered. We go for a drink at the Taj Hotel opposite (rum and sodas), and then have dinner at the Oberoi's Indian Restaurant (it's very difficult to find anywhere that serves authentic Sri Lankan food). We dine on tandoori king prawns, lal mas (a Rajasthani speciality that is hotter than hell), chicken biryani, roomali roti and rice, accompanied by Lion beers.

Returning to the Galle Face, we drink a celebratory bottle of mineral water on the terrace by the ocean. It is a truly superb, quite unreal setting.

16.4.99. After having passed a fitful, hot night, I awake at 8.45. We eat breakfast on the terrace: poached eggs and bacon, toast, papaya juice and coffee. A cab arrives at 10, and an hour later we are at the airport, where we find we have been upgraded to First Class, seats 2A and 2B. We have drinks in the First Class lounge.

The Maldivian archipelago located 300 miles south-west of the southern tip of India and 450 miles west of Sri Lanka is a beautiful string of 1,190 low-lying coral islands scattered across the equator in the vast expanse of the Indian Ocean. On the hour-long flight to Male, champagne is served all the way, which is just as well since Male itself is a dry island. On arrival, we are met by a representative from the Soneva Fushi resort, and our luggage is transferred to a seaplane for the 45-minute flight to Soneva's resort on the island of Kunfandhoo. This is a five-star-plus Robinson Crusoe island, where we are accommodated in a superbly appointed cottage with a beach entrance to the Indian Ocean. No shoes are required (indeed, the slogan of the place is 'No News, No Shoes'), as everything – including the bar and restaurants – is on sand. The highly professional general manager here is Alasdair Junor.

There is an excellent bar and two restaurants, one at each end of the island, one French, and the Me Dhuniye offering a splendid themed Eastern buffet, which changes every night, from Thai to Chinese to Indian to a fish menu, etc.

I spend four hours a day, two hours in the morning and two in the afternoon (thereby splitting the staff into two shifts) conducting training in all aspects of wine and spirits. I swim, read, have lots of wonderful massages and reflexology treatment, scalp and foot treatments.

All in all, we spend a glorious ten days in idyllic surroundings, returning via a day in Male, where a visit to the local fish market is a must. We get back to London on 25 April at 9.15 a.m. on an Air Lanka Business Class flight.

30 October–7 November 1999

30.10.99. A taxi arrives at 9 a.m. to take me to Heathrow Terminal 4. The driver curiously chooses the scenic route via the M25. On arrival at 10, I check in for Air Lanka Business Class flight UL 506, seat 5G, to Colombo – having been informed there was no First Class service on this flight, breezing straight through while the Economy check-in desks were dealing with a three-deep queue.

I have immense difficulty finding a decent range of books, although this terminal is otherwise well equipped for shops. I eventually settle on the latest Stephen King novel and venture into the British Airways Business Lounge. It turns out to be almost totally full, although I finally manage to find an odd seat and settle down with a Grolsch beer. The flight is scheduled for 11.50, and we take off about half an hour later.

Seat 5G is situated in the middle, where there is the smallest amount of legroom, and only now do I discover that there is also a First Class section, which is only half full. I try to compensate by drinking copious quantities of excellent Pol Roger champagne.

The meal served is lobster salad, followed by lamb curry and rice, and then cheese with Taylor's port. Over bourbon and soda, I watch a couple of indifferent films, before sleeping and reading. Dinner is kebabs and fruit and more Pol Roger, and we arrive in Colombo at 4.05 a.m. local time.

31.10.99. We are transferred to the Business Class lounge, where I drink a couple of Johnnie Walker Black Labels with soda to revive me from the journey. Some chap nearby is snoring like an express train.

The onward flight is UL 101 to Male at 7.05 a.m. This time I'm in seat 1G in First Class, and we are served a breakfast of poached eggs with spinach, and coffee. It's a 90-minute flight and we arrive in Male at 7.35. A transfer bus takes us to the twin Otter seaplane, which gets to magical Soneva Fushi resort at 10 a.m. local time.

After a very hard massage at noon, I go to the lunch buffet and have stir-fried beef and noodles and a couple of beers, and then sleep for an hour. When I wake up, I find it has started to rain, and I while away the afternoon swimming, sleeping and reading.

I begin the evening in the bar at 7 with a couple of Scotch and sodas, and have talks with various members of staff. The Me Dhuniye Restaurant on the other side of the island has been transformed into an à la carte venue serving East-meets-West fusion food, and I have a very good filet mignon steak with Chinese noodles and a coconut and pineapple sauce, accompanying it with two glasses of Miranda Australian Chardonnay.

After meeting with Klaus Rauter, the wonderfully eccentric Austrian executive chef, I go back to the bar at 10, and fall into a very interesting conversation with a banker from Jakarta. I am in bed at 11.30, and go out like a light.

1.11.99. After awakening at 8.45 a.m., I have a breakfast meeting with Klaus at 9 over coffee and rolls. We arrange staff training sessions from 3 till 6, Monday to Thursday inclusive. I spend the next three hours revising their extensive wine list.

At 12.30, I have a beer in the bar, where a snake has managed to get in. Lunch at 1 is grilled job fish with rice and Chinese vegetables, and I have a further meeting with Klaus at 2. Staff training for nine people then takes place, as arranged, between 3 and 6, and proves to be quite exhausting. I have a beer at the end of it, and then swim and read for a while, before embarking on a couple of rums with soda before dinner.

Klaus and I eat in the main restaurant at 7.30, pasta with chicken, paired with Inniskillin Chardonnay from Canada. Afterwards, I have a few more drinks in the bar.

I get to bed at 1 a.m.

2.11.99. Awakening at 8, I go for a pre-breakfast swim, before settling down to fruit, eggs and coffee. I sit on the sunbed by the sea and proof-read the final version of the wine list, having a chat with a lovely Portuguese couple from Oporto who are staying in the next-door cottage, and going for another swim at 12.30.

After changing, I have a beer in the bar and then deliver the final proof of the wine list to Klaus. Lunch is grilled kingfish and noodles with chilli and mushrooms, accompanied by a large draught San Miguel beer.

Wine school with a class of six people lasts from 3 until 5.30, and then I wander over to the manager's drinks party on the nearby sandbank, a sand spit stuck in the middle of the Indian Ocean, ten minutes by speedboat from the resort. What a stunning setting! The weather is perfect.

Back in the bar at 7.30, I have a large rum and soda, and then go to the seafood barbecue for dinner. With job fish, kingfish, lobster tails, curries and so forth, I drink a glass of white Côtes du Rhône, Domaine de Becassonne, and whisky and soda later, in the bar.

I am in bed at 11.

3.11.99. Having woken at 8.45, I go for a swim in perfect weather, before breakfasting at 9.15 on mango juice, fresh fruit and coffee. I book a reflexology session for noon, and then go for a sail on a Bobcat 215 catamaran with the instructor. He is already booked, but takes me out for 45 minutes and nervously lets me take the helm, as this is my first attempt at sailing. The sea is very calm, and we sail out as far as the sandbank.

Back at 11.45, I attend what turns out to be a fabulous hour of reflexology, followed by a much needed beer in the bar, and then a lunch at 2 of grilled kingfish, sweet-and-sour job fish, and noodles with everything.

Lectures take place from 3 till 6. They are a good crowd today, including the chef, Lal, who has agreed to let me watch him at work in the kitchens tomorrow.

In the evening, I shower and change, and have a meeting with Klaus, and I am pleased to see the new wine list is already in operation. After a rum and soda, I walk over to the Medhuniye Restaurant and have another rum, before dining on lamb fillet with sautéed onions, accompanied by a glass of excellent 1997 Châteauneuf-du-Pape, Château Fortia, and two of a delicious Barsac, 1989 Château Nairac.

I make it to bed at 11.30.

4.11.99. Awakening at 8 a.m., I walk along the beach and go for a swim off the Point. The sun is hot today. I settle to a 9.30 breakfast of fruit, scrambled eggs and coffee, and then at 10.30 go for an hour-long Thai massage, which is very relaxing. The newly built spa has rooms that are half-open to the sky, with a waterfall gently cascading down a tiled wall, contributing to a great feeling of serenity.

I decide to take another walk along the beach, this time the long way round the whole island, which takes around 45 minutes. As it's extremely hot by now, I go for a dip, then rest and read.

At 1, I have a beer in the bar and meet Rienzi, the new food and beverage assistant, who is full of questions. We have lunch at 2, grilled mullet with noodles and all the extras, and a large beer. Between 3 and 6 in the afternoon, I take my final staff training session. It is still intensely hot, and after a small beer, I return to my room.

After another swim, I venture into the bar at 7.30 and have a couple of rum and sodas, before going to a dinner at 9 of chicken curry, dhal and rice, followed by a whisky and soda.

I go to bed at 11.30.

5.11.99. I start the day with an 8 o'clock swim, before breakfasting on orange juice, fruit and coffee.

At 10, I attend the cookery demonstration with chef Lal at the Me Dhuniye Restaurant. He shows me some great sauce recipes. His garam masala is a blend of mustard seed, cardamom, cloves, cinnamon, fenugreek, dill and turmeric, while the curry oil is a sieved reduction of olive oil, curry leaves, garlic, ginger, curry powder, salt and pepper. The curry sauce is composed of curry leaves, shallots, garlic, cinnamon, cloves, cardamom, salt and pepper; he heats the oil, adds those ingredients, and then stirs in some fish curry powder, turmeric and coconut milk, before straining it.

His base sauce is founded on a stock made from seven litres of water, with browned bones, carrots, onions, garlic, tomato and celery, which is simmered for five or six hours until it is reduced to two litres, whereupon he sweats some garlic, celery and shallots, adds the reduced stock and strains it. The white sauce involves sweating garlic, shallots and celery in oil, then adding whipping cream, boiling it and finishing it with Parmesan. Some sauces may be thickened with a roux of melted butter and flour, while the fish sauce is a quick-fried mixture of chopped parsley with capers, lemon juice, salt and black pepper in oil.

From 11 until 12, I have a wonderful Swedish massage with Eva, and then, feeling thoroughly relaxed, take a half-hour stroll. Lunch is kingfish, with noodles and all the trimmings, accompanied by beers, after which I sleep, read and swim until 4.30.

An hour later, I have to conduct a tutored wine tasting on the sandbank, with twenty guests arriving at 6. It's an amazing venue for a tasting, watching the sun go down while talking and sipping, standing in the sand on a sandbank in the middle of the Indian Ocean. We taste the 1998 Taltarni Australian Sauvignon Blanc, 1995 Inniskillin Reserve Canadian Chardonnay, 1997 Echeverria Chilean Chardonnay, 1993 Carpineto Chianti Classico, 1989 Château Beaumont and 1993 Clos du Val Californian Cabernet Sauvignon.

Returning to the bar at 7.45, I have a couple of rum and sodas, and then eat dinner at 8.30 – filet mignon and vegetables, with a 1993 Bardolino Classico. After a final whisky and soda, I'm in bed at 11.30.

6.11.99. After a 9 a.m. breakfast, I spend the morning reading, sleeping and swimming, and then go for a beer at noon.

At 1, I have a special massage conducted by a 6" 3' female Swede. It's called 'the alignment procedure' – putting my muscles and spine back in line – and almost kills me, but it's an incredible experience, and I emerge feeling superb. After an hour of this, I feel I've earned a very large beer.

Over a lunch of job fish, and noodles with all the extras, I have a couple of espressos, and then settle my bill of $590, which is just for massages and drinks.

I shower and change, and then take the 4 p.m. seaplane, via another small island, to Male, arriving at 5 local time (back one hour). After sitting surreally in the Business Class lounge watching CNN news with a glass of water, since no alcohol is served, we are boarded at 8 on to the 8.25 Air Lanka First Class flight UL 102 to Colombo. I'm in seat 1G.

Lashings of Pol Roger are served, which seems quite luxurious after the dry airport lounge. My seat is once again a middle-aisle seat at the front, with limited legroom, and positioned right by the kitchen. I ask to be moved, and am reallocated to 3B, which is perfect. Dinner is smoked salmon, followed by chicken in a tasty sauce, with more Pol Roger.

We land in Colombo at 9.30, and I go to the Business Class lounge for a Chivas Regal and soda and two spells of sleep, one of an hour, one half an hour.

7.11.99. Flight UL 505 to London boards at 1.40 a.m., and I'm in seat 3B in First Class. We take off at 2.30, and are served with more Pol Roger, smoked salmon, Parma ham, tandoori prawns and chicken Kiev. I watch a film, and then sleep for four hours. I'm in quite a comfortable seat with nobody next to me.

At 6.45 a.m. local time (four hours back), a breakfast of scrambled eggs with ham is served, and coffee, and we come in to land at 8.45. It's been a great trip.

23 September–7 October 2000

23.9.00. My initial travel arrangements are as follows: Emirates Business Class flight EK 002 London to Dubai at 13.45, arriving 23.30 local time, and then Business Class flight EK 814 at 3.55 on the 24th, Dubai to Male, arriving 8.55.

The courtesy limousine from Emirates arrives at 10.30 to go to Heathrow Terminal 3, where I am upgraded to First Class. Sitting in the First Class lounge, I eat a round of roast beef sandwiches, accompanying them with Laroche Chablis, as it seems they have rather curiously run out of champagne. We board the plane at 1.45, and I'm in seat 1J.

Charles Heidsieck champagne is served, and I peruse the leather-covered menu. After taking off at 2.15, we are served an aperitif of 1993 Dom Pérignon, with caviare and all the trimmings. The main course is beef in red wine sauce with tomato rice, all served on real china from a trolley; very civilised. Copious quantities of the 1993 Dom Pérignon are served throughout the flight. Each seat is equipped with an individual video player, and one chooses from a library what to watch. I opt for a recent Woody Allen film, *Sweet and Lowdown*, and *The World is Not Enough*.

We arrive at 12.15 a.m. local time. The temperature in Dubai is 35°C. It's a very impressive airport with an excellent duty-free area, but I discover that on this next leg of the flight, there is no First Class accommodation. I'm in seat 2B in Business Class, but notwithstanding that, I wait in the First Class lounge, where club sandwiches and hot food are on offer, and the ambience is all leather and palm trees. I have a couple of Johnnie Walker Black Labels, and sleep for an hour in the massage chair.

The plane eventually leaves Dubai at 3.55 a.m., and we are served champagne, delicious warm snacks, and then a large Johnnie Walker and soda. I sleep until 7.30.

We land in Male at 9 a.m. local time, to find it's pouring with rain. A 45-minute seaplane journey takes me to the Soneva Fushi resort, where I am met by all the staff, who by now consider me one of the family. Alasdair Junor and his wife Anna are sadly just leaving, at the end of his two-year contract as general manager. I check into room 9, and later have lunch with chef Klaus – pasta and meatballs, with a small beer. I then sleep until 3.30, and go for a massage at 4. It's still raining cats and dogs.

I meet Klaus for drinks and dinner at 7. After a couple of rums and soda, we eat in the main restaurant. The main dish of beef in a dark sauce is very good, and I accompany it with a glass of fine South African Merlot. After a final nightcap, I'm in bed at 10.

25.9.00. I am woken by an alarm call at 8.30 a.m., having slept well. It's still raining heavily, and at 9, I have a breakfast of omelette and bacon, with fruit. At 10, I have a massage, and then go to an 11.30 meeting with Klaus to discuss many new additions to the wine list, followed by lunch at 1.

From 3 till 5, I conduct the first staff training session, and then another from 5 till 6.30. At some point during the day, I stubbed my toe very badly, to the extent that I am not sure whether it might not be broken. Back in my room, I take a hot bath, and then limp to the bar.

Klaus and Serge, the assistant manager, join me for drinks, and at dinner I eat a not particularly good dish described as 'runner fish on kale', accompanied by a glass of mediocre 1997 Vergelegen South African Chardonnay. With cheese, I have a glass of the very good 1993 Swanson California Cabernet Sauvignon.

Over a digestif of J&B whisky in the bar, I fall into conversation with a very wealthy German woman and her daughter, who seem to spend all day, every day, in the spa having various luxury treatments. I am bed at midnight. It has rained all day.

26.9.00. Awakening to an alarm call at 8.30, I find it's a little brighter, and there is no rain, for the time being at least. I go for a swim but my toe is killing me; I'm limping badly and it looks terrible, black and blue and practically the size of my ankle. Breakfast at 9 is mango and melon, followed by poached eggs on toast with bacon.

At 10, I go to the spa for a wonderful 30-minute Thai massage treatment on the back, head and neck, then 15 minutes on each foot, carefully avoiding my toe. It's so relaxing, I keep falling asleep. At 11.30, I meet with Klaus, and we discuss their new wine cellar, which has been built deep into the ocean, and the programme of weekly tutored wine tastings for the guests.

A brief respite from the rain accompanies our 12.30 lunch, a duo of grilled Job and kingfish with noodles and a small beer, so we are at last able to eat sitting outside on this idyllic paradise island. From 1 till 3, there is staff training, and then I have beer and a rest. It is now raining heavily again. Another training session follows, from 4 till 5.30, and I walk back to my room in the pouring rain to get ready for the manager's drinks party, which will not now take place at the sandbank. My toe is still causing me tremendous discomfort.

At 6.30, I shower and go to the party in the bar. A buffet dinner follows, at which I meet Charles Morris, the new general manager, and his charming wife Jacqueline, who was born in Paris but is Chinese. The event is great fun, and we dine on grilled lobster, beef and a chicken stir-fry, served with Léon Beyer's Alsace Riesling and Clos du Val Californian Cabernet Sauvignon, both drinking very well. I then drink a couple of J&Bs on the rocks in the bar, and make it to bed at 12.

27.9.00. I awake at 9.30 after a fitful night, during which I kept waking up as a result of my having set the air conditioning too high. It's cloudy but dry, with a slight breeze, and I take a walk along the beach before breakfasting at 10.

At 11.30, I have a meeting with the food and beverage managers, Niro and Farisha, on the subject of how to organise and tutor future wine tastings in the new cellar. After a 12.45 lunch, I have a 2 p.m. meeting with the kitchen team, including Troy, a new chef.

Back in the spa at 5, I have another superb hour-long massage, Swedish this time, on the back, neck and head only, followed by an hour-long facial, the result of which is quite amazing. I look brand new!

At 7.30, I meet Klaus and his attractive young Thai wife for drinks, and then we go to dinner at the Me Dhuniye Restaurant on the other side of the island. Prawn triangles with a dip are followed by sliced roast pork in Szechuan sauce with roasted vegetables. Afterwards, I have a large J&B with ice in the bar, and am in bed at 10.15.

28.9.00. Awakening at 7.30, I eat a hearty breakfast at 8 of mango, scrambled eggs with baked beans, pear juice and coffee. Half an hour later, it's raining again.

At 9, I take myself off for another Thai massage, and receive an hour of superb treatment from Umi. I have the morning off, and so I swim and read, and take a phonecall from Rienzi, the former food and beverage manager. He wants to see me, and so we arrange to meet in Male on Saturday at the new airport hotel on Hulhule island, which isn't dry like Male.

I have a large beer at 12.45, and then lunch at the barbecue. The weather seems to be improving. After a training period with bar staff from 2 p.m., I return to my room at 3.15, and then do some swimming, reading and sunbathing, during the course of which I get a little burnt.

After a 5 o'clock shower, I go to the bar and have a couple of large rums, and then leave at 6 for the Sandbank. At 6.30, there is a guest wine tasting for 20 people, which is a great success. After that, I return at 8.30 for more rum and a curry dinner with the staff.

I am bed at 10.30.

29.9.00. Rising at 8.30, I breakfast on omelette with onions and tomato and crispy bacon, with pear juice and coffee. From 10.30 till 11.45, I take staff training with the bar staff, before returning to my room and going for a swim.

Lunch is seafood and fish with noodles and beers, after which I repair to the spa from 2 till 3.30 for reflexology treatment on my feet, neck and head. Once again, I fall asleep under the influence.

Later, after changing, I have a couple of rums in the bar where some local musicians are playing, and then walk to the Me Dhuniye Restaurant, where I accompany a Thai chicken curry and rice with two glasses of the very good 1999 Rovalley Ridge Australian Shiraz. I make it to bed at 10.30.

30.9.00. Upon receiving my 6.15 a.m. alarm call, I shower and pack, leaving at 7.15 for Male. On the way, we make a stop to collect some people from another island resort. We reach Male's airport island, Hulhule, at 8 a.m. local time (which is one hour back from Soneva Fushi).

The new Airport Hotel was only opened in August of this year, and as it is not on the mainland of Male, it is allowed to serve alcohol (although not to the native Maldivians). I have a very nice breakfast here of an omelette with bacon, mushrooms and onions, with apple juice and coffee, and then sit by the pool chatting to Renzi in lovely weather.

At 7, I check in at the airport for the 8.25 Business Class flight VL 102 to Colombo, seat 2C. The airport lounge is dry. The flight takes an hour and 45 minutes, and we are served with Moët et Chandon and a chicken curry, arriving in Colombo to pouring rain again. I am collected at the airport and delivered to the four-star Royal Oceanic Hotel, where I am given the Royal Suite (300). After a large Johnnie Walker Black Label, I go to bed at 11.30.

1.10.00. Waking at 6.30 a.m. to an alarm call, I find I have been bitten to pieces.

I have a 7 o'clock meeting with the charming Hiran Cooray, managing director of Jetwing Hotels (of which there are fifteen in Sri Lanka, including the Royal Oceanic), with a view to my acting as wine consultant for his group.

A car then takes me back to the airport in pouring rain, arriving at 11, where I check in for the Business Class flight UL 141 to Bombay. In the Business Class lounge, I drink a Chivas Regal, and we take off at 1.10 on a two-hour flight. Spicy lamb and rice is served, along with delicious Pol Roger champagne. We arrive in Bombay in temperatures of 39°C, and I am driven to the Ambassador Hotel, where I am put in room 204.

At 6, I go for a walk down to the beachfront and see dozens of large rats scuttling along the beach. It starts to rain. Back in the hotel's Flavours bar (which doubles as the breakfast room, as well as the disco and nightclub), I down a couple of large rums. The 14th floor bar is currently closed for refurbishment.

Dinner at 7.45 is at the revolving Indo-Chinese Pearl of the

Orient Restaurant on the 12th floor. I eat prawn dim sum and prawn dumplings, followed by stir-fried Szechuan lamb with char siu rice, and drink a large Kingfisher lager. The portions are as huge as ever, and I find I am very tired. I go to bed at 10.30.

Signs spotted in Colombo:

Hairdressers – Ledis and Gints
Garage: we specialise in tinkering

2.10.00. I get up at 7.30 a.m., take a shower and then, a half an hour later, settle down to a breakfast of two fried eggs on toast with bacon, and mango and sweet lime juice.

At 9, a car arrives to take me to a meeting with Arvinder Gill, marketing manager of Chateau Indage Vintners Ltd (CIVL), our new joint venture company, plus Ashok Sood, sales manager. I give them an update, as well as a piece of my mind regarding the various delays we have experienced to date. After the meeting, another car takes me to the domestic airport terminal at noon, where I check in for Indian Airlines flight 658 to Delhi. I am unable to upgrade, even with the offer of payment, as the flight is full and overbooked. Furthermore, to add to my frustration, all the airport bars have gone dry for the day in honour of Gandhi's birthday.

We take off at 1, and I find myself crammed into seat 16F by the window. I had quite forgotten how cramped and claustrophobic Economy Class is. We are given an orange juice, and then chicken curry, rice and dhal, and after two hours of flying, land in Delhi in temperatures of 39°C.

Gagan, from the Indage's Delhi office, is here to collect me. He is a young, dynamic fellow who will go far. We drive to the brand-new five-star Nikko Metropolitan Hotel, which is also having a dry day (what is going on?). There, we have a full meeting, and then go to the Gaylord for dinner (the oldest Indian restaurant in the city, established in 1952). The food, a chicken curry and dhal with naan, is indifferent. I retire at 10.30.

3.10.00. I rise and shower at 8.15. The facilities in the room are splendid. Breakfast at 8.40 is sweet lime juice, an omelette with ham, sausages and hash browns, toast and coffee. I work in my room until 11.15, and then an hour after that, Gagan collects me. He is late because President Putin of Russia happens to be visiting Delhi, and all the traffic is in more chaos than usual.

Our first appointment is at the Hotel Nikko Metropolitan with the food and beverage manager and purchasing director, and then we proceed on to the Oberoi and a very ordinary lunch of lamb curry with buttered naan. After lunch, we visit the food and beverage manager at the Meridian Park Hotel, and then return to the Nikko.

There, I embark on my favourite Old Monk rum with soda, and meet with the bar manager, and then with the general manager, Gerhard Schaller, who used to be food and beverage manager at the Grosvenor House in London. We have dinner in the only restaurant that is open, the coffee shop – a very good chicken dish with buttered naan. There is also a supposedly authentic Japanese restaurant, which closes at 9 p.m., but as a result of having had one too many rums, I've missed it. The Sandpiper beer I drink, made by Inertia Industries of Haryana, is served in a silver wine cradle with a lock at the top. The hotel has only been open eight weeks, and is a quite soulless, international place.

I am in bed at 10.30.

4.10.00. The day begins with an 8 a.m. breakfast of poached eggs on toast with bacon, sweet lime juice and coffee. I am checking out today for the Jet Airways flight back to Bombay at 20.25.

A car collects me at 11.15 for a meeting with the food and beverage manager of the Radisson Hotel, and then for another at the Taj Palace. We have lunch at Baluchi, the finest restaurant in Delhi, located in the deer park: rogan josh with buttered naan and two Sandpiper beers.

Back at the office, I work for a while, and then meet with the manager of the Delhi office, Rajiv Kaushal, at his home, where he is recuperating from a heart bypass operation. He is only 49. We have a couple of beers, and then I'm driven to the airport to catch the Jet Airways flight 312 to Bombay, which has been delayed until 8.50. I have a large Monk rum and (warm) soda in the bar.

On our arrival in Bombay at 11, it starts to rain. There is no car waiting, and so I am forced to take a taxi to the Ambassador, where I arrive, shattered, at midnight. After having a whisky in the room, I retire at 1 a.m.

5.10.00. I awake at 7.30, shower, and am eventually collected at 10.30 for the day's appointments: 11 a.m., the Marine Plaza Hotel; 12, the Oberoi, where I spot Mrs Putin; 1, the Indigo Restaurant; 3, the Ambassador; 4, the Taj; and at 6, a meeting with my business partner Ranjit Chougule.

I have dinner in the revolving restaurant of the hotel at 9.45, and collapse into bed at 11, exhausted.

6.10.00. I rise and shower at 6.30 a.m., work for a while, and then at 9, take a breakfast of scrambled eggs with bacon and toast, sweet lime and mango juice and coffee. Arvinder arrives to collect me at 10.

We have appointments at the Leela Hotel, the magnificent Regent (a new seven-star hotel), the Orchid, the only Eco hotel in Bombay, the Club, and the Sun n Sand Hotel, fitting in a snack lunch at the Club.

Back at the office, I have a final meeting with Ranjit, and we go to his house for drinks. Dinner is at the Indian Summer Restaurant, just along from the Ambassador, an assortment of very good dishes selected by him, and I am in bed by 11.

7.10.00. I manage to wake up at 1.15 a.m. without an alarm call, shower and pack. Checking out, I take a cab to the airport and check in for the 4.30 Emirates First Class flight from Bombay to Dubai, seat 2C, arriving at 6.45, with the onward flight from Dubai to London, seat 2J, scheduled to arrive at Heathrow Terminal 3 at 12.15 p.m. local time.

After a coffee in the First Class lounge, we board at 4.20. There are only twelve seats and four passengers in First, and they are huge seats with loads of legroom. We are served Lanson 1988

Noble Cuvée champagne, which is starting to show its age (but it may perhaps just be this bottle), and then a breakfast of fruit, croissants, a mushroom omelette with tomatoes, and toast, all top-class. I sleep for an hour, and then we arrive in Dubai.

The First Class lounge here is superb as always, and I take some juice and coffee, before boarding the onward flight EK 001 to London. This departs at 8.45 local time, and we are served 1993 Dom Pérignon with caviare, and then 1991 Château Calon-Ségur with duck. During the flight, we pass through an amazing electrical storm, with ferocious lightning. I take my mind off that with the film, the excellent *Green Mile* with Tom Hanks, and after drinking more Dom Pérignon, I fall asleep.

We arrive at Heathrow Terminal 3 at 12.15. What a trip this has been! I wonder how I am still alive...

7–15 September 2001

7.9.01. A courtesy car from Emirates Airlines collects me at 11 a.m. to take me to Heathrow Terminal 3. I'm booked on to a Business Class flight (First Class is full) to Dubai, seat 8B. I have two Bloody Marys in the Red Carpet lounge, and learn that the departure has been delayed to 2.15.

The plane is a 777–300, and I'm in an aisle seat right by the kitchen and loo. Lanson Black Label champagne is served as an aperitif to a lunch of very good tuna salad, accompanied by Fèvre Chablis 1er cru 1999, chicken and rice with a fine Montes Alpha Chilean Merlot, and then cheese with Taylor's 1994 LBV port. After eating, I sleep for a while, and we arrive in Dubai at midnight local time (9.30 p.m., according to me).

8.9.01. I spend a while in the Business Class lounge at the airport, and then have a walk around the huge, excellent duty-free section. The facilities in the lounge are very good, and I partake of some smoked salmon sandwiches and a Johnnie Walker Black Label with soda. It's not quite as good, of course, as the First Class lounge I used last time, but there is still a range of hot food served at all times of the day, cooked breakfasts, and so forth. It's quite a difficult four hours to pass, but we board the plane again eventually at 3.30, and we're off again at 3.45 a.m. on flight EK 884 to Male, a four-hour flight.

I am woken by breakfast being served, scrambled eggs in a pancake with juice, coffee and a croissant, and we land at 8. I'm first away as I only have hand luggage, and am taken to the VIP lounge for a Trans Maldivian Airways flight at 10.30 to Soneva Fushi resort.

I'm in room 57 at the resort, which is large and next to the ocean. I meet with Remon, the executive chef, Sonu Shivdasani, the owner, and Marc Aeberhard, general manager of their other resort, Soneva Gili. We have a lunch of pork and noodles. I book myself in for two daily sessions at the spa. Later, after a very large

San Miguel lager, I go to my first massage, from 4.30 till 5.

In the evening, I meet the food and beverage staff for drinks, and we are joined by Sonu and six guests for dinner at the Me Dhuniye Restaurant. The kitchen there is headed by a talented young Canadian chef, Rahoul, who cooks satay, seared beef, lobster, duck, and a chocolate dessert. With these dishes, we drink a delicious Goldwater New Zealand Sauvignon Blanc, a well-made 1996 Los Altos Cabernet Sauvignon from Chile, a superb 1988 Gevrey-Chambertin Vieilles Vignes, and Quady's Essencia Californian Orange Muscat.

I make it to bed at midnight, completely shattered.

9.9.01. After having woken twice during the night, I get up at 9 a.m., and eat a breakfast of fruit.

My first training session is from 10 till 11.30, and then I go for my hour-long massage at midday. An extensive buffet lunch is served by the ocean; I select barbecued monkfish with noodles, and draught San Miguel lager, and then I take my second session from 3 till 4, followed by my second massage from 4.30 to 5.30. As the easiest way to get around the island is by bicycle, I decide to try but, not having ridden one for over forty years, I fall off, badly bruising my shin, much to the amusement of the staff, who suggest that I might like to use the tricycle from now on.

Later on, after a shower, I meet up with Edwin, the chef of Soneva Gili, and Remon, the Fushi chef, for dinner. Rahoul, cooks for us – foie gras, lobster and lamb, all superb. We drink the brilliant 1997 Château Fortia, Châteauneuf-du-Pape, and the excellent 1998 St Clair Cabernet/Merlot from New Zealand.

After falling off the bike twice on my way home, I make it gingerly to bed at midnight. I am determined not to succumb to the tricycle.

10.9.01. Following a 9 a.m. breakfast, I take my first staff training session from 10 till 11.30, and then go for my 12 o'clock massage. Lunch is barbecued job fish and noodles with a large beer, and then I rest before the next training period, from 3 till 4. An hour-long massage from 4.30 to 5.30 includes aromatherapy treatment, and then between 6 and 7.30, I conduct a tutored wine tasting in

Wine-tasting in the Maldives.

the wine cellar. The cellar is temperature-controlled, and so the guests are provided with fleece-lined anoraks and hot-water bottles for their feet.

To start the evening off, I go to the main bar for a couple of well-deserved rums, and then end the day with chef Lal's house curry and two glasses of red wine, one Chilean, the other Australian. I am bed at 10.30.

11.9.01. I'm up at 7.45, go for a swim half an hour later, then shower and have a breakfast of fruit at 8.45. Staff training takes place between 10 and 11.30, and at midday, I have a Thai massage. At 1, I go to lunch, kingfish with rice and noodles and a large beer, and then take staff training from 3 till 4.30.

At 6 is the manager's cocktail party on the sandbank, a spectacular setting for a party, surrounded as it is by the ocean, after which, returning to the resort, I go to the dinner buffet, and eat grilled lobster and much else besides, sitting and chatting with some of the guests.

I get to bed at 10.30, having got through the day without falling off the bicycle.

12.9.01. I awake at 8.30 to news of the terrible disaster from the terrorist attack on the World Trade Centre in New York the day before. Everyone is in a state of absolute shock.

After swimming and showering, I breakfast at 9 on fruit and coffee, and then take staff training as usual from 10 till 11.30. My spa treatment at midday is reflexology, followed by my usual grilled fish lunch. The afternoon training session goes on from 3 till 4, and then I have a relaxing facial from 4.30 to 5.30. I feel I emerge looking ten years younger, but then I do have a strong imagination.

At 6, I meet with Sonu and guests, and conduct a wine tasting on the sandbank, standing barefoot at sundown – a quite bizarre setting.

Back at the resort at 8.30, I have dinner with Sonu and two American guests. We drink an amazing 1985 Hermitage, Domaine Grippat, which still needs time, but goes very well with a dish of grilled lamb. I am in bed at 11.30.

13.9.01. I awake at 8. It has been raining all night long, and is still doing so. Breakfast at 9 is eggs, bacon, sausages and beans.

At 10, I take a training session for the bar staff, covering spirits, etc., before going for my 12 o'clock massage, Swedish-style today. The lunch buffet seems to be loaded with more food than in previous days, and I help myself to sushi, as well as a chicken and pork stir-fry.

I have a meeting with chef Remon at 2 to discuss new additions to the wine list. From 4.30 to 5.30, I have another reflexology session, and then further staff training from 6 till 8. It's still pouring with rain.

The evening begins with drinks in the main bar. My regular order – dark rum with fresh lime juice and soda – has become known as 'Jeffrey's Cocktail'. I fall into conversation with an English honeymoon couple from London, and go with them for dinner at Me Dhuniye. The restaurant is serving a delicious Thai menu tonight, and with it we have a bottle of very good Don David Argentinian Malbec 2000.

I get to bed at midnight.

14.9.01. After getting up at 8 a.m., I take a light breakfast of fruit and coffee. It's overcast today, but at least there's no rain.

The day's business opens with a meeting with Edwin, executive chef of Soneva Gili, after which I have a Thai massage from 12 till 1. Lunch is grilled job fish, with noodles. In the afternoon, I read on the beach for a while, although it continues overcast, and then have a wonderful facial from 4.30 till 6. I am still convinced it is working... or at least my imagination is.

Drinks in the main bar to a background of live music from local musicians start off an evening that continues with dinner at Me Dhuniye with Charles and Jacqueline Morris. Chef Rahoul has prepared prawns tempura (with which we drink Léon Beyer's Alsace Pinot Blanc), lobster wrapped in an omelette, and beef in sweet soy (accompanied by Don David Argentinian Malbec).

I am in bed at 11.30, having fallen off the bike again and crashed into one of the road lights.

15.9.01. Awakening at 8 a.m., I breakfast on fruit and coffee, and finish my packing. I catch the small seaplane to Male at 10, arriving an hour later in pouring rain once more.

There, I check in for the Business Class flight to Dubai (seat 2F), with an onward journey by First Class flight from Dubai to London (again seat 2F).

The first flight leaves at noon, and has good on-board catering, accompanied by Lanson champagne, and I watch a film and sleep. We land in Dubai at 3. Taking off again at 4, I'm in First Class, and the Dom Pérignon and caviare are soon flowing.

We arrive at Heathrow Terminal 3 at 8.35 p.m. local time. It's been another great trip, even though I am covered in bruises from my escapades on the bicycle, but of course looking much younger from the facials.

4–11 September 2002

4.9.02. At 6.30 p.m., I am collected by a courtesy car from Sri Lankan Airlines and taken to Heathrow Terminal 4, arriving at 7.45. There, I check in for the Business Class flight UL 502 to Male, departing at 21.35. I'm allocated seat 2H, and then informed that the flight has been delayed to 23.45. I am handed a food and drink voucher worth £16. Leaving my cases in the Business Class lounge run by BA, I go straight to the Caviar House buffet bar and order a plate of smoked salmon at an overpriced £14.95.

Back in the lounge, there is no champagne on offer, so I settle for a Glenfiddich and water. Further delays mean that eventually our flight is the only one left on the notice board. We finally board at 12.45, only to be told there will be a further 45-minute delay. Being plied with Lanson Black Label eases the suffering somewhat, and we depart at last at 1.30. The plane is full.

5.9.02. The meal service begins with a salad of duck magret, followed by chicken curry with rice and vegetables, accompanied by more Lanson, after which I sleep. Upon awaking, I watch an awful film – *Bad Company*, with Anthony Hopkins. Breakfast is scrambled eggs, chicken sausages (which taste as bad as they smell), croquette potatoes, grilled tomatoes and mushrooms, with fruit, croissants, apple juice and coffee.

The local time is now noon (four hours ahead of UK time). We are due to land at 3. Arriving in Male, I transfer to the seaplane to Soneva Fushi, and reach my destination at 5.

I celebrate my arrival with a swim in the warm Indian Ocean, and then have dinner with one of the guests who had been on the plane with me. Poached lobster is served as a starter, and followed by grilled jackfish with a cardamom crust, partnered with an excellent 1999 Goldwater New Zealand Chardonnay.

6–8.9.02. The next three days are taken up with the chefs' conference, at which the chefs and food and beverage managers from Soneva Gili, the Evason resorts in Phuket and Hua Hin in Thailand, and the Ana Mandara resort in Vietnam, will be present. The chefs demonstrate their skills by means of tastings of some of their signature dishes, the recipes for which are to be published as *The Six Senses Cookbook*, reflecting the regional cuisines of each location represented. I am on hand to provide suggested appropriate wines.

These are as follows:

Ana Mandara
Snapper sashimi – New Zealand Sauvignon Blanc
Sushi rice prawns – Alsace Pinot Gris
Marinated duck breast, ginger and star anise – cru Beaujolais

Evason Phuket
Tuna carpaccio – Alsace Riesling
Star anise duck salad – Chinon (chilled)
Snapper fritters – Somontano unwooded Chardonnay
    from Spain
Snapper with coriander – Australian oaked Chardonnay
Saffron pannacotta – California Orange Muscat

Evason Hua Hin
Black pepper with spinach Caesar salad – South African
    Pinotage
Asian minestrone – rosé champagne
Grilled veal chops – Rully
Zabaglione – white port (chilled)

Soneva Gili
Lobster and tuna tartare – vin de pays d'Oc Viognier
Antipasti – Chablis
Tenderloin of beef – young cru bourgeois claret
Tuna saltimbocca – Gavi di Gavi
Pina Colada mousse – German Beerenauslese

On the evening of Sunday 8th, the celebrity chef Vladimir Scanu, an Italian from the Equinox Hotel in Singapore, prepares the most fantastic eight-course feast, with wines to accompany selected by myself.

Chef Vladimir's Signature Menu

Amuse bouche
Star anise marinated ahi tuna, melon and green papaya pickles
(NV Moutard Père et Fils, Réserve champagne)

First course
Scampi and crab Bloody Mary, Thai basil oil
(1999 Echeverria Chilean Sauvignon Blanc Reserva)

Second course
Lobster-lemongrass cappuccino
Celeriac – cashew nut dumpling
(1998 Les Pierre Vineyards California, chardonnay)

Third course
Yuzu roasted Murray cod
Fondant and raw daikon, coconut – black truffle sauce
(1999 Alsace Gewürztrainer, domaine Léon Beyer)

Intermezzo
Coriander – goat cheese sherbet

Fourth course
Pan roasted guinea fowl
Braised root vegetables, red wine-ginger jus
(1996 Brunello di Montalcino, Carpineto)

Dessert
Five spice roasted pineapple
Kaffir lime ice cream, natural jus
(1997 Miranda Golden Botrytis, Riverna, Australia)

9–10.9.02. I spend Monday in the spa, and have dinner with the resort owners.

The following day, I take the 7.30 seaplane to Male. A 15-minute speedboat ride takes me to the Taj Exotica island resort, which is quite small but very beautiful. My cottage, 124, is on stilts in the ocean. There are thirty cottages out in the ocean like this, and a further ten on the beach.

I have a lunch of pad thai noodles with a Torres Spanish white wine, before visiting the spa, where a mandara massage is performed by two Thai girls working in unison for one hour. This is followed by a facial, after which I feel absolutely exhausted, but rested too.

At 7.30, I have drinks in the bar. There is a seafood and fish restaurant at one end of the resort near the spa, and a fusion restaurant at the other, all of five minutes' walk away. The gym is also on stilts, and there is a sunken bar with glass floor.

Dinner at the seafood restaurant is a disappointment. Lobster ravioli is tough and cooked in an overpowering brown sauce. Curiously, for a place specialising in fish and seafood, the special of the day is tournedos, which turns out to be stringy and tasteless. The wines with which we finish the evening, a glass of Gewürztraminer and one of Australian Cabernet, are of reasonable quality.

The rooms are very comfortable, and I sleep well.

11.9.02. After breakfasting at 8 on poached eggs on toast with bacon, and carrot and orange juice, I take the speedboat back to Male.

Later on, I board the Sri Lanka Airlines Business Class flight UL 502 direct to London. Flying time is ten hours. Once again, we are served with Lanson Black Label, and then a rather dried-out fish curry with rice.

We land at Heathrow Terminal 3 at 7.40 p.m. local time.

Africa and Seychelles
1993–2002

South Africa
17th–25th July 1993

17–18.7.93. I arrive at Heathrow Terminal 1 at 6 p.m. for South African Airlines flight SA 231 to Cape Town, and am upgraded to Business Class. After a gin and tonic in the Gold Lounge, we board the 747, and take off at 8.15. I'm in seat 33E.

Laurent-Perrier champagne is served before a starter of smoked salmon, after which vegetarian or meat dishes are offered. The meat alternative looks highly suspect. When I ask the air hostess what kind of meat it is, she is unsure, so I cautiously opt for the vegetarian pasta dish. There are various indifferent South African wines, followed by port and the delicious South African liqueur, Van der Hum. At around 11, I drift off and pass a fitful night, awakening at 5.

Breakfast is served at 7 (a steak and scrambled egg), and we make our arrival at 8.30. I hire a car at the airport, and drive to the Victoria and Alfred Hotel, which is located in the nineteenth-century harbour. This was redeveloped in the 1990s, housing many shops, trendy restaurants and bars. The hotel is a well-appointed four-star establishment, and I am in room 213 overlooking the harbour, with a stunning view of Table Mountain. I immediately unpack, shower and shave, and then take a leisurely drive to the Cape of Good Hope, passing through attractive coastal resorts such as Clifton, Camps Bay, where Clare lived for four years on this beautiful stretch of coast, the moneyed enclave of Llandudno, and the nudist beach at Sandy Bay. Lastly there's Hout Bay, which is a delightful fishing port and the headquarters of the Cape Peninsula's crayfish fleet, where keen fishermen flock for the snoek harvest in June and July and to attend the annual Hout Bay Snoek Festival. In the valley nearby I found the country's largest bird park, The World of Birds, a superbly landscaped series of aviaries with more than 3,000 birds of 500 different species.

Beyond Hout Bay the road takes a dramatic turn towards

Chapman's Peak, a crusty millefeuille of layered multicoloured sandstone cliffs skirting a 2,000-foot drop and with stunning views along the coast before the road drops towards the flatlands around Noordhoek, and on to the sea-swept village of Scarborough, a hamlet of holiday cottages behind a rocky shore.

As the road swings inland it joins the east coast route, funnelling into an 8,000 hectare protected conservation area, a peaceful floral reserve and animal sanctuary. At last I reach the Cape of Good Hope, where I make an exhausting climb to the top to appreciate the astonishing views of the confluence of the two great oceans. After a short bus ride in first gear, we climb again, this time to Cape Point, then a stunning drive to the end of the earth, Cape Agulhas, the most southerly tip of Africa – quite breathtaking.

A late lunch is at a restaurant in the wildlife reserve, I enjoy the local fish, knipper, served with salad. Journeying back to Cape Town, I stop briefly at the naval port of Simonstown and see flocks of miniature penguins. In the centre of town I found a statue to an unusual old sea dog, Able Seaman Just Nuisance, a great Dane who befriended the sailors stationed there during the Second World War and was later formally co-opted into the Royal Navy and buried with full naval honours. By Fish Hoek, where the coast railway runs so close to the Indian Ocean that the spray splashes against the carriage windows, I saw a family of whales very close to the shore. Nearby, was Peers Cave, one of South Africa's most important archaeological sites, was once the home of Fish Hoek Man, estimated to have lived some 15,000 years ago. Interestingly enough, Fish Hoek is the only dry town in Southern Africa. The father of the town, Lord Charles Somerset, was so concerned about the influence of the drunken sailors in the adjoining naval base that he banned all sales of alcohol within the municipal limits.

Moving on, I reach the resort of Muizenberg with its glorious white sands and Victorian bathing boxes. From Muizenberg, the road in one direction, continues along the southern coast to join the famous Garden Route, 220 km of some of the finest scenery in Southern Africa; the other direction slips inland back towards Cape Town and the wine route around the Constantia homesteads. Back in Cape Town, a late cable car takes me to the 1,087-metre top of Table Mountain, where it's as chilly, as one would expect for this time of the year, but the views are well worth the visit.

Back at the hotel, I have a quick pint of Castle lager in the bar, and then take a good look around the new complex built on the docks. It's an excellent development, with an amphitheatre, Mitchell's Brewery, and more than forty shops, restaurants and bars, similar in its way to Fisherman's Wharf in San Francisco.

Dinner is at the Green Dolphin Café, where there is live modern jazz. I have gravad lax, followed by an ostrich steak, which in terms of both appearance and taste is not unlike ordinary beefsteak, but with a very slight gamey aftertaste. With these dishes, I drink Boschendal chardonnay and Groot Constantia Pinotage 1990, which turns out to be drying out somewhat.

I am in bed at 12, quite exhausted. All in all, it's been a fabulous day, crammed with stunning scenery and views, and with friendly and helpful people on hand.

19.7.93. My alarm call awakes me from a deep sleep at 7 a.m. After a quick coffee, I leave at 7.30 for Paarl, 50 km from Cape Town, to spend the day with the KWV Winery. Formed in 1918, the De Ko-Operatiewe Wijnbouwers Vereeniging van Zuid Afrika Depakt had far reaching statutory powers to rid the South African wine industry of its surplus. I take breakfast (an omelette and bacon with all the trimmings) at the five-star Grand Roche Hotel in Paarl, a seriously over-the-top hotel in an impressive setting, which opened last year.

I arrive at the KWV at 9.30. A video presentation and cellar tour ensue, and then after an extensive tasting of mainly commercial wines, we lunch at La Borie on oysters with mushrooms, and a huge rump steak.

In the afternoon, I visit the Backsberg Winery, and meet the very personable Michael Back. The wines are quite superb, as is confirmed by the full tasting we undertake. I then drive east to Franschhoek, and up the mountain road to some magnificent sites, arriving back at the hotel at 7.

Later, I repair to the Santa Anna Spur, a noisy but fun Tex-

Mex restaurant on the waterfront, for an enormous portion of spare ribs, washed down with Castle lager. I am in bed by 10.30.

20.7.93. An alarm call wakes me at 6.45 a.m. After coffee, I drive to the beautiful university town of Stellenbosch, which lies at the centre of South Africa's premier wine producing district, and the Welmoed Co-op, which owns a large rambling winery, where I enjoy an extensive tasting.

Then it's on to Boschendal, arriving at 11.15. Here I enjoy a very good meeting and a full tasting of their excellent wines, in the company of the Development and Wine Production managers. This is followed by a fine lunch at their restaurant. It's a superbly restored old Dutch Cape estate, producing top-quality wines.

At 2.30, I go for a tasting at McLeod Wines, a wine-broking firm, and then take off on a sightseeing trip up the north east mountain route, and almost as far across as Worcester. Once again, the views are marvellous.

Back at the hotel at 7, I change and then go to Camps Bay for dinner at Blues, a very commendable place, similar in feel to Quaglino's in London. I am in bed at 11.

21.7.93. After an 8 a.m. alarm call and coffee, we drive to Belleville to see Fanie Augustyn at Vinfruco. We have an interesting tasting of fairly commercial low-cost wines, and then go to visit several of the wine co-ops.

At 2.30, I leave for a meeting with Sonop Farm, a Swiss-owned concern seemingly in the middle of nowhere, but actually just outside Paarl. The wines we taste are not showing well, but the drive is worth it. After this, I travel to Malmesbury, and then on to Yzenfontein Point on the coast, a twee holiday resort, but blessed with lovely beaches and sumptuous views.

Continuing on along the coast, I pass through Cape Town and on to Stellenbosch for dinner at De Volkscombuis. In a classical Cape house or cottage is a restaurant serving authentic local food. Mixed Country Platter is comprised of springbok pie, chicken and mushroom pie, lamb cooked in wallflowers, and bobotie with cooked peaches – all quite excellent.

I am back at the hotel at 10.30.

22.7.93. The day begins with a superb cooked breakfast. I then drive to Stellenbosch for a meeting at the Distillers Corp, otherwise known as the Bergkelder. After visiting several of their estates, I am taken on a tour of the bottling plant and cellars.

Lunch is at De Volkscombuis again, with the excellent springbok pie. I leave at 3.30, and drive to Bettys Point, around the cove and then back via the Houw Hoek Inn, built in 1779, the oldest licensed hotel in South Africa.

I arrive back at the hotel at 7.30, and shortly afterwards depart for the docks, and dinner at Jelly Roll Morton's, ribs and beer. I am in bed at 10.

23.7.93. Another full cooked breakfast starts the day at 8, after which my first appointment and extensive tasting is with Nederburg, an historical farm set in the beautiful Paarl Valley dating back to 1792.

My second meeting, and lunch, are with Boschendal, at their new superb Vergelegen Estate in Somerset. We lunch outside on yellowtail fish with salad. It's the most amazing set-up, a national monument no less, with listed flora such as camphor trees, and the winery built into a hillside. The tasting confirms the fantastic quality of the wines.

In the afternoon, I visit Klein Constantia, another impressive estate, with a new modern winery tastefully attached to the famous old farm. The full tasting includes a deliciously rich 1979 Constantia.

I am back at the hotel at 6.30. Drinks at 8 are followed by a hamburger dinner, and I am in bed by 10.

24.7.93. I start the day with coffee at 8.30, and then drive into Cape Town for some sightseeing. The city centre stretches out from the main train station, which houses one of the city's endless flea markets, full of ethnic knick-knacks and old clothes. Heading north from the station is Adderley Street, in pre waterfront days the main shopping street, and still home to assorted department stores. Unlike in the waterfront, however, it is evident they we are now in Africa: street vendors are everywhere. Drift south and east from Adderley Street and the shops become more interesting. In

Greenmarket Square there is a pleasant arts and crafts market. Along Church Street there is an array of shops selling antiques. Keep going down to Wale Street and there is St George's Cathedral, for a long time Archbishop Tutu's stronghold, and the parliament buildings. Past the cathedral, Wale Street meets the most intriguing of Cape Town's shopping streets, Long Street. This is the heart of alternative Cape Town, where the backpackers who are beginning to flock to the region have their hostels, and the clothes reflect the internationalisation of street style. My jaunt also takes in the flower market at Trafalgar Place and the Malay quarter.

After that, I drive to Stellenbosch, South Africa's second oldest town, do some shopping and have a proper look at the pretty leafy old university town itself.

Then it's on to Boschendal for a roast lamb lunch with the managing director, Don Tooth. We take a tour of their magnificent estate, including the Rhodes fruit farms, which is all part of the Anglo-American/De Beers group.

Back at the hotel, I do some more shopping around the wharf area. Dinner at Clementine's in Wynberg is ostrich and kidney pie, very good. I'm in bed at 11.

25.7.93. Breakfast at 8.30, after which I drive to a small game reserve near Franschhoek, stocked with cheetahs, eland, zebra and baboons. There are ravishing views from the top of the mountain. We have lunch in Franschhoek (springbok, etc.), where I inadvertently leave my credit card behind.

Arriving at the airport at 3.30 for the return flight, I find an upgrade has been arranged, but the flight back will be via Johannesburg, where there will be a two-hour wait.

Food notes: bobotie is baked mince, often served with apricot chutney. *Bredie* is a rich ragout of mutton in tomato sauce, while *sosaties* are kebabs.

Zimbabwe
7–16 February 1995

7.2.95. Arriving at Gatwick North Terminal at 3 p.m., I check in for the Business Class Air Zimbabwe flight UM 725 to Harare, departing at 6. It's a Boeing 767, and I am allocated seat 2F and given VIP status on my boarding pass. I go to the BA Club Lounge for coffee, snacks and drinks.

We take off at 6.30, and Moët et Chandon is served with the canapés. The dinner is veal with potatoes and salad, followed by cheese, all very good, well cooked and presented.

I read and reflect on the country situated in south central Africa between the Limpopo and Zambezi rivers. It is bounded by Zambia to the north and north-west, by South Africa to the south, by Mozambique to the east and northeast and by Botswana to the southwest. The country covers 390,000 sq.km, and since independence in 1980 and the election of Robert Mugabe has gradually instituted a number of changes to encourage foreign investment, particularly in priority projects, including allowing foreign ownership of up to 100%; how this will work alongside government commitment to indigenisation and greater black ownership remains to be seen... While market reforms point to economic growth, unemployment is estimated at 30% of the workforce and rising – with some 200,000, school leavers chasing around 50,000 jobs. Meanwhile, high inflation, fixed salaries and deteriorating social services make life miserable and are eating away at the advantages of fifteen years of independence.

The history of the wine industry in Zimbabwe dates back more than fifty years, to the days when it was Southern Rhodesia. Then, the plantings were entirely of hybrid vines, producing cheap, often undrinkable table wines under brand names such as Flaming Lily, White Thunder and Golden Eagle. With independence in 1980 came a fresh wave of change, with free education, medical care, and revitalised industries with a desire to increase exports. This last development led the country's three wineries to pull up their vines, and replant with grafted *Vitis vinifera* varieties such as Chardonnay, Chenin Blanc, Cabernet Sauvignon, Merlot, Cinsault, etc.

Breakfast is served at 5 a.m., and we arrive at 6.30 local time – two hours ahead.

8.2.95. At the airport, I am collected by David Simleit, the owner of both Meadows Estate Vineyards and a prestigious wine shop, Phillips Cellars, in the centre of Harare, and driven to the five-star Meikles Hotel, where I am assigned the opulent Imperial Suite 1010 on the tenth floor. It consists of two large bedrooms, a very large sitting room, a huge bathroom with walk-in shower, and so forth.

At 8.30, Greg Guy, the sales director of Phillips Cellars, collects me, and we walk to the wine shop, which is attached to the very old but attractive cellars. I have a tasting of their own excellent Meadows Estate wines, and then we drive on to African Distillers, who are the only spirit distillers in Zimbabwe and also own Stapleford Wines, which consists of three wine estates and a large winery at Gweru. At their Harare offices, I undertake a blind tasting of the products of all three estates. At the end, I am prevailed upon to read my tasting notes out loud, and give my marks out of 20 for each wine. This is something I do not normally do, but given that the wines are of high quality, particularly the 1992 Cabernet-Merlot, I succumb.

We then have a fine buffet lunch in their cellars – oysters, smoked salmon, prawns, and many other local specialities – alongside which their very good sparkling wine shows well. Afterwards, we take a tour of their cellars in the company of the winemaker and marketing manager.

Back at the hotel at 4, I take a nap until 5.30, and then go for drinks in the ground-floor Explorers Club bar, an experience not to be missed, with waiters immaculately attired in Panama hats and safari suits, serving ice-cold Zambezi lager.

At 7.30, I am collected for a dinner with the three vineyard owners of Zimbabwe. We go to a steakhouse where, thanks to lovely weather, we eat outside. I am recommended to have the rump steak, which is self-cooked on a sizzling stone, and can be dressed with various sauces. It covers almost two plates. We accompany the food with many different local wines from the three producers, followed by a superb South African Rustenberg 1971.

I am back by 11.30.

9.2.95. I awake at 7.30, and have some coffee.

The main visit of the day is to the Mikuyu Winery owned by Cairns Foods, a 90-minute drive. We conduct a tasting of the very good 1994s, and then have drinks and lunch sitting outside their guest house. It's very warm. Lunch begins with crocodile tails, tasting like a cross between chicken and fish, followed by ostrich stew, and then a tour of the winery. We get back to the hotel at 6.

At 7.20, I am collected and driven to a restaurant called Le Français, where we dine on smoked marlin with an excellent 1994 Mikuyu Merlot, and then chicken piripiri, the spice 'temperature' of which necessitates numerous bottles of very cold lager with the vaguely familiar name of Bohlinger. We round the day off with a nightcap in the hotel bar, and I am in bed by 11.30.

10.2.95. The day begins with a 7.30 coffee, and at 9.30 David Simleit arrives and kindly takes me to the airport's domestic terminal, from where I will take Air Zimbabwe flight UM 0226 (seat 15C) to Kariba, the world's second largest man-made lake. Finally completed in 1963, it covers more than 5,000 sq km, is 281 km long and at its widest point is more than 40 km across. Before the dam was built, the Zambezi Valley was hot, infertile, infested with tsetse flies and almost uninhabited except for the Tonga people.

From there, I take a small plane, BA 146, to Hwange. The ride is very bumpy, as well as being extremely hot and humid. We continue on for another hour to Hwange National Park, which is a huge slice of Zimbabwe – 14,000 sq km. It has been set aside purely for the purpose of conserving wildlife in its natural habitat. From there we have a ten-minute bus transfer to Hwange Safari Lodge. I'm in room 233, which turns out to be pleasant and comfortable.

At 1.45, a barbecue lunch by the pool is laid on, and we get through a fair amount of Zambezi beer. Later in the afternoon, at 4, we embark on a splendidly well-organised safari, during which we see elephants, cheetahs, giraffes, warthogs, kudus, zebras, wildebeest, black and side striped jackal and more.

We get back to the hotel at 6.45, and have drinks outside to the accompaniment of a local singing group. There are wood fires at various places in the grounds, and a choice of a barbecue or formal restaurant. We enjoy the compelling sight of various game animals hovering, attracted by the lights. After numerous gin and tonics, Zambezi lagers, and rum and sodas, we opt for the outdoor roast pork barbecue, watching the elephants, zebras and impalas wandering nonchalantly by. It's a balmy evening, quite magical, and I wish my family were here to see it. *Quel dommage!*

11.2.95. An alarm call wakes me at 5.30 a.m. for the 6 o'clock dawn safari. This time, we see lions, buffalo, lots of elephant calves and giraffes. A beautiful dawn comes up in clear skies, and the temperature is already mounting into the 80s by 8.30.

At 9, I have a full breakfast of eggs, bacon, sausages, baked beans, tomatoes, potatoes and onions, with toast and coffee to follow. Shortly after, we take the bus back to Hwange airport, and board a very small plane to Victoria Falls (of which we get a sumptuous view from the air) a half-hour flight. We arrive in cloudy, thundery conditions, and take the bus to the five-star Elephant Hills Hotel, which is an architectural monstrosity but enjoys a superb location overlooking a golf course within sight of the Falls. I am checked into room 312.

At noon, we have drinks at the poolside bar, and then the heavens open up, quite dramatically. After numerous drinks, we have a buffet lunch of beef stew and rice, after which, at 3, we take a coach to the crocodile farm. A full range of beasts is accommodated there, from a newly born infant, which I hold, to enormous, terrifying five-to-seven-year-olds. 3.45 is feeding time. They dine on elephant meat, an incredible sight. We are told they are the only creatures that eat their own kind.

We then take a bus to the jetty for a trip down the Zambezi River, which is the fourth largest river in Africa, 2,700 km, during which we see hippos and crocodiles floating by, a stunning prospect. After this, another coach takes us to an African village for an absorbing display of dancing and singing by locals in masks.

Back at the hotel at 8.30, we have an appalling alfresco dinner of tasteless smoked crocodile tail, followed by undercooked chicken piripiri, partnered by the superb 1994 Mikuyu Cabernet/Merlot. Afterwards, I take a leisurely walk around the casino, before going to bed at 11.30.

12.2.95. Awakening at 8 a.m., I do a spot of sunbathing on my private balcony, but the sun is very hot. After a full cooked breakfast, I take a 9.30 coach to an African arts and crafts village. There is a tour of the village huts, and I have my fortune told by a witch doctor, who tells me I will evidently travel a lot (!). The central attraction is the amazing 1000-year-old booba tree.

Then I take a long, absorbing walk by the magnificent 1,700 metre wide Victoria Falls, where the views are superb, getting quite wet from the fallout. A bus takes me to the Victoria Falls Hotel, a place with a splendidly colonial ambience (Best Rooms, 82 and 143; best suites 23,24,25,26). I have drinks on an outside terrace, and go inside for the buffet lunch, as it's now very, very hot.

At 4, I take a bus to the airport for the one-hour flight back to Harare. There, I'm collected by David Simleit, have a quick shower and change, and then go to a formal dinner in the hotel with his family and members of staff. Numerous gin and tonics are followed by smoked salmon and an obscenely large rib of beef, accompanied by Meadows Estates wines. I am in bed by 12.30.

13.2.95. After a full breakfast in the hotel, I am collected by the marketing director of African Distillers (Stapleford Wines) for a visit and tasting at their winery. We have a buffet lunch and a meeting with the other directors.

At 1.30, I am put into their private six-seater Cessna plane for a visit to their Bertrams Winery in Gweru, which has state-of-the-art installations and a superb vineyard. We taste some of the potentially very good 1995 wine – Chenin Blanc, Colombard, Muscat, Trebbiano and Pinotage.

Later, I take the plane back to Harare, a considerably less

bumpy ride this time, arriving back at the hotel at 6.30. I'm collected at 7.30 for dinner at Alexander's. We eat grilled bream and another embarrassingly large T-bone steak, paired with a well-balanced Stapleford Chenin Blanc and the excellent 1992 Cabernet-Merlot. I am in bed at 11.

14.2.95. The day begins with a 7.30 breakfast, after which I am collected at 8 by David for a tour and tasting at Meadows Estate, an hour's drive from Harare. The vineyards are located in the most beautiful setting, and one tours them by ox cart. The estate specialises in white varietals such as Gewürztraminer, Chardonnay, Chenin Blanc, Colombard and Bukettraube (an aromatic grape, originally German). There is also a lovely guest house but no Winery, all the wines being made under contract by Cairns.

I return to the hotel at 10.30 for a quick change and shower, and then there is a full meeting in the hotel boardroom of the ZVEA (Zimbabwe Vintners Export Alliance), of which I am chairman. We then proceed to sign the protocol agreement. An official press conference follows, and local TV turns up to film the event. There is a buffet lunch afterwards.

At 2.30, I take a tour of various wine shops, and stop for a drink of draught Bohlinger beer at a local pub. Then I drive to David Simleit's house, Tanglewood, which is in an enviable location with sumptuous views. Stepping into the breach, I cook a barbecue wok supper – fillet of beef, chicken, pork and stir-fried vegetables which, I have to say, all tastes excellent. The food is accompanied by a slightly tired 1971 Trimbach Edelzwicker from Alsace, and a 1958 Château d'Yquem (mahogany-brown, slightly musty on the nose, but full and rich, with barley-sugar on the palate).

I am back at the hotel by 12.30.

15.2.95. I awake at 8.30 and have coffee, and then work until 12 in the dining room of my suite. At noon, I am joined by the directors of Stapleford Wines, Meadows Estates and Cairns/Mikuyu Estates for a full meeting and sandwich lunch to finalise the export programme of their wines for the UK market.

They all leave at 2, and I continue working until I am collected on my checkout at 5.30.

We go to Phillips Central Cellars for a final briefing over whisky and sodas, and then I am driven to the airport for 8 o'clock. I check into Air Zimbabwe Executive Class flight UM 724, and am given seat 2B in the VIP section. I drink another whisky and soda before the departure, which is at 10.15. It's a turbulent flight, 10½ hours, during which I manage to sleep well, and arrive at Gatwick at 6.30 a.m. local time on Thursday 16th.

Zimbabwe
5–9 June 1995

5.6.95. I check in at Gatwick North Terminal for the Air Zimbabwe flight UM 727 for Harare, via Frankfurt, departing at 2.30 p.m. The plane is a 767, and I'm in a pre-reserved Business Class seat, 2A. Before boarding, I have a coffee in the Club Lounge, and learn that the flight is delayed. It is now scheduled for 4 o'clock, but eventually takes off at 5.35. It seems that the plane was broken somehow, and engineers had to be called to fit a new part.

I drink a glass of cava (there is no champagne available). After 90 minutes, we land in Frankfurt, having circled at great length before being allowed to do so. There are only six people in Business Class, and the air hostess reeks to high heaven. We spend 55 minutes on the ground, and eventually take off again at 8.

Nederburg sparkling wine is now served, prior to a dinner of marinated beef, followed by roast lamb and cheese, accompanied by a thin Château Plaisance 1993 and Sandeman's port. The film is *Street Fighter*. No menu is handed out, as it apparently hasn't been printed yet, and there is no film programme for the same reason.

6.6.95. I sleep for four hours and awake again at 4.15 a.m., one hour ahead. I have a sore throat yet again, and resort to the Disprin. It really is either sod's law or psychosomatic.

Breakfast, served at 5.15, is scrambled eggs with asparagus, tomatoes and mushrooms, fresh fruit and coffee. At 5.45, there is a superb sunrise, all red and burnt gold. We arrive in Harare at 6.35, where Greg Guy and David Simleit are waiting to collect me. After coffee (it is still only 7.30 a.m.!), we undertake a tasting of 22 Meadows Estate wine cask samples.

I am then taken to the guest house of AFDIS (African Distillers), a magnificent place set in its own grounds, with a swimming pool, fully stocked bar room and full-time maid.

At 11, I am picked up again by AFDIS for a wine tasting of seventeen tank samples from their Stapleford Winery and a meeting with their managing director, Ian Godden. We go to lunch at Squabbles, a restaurant in the Highlands area, where, after a couple of Zambezi beers, we dine on tournedos steaks in cheese and mushroom sauce with chips, carrots and beans, a rather clumsy meal.

Back at the guest house at 3, I read in the garden for a while. It's a beautiful sunny day (22°C+), and I eventually succumb to sleep. Awakening again at 5, I shower and then have a whisky and soda in the bar.

Dinner with Ian Godden is at a Portuguese restaurant, and includes giblets, prawns, chicken piripiri and salad, with a South African wine called Gacia, something like vinho verde in style. We finish with crème caramel and ice cream with whisky. Ian is great company.

I am back the guest house at 10.30.

7.6.95. I awake at 8.30 to a beautiful day, the temperature already 25°C. After a coffee in the garden, I am collected at 10, and driven to Meadows Estate Winery. Here, we taste various blends and grape varieties, such as Bukettraube, L'Étoile, Chenin/Chardonnay and Colombard/Chardonnay, as well as some Pinotage and others. We tour the vineyards on an ox-cart, drinking Zambezi beers – great fun. Lunch is a barbecue in the garden, lamb chops with salad and cheese.

Once back in Harare, I do some sightseeing, taking in the Parliament building, which was originally built as an hotel in 1895, the National Botanic Gardens, 58 hectares of indigenous vegetation, the museum and National Gallery. I then go shopping, which is somewhat limited, before returning to the guest house. A quick shower and change, and then I make my way over to the Sheraton Hotel for a wine tasting attended by 200 people. All the wines are tasted blind. There is a selection of 40 different wines from South Africa and Zimbabwe, and as I am the guest of honour and guest speaker, I have to comment on them and give a comparative quality assessment as between the two countries. The result runs 60/40 in favour of the Zimbabwean wines.

Dinner at the hotel begins with smoked crocodile tail, which is followed by an impala steak, served with Meadows Estate L'Étoile 1994. I have drinks afterwards in the bar, and return to the guest house at 12.30.

8.6.95. I begin the day much as yesterday, awakening at 8.30 and taking coffee in the garden, in temperatures of 25°C+.

At 9.30, Alan Buchanan, the managing director of the Cairns Mikuyu Winery, collects me. It takes about an hour and a half to get there, and we spend a full morning tasting and blending, selecting some superb blends of Chenin Blanc, Merlot and Pinotage.

Lunch is in their guest house, and consists of roast beef and ham with salad and cheese, with which we drink their méthode traditionelle sparkler, a Cabernet Sauvignon and a selection of other wines.

Back at the house at 4.30, I get into conversation with some of the other guests who have just arrived. One is the coach of the Zimbabwe national women's hockey team. Another is the Africa director for Bols liqueurs. Both are Dutch.

After two large whisky and sodas, Greg collects me at 7.30 to go to dinner with David and Jacky Simleit at their home. We eat rollmops and chicken curry, accompanying them with a full-bodied 1987 Alleslost South African Cabernet Sauvignon, 1990 Groote Shiraz, and a rich 1986 Furmint Adelose.

I am back home by midnight.

9.6.95. I start my packing at 8 a.m. and have a coffee at 9. The weather is, if anything, even more splendid, now above 28°C and intensely sunny. It feels very civilised taking coffee in the garden by the pool. I finish my packing.

At 10.30, I have a meeting with Perry McQueen, president of Zimtrade, who are supposedly there to promote Zimbabwean produce in the export markets. Disappointingly, he is not the top man, so the two hours we spend talking will be something of a waste of time.

We go to Wombles steak house for lunch, which begins with Hunters beer, made by a local brewery. This is followed by

Mikuyu Vat 10 Colombard, Meadows Estate L'Étoile, and the superb 1992 Stapleford Cabernet-Merlot from AFDIS. With these, we eat sardines, and then a gigantic T-bone steak with all the trimmings.

Back at the house, I have drinks with Ian Godden, Greg, David, and his secretary Dale. Greg then drives me to the airport at 8, where I am booked on Air Zimbabwe flight UM 724 in Business Class, seat 1A. I have a Famous Grouse and soda in the Executive Lounge, which is designed like an Indian tandoori Restaurant.

We take off at 10.35, and are fed on veal and boiled potatoes, with the Château Plaisance 1993 again. I sleep from 11.30 until 5.30 a.m., waking shortly before landing.

Zimbabwe is a country whose wines, I feel, have great potential.

Zimbabwe, Tanzania and Zanzibar
24 April–3 May 1997

24.4.97. I arrive at Gatwick North Terminal at 4.30 p.m. and check in for Air Zimbabwe flight UM 725 to Harare. I am upgraded to Business Class, seat 1A. After buying a new camera for Holly, I repair to the Executive Club Lounge for a Glenmorangie 18-year-old, and am joined by wine importer Guy Anderson.

The plane takes off at 7.30, and we are given Moët et Chandon with toasted nuts. Dinner consists of Parma ham with guava, roast lamb with roast potatoes, and cheeses, and I follow it up with a couple of Ballantine's and sodas. After watching the film *Toy Story*, I sleep soundly from 11.30 until 5 a.m. The plane appears to be two-thirds empty, but I notice Bruce Grobelaar, the Zimbabwe goalkeeper, in the seat behind me.

25.4.97. We land at Harare at 6.15 after breakfast on the plane. I decline the sausages and scrambled eggs, but go for the croissants, coffee and a couple of glasses of apple juice. Bess Scott, of Cairns Mikuyu Winery, has come to meet me, and we check in to the five-star Meikles Hotel in Harare.

We then drive to the winery, which takes 2½ hours, and once there, embark on a mammoth tasting of well over 50 wines. Guy and I are involved in blending three of the whites (Chenin Blanc/Colombard, Chardonnay/Pinot Blanc and Chenin/Muscat) for the UK retail market. Sadly, the reds in the 1997 vintage have not been up to the standard of previous years. As the assemblage of our final blends will take some time, I have decided to spend a few days in Tanzania and Zanzibar.

A buffet lunch at the winery guest house comprises cold meats, salad, pizza and cheese, accompanied by a well-made Mikuyu Pinot Blanc. I return to the hotel at 4.30 and shower, and then we meet for Zambezi beers in the hotel's ground-floor bar at 6.30, which is decorated like a colonial shooting lodge, with waiters in panama pith hats. At 7, Bess Scott arrives and drives us to the head office of Astra, the holding company of Cairns Mikuyu, where chief executive Tim Johnson and his wife host a dinner for twelve. We drink Cairns' delicious Mikuyu sparkling wine and then the Mikuyu Chardonnay 1994 with poached salmon, fillet steak and cheese. Some French antiques follow these: the full and rich 1966 Château Grand Barrail Lamarzelle Figeac, 1962 Château Cissac, in perfect condition, and my own contribution, the 1966 Liger Belair Volnay, which has survived the journey extremely well. There is also an assortment of Australian reds, including 1979 Penfolds Grange, and vintage ports back to 1955.

I make it back to the hotel by 11.30, feeling very tired, but surprisingly have difficulty sleeping.

26.7.97. I awake at 8.45 a.m., and have breakfast on the first-floor Pavilion Terrace at 9.30. It's a hearty spread of apple juice, scrambled eggs, bacon, sausages, baked beans, tomatoes, toast and coffee.

At 11, a courtesy bus will arrive to take me to the airport for what is supposed to be, according to my ticket, the 12.20 p.m. Air Tanzania flight TC 763 from Harare to Dar-es-Salaam. On checking at the hotel desk, however, I find that the flight is actually 11.20 and it's already 10.45. I then depart in a mad rush via an English-style black cab, which costs Z$100 (ie. about £5). I arrive at 11.05 to find that the flight was in fact originally scheduled for 11.10, but has in any case been delayed until 12.20. I stand in a long queue to check in.

I pay Z$10 for a cold Zambezi beer in the very humid departure lounge. On checking the itinerary, I now find that the travel agent has booked me into the Pemba Hotel, which is on an island off Zanzibar, not the Tembo in Zanzibar. Should be interesting to see what happens if and when I arrive. We eventually take off at 12.55 in temperatures of 32°C. I'm in seat 14A on the 737 and the flight is almost full.

Lunch arrives. After a Castle lager, a tray is put in front of me. The starter looks completely unrecognisable, and the stewardess doesn't seem entirely sure as to what it is either, but hazards a guess that it might be some sort of crabmeat and pasta salad. It is intended to be followed by the contents of a sealed container marked 'Beef'. This is so inedibly tough that I facetiously ask the stewardess whether it might be rhino meat with the skin left on. Quite straight-faced, she replies that she will find out for me, and returns equally deadpan to announce that no, it is indeed beef. I settle in the end for a cheese roll with a quarter-bottle of Nederburg Steen 1996, served warm naturally and apparently in a state of secondary fermentation. The pudding looks like a smoked salmon sandwich set in a sea of blood. I decline, of course, but this is certainly an interesting airline.

We arrive at 4.30 (local time is one hour ahead of Zimbabwe). My connecting flight to Zanzibar is at 7.30, leaving me with three hours to kill at Dar-es-Salaam Airport. There is no air conditioning, and it must be well over 30°C, with crushing humidity. The countryside looks quite green, and they have evidently just had a lot of rain. The bar is on the roof in what must be 35°C. There is no lift, and I decide not to take my suitcases all that way with me in these conditions, leaving them with the information desk. Finally, drenched in sweat, at 6.15, I check in for my flight on an 11-seater plane, and appear to be the only passenger in the 'departure lounge'. I pay US$2 for a much needed Kilimanjaro lager, and eventually board the plane at 8.

It's a twin-propeller plane from Jambo Airways, and I am one of five passengers. We take off at 8.15, and arrive at 8.35. The humidity is just as intense. I am forced to open my suitcase at a joke of a customs desk in Zanzibar Airport, where they take an inordinate interest in my unwashed clothing.

My taxi ride to the Tembo Hotel in Stonetown is in a 1953 Austin, which needs a push-start at every stop. Nothing on it seems to work, including the headlights. It's a 10-minute drive, US$10. The hotel is a magnificent example of old Zanzibar architecture, in need of renovation but beautifully located, overlooking the ocean. However, much to my horror, I discover it does not serve alcohol. I am given room 14, a sizeable room full of old Muslim furniture, and a large bed with mosquito netting. The bathroom is also spacious, and has a sunken bath. After washing and spraying myself with repellent, I walk to the Chit-Chat

Restaurant through narrow streets, where I am continually accosted by people offering taxis, guided tours and even someone's sister, arriving at the restaurant at 9.30.

It's an old, small, run-down place staffed by three people. I order chicken xacuti (a coconut-based chicken dish) with rice and Tusker beers. The food is acceptable, although tepid, and the bill comes to about £4.50. Afterwards, I go for a local Serengeti beer at a bar opposite my hotel which is full of German businessmen and very, very young prostitutes. I am propositioned by some that look younger than my daughters, naturally declining the offer, and am back at the hotel by 11.

The population of Zanzibar is 600,000, that of the neighbouring island of Pemba 200,000, and 80% of the export business of the latter is cloves. The place to be at 6 p.m. is a sunset view on the terrace of the Africa House Hotel, formerly the English Club, and the good news is it is licensed.

27.4.97. I eat a self-service breakfast on the beach terrace of the hotel: bungo juice, a croissant and instant coffee. There is no water in the room, so I am not able to shower; I am assured by the manager it will be working by tonight.

I book a three-hour walking tour of Stonetown from Cheema Travel, with an excellent guide by the name of Mawlidi Kigwa. Stonetown is being beautifully restored, thanks to the generosity of the Aga Khan. A fascinating itinerary takes in the famous door at Tippu Tip's House, the orphanage built in the late nineteenth century, the House of Wonders, the People's Palace, the Big Tree, Creek Road and Daranjani market, which sells fly-infested meat and live chickens (when you buy one, they chop its head off – what could be fresher than that?). Then it's on to the Christian Cathedral, the Peace Memorial Museum, the High Court of Justice, the Africa House Hotel, the magnificent new five-star Serena Inn Hotel, which is right on the beach and owned by the Aga Khan, and St Joseph's Catholic church. Having walked for three hours, my brand-new plimsolls have given me huge blisters on my little toes.

Back at the hotel by 1, I pop across the road for a very necessary 50cl bottle of Serengeti beer. Lunch at the hotel is kingfish stewed with green bananas, which is quite tasty, but as before served tepid. I accompany it with soda water! Afterwards, I take a dip in the hotel pool, then read and sleep. Returning to room 14, I find there is still no water – the manager informs me that he is unable to find a plumber – and so I request a move.

Room 207 is in the newer extension of the hotel, overlooking the pool and the Indian Ocean, but sadly there is no balcony. It's a slightly more modern room, and in a strange way, not as nice. Anyway, I am able to shower at last and wash my hair, and I book a table for dinner on the rooftop at the highly recommended Emerson's Restaurant.

I decide to walk, following the map I have been given by the travel guide. Theoretically, it's a mere five minutes, but after half an hour, I have to stop and ask, and am shown the way by somebody kind. The main problem seems to be that the map shows left as right and vice versa, though not entirely consistently. That, coupled with the fact that the restaurant has no sign outside, contrives to make the expedition something of a challenge. Emerson's looks a little like a building site but, nothing daunted, I climb the four flights of stairs to the roof terrace, which turns out to be amazing. It feels like a pagoda stuck on top of a roof. You must remove your shoes and sit on low cushions. It caters for a maximum 20 covers, and the sunset view is outstanding. At 6.30, a great wailing from the mosques fills the air.

I begin with a couple of gin and tonics, drunk to the sound of constant bells. Although I have something of a problem with eating in a squatting position, the food is certainly immaculate. A very tasty mixed dish of potato cake, vegetable samosa, lobster claw with chilli, shredded lemon chutney and shredded coconut is followed by more slightly chillied lobster, grilled kingfish masala with coconut, cinnamon and tomato rice, chocolate cake with some sort of strange liqueur, and guava ice cream. I drink a couple of Tusker beers with it, and have a whisky and soda digestif. While there, I meet a nice Swiss couple – both teachers – from Zürich.

28.4.97. I breakfast at 8 on scrambled eggs on toast, bungo juice and coffee, and am then collected at 9 by car for a drive to Kizimkai beach on the extreme southern tip of the island. The drive takes us through some superbly impressive trees and foliage, and then the tarmac road runs out, and the journey continues on a dirt road full of potholes. We arrive at 10.45.

The beach 'resort' consists of three huts at a tariff of about £2 a night. It is extremely basic and there is only one communal loo, which is flooded. Readying myself for a swim with the dolphins, armed with snorkel, flippers and mask, I wade out to a boat, which turns out to be half full of water, through a very choppy sea. Eventually, I catch sight of the dolphins, a superb experience. It's very overcast, and in due course starts to rain. This means I am unable to swim, as the water fills up with jellyfish during the rainy season.

Lunch, back at the resort, takes an hour to prepare and, when ready at 2 p.m., consists of grilled kingfish and chips. Not bad, and hardly expensive at about £1.80. I drink Sprite, as there is no alcohol.

Afterwards, I am driven to the Jozani rainforest for a brilliant one-hour walking tour, and then to another area to see the famous red monkeys, which are indigenous only to Zanzibar.

Delivered back at the hotel at 5, I have a cold beer in a bar opposite, which I now discover is called Le Pêcheur. I shower and arrange to have dinner at 7 with the Swiss couple I met at Emerson's. We have two large gin and tonics at Le Pêcheur at 6.30. Their 18-year-old tour guide recommends a terraced restaurant called the Oman, which we have a look at but decide against. We settle instead for the Camiors, a Goan Restaurant in what was originally Freddie Mercury's family house. I eat a good crab curry with coconut and rice and drink two Lion beers, all for £5, and am back at the hotel by 9.30.

29.4.97. After breakfasting at 8 a.m. (bungo juice, scrambled eggs, toast and coffee), I am met by the guide at 9 for the five-hour Spice Tour and a visit to the slave caves. It looks as though it's about to start raining and the wind is rising. In fact, it stays clear, and becomes hot and sunny by midday.

We drive north via the ruins of Marhubi to the Kizimbani spice area and visit a number of farms, some privately owned and some owned by the state. Everywhere, I smell cloves, vanilla, cinnamon, lemon grass, cardamom, pepper, ginger, chilli and turmeric. Some growers are experimenting with coffee and cocoa. There's fruit too in abundance: starfruit, mango, lime, passion fruit and bananas. Among the oddities are durian, a green spiked ball of a thing that smells absolutely appalling when opened and tastes like a kind of fruity potato, and the lipstick plant.

From there, we go to the Kibweni Palace, built in 1915 as a summer palace for the ex-sultan, and then to the original Persian/Turkish baths at Kidichi, which was full of bats. After that, we continue on to the far north of the island to see the slave caves at Mangarwani beach, quite a disturbing prospect when one thinks back to what they were used for, and from there to an amazing natural cave with fresh water on the north-west coast.

We then proceed on the usual shocking roads to Fuji beach, where we will have lunch with Mawlidi, our guide, who disappears at regular intervals to the mosque. Our driver Swalli looks to be easily over 80, but when we ask him, he estimates his age at something between 55 and 60, but isn't sure.

The restaurant is situated on a terrace on the beach, and is quite run-down. We are the only customers, as it's out of season. I drink two 50cl bottles of Safari lager, and eat a fish called changu, which is a bit like bream, in masala sauce with maize and chapatis. The fish is full of bones, and there is a plague of flies, a complete invasion in fact, making it almost impossible to eat. They even give you a cardboard lid to put over your glass of beer to keep the flies out, a total nightmare. The others are seemingly unperturbed and allow the flies to settle and wander all over their faces, bodies and food. Eventually, seeing my distress, they call over the waitress, who produces an enormous canister of insecticide and proceeds to spray it all over the table and the food. What a farce!

We drive back to the Tembo, arriving there at 4, and I have a much needed swim and sleep. Later, I meet the Swiss couple, Andreas and Hilda, at the newly built five-star Serena Hotel, which was only completed on March 14th this year. It too is owned by the Aga Khan. We pay $5 for a gin and tonic (about three times the usual) and $2 for a beer.

After aperitifs, we go to dinner at 8 at the Maharaja, an Indian restaurant nearby, where I have a couple of Kilimanjaro beers, an honest lamb curry and naan. I'm back at the hotel by 10.

30.4.97. I breakfast at 9 after a tremendous thunderstorm with incredible rainfall. I pack and phone home, and then suddenly the weather is sunny, warm and humid. I change 300 French francs, the only foreign currency I have left, as I have discovered that if payments are made by credit card, you pay an extra 10% for the privilege.

I take a walk around Stonetown at 11.30, and buy two beautifully carved wooden hippos by the docks for $2. I can't resist returning to the Serena for drinks and lunch. It is truly a superb hotel. I arrive at 12.15, just as it's starting to rain yet again. The rooms are US$180–500 bed and breakfast. The restaurant has wonderful views, which I appreciate from a table in the window. I have a Serengeti beer on the terrace and then two more with lunch at 1.30. Lunch is a pan-fried fillet of barracuda in a green coconut sauce, served with spinach, boiled potatoes and carrots, and another green vegetable that looks like a shrivelled cucumber. The portions are small, but it's all well cooked. It's $5 for the meal and the same for the beers. The hotel is full of Germans. At 2.30, the rain stops.

I return to the Tembo and pay a bill of $270, plus 10% for the use of the credit card, a scandalous charge. I sleep on the terrace for a while, but am awoken by the receptionist, who informs me that they have omitted to charge me for my call to London – US$54 for nine minutes. This surely has to go in *The Guinness Book of Records*.

I read until 7, and then have two large gin and tonics in Le Pêcheur opposite. I have dinner at 8 in their restaurant, good grilled kingfish and chips in large portions, with a Safari beer. The bill is £5. A live guitarist sings in many different languages.

At 9, I take a cab to the airport, $7. I am the only passenger boarding the flight here, and therefore the plane can take off straight away. It starts to leave at 9.35, an hour ahead of schedule, when a fire breaks out in the cabin, just next to the cockpit. All passengers who were on this Cape Town to Dar es Salaam flight, and who have been routed via Zanzibar just for me, are now evacuated. We all wait three hours in the stuffiness of the airport for a plane to be diverted from Nairobi to collect us. We finally arrive at Dar-es-Salaam at 1.30 a.m.

I am then taken on a 90 mph taxi drive in a broken-down old 1950s wreck with no lights. At 2, we arrive at the Agip Hotel and I am given room 212. For US$90 a night, the room is frankly disgraceful. The view from the window overlooks a rubbish tip.

1.5.97. I awake at 7.30, and after showering, have breakfast in the dining room – lemon juice, poached eggs, bacon, toast and coffee. At least, I order poached eggs, but what arrives, half an hour later, are two fried eggs with a tomato. The yolks are pale grey.

At 9.30, my car and driver/guide for the city tour, organised by Avis, arrives. It's $34, including a lift to the airport. We visit the roof of the Kilimanjaro Hotel, which commands a fine view of the coastline and city, and then drive to various beach resorts along the coast, past the President's villa, the embassies and so forth. There is much new development in evidence, undertaken by Indians and other Asians. We drop in at the fish market by the sea, which is absolutely incredible and a must to visit (lucky I have a guide with me to explain it all).

From there, it's off to Mwenge, a wood carving market, and then to the general market, which is both an outdoor and indoor affair on three floors. It sells everything from meat, fish, vegetables, fruit and rice to all manner of household goods, and is seething with people. Once again, I am lucky I have a guide with me. On the drive back, we stop off at the five-star Sheraton Hotel, a very impressive place that opened in 1996, and then arrive back at my own hotel at 1.

I have a light lunch of spring rolls with teriyaki chicken kebabs and two Safari lagers. Then I settle the outrageous bill of US$95 plus 20% tax for what was basically a two-star hotel room.

Fish Market, Dar-es-Salaam

I'm driven to the airport by a friendly Avis driver, who tells me he earns T$25 an hour. Once there, I check in for Air Zimbabwe flight UM 773, Dar-es-Salaam to Harare. We are scheduled to take off at 4.05, but in fact leave 30 minutes later. It's a 2½ flight. I watch the in-flight film and eat a snack meal.

We arrive at 5.45 local time, which is one hour behind Tanzania. David Simleit meets me and we drive to the Harare Club, where I am put in room 33. As it's May 1 and a public holiday, everything is closed, including the club. Eventually, a security guard is persuaded to let us in. My room is old-fashioned, in the colonial style, with no air conditioning, in what is clearly a very exclusive place.

I shower and change, and then we drive to David's house for a gin and tonic. From there, I go with David and his wife Jacqui to Buckler's Lodge, a five-star restaurant out of town. Our five-course set menu comprises: mixed smoked fish (tuna, swordfish and marlin); prawn and corn soup; giant prawns with rice and vegetables; chocolate mousse; and cheese. With this spread, we drink an excellent 1984 Meadows Estate L'Étoile, 1986 Meadows Gewürztraminer, Evans & Tate Sauvignon-Semillon, Evans & Tate Shiraz and a superb old Seppelt's Australian tawny port. I'm back at the Harare Club at 11.30, extremely tired.

2.5.97. I awake at 6.30 a.m. to lovely weather, blue skies and 25°C. This is indeed a very smart club (it's just a shame the rooms don't match). I take breakfast in the Flame Lily Room – mango juice, two poached eggs, bacon, grilled tomato, toast and coffee. I await Guy Anderson, who has been paragliding in the Eastern highlands of Zimbabwe on the Mozambique border. He arrives at 9.30, and then I check out of the Harare Club (good value at $20 B&B).

We drive to the Lion and Cheetah Park, which is 25 km out on the Bulawayo road, admission Z$100. This is a superb experience. The animals roam wild, run right up to your car, and there are lots of them. It's a very fine day, 26°C and sunny.

We have lunch by the pool at the Sheraton Hotel, spare ribs with two Bohlinger beers, and then we drive to AFDIS for an interesting tasting of their excellent Stapleford wines.

From here, we drive to the Cairns head office at Astra Park to collect our driver, Freddy, who will take us to the airport. We are upgraded to Business Class, which has three rows of eight seats.

On the flight, we are seated to one side, but are then asked if we could move to the other side, as President Mugabe's young pregnant wife and various kids have arrived, and the staff obligingly remove three rows in order to install a double bed for her. All this delays the flight for two hours. I drink Nederburg sparkling wine, and eat smoked salmon, followed by ostrich stew with rice, and then sleep for six hours. On waking, I am treated to a breakfast of rock-hard poached eggs, sausages, toast, apple juice, etc.

3.5.97. We land in London at 8.15 a.m. What a fascinating trip this has been.

Seychelles
28 March–13 April 1998

A Rare Family Holiday: Clare, Holly, Toby and Myself.

28.3.98. We are booked on flight BA 2069 via Nairobi to Mahé, scheduled to leave from Gatwick North Terminal at 22.05. We take off one hour late. I am in a row of four seats in a centre row (42) in the last cabin at the back, having originally been allocated seats 28/29 or 30/31, with extra legroom, or an upgrade to Business Class against the number of mileage points collected. On check-in, the BA rep denied that there was any mention of an upgrade in the computer, and then told me that seats 28/29 were not bulkhead seating. On arrival on the aircraft, I discovered that, much as I had thought, they were.

The plane is full, and I am not looking forward to the 11-hour flight. We are crammed in like cattle, with screaming babies everywhere. I therefore take a sleeping pill. Much as I had feared we are in the worse seats in the aircraft. I am the last to be served a whisky and soda. The food offered is some inedible chicken dish with very hot curried potatoes. Toby's vegetarian dish of rice covered with cheese and spinach looks revolting. Nobody else dares risk dinner. What a joke BA food is.

29.3.98. I read and sleep until 5.30 a.m. Breakfast comes round at 6, and consists of an ice-cold stale croissant, yoghurt and an indescribable cake. Even the coffee is stewed. The stewards, without exception, seem to ignore the call bells. Why anyone would choose to fly BA is beyond me.

We land in Nairobi at 10 a.m. local time, and are on the ground for two hours. Clare is feeling unwell. I attempt and fail once again to get a change in seat or an upgrade for the remaining leg of the journey. We take off again at noon.

As food and drink are served again, I take a couple of gin and tonics, and a little bottle of Domaine Virginie Marsanne 1997.

There is another appalling chicken dish in some unknown sauce (even the stewardess is unsure what it is), served with undercooked sweet potatoes.

We arrive in Mahé, 4 degrees south of the equator, (the largest of Seychelles' 115 granite and coral islands, owned by the British until 1976) at 3.45 p.m. local time, having queued for half an hour at Passport Control in very high humidity. The temperature is 33°C. For some strange reason, a Mini Moke and two taxis are waiting to take us, and our bags to the Sunset Beach Hotel, a 20-minute ride away, an amazing tropical resort on the north west coast.

The hotel is superb, and affords us a great reception with cocktails. We are in two adjacent bungalows, 12 and 14, right on the beach, the best rooms in the hotel. A complimentary bottle of South African sparkling wine is provided. I go off for a much needed swim in the Indian Ocean, quite magical.

After a shower, I take a gin and tonic in the Pool Terrace bar. Then we have an excellent table reserved, by the open window, in the restaurant overlooking the sea. Dinner is crab bisque, smoked fish salad, and red snapper in Creole sauce, with an accompanying chilled bottle of Bardolino Chiaretto, a light and refreshing Italian dry rose. Afterwards, we take our nightcaps on the terrace looking out over the waves. It is quite humid, and during the night there is a tremendous thunderstorm.

30.3.98. Awakening at 9, I go straight for a swim in the ocean, which is a mere ten feet from our bedroom. From the breakfast buffet, I have a light breakfast of two fried eggs, bacon, sausage, mushrooms, tomatoes and fried bread, with juices and coffee.

We go for a drive in our Mini Moke around the island, which is the largest in the Seychelles – 27 km by 8 km – with Victoria, the world's smallest capital, named after the British monarch, and main port housing 90% of the population. Mahé is typical of the granite islands, being mountainous and covered with jungle vegetation. Its highest point, indeed the highest point in the Seychelles, is Morne Seychellois at 905 metres. There are miles of superb, unspoiled coastline, stretches of virgin beach and palm trees, exactly as in the picture books. We stop off for a Seybrew (the local beer) at the Plantation Club on the south west coast – a ghastly complex, 200 rooms full of the wrong people. Then we drive on around the southern tip, and stop off for lunch at Oscar's overlooking the ocean. I opt for job fish in lemon wine, with half a litre of rosé. Holly and Clare have prawns, Toby has chicken kebabs wrapped in smoked bacon. This is a good restaurant indeed.

Arriving back at the hotel at 5 p.m., I take another much needed swim. We have gin and tonics on the terrace, before going to the manager's drinks party at 7, where there is lethal rum punch galore with nibbles. At 8.15, we embark on a fine buffet dinner. Conditions are now very humid and overcast, so dinner is served in the dining room rather than by the pool. Red snapper and onions are followed by roast beef, accompanied by Bardolino Chiaretto. After dinner, we play snooker, and dance to a live group, and round things off with a nightcap on our patio by the sea.

31.3.98. I awaken at 8 a.m. with severe cramp, owing to lack of water, I presume. (I really ought to drink more of the stuff.) It is overcast and raining a little. I go for a swim in quite a choppy sea. We book a glass-bottomed boat trip for tomorrow, to visit Cerf Island, in the St Anne Marine National Park, including a Creole barbecue lunch on the beach. I hope the weather improves.

We take lunch at our hotel, a beef curry with our usual intake of gin and tonics, beer and wine. It is still raining.

I sleep for an hour and a half, and then get up and play some snooker. We drive in the drizzle to see some nearby hotels, the Best Western, an awful place; Le Meridien Fisherman's Cove, which looks very good; the Coral Strand, a good location but very downmarket; the Auberge Club des Seychelles, good location but no beach, and the Northolme, which is the oldest hotel on the island with just 19 rooms. It's old-fashioned and run-down, but is situated high up and has a nice view and a literary history that boasts Ian Fleming and Somerset Maugham among its guests. Our hotel is without doubt the best of the bunch.

Later, we have drinks on our terrace, and then go to dinner at 8.15. We have fish balls, followed by red snapper, or 'Bourzwa' as it is called locally, in a saffron and shrimp sauce, with another bottle of Bardolino Chiaretto (the first bottle of which is oxidised). The choice of wines is somewhat limited, to say the least.

We are in bed by 10.30, but I have difficulty sleeping.

1.4.98. Up at 7.30 a.m., I swim in the ocean. The weather is fantastic once again: there are blue skies and the water is calm. Breakfast at 8 is sausages, bacon, scrambled eggs, mushrooms and fried bread, with coffee and juice.

We take a minibus to the harbour, where we board the boat at Victoria Harbour for the Marine Park, which is on the other side of Mahé. On the way, we feed the fish. The seas have astonishing coral formations here, and there is a huge variety of fish – sailfish, marlin, tuna, wahoo and rainbow runner. Eventually, we transfer to a submersible boat, like a mini-submarine, which travels on the ocean bed, where we get exquisite views of the coral and tropical fish.

Installed back on the first boat, we do some swimming and snorkelling, and then head off to Cerf Island for Seybrew beers and a buffet lunch cooked by 'Mother', as she is known. (The island has only thirty inhabitants.) She offers us sailfish in demarara sauce, curried tuna, chicken with coconut, and white and yellow rice – all superb.

After lunch, we walk around the island, and then take a slow cruise back among the adjacent islands. There is Round Island, Long Island, where the prison is, and Moyenne, which is privately owned by a Yorkshireman, who bought it in 1962 for £8000 and lives alone there.

Arriving back at the hotel at 4, I swim and shower, and then go for a drive in the Mini Moke to the remote North Point of the island.

Returning at 7, we have cocktails on the bar terrace, and then go to dinner at 8.30: fish soup, red snapper and onions, roulade of grey jackfish, and rice, followed by bananas cooked in a sweet, thick, sticky red sauce. Tonight we drink two halves of Bardolino Chiaretto, as they have run out of full-size bottles, and the day ends at 10 with another dramatic cloudburst.

2.4.98. This will be our last day on Mahé. I begin it at 8.30 with a swim in perfect weather – blue skies and a calm sea. It's 30°C and the humidity is 75% (which is in fact the year-round minimum). Another light breakfast at 9.15 comprises two fried eggs, bacon, sausage, tomatoes, mushrooms and fried bread, with juice and coffee. God, I am starting to be unable to get into my clothes.

We drive north for a fascinating visit to the perfume maker, who uses only herbs in his products, and then head south, intending to stop at the Sundown Restaurant for lunch, but they only open at 1.30 p.m., so we buy drinks next door, and then take a drive through the tea plantations.

At the Baptista Restaurant on the south-west coast, we have lunch on the beach. There are grilled prawns from the barbecue to start, followed by grey job fish, accompanied by a number of Seybrew beers and a 50cl bottle of off-dry South African rosé.

Later on, calamity nearly strikes, as we all but run out of petrol in the Forêt Noire; but by some miracle, we stumble on a petrol station in the middle of nowhere. At 3.30, we take the Spice Trail through the rainforest, a very humid, high-altitude trek, where I am bitten half to death by giant mosquitoes. The Trail itself is a most informative and worthwhile experience. Then we drive round the island and back to the hotel at 5, and swim in the pool in the still perfect weather.

At 7, of course, it's time for aperitifs, with dinner at 8.30. This consists of a smoked fish platter, grilled tuna Creole and rice, and with it, I order what is described on the wine list as 'PJ Belle Rosé' at around £32, but it turns out not to be Perrier-Jouët Belle Epoque, but a most disappointing off-dry Pierre Jourdan rosé from South Africa. Malt whiskies on the patio finish off a humid, but highly rewarding, day in style.

3.4.98. Following breakfast at 8.30, we pack in two separate lots. One batch of luggage is for Bird Island (a 10 kg allowance per person), and the rest will be staying at the Reservations Office on Mahé. We drive the Mini Moke, accompanied by taxis, to the airport, having checked out at 9.30. The hotel bill comes to £2,150.

We arrive for a 10.30 departure on a small 20-seater plane for

Bird Island, Seychelles, March 1998, 'Esmeralda'

the half-hour flight to Bird Island. It is so named because it houses a bird sanctuary, which is home to many species of rare bird (terns, noddies, etc.), as well as giant land tortoises, including Raphael, Jeremy and Esmeralda – the last a male who is 203 years old and weighs 305 kg! They have no need to hibernate, as the temperature is constantly high. The island is two miles around the perimeter, all pure white sand and blue seas.

We are staying in cottages 25 and 26, which are right at the end of the resort, nearest the beach – lovely open wooden cottages, with four-poster beds equipped with mosquito nets. There is a central open bar and restaurant, where we have a buffet lunch of curried pork, sailfish, job fish, rice and salads, and a 50cl carafe of rosé. The surroundings are pure magic.

Afterwards, we walk to the west side of the island, where there is more wind and wavy seas. The east side, by contrast, is calm, and perfect for snorkelling as the translucent turquoise sea is full of amazing fish. At this time of year, the island is a nesting ground for millions of white fairy terns, sooty terns, brown noddies, grey doves and many other breeds.

Following a good sleep, I swim in the calm, warm sea, and then take a drink on the terrace, where there are friendly lizards and not so friendly mosquitoes in abundance.

At 8, we go up to the restaurant, and play cards and pool, before dining on fish curry, chicken, rice and salads from the buffet, accompanied by a good bottle of Provence rosé. Afterwards, we find our way back to the bungalow with torches, so as to avoid stepping on the crabs. After a whisky nightcap, I am in bed at 11.

4.4.98. I awake at 8 after a fitful night's sleep. It's hot and humid, bearing in mind we are only two degrees from the equator, and there is an abundance of mosquitoes and flies, but nothing can spoil the magical atmosphere. After going for a swim, I take a much lighter breakfast of two poached eggs on toast, with coffee and mango juice.

We go to explore the southern part of the island, but I disastrously neglect to apply any sunblock. I spend two hours in the ocean, gathering loose coral in temperatures of 35°C and more.

During the buffet lunch of fish curry, chicken, salads and rice, I realise I have badly burned my thighs and lower legs, and am beginning to be in serious agony. I try to read and sleep fitfully through the afternoon.

At 7 p.m., I just make it down to the bar in excruciating pain, but I can barely walk. As we're on such a tiny island with no doctor or nursing facilities, the manager has to have first-aid training as part of his job. It is suggested I see him, and with a look of horror at the sight of my burned legs, he applies a wonderful soothing cream called Biafine, which relieves the pain somewhat. Dinner is a barbecue, with blue marlin, pork, chicken, jacket potatoes, rice and salads, with 50cl of rosé. I repair to bed at 9.30 in extreme pain.

I pass a fitful night, but the cream is gradually working, and I awake at 7 a.m. a little more relieved from the agony.

5.4.98. It's a broiling hot, but slightly overcast, day. The first thing to do is to apply more cream to my burned skin, and anti-sting ointment for the mosquito bites. Breakfast at 8.15 is poached eggs, papaya and coffee.

At 9, dressed in a sarong to protect my legs, we embark on a nature tour to view the stunning variety of bird life: lemon and brown noddies, fairy and sooty terns, all just arriving for the season, thousands of them flying above and about the bird sanctuary. This is followed by a swim, a couple of beers and then lunch: fried fish, sausage curry, rice and salads, accompanied by 50cl of off-dry South African jug rosé.

After reading and sleeping for a while, we take a walk round the whole island. It takes about an hour, and demonstrates the amazing contrasts there are between the constant breeze and waves off the west coast and the calm seas and humidity to the east.

There's time to fit in a little more reading, before repairing to the bar at 7 for rum and sodas, and then dinner at 8, which is grilled fish and rice with a bottle of the Provence rosé (£16). I am in bed by 11.

6.4.98. I take breakfast at 8.30 after what can only be described as another fitful night. I have been bitten again in places that even I find difficult to imagine one can be bitten in. We pack and then settle the bill for the extras, which come to around £200, bringing the total cost of three nights on Bird Island to £2,100.

The 12.45 flight to Mahé is slightly delayed to 1 p.m. It's a half-hour flight, and our connection to the island of Praslin is 1.30, making it very tight. We eventually arrive at 1.50, to be met by immediate confusion over the car hire. We are booked with Vallée Car Hire, but what we are presented with is a different car under a different name and hotel to us. This turns out to be a cowboy company called Prestige. When I try to confirm the booking details, the driver tries to sign me up for a jeep at 350 rupees a day. We eventually track down the rep from Vallee Car Hire, who had fallen asleep behind a tree and forgotten to bring our car. He then agrees to deliver a Mini Moke to our hotel, the Paradise Sun, at 9 a.m. tomorrow. A taxi to our hotel costs 125 rupees.

A further unsatisfactory scene awaits us on arrival. Although the reservation was made last November, and a 50% deposit paid, for rooms 23 and 24 (the best cottages on the beach), it turns out they have already been allocated to friends of the general manager, who have decided to arrive at the last minute. Confusion reigns. We are offered 49 and 51 instead, amid much bowing and scraping and apologies from the general manager, Mr Roche, who is impressively decked out in gold chains. We settle eventually on 51 and 52, where the view isn't bad, and we will be accorded a 50% reduction in the bill.

The beach is glorious and a swim soon washes away the aggravation, as do aperitifs on our terrace. A buffet dinner is served on Mondays, Wednesdays and Fridays in the Beach Restaurant. It is a generous one too, comprising job fish, tuna, mullet, snapper and chicken. We drink a bottle of acceptable 1996 Bellingham South African rosé. A live group plays, and during the course of proceedings all the under-managers come over to apologise again for the mix-up over the rooms.

I am in bed by 10.30.

7.4.98. We spend the day driving around this very pretty island. When the Frenchman Lazare Picault first came upon the 37 square kilometre island of Praslin on June 10th 1744, in virtually uncharted waters of the Seychelles, he called it the Island of Palms, so impressed was he with its unbelievable lush vegetation. A century ago, General Gordon of Khartoum visited the island and became convinced that it was the location of the original Garden of Eden. He developed this idea when he saw the strange shape of the coco de mer, the enormous coconut, which resembles a female pelvis.

Lunch is at Bon Bon Plume, involving an extraordinary journey to this restaurant right on the beach. We also take a look at Capri Restaurant, which looks awful, and at Les Rochers, rated as the best restaurant on Praslin, where they specialise in curried fruit bat.

Later, a light dinner in the hotel restaurant finishes a delightful day.

8.4.98. I begin the day with a 7 a.m. swim. What a glorious day it is too: blue skies, sunshine and breeze. We have a full cooked breakfast at 8.30.

We then take the Mini Moke to Vallée de Bai, the protected nature reserve. A guided tour for four is £25, lasts 90 minutes, and takes in the rare black parrot, bulbul, blue pigeon, sunbird and the bizarre coco de mer trees, both male and female (the female nut to me has the precise appearance of a vagina). All in all, it provides a fascinating insight into the richly varied plant and bird life of Praslin.

Lunch is taken at the excellent Indian Island Lodge Hotel, right on the beach – local fish, prawns, beers and rosé wine – and is preceded and followed by a swim.

Afterwards, we take the Mini Moke to the top of the island, up roads riddled with huge potholes. We labour up 30% inclines in first gear, with the engine overheating, and are rewarded with breathtaking views from the peak, from where one can see many of the other islands.

Arriving back at the hotel at 5, I take another swim, and then we avail ourselves of the Beach Restaurant's buffet and barbecue dinner of various fish and meats. This really is an excellent location.

9.4.98. Following my 7 a.m. swim, we reserve sunbeds by the ocean for later. Breakfast at 8.30 is scrambled eggs, bacon, sausage, baked beans, mushrooms and tomatoes (I am beginning to look like the Michelin Man), following which I laze, read, swim and sleep by turns. It is a slightly overcast and humid day.

At 1 p.m., we take the 15-minute walk to the expensive La Réserve Hotel, situated in Anse Petit Cour, the next cove. This is a disappointing place that gives the impression of trying to be smart. It has a small, unkempt beach and no swimming pool, but boasts an incredible location for its restaurant, on a jetty that projects into the ocean, where we have superb grilled parrotfish with hot Creole sauce and very good octopus curry, washed down with a carafe of South African rosé. Dessert is intended to be a crêpe flambéed with rum and served with chocolate sauce and fresh fruit salad. It gets returned, as it hasn't been flamed and there is no chocolate sauce. The bill for four comes to about £60.

I read, swim and sleep once more in the afternoon. After tea at 4, there is a coconut-opening demonstration. Toby takes himself off, determined to open one, and actually succeeds. Later, we have cocktails on the terrace, followed by the buffet and barbecue dinner in the Beach Restaurant, as last night, to the sounds of a live reggae group. I am in bed by 11.

10.4.98. After a swim at 7.15 a.m., we reserve sunbeds again under the palm trees, staying around the hotel throughout the day. Lunch in the Beach Restaurant is fish curry. Holly and Toby go off for a scuba-diving lesson. An excellent Creole cookery demonstration takes place, and later there is a bonfire and dancing. We round off the day with the 8 o'clock barbecue.

11.4.98. Our anniversary is a hot day with a slight breeze. I begin with my usual swim at 7.30 a.m. convinced that all this exercise will reduce the extra weight I seem to have accumulated.

Today we shall go to the neighbouring island of La Digue, the fourth largest island, with its giant granite boulders and population of Paradise Catcher birds. A small speedboat leaves from the beach outside the hotel at 10. It's been organised by the gregarious Lesley, a very dark-skinned South African. The crossing to La Digue takes 20 minutes.

Once there, we hire bicycles to get us around the little roads, favouring them over the ox carts, the other mode of transport. In fact, I haven't been on a bicycle for forty years, but I just manage to control the thing after crashing into Clare a couple of times (I was to gain a little more cycling experience in the Maldives). We visit the farm and President's house where our Prime Minister, Tony Blair, stayed.

Lunch is taken in a small restaurant, and consists of grilled local fish, rice and salad, with a number of Seybrew beers. Afterwards, Holly and Toby go off with a group on an arduous journey to the famous beach, Grand Anse, where the Bacardi advert was shot. The tide is very high. Clare and I embark on a gentle bike ride around the island. The La Digue Lodge Hotel looks smart and has a good location. We go up to Plantation House, set in the midst of a coconut grove by the sea with its splendid array of plant life, and then back to the pier at 4.30. The others have been delayed, so we take the boat back at 5.30, and have drinks on the terrace.

For our anniversary, the hotel has organised a table on the beach for dinner with Bellingham sparkling wine waiting in ice buckets. Our food, served by the head waiter, Dan, comprises pea and ham soup, assorted hors d'oeuvres and smoked fish, a whole grilled jackfish, prawn kebabs, oxtail, pork, corn and vegetables, the latter served by the chef. The pièce de résistance is an anniversary cake with a sparkler in it, completing a thoroughly romantic scene. This is a very professionally run hotel in a superb location.

12.4.98. After a 7 a.m. swim, we have drinks on the beach. Lunch, later, is chicken curry. We are back at the airport at 5.30 for a flight to Mahé, from where we will pick up the 7 p.m. connecting flight to Gatwick, via Nairobi. Once again, we have to endure BA and dreadful seats (row 35). I sleep until Gatwick.

We get in at 6 a.m. It's snowing.

Morocco
13–23 April 2002

13.4.02. Clare and I arrive at Heathrow Terminal 1 by taxi at 1 p.m., for the British Airways flight BA 6918 to Casablanca, scheduled to leave at 15.40 but delayed until 16.40. The plane is full, but they manage to find us two seats together right at the back. Ah well – what does one expect using Air Miles?

The Tap and Stile pub in Terminal 1 is a pathetic excuse for a bar, with no dry white wine and – calamity! – no champagne. I settle for a large Bloody Mary. Somebody should at some stage have instructed the barmaid that Tabasco is not the same thing as Worcestershire sauce, because the finished article almost has me in need of an oxygen tent.

As a result of our being seated at the back of the aircraft, there is nobody else between us, but the seats don't recline. They are also right by the loos, the endless queues for which make the journey a nightmare. A much needed bottle of Charles Heidsieck mis en cave 1997 goes down very well after take-off. BA's traditional attempt to produce any kind of edible food has just as traditionally failed. The salmon with mashed potatoes is reminiscent of Billingsgate after a week's holiday, and is totally inedible.

The weather forecast for Casablanca is rain and cold, we learn, and we duly arrive at 6.30 local time (one hour behind) in torrential rain. A courtesy car from the Royal Mansour Meridien is waiting for us. The chauffeur explains in French patois that it has been raining for the past two days, but is sure to stop tomorrow – 'just for you'. The hotel is 25 km from the airport in the old part of town, very near the medina and the souks. Casablanca has become the industrial capital of Morocco, with high-rise office blocks much in evidence. The newly built Hyatt Hotel has opened a Bar Casablanca based on Rick's Bar in the film, where the pianist endlessly plays 'As Time Goes By'.

We kick off our first evening with drinks in the hotel's

distinctly colonial-looking conservatory bar, the Winter Garden (there is also a bar on the ninth floor with a great view), with a five-year-old rum and soda. The Royal Mansour is generally reckoned to be the best hotel in the city, and was designed by the architect of the Georges V in Paris. Room 209 is £300 a night.

The hotel restaurant where we have dinner is called Le Douira, and serves authentic Moroccan food. We sit on low comfortable sofas, and listen to very good traditional music from a guitarist and singer. From the menu, we choose pastilla aux pigeons (minced pigeon with dates and onions in a sweet pastry case), pastilla aux fruits de mer et épinard (mixed white fish and prawns with spinach in a savoury pastry case), tagine de lotte m'charmel aux poivrons et tomates (monkfish tagine with peppers, tomatoes and olives, which is quite spicy but not great), and tagine de poulet beldi m'hamas aux amandes grillées (a dispiritingly greasy chicken tagine with grilled almonds and way too many olives). With the food, we drink S de Siroua rosé 2000 at 200dh (dirham), a well-balanced, deeply coloured, dry Cabernet rosé with a clean finish.

We retire at 11.30.

14.4.02. Breakfast, at 8.30, is served in the Colonial Terrace breakfast room, and consists of an omelette with onions, bacon, sausages, etc., and a superb range of fruit juices, from which I choose peach.

A guided visit to the Grand Mosque of Hassan II has been arranged for us at 10. Completed in 1994, it sits on a vast platform of reclaimed land to the west of the port. It is the largest mosque in the world outside Mecca, with a prayer hall that can accommodate up to 25,000 faithful, and cost over $1bn to build. The interior is a feather in the cap for Moroccan architecture, purely on account of its grandiose size. A glass elevator carries you up the side of the colossal minaret (the tallest in the world, at 700ft), which is topped with a green laser beam pointing in the direction of Mecca.

Abdullah, the driver of our air-conditioned Mercedes, later takes us down to the beach resorts along the Corniche, which look very similar to Southend or Blackpool, and to the smart residences of the rich, an area more reminiscent of Beverly Hills.

After returning to the hotel, we take a walk to the Hyatt for a 50cl bottle of a local beer, Flag, in the famous Bar Casablanca. The place is filled with memorabilia from the film, the waiters are all dressed as Humphrey Bogart in trench coats and fedoras, and as noted, the pianist plays *that tune* ad nauseam.

Leaving that behind, we take a long walk through the medina, each section of which specialises in a different kind of produce – spices, fish, meat, pulses, musical instruments and so forth. Watch out for the young teenage guides who offer to chaperone you free of charge through the medina, and are really only working on improving their English. At the end, they hassle you for a fee, expecting to receive at least £10.

Back at the hotel at 1.30, we take lunch in the Winter Garden brasserie, lamb chops and vegetables accompanied by a 2000 Guerrouane rosé, a light, dry wine with fairly high acidity, but perfect for lunch. By now, the clouds have cleared, resulting in lovely afternoon conditions.

At 5.30, I go for a Turkish bath, followed by a one-hour massage.

Dinner tonight will be at a restaurant called La Mer, reached by means of a £5 petit taxi. The place is situated on the coast by El Hank lighthouse, and has a majestic view over the rocks out to the Atlantic Ocean. Entering it is like stepping back fifteen years, with over-attentive waiters in white jackets and bow ties, and notably indifferent cooking – a place clearly resting on its laurels. In the international section of the wine list, under Portugal, I find 'Mathew's Rosé'…

A bottle of the S de Siroua rosé 2000 accompanies filet de rouget (a passable warm red mullet on potatoes), gratin de poissons (a clumsy mixed seafood dish with a cheesy top, flashed under the grill), loup florentine (sea bass and spinach in a white sauce made with mustard), a tepid timbale of rice, and brochette de loup (skewered sea bass), with another tepid timbale of rice and a portion of undercooked ratatouille. A petit taxi takes us back to the Royal Mansour for a large green Chartreuse, which happens to be old stock from a bottle about twenty years old. Excellent.

We retire peacefully at midnight, having decided that Casablanca only really needs a couple of days maximum to take it all in.

15.4.02. The day dawns with blue skies, just spotted with a little cloud. When we go down to breakfast at 8 a.m., we find the resident pianist from last night still playing. Is she just completing a night shift?

At 9.30, we take the Marrakesh express train, with seats in the First Class compartment. The route takes you through the villages of Berrechia, Settat, Khemisset, Benguerir and Bou Nagar. To the east of Settat lies the desolate phosphate mining region and Morocco's greatest river, the Oum Erbia. About 50 km west of Settat is the impressive Kasbah de Boulaouane, and the revitalised vineyards famous for their Gris de Boulaouane. The train then rumbles on through vast expanses of scrubland, dotted sporadically with farms, ending its three-hour journey in Marrakesh.

On arrival, we find a liveried chauffeur waiting to collect us and take us to the La Mamounia Hotel. Built in 1923, this is the city's premier hotel, with 171 rooms and 57 suites, and featuring wonderful original tiles and mosaics. There are also five Restaurants: Moroccan, Italian, French (all very smart, and requiring jacket and tie), a brasserie and a poolside buffet. Churchill was a frequent visitor here and painted many pictures in the 32-acre gardens, which were once the royal grounds. Our superb de luxe room, 116, has a balcony overlooking the gardens.

A buffet lunch by the pool begins with Casablanca beer, and also includes a bottle of Cuvée du Président Cabernet rosé, a full-bodied, dry rosé of good length, which makes a perfect partner for my couscous.

After a swim, we take a walk to the souks and the main square, the sprawling market of Place Djemaa el Fna, overlooked by the magnificent twelfth-century Koutoubia minaret is a cacophony of cars, mopeds, donkeys, jugglers, story tellers, fortune-tellers, snake charmers, and various food stalls selling snails, liver, hearts, and goat's head soup, all cooked in situ. We sip mint tea on the terrace of the restaurant Argana, overlooking the whole square – what a sight, straight out of *The Arabian Nights*. Wandering on through the warren of winding streets in the medina, we encounter shops and stalls purveying virtually anything one could imagine, with spices, pulses, musical instruments, carpets that are woven on the spot, shoes, brassware, and much else vying for one's attention. We return to the hotel at 6.30 by horse-drawn carriage.

Later, we have drinks – Dewar's and soda – in the Churchill Bar, a piano bar adorned with photographs of jazz musicians that constitute an entertaining, and quite demanding, quiz. While trying to identify all the musicians, I spot a mistake. A picture that I am convinced is of Eric Dolphy has been captioned Charles Mingus. Sure enough, when I mention it to the barman, he confirms that many other guests have pointed this out, and I am given a free drink for spotting it.

At 8.30, a petit taxi takes us to Le Toblis, a restaurant in the Riad Catallina, in the heart of the medina. We sample ten starter dishes, served in similar style to a Greek meze: sweet tomatoes in cinnamon (**); liver and olives (***); a spinach and cheese pastry (***); aubergine (*); celery and mint (**); tomatoes, peppers and onions (*); courgettes in parsley (*); sweet peppers (*); ratatouille (**); and leavened bread. These are followed by a brilliant tagine of small chicken (poussin), slow-cooked with raisins (****), and that in turn by a first-class lamb tagine with onions and artichokes, cooked in a superb stock (***). These are succeeded by good vegetable couscous (**), and the repast concludes with poached pear in an orange marinade with strawberries and blanched almonds. With regard to tagine, the top restaurants clearly know how to cook it so that it avoids greasiness. The dishes are slow-cooked, with the skin being left on the chicken, the fat on the lamb and so forth, in a sealed earthenware pot.

With the food, we drink two bottles of Cuvée du Président rosé. The wine waiter tells me that, although they don't have it, I should try a local brandy that is made from figs.

This really is a restaurant you have to know about. It would be almost impossible to find it without a guide, situated as it is right in the middle of the medina. It should by rights be advertised with the slogan 'Come hungry', as there is no indication in any of the write-ups that it serves a fixed menu.

16.4.02. On another day of what looks to be perfect weather, we breakfast at 8 a.m. from a full buffet for £12. There are numerous cereals, scrambled eggs, sausages, bacon, potatoes with onions, tomatoes in garlic, two types of soup, various breads and superb coffee.

At 9.15, we are taken on a guided tour of the souks, on foot. These are the markets of the medina, occupying a maze of very narrow streets to the north of Djemaa el Fna. Business peaks in the late afternoon. The main entrance to the souks is at the opposite end of the square to the Koutoubia minaret. An alley directly facing the Café de France, just left of the Restaurant al Fath, takes you to the potters' souk. Forking right off this is the route to the apothecaries' souk, where you can find all the spices, roots and herbs used in medicine and magic spells. Here one can buy mandrake root, a well-known aphrodisiac, the Viagra of Morocco. Following the streets onward, one finds leather and wooden goods, silks, antiques and clothes. Realistically, it would take a good two days to explore it all fully.

Our guide claims to remember taking Winston Churchill on just such a tour as this. It proves to demand a supreme effort to keep up with him as he weaves his way through the endless covered alleyways. The first stop takes us to the section selling herbs, spices, cures and lotions, where we are accorded a full initiation into the various oils and aromatics, including a neck and back massage and a most interesting lecture.

After another twenty minutes of breakneck walking, we arrive at our second stop, the carpet emporium, which extends over six huge, cavernous underground rooms, crammed with carpets and tapestries from the Lower and Middle Atlas Mountains. Our guide then proceeds at his usual rate of knots through never-ending winding alleyways, each section specialising in its own specific range of artefacts or produce. In one part, we see construction work at its most basic going on: a hole in the ground just big enough for one man, in which he works hoisting up bucket after bucket of black mud. As this is going on in the middle of an already extremely narrow pathway, chaos ensues. He has put down only a single foot-wide plank to act as a walkway, although this is a two-way pedestrian thoroughfare and the street is only about four feet wide altogether. Having spent twenty minutes negotiating the plank, I console myself with the purchase of a bright red fez, à la Tommy Cooper.

A brisk walk takes us back to the hotel for a well-deserved Casablanca beer or two, followed by a light lunch of ravioli stuffed with fresh herbs, Caesar salad and a chilled bottle of Cuvée du Président rosé. A walk around the river and garden, with an excellent massage to follow, sets us up well for the night ahead.

A bourbon and soda in the Churchill Bar at 7.30 is accompanied by a live pianist and singer, Paul Balfour, a fine entertainer from Las Vegas. Surveying the photos of jazz musicians again, I come upon another two mistakes. We have dinner in the Moroccan restaurant in the hotel, which is beautifully furnished in traditional style. Lamb and lentil soup precedes pastilla made with minced rabbit and raisins, and tagine of veal, onions and tomatoes. Another bottle of the Cuvée du Président turns out to be slightly corked. A highly accomplished belly dancer performs as we eat.

We continue the evening with a visit to the hotel casino, which has a section of slot machines, and another of roulette and blackjack tables. I opt to play at the quiet roulette table, and discover that it has a minimum 50dh bet (about £4). I put 50dh on 10 black, and what should come up but – 10 black! The croupier is stunned as I walk out with 2,500dh (£150). Returning to the Piano Bar, we meet Guy Barker, the well-known British jazz trumpeter, and round off the evening enjoying copious drinks with him and Paul, the pianist, until 1 a.m.

17.4.02. The weather today is overcast and cool. We breakfast at 8.30 in the Bar du Soleil on croissants and espresso, and then begin the day with a city tour at 9.15, our guide for which, Mohammed, curiously has only four toes on each foot.

We start with the Koutoubia mosque with its 252 ft minaret, and then continue at the mid-twelfth-century gates of the Kasbah, which were built by Sultan Abd el Moumen at the same time as the Koutoubia mosque. The El Mansour mosque, also known as the Masque of the Golden Balls, is reached by a tortuous drive through tiny alleyways, past tiny shops selling chicken and rabbits killed, plucked and skinned while you wait, and then we press on to the Tombs of the Saadian Princes, where our special guide is a one-legged, one-eyed man who looks as though he has been resurrected from the tombs himself. They were built in the sixteenth century by Ahmed el Mansour, and were walled up around a hundred years later by the vengeful Sultan Moulay Ismail. They then lay forgotten until 1917, when their existence was revealed in French aerial photographs. A passageway was cut through the wall, exposing the sumptuously decorated pavilions where the Saadian imperial families lie buried.

The Bahia Palace dates from the nineteenth century, and is set in two acres with separate chambers for the harem, and each room boasting a differently carved ceiling, while the Ben Youssef Medersa is a religious school and college founded in the fourteenth century, decorated in the Andalusian style, currently undergoing impressive restoration of its rich mosaics, filigree stuccowork and intricately carved ceilings.

Back at the hotel, we eat a buffet lunch by the pool of kebabs, steak, lobster and salad, accompanied by another bottle of our favoured Cabernet rosé, following which the hotel manager kindly conducts us on a mini-tour of the hotel suites, including the Winston Churchill suite, which is adorned with some of his original paintings and memorabilia. It costs £1,000 a night. The Presidential suite on the fourth floor is comprised of two bedrooms, two large sitting rooms and a drawing room, and is £3,000 a night.

Leaving the hotel again, we walk to the Place Djemaa el Fna, and the Riad Tamsna, which has been beautifully restored to house an art gallery, tea house and bookshop. This is very difficult to find, as it is hidden among a myriad alleyways. A map is most definitely needed. We head back to the main square, which is by now filling up with snake charmers and street dentists, the latter proudly displaying their most recent extractions.

Over drinks in the hotel's Piano Bar at 8, we meet up with Guy Barker again, and then all go to dinner at Dar Marjana in the old part of the medina, a cleverly converted riad, which serves a fixed-price menu of 550dh (around £30, inclusive of all wines).

We start with 12 meze dishes, and then go on to a dish of baby pigeon cooked in a sort of pasta wrapping, tagine of lamb, couscous, and almond filo pastry. The Cuvée du Président rosé is served in unlimited quantity, and we finish off with a tot of mahlia, the fig brandy I have been searching for – an interesting experience. Guy has been great company, amusing us with a seemingly unlimited stock of stories.

Back at the hotel bar, we have a final bourbon nightcap, and get to bed at 1.30.

18.4.02. After a full buffet breakfast at 8.30, we check out an hour later, and pick up a Toyota from the budget car hire for £100 a day.

We're heading for Ouarzazate on the N9. The road passes through various villages – Ait Ourir, Ait Barka, Taddert and Amerzgane – that are typical of the northern slopes of the High Atlas, where corn can be seen ripening in the sun on the packed earth roofs of the stone houses. The road then continues across the territory of the powerful Glagva tribe, where a number of ancient kasbahs and fortified granaries can be seen. We then reach Taddert, a characteristic Moroccan mountain village set among walnut trees, which used to be the first staging post on the caravan route between Marrakesh and Ouarzazate. Traders still gather here to sell semi-precious stones and fossils that they have found in the mountains.

We then enter the Tizi N'Ticka pass, which climbs to a height of 7,415 ft, the road winding over tortuous bends. Sadly, conditions are misty, and so we are unable fully to appreciate the reportedly astonishing views.

Finally, at 2 p.m., we arrive at the Meridien Berber Palace Hotel in Ouarzazate. This is a new Saharan town, created as a garrison by the French in the late 1920s, with an array of modern hotels set along the main highway. During the 1980s, it was a boom town that was also home to film studios. *Lawrence of Arabia* was made here in 1962, and *The Sheltering Skies* in 1990. The town didn't quite survive on soldiering and film-making, however, and today it looks shabby and run-down, rather depressing, although the kasbah is certainly worth a view.

The Berber Palace was built in the 1990s, and is a replica of an ancient palace. We are given a small suite, 222, which is quite stark, dark and basic. Lunch by the pool is Flag beer and a bottle of Ksara rosé from Meknes, a light wine with fairly high acidity. These accompany chicken salad and a rather dry club sandwich. It then starts to rain, and continues to do so until 5.30, at which point I have what turns out to be a disappointing 30-minute hammam and sauna.

The hotel is in need of complete refurbishment and renovation to maintain its five-star classification, and the poor service and lack of attention to detail do little to alleviate matters. Later, we have drinks – a Black & White and soda for me – in the large, unattractive bar, which has no atmosphere at all.

Dinner is taken in the Moroccan Restaurant on the first floor of the hotel, which used to be their nightclub, and is quite ornately furnished with sofas and low tables. The fixed-price menu is 550 dh, and comprises a shared pastilla of pigeon, couscous royale with lamb (which is very disappointing, containing too much couscous and not enough of anything else), and a quartet of poor chicken kebabs for Clare. The bottle of Ksara rosé we order has to be sent back as it has oxidised, but the 2000 Président rosé with which we replace it is as excellent as ever.

As we have an early start tomorrow, we retire at 10.30. We are driving to the valley and gorge of Dades, which rambles eastwards of Ouarzazate, and is the harshest and most desolate of the southern valleys.

19.4.02. Setting off at 8 a.m., we drive through Skoura, a souk village 30 km east of Ouarzazate, through the Valley of the Roses and the village of Kelaa des Mgouna, which is famous for its rosewater, and thence to Boumalue, a bird-watcher's haven.

The Dades Valley and gorge is formed of high limestone cliffs and weirdly shaped erosions. We drive 25 km through the valley and into the gorge itself, with its majestic scenery. Four kilometres further on, the road begins to turn into a hairpin corniche, offering the most awe-inspiring views I have ever encountered, and passes the Hill of Human Bodies, so named for its strangely shaped rock formations. After 60 km, we come to Msemrie, after which you need a four-wheel-drive car.

Heading back, the views are equally stunning, but seen of course from a different perspective. The whole round trip takes six hours, with only one short stop for water, and has to be considered one of the world's finest drives.

Back at the hotel, we shower and have drinks in the bar. Of the six whiskies listed, only two are actually in stock – Ballantine's and Black & White. After a couple of those with soda, we go to a locally recommended restaurant, Fint, set high up overlooking the kasbah in a wonderful setting, which we make the most of by sitting outside on the terrace. Sad to say, though, we are the only patrons.

We eat briourte panaché, deep-fried beef with spices in what looks like a spring roll, together with egg in filo resembling a samosa, then beef tagine with vegetables, which turns out to be the best tagine we have tasted thus far. A bottle of Guerrouane rosé 2000 is light and fresh, and we also enjoy the Sidi Ali mineral water.

Returning to the hotel for a nightcap, we find they are now down to one whisky only – the Black & White. We turn in for an early night, as we shall have another early start in the morning.

20.4.02. We breakfast at 6.30 on carrot juice and omelettes, and then check out. The room was £100 a night, and I leave an appropriate note for the manager with my comments.

Taroudant, a four-hour drive, is our destination today. We head out along the N9 once again, passing through Tazenakht, a carpet-making centre, Taliounine, where saffron is grown in the surrounding hill country, harvested in September and October and sold through the cooperative in town, Aoulouz, an ornithological centre, and Ouland Behil, with its extinct volcano. The remaining drive proceeds through expanses of scrubland and sleepy villages, until you reach Taroudant, with its majestic red ochre circuit of ancient walls. It is one of the most elegant towns in Morocco, a friendly, laid-back place with a sixteenth-century market, open for business on Thursdays and Sundays, and a regional souk where Berbers bring in their wares.

Driving through the town, I contrive to get us slightly lost, forgetting how very strict the police are with regard to speed limits, which are no higher than 20–30 mph in the town centres. I am duly stopped by an absolutely furious policeman pointing at the car and screaming the word, '*Vitesse!*' Pleading ignorance of the French language – 'No French speak!' – I politely point out that the car is a Toyota and not a Vitesse, and naturally he lets me go without another word.

One kilometre to the west of the town is situated the Gazelle d'Or, one of the finest – if not the very finest – hotels in Morocco. It was built in the 1920s as a hunting lodge by a French baron, and was converted into a five-star hotel after the Second World War. Thirty-two cottages are set in acres of gardens and orange groves, and each cottage is like a private suite with its own terrace and garden. It is, quite simply, one of the greatest hotels I have ever stayed in (and £500–1,000 a night).

We settle straight away to an indifferent poolside buffet lunch of red mullet and salads, accompanied by a bottle of the Président rosé. The afternoon continues with a swim and a massage, and the temperature hits 31°C. It is quite something just to relax on the terrace outside our cottage overlooking the magnificent gardens.

In the evening, I shower and change for dinner. A jacket and tie are required. We begin with drinks on the terrace outside the restaurant. I have a J&B and soda, and Clare orders a bourbon sour, before deciding that she would like a straight bourbon with soda as her second drink. Neither of two waiters seems capable of understanding the latter order, and I try to assist by explaining that the bourbon on their list is Four Roses. This only partially helps in that the drink that then arrives is another bourbon sour. The second attempt is literally four roses, a bouquet in a vase, with a bottle of soda.

Dinner is a fixed menu that changes daily, as you can only stay full or half board. We decline the soup and pudding, but opt for farfalle with salmon in a cream sauce, and then mechiou, slow-cooked shoulder of lamb in its skin, served with a beetroot crisp and mangetouts, and accompanied by a small bowl of ground cumin. This is a dry and boring dish. We finish with a creamily pleasant Moroccan goats' cheese. With the lamb, we drink 1998 Les Coteaux de l'Atlas 1er cru red at £25, which comes in a smartly presented and serial-numbered bottle, and is deeply coloured, with a nose of Cabernet Sauvignon, medium body and a good finish.

Sadly, the cooking lets down an otherwise superb and unique establishment. This is a very old-fashioned place – not in decor, which is excellent, but in old-school politeness – which extends to the courtesy that residents are not asked to sign for any food or drink they order.

21.4.02. I rise at 8.30 to be greeted by another fine day, with 31° of heat and just a slight breeze, and go for a refreshing swim. Breakfast is served only on the terrace of your cottage or villa, and consists of fresh orange juice made from the produce of their own gardens, croissants with home-made honey, and coffee.

Checking out at 11.30, we drive to Essaouira, some 350 km distant along the N10, through Ouland Tema, Inazgane Ait Mello (which boasts a good restaurant, La Pergola), and on to the Atlantic port of Agadir, first colonised by the Portuguese in the fifteenth century and reclaimed by the Saadians in the sixteenth. It suffered a huge earthquake on February 29th 1960, with 15,000 people killed and 50,000 left homeless. The town was completely rebuilt in 1960s style, and now lacks all soul. It still has a large working port, though.

The N1 road follows the Atlantic coastline with stunning views as you meander along the twisty roads, passing through Taghazoute, a fishing village, a smart village called Paradise Place, the lighthouse at Cap Rhir, Tamanar, Simou, and then through the argon tree forests that are scattered over the sides of the High Atlas Mountains. The berries of these trees yield argon oil, and attract tree-climbing goats when ripe.

Eventually, we arrive on the coast at Essaouira, a thriving seaside and fishing port where Orson Welles filmed his celebrated *Othello* in 1952. It is a walled Atlantic port 173 km north of Agadir, and one of the loveliest destinations in Morocco. In ancient times it was known as Mogador, and the purple dye extracted here from local shellfish was used to create Rome's 'imperial purple'. The attractive present-day town is over 200 years old, and was built originally as a military fort.

We check into the four-star Hôtel des Îles, which overlooks

the sea and the port. After a Flag beer by the pool, we take a walk along the twelfth-century ramparts and through the souks, which specialise in wooden objects, chessboards, large dice, picture frames and bowls of all sizes, all beautifully hand-made. A stroll around the very busy fishing port brings us eventually back to the hotel, where we go and have drinks in the bar (Black & White and soda).

Afterwards, we walk to the end of the port to a wonderful Restaurant called Chez Sam, which luxuriates in a sumptuous setting, and naturally specialises in fish and seafood. We dine on six local oysters, samosas of fruits de mer, nine superb grilled sardines, tagine de poisson (simply the best ever, made with sea bass, preserved lemon, carrots, onions and tomatoes), and a whole grilled langouste for Clare, which is also excellent. We drink our preferred Cuvée du Président rosé, and finish with the highly recommendable mahlia fig brandy. The total bill comes to 900 dh (about £55).

22.4.02. We breakfast at 8 on omelette, scrambled eggs, croissants, and fresh orange juice, which has just been squeezed. Checking out, we pay a bill of £40 for the room for both of us, and then drive north to Casablanca through the Chiadma region, where the Regraga tribe was the first to bring Islam to Morocco. Passing the Iron Mountain, we continue along the new coast road with its breathtaking views of the Atlantic, to the large, sprawling town of Safi, sardine capital of Morocco. It also has the largest phosphate plant in the country, belching out noxious fumes, as well as an old medina and sixteenth-century castle.

We then follow the coast road through Had Harrara, Sidi Beddouza, Cap Beddouza, Qualidia (where all the major oyster beds are), Jorf Lasfar, another phosphate town, and Moulay Abdallah, which has a twelfth-century monastery where, every August, up to 200,000 people come to the Moussem religious festival, and 15,000 horses take part in the parades. The magnificent views continue along the coast road until you reach El Jadida, whose ramparts follow the line of the beach. This is a

Atlas Mountains, Morocco

very busy fishing port, and an immaculately clean and well-laid-out town.

Here, we have lunch at Restaurant Le Port, situated right on the tip of the harbour. Grilled prawns and sea bass are all very fresh and excellent, and well accompanied by Flag beer.

Driving for another 100 km, we eventually make it back to Casablanca, where we check in once more at 3.30 to the Meridien Royal Mansour. This time, we're in room 122. Our total drive has been 1600 km.

Having worked up a thirst, we go to 'Rick's Bar' at the Hyatt for a J&B and soda, sipped to the strains of a very good female jazz pianist and vocalist. Opposite our hotel is a street of many cheaper restaurants offering 'eat as much as you can' deals for a fixed price of £5. The name of the street is Rue du Belly Out. Resisting these enticements, we go to dinner at the Bretagne, reputedly the finest restaurant in the whole of Morocco, a petit taxi taking us the 10 km to the Croisette beach.

Situated hard by the ocean, the restaurant is of very smart modern design, very French, with no Moroccan dishes at all. The chef-patron is André Halbert. Our dinner is composed of crab cakes on a bed of potato, leek and artichoke, in a reduction sauce made with crab and squid ink, which has an excellent balance of flavours, superb roasted suprême de loup served with an aubergine and lentil sauce, and saddle of hare in a mustard sauce, served with brilliant pomme purée in argon oil, accompanied by (of course) the Cuvée du Président rosé. The total bill is about £40, and the place undoubtedly deserves a Michelin star.

Outside, the petit taxi is still waiting...

23.4.02. We eat a full cooked breakfast at 8 a.m., then check out of the hotel, and take a car to the airport for our 11.15 flight to London Heathrow Terminal 1.

Morocco is a fascinating country, which, as this trip has demonstrated, is well worth a revisit. The best hotel is La Mamounia in Marrakesh, and the best Restaurant, Chez Sam in Essaouira.

The Caribbean
1994

8–16 March 1994

8.3.94. I take a taxi to Victoria station at 7 a.m. and board the Gatwick Express. The train turns out to be defective, however, and we all have to change, eventually reaching the airport at 9.30.

The plane is full, so there is no chance of an upgrade. It's a 747, British Airways flight BA 255 to Barbados and Trinidad. Although the seat was pre-booked, the allocation has gone dreadfully wrong. I am stationed at the back in 25B by the loos, with a howling draught and no legroom, whereas I should have been in 26B, which has plenty of room to stretch out. It's impossible to sleep, of course, with all the traffic going to the loos, and only enough legroom for a five-year-old. The food is indescribably bad; the only redeeming feature is the film, *Mrs Doubtfire*.

We land in Barbados at 4.45 p.m. local time, four hours behind the UK. The flying time has been 8½ hours. We must wait for a change of crew for the onward 40-minute flight to Trinidad, and eventually arrive in Port of Spain at 6 p.m.

It's intensely humid, and proceedings over the hire car turn out to be quite hilarious. Although I have a paid confirmation from a well-known hire company, there is no desk, nor anyone from that organisation, at the airport. After a number of irate phone calls to their head office, a car miraculously appears. I drive to what is described in their brochure as a guest house, the Pelican Inn, Coblentz Avenue, which turns out to be rooms that are normally rented by the hour, above the local gay pub. Room 830 is basic but clean, and at least has air conditioning.

After a Carib beer in the bar, I drive to the Hilton Hotel, which has been constructed with the reception, open-air restaurant and pool on top, with the rest of the building descending through the side of a mountain, so that the guest rooms face the sea. I drink rums with soda and lime, and listen to the steel band for a while.

Then I drive into town, which was originally protected by four forts. Today only two remain: Fort George, built in 1804, and Fort Picton. Then it's on to the Monsoon Restaurant, corner of Tragarete Road and Picton Street in Newtown, for a very good Indian/Creole dinner of shrimps and yams, sweet potatoes, roti and hot sauces, accompanied by Carib beers.

I get to bed at 10.30 p.m. (2.30 a.m. on my body clock), and sleep surprisingly well.

9.3.94. I begin the day with sweet lime juice and coffee on the terrace at 7.30 a.m., after which I drive through the smart district of Maraval along the north coast road to Maracas Bay. Here, there are superb virgin beaches, which are quite deserted and sadly lacking in any facilities. From there, I head towards Las Cuevas Bay, which has a similar feel, except that it boasts a basic bar/restaurant.

After a swim in the Caribbean, I have beers and a fun lunch, which begins with a shark burger, and is followed by more shark with rice and rum in the company of the local fishermen.

Next stop is Blanchisseuse and the North Bay beach, a surfer's paradise, again completely lacking facilities, but a good spot for an afternoon nap. By the time I drive back to the hotel, it's raining. Back there, I shower and pack.

Following a final round of rums on the terrace, I head off to the airport for the one-hour flight to Georgetown, Guyana to meet with Demerara Distillers Ltd, who have the exclusive concession for producing rum in Guyana.

I am met by a black-clad driver in a black Mercedes with blacked-out windows, very Mafia-like, together with the director in charge of hospitality. It's extremely humid as we drive through Georgetown to their head office, where I shall be staying in the penthouse suite. There are two suites in fact, with sitting room, dining room and terrace, staffed by a housekeeper and cook. It's all superbly well appointed, with stunning views over the town towards the sea. After a late supper of rum and sandwiches, I am in bed by 11.

10.3.94. I awake at 6.30 a.m., and am relieved that there is air conditioning in the bedroom, as the rest of the rooms are very humid. The cook has prepared a breakfast of sausages, baked beans and onions, fruit and toast.

At 9, I have a meeting with the managing director, we then visit three of their distilleries and conduct a most fascinating tasting by nosing over fifty new rums, after which we cross the Demerara River on the floating bridge to their Uitvlugt Distillery for lunch. The buffet comprises soup made from local vegetables with hot sauce, duck, fish, shrimps and rice, as well as delicious milk tapped from young coconuts. Following lunch, we pay a visit to the market at Parkin. I return to my room at 5.

After aperitifs at 7, we go to dinner on the terrace at Palm Court, a Chinese restaurant on the main street. There are prawn and chicken dishes, noodles and so forth, all quite good. During dinner, it starts to rain and so we move inside. It develops into a torrential storm, very unusual for March, and rains all night, which seems to contribute to the already very high humidity.

Back at the suite, I find a huge lizard in the loo, reminiscent of a prehistoric monster. This is indeed a strange country – 12 feet below sea level surrounded by dykes built by the Dutch, constant extreme humidity and mosquitoes the size of Wellington boots. There are no railways, credit cards, buses or trams, the roads are in such a poor condition as to make whatever little driving there is a nightmare, and most transport is by river boats.

I make my way to bed at 11.

11.3.94. After an 8 a.m. breakfast of onion omelette and fruit, I meet up for discussions regarding the introduction of a 15-year-old dark rum for the export market. We follow it up with a buffet lunch of delicious barbecued chicken at the penthouse.

In the afternoon, there is time to do some sightseeing, despite the fact that it is still very humid and raining. Georgetown, the chief port, capital and largest city of Guyana is situated on the right bank of the Demerara River estuary. It was chosen as a site for a fort to guard the early Dutch settlements. The city was designed largely by the Dutch, and is laid out in a rectangular pattern with wide tree-lined avenues and irrigation canals that criss-cross the city. Most of the buildings in the city are wooden with unique architecture dating back to the eighteenth and nineteenth century. We see St George's Cathedral, the world's tallest free-standing wooden building completed in 1892, the Victoria Law Courts, designed by C. Castellani and opened in 1887, the very colourful Stadbrook market, the clock tower which can be seen for miles around and the botanical gardens. These house one of the most extensive collections of tropical flora in the Caribbean, and are beautifully laid out with ponds, canals, kissing bridges and a bandstand where you may be lucky enough to hear a concert by the police band. Lastly we saw Umana Yana, an unusual thatched building, built in 1972 by native Wai Wai Indians, where ministerial dignatories meet, and then we repaired to the Forte Pegasus, a very good hotel, for drinks.

At 8 p.m., there is a dinner for twenty people at the renowned Georgetown Club, a members-only gentlemen's club. It turns out to be a superb evening. Two of the guests play guitars after dinner. We dine on chicken and fish, and drink Chilean Sauvignon Blanc and a prodigious quantity of rum.

I'm back at the penthouse by 12.15 a.m.

12.3.94. After a 7.30 coffee, I go by a small six-seater private plane to visit the Kaieteur Falls, the highest continuous waterfall in the world, with a 741 ft vertical drop. Stretching 822 feet, the falls are twice as high as Victoria Falls, and almost five times as high as Niagara, with a width varying between 250 feet in the dry season to 400 feet at the height of the rainy season. This is situated in the middle of the rainforest, and is only accessible by a long walk through the undergrowth following our guide, who uses a machete to see us through, a remarkable experience. Then it's on to the Rock View resort at Annai for a barbecue lunch at a gorgeous setting deep in the savannah, and from there, to the Orinduik Falls for a swim. During the course of this journey, we fly over miles and miles of rainforest. From about 500 feet up in the air, the treetops look like so many bunches of broccoli. I also get a glimpse of the top of the flat mountain featured in the film *The Land That Time Forgot* – all in all, an unforgettable trip.

Nosing new rum, Guyana

Main road, Georgetown, Guyana

Local pub, Georgetown, Guyana

Georgetown, Guyana

An unwanted guest

Kaieteur Falls, Guyana

We're back at 6 for dinner, followed by drinks at Pegasus to the accompaniment of a steel band, and then more drinks and dinner at Palm Court, to the less melodious strains of a dreadful reggae band. I discovered that the forest mosquitoes had covered my entire body with bites, and I look as though I have a severe case of measles.

I am in bed, bitten to pieces, by 11.

13.3.94. The day begins with breakfast at 8 a.m., and then I must be at the airport by 11.

I'm booked on a noon flight by Air Liat to Bridgetown, Barbados. It's a twin-engined plane and the flight takes two hours, but the aircraft is something of a joke, with many malfunctioning features, including the loos and seat belts. It's crammed solid and unbearably hot.

When we arrive in Bridgetown, the sun is shining and the weather altogether stunning. I hire an open top Mini Moke and drive along the west coast to the St James district, past the magical-looking Sandy Lane Hotel to the Coral Reef Club. The rooms are in a series of cottages, and mine overlooks the beach and sea. There is a large balcony with sunbeds.

I take drinks and dinner in the open-air dining room: lobster wontons, chicken stir-fry, Argentinian Chardonnay and lots of rum. The food is very average and the service poor, but the setting is enchanting. I am in bed at 10.

14.3.94. Awakening at 7 a.m. to the sounds of waves lapping on the beach, and the sight of the sun rising, I take breakfast on my terrace. There are scrambled eggs and bacon, a croissant and coffee.

I spend the morning driving around the island, going north up the west coast through Holetown, where the first settlers landed in 1627 in the ship, *Olive Blossom*. The site reminded sailors of Limehouse Hole on the River Thames, hence the name Holetown, Driving on to Speightstown, once known as Little Bristol, this town was a bustling sugar harbour with several military forts, and then across through Portland and Greenland to the more remote eastern side, where there are beautiful coral reefs, but no hotels and no swimming allowed. The interior of the island turns out to be quite boring, consisting mainly of sugar cane fields. I have a beer in an isolated, run-down hotel near the coast, and get back to the Coral Reef by noon for a piña colada and superb buffet lunch.

I sleep for an hour on the beach, swim a little and then read until 5.30. After showering and changing, I have aperitifs at 6.15, and then drive to the sumptuous Sandy Lane Hotel, where Lord Forte (the then owner) is having a drink on the terrace. What a stunning location for a hotel! Afterwards, it's onwards to the Cobblers Cove on the north-west corner of the island. It's small but full, and rather like an English country house hotel in feel. After a couple of drinks there, I make my way back to the Coral Reef, where an enormous Bajan buffet is served, with live music to accompany, all in the open air. The weather in the evenings is superb. I get to bed at 10.

15.3.94. I awake at 6 a.m., read for a while and then start my packing, before taking a full English breakfast, overlooking the sea, at 8. A lazy morning is taken up with reading and sunbathing, and is followed by a massage at 1 p.m.

I eat a buffet lunch at 2.15, and then some time later take the southern route back to the airport, arriving at 7. Our flight to Gatwick is at 9.15.

Trinidad Specialities:

Plantain chips. Accras – codfish balls. Bol Jon – salt cod. Callalou soup. Pepperpot – meat stew. Guava cheese – a pudding. Kachouris – chickpea fritters. Poulouris – split-pea balls. Sahinas – fritters of split peas and saffron. Carib beer.

Barbados Specialities:

Callalou soup. Flying fish. Kingfish. Pepperpot. Sancoche – a special soup. Mauby – a non-alcoholic drink.

Recommended Barbados Restaurants:

Raffles and La Maison in Holetown
Reids in Derricks, St James
Bagatelle in St Thomas
Joseph's in St Lawrence

6–13 September 1994

6.9.94. My travelling companion for this trip, Tim Bartley, collects me at 8 a.m. and we drive to Gatwick Airport, where we check in for a Caledonian charter flight 877 to Barbados. The seat allocation is 23A and B, as requested, which have plenty of legroom.

After getting through a bottle of Piper-Heidsieck at the airport, we take off at 11.30. A quarter-bottle of Lanson on the plane is £5, and takes twenty minutes to chill and serve. Obviously, they aren't used to anybody ordering champagne. Lunch is beef and overcooked vegetables, with a strange German-bottled vin de pays. I catnap a couple of times, we have tea and sandwiches, and then land in Tobago after eight hours. About half the passengers get off; we refuel and then take off again an hour later. It's another thirty minutes' flying time to Barbados.

Once there, we take a taxi to the Southern Palms Hotel in the rather run-down St Lawrence district – a seedy establishment, but the best in the area. Suite 233 overlooks the sea, but it's overcast and raining.

We go for a walk. Divi Apartments are holding a welcoming party, which we manage to gatecrash, and are lavished with unlimited rum. Back at the hotel, we have a dreadful meal of prawns in hot sauce. Thunder and lightning continue all night.

7.9.94. I awake at 6 a.m. and take a walk along the beach. At 7.30 I have breakfast, and then at 9.15 we are to take a small plane to Georgetown, Guyana. The bill for the hotel, including last night's dinner, is almost £200 – somewhat overpriced, I would say. We arrive at the airport at 8.30, only to find the plane has been delayed, so we have a couple of beers in the bar, and eventually take off two hours later, arriving in Georgetown at 11.30. Owing to its position below sea level, the humidity is incredible.

We drive to the Georgetown Club, where Tim and I will be sharing the tiny room 3. The Club is a very old colonial building with snooker tables, an old-fashioned restaurant and bar, shuttered windows and no air conditioning.

Taking ourselves to the Tower Hotel, we order beer and a snack. This is quite a nice place, but claustrophobic. Afterwards, we take a walk to the well-appointed Forte Crest, and then take a cab back to the Club, where we play some snooker.

We're collected at 7.30 by Demerara Distillers Ltd for a buffet dinner in their office penthouse on the fifth floor. There is a cocktail party, with various agents from around the world, which includes a farewell celebration for their Dutch agent. We leave at 10 and go for a drink at the Palm Court, getting back to the Club at around 11.30. It's very, very humid.

8.9.94. A sunny morning. After breakfasting at 8 a.m. on bacon and eggs, we are collected at 8.30 to be driven across the floating bridge to the Uitvlugt Distillery. We are given a tour of the complete rum production system, and then the heavens open for a truly incredible downpour.

Lunch in the local hospitality room is a buffet in the presence of the general manager, and company secretary. After this, we visit the famous colonial cricket club Bourdha, which still sports huge leather armchairs, and a wonderful collection of trophies and old photographs.

Then it's back to Georgetown at 6. At the Club, we play some more snooker, and are then collected at 8 to be taken for a chicken dinner at the Palm Court. It's still extremely humid. We are back by 11.30.

9.9.94. After a 7.30 breakfast, I am collected at 8.30 for a full tour of the Diamond Distillery, gas plant and Pepsi Cola plant, for whom they undertake the bottling. Lunch is at a deserted local club, a fairly good range of chicken, fish etc. In the afternoon, there are further visits, but I am very hot, bitten by huge mosquitoes, and tired.

Returning to the Georgetown Club at 6, I shower, then stroll round the corner to the Caribbean Rose Restaurant, 175 Middle Street. It's an open-sided place situated on the top floor of a building, serving very good spicy food. Back at the Club, I repair to bed at 11.30 to write some postcards.

10.9.94. Following an 8 a.m. breakfast of fried eggs and bacon, I pack to leave. I'm booked on a 12.15 Air Liat turbo-prop plane to Bridgetown, Barbados. There is an hour's delay, and conditions at the airport are intensely humid.

We eventually arrive in Bridgetown at 3, and taxi to the Tamarind Grove Hotel, where I have suite 205. This and 305 are the best accommodation in the hotel, right on the beach. It's altogether a superb location, although the bar and restaurant are set back just a little too far.

I take a Cockspur 151 rum and lime before dinner, which turns out to be appalling international cuisine. Tim is sick from the clam chowder. It's raining. I'm in bed by 11.

11.9.94. Waking at 7, I stroll along the beach to the magnificent Sandy Lane Hotel, whereupon it starts raining again. After breakfast, the sun comes out and it's suddenly lovely. I swim in the sun and have a beer.

Later, we take a free water taxi to the hotel's sister establishment, the Coconut Creek, for a buffet lunch. The food isn't bad, and the bill comes to B$80. Back at the Tamarind, I swim some more, and then sleep beside the pool.

In the evening, we have drinks at the Sandy Lane, and then take a taxi to the Beach Club. It seems it's Ladies' Night, and the place is full of the worst kind of English tourists. For the equivalent of £7, one can have unlimited drinks. In the midst of things, I witness somebody's handbag being snatched, which causes an almighty confusion. We taxi home at 11.30, having had no dinner.

12.9.94. I breakfast at 8 a.m. on poached eggs and bacon, and then go for a swim in the pool. We spend the day on the beach, enjoying the lovely weather, lunching by the pool (on chicken creole – dreadful). It is a shame that the hotel is so good, and yet the food so objectionable.

Happy Hour is 4.30–5.30, and I drink a Cockspur 151 rum and lime. 6.30 is the manager's drinks party, followed by an appallingly bad buffet and floorshow. I'm in bed at 10.30.

13.9.94. The day dawns wet and humid. Despite that, I breakfast on my terrace at 9 a.m. (scrambled eggs, bacon, sausage, mushrooms and tomatoes, toast and coffee), enjoying the superb views, but again having been bitten to pieces the previous evening.

Afterwards I pack, and later lunch by the pool, accompanied by Bloody Marys. It's still raining.

At 4.30, we take a taxi to the airport for a 6.45 flight home. We are given seats 1A and B in Business Class. I have a slightly upset stomach, which is not surprising, considering the awful food at the hotel.

Italy
1995–2002

Verona
28–29 November 1995

28.11.95. The 12.20 British Airways flight from Gatwick North Terminal to Verona takes just under two hours. An overpriced journey is marked by dreadful service and food; I fail to understand why British Airways is so consistently bad in these departments.

At the airport, I am collected by a driver from the Pasqua Winery and taken to the three-star Hotel Maxim, which is 2 km out of town.

After a meeting and extensive tasting with the directors of Pasqua, whose wines I find quite commercial, we go to dinner at Nuovo Marconi, 4 Via delle Fogge, in Verona. There is an excellent range of different Italian dishes, from which I try a very good risotto made with mixed fish, accompanied by an indifferent selection of their wines. I stroll around the old walled city, taking the truly beautiful Piazza dei Signori, the Palazzo di Commune with its neoclassical façade, the imposing medieval Torre dei Lamberti, 83 metres high, and the Piazza delle Erbe, once the site of an ancient Roman forum. This last is home to the Arena, one of Verona's most famous monuments. Built in the first century AD, it has been expertly preserved, making it one of the world's most treasured operatic theatres. I then visit Juliet's house, where Shakespeare's heroine was said to have lived, and where the famous balcony is now a place of pilgrimage for many star-crossed lovers.

I'm back at the hotel at midnight.

29.11.95. The day begins at 9.30 with further tastings (again I am distinctly unimpressed by the quality), and then we go to lunch at Trattoria San Basillio, 9 Via Pisano. Here, we eat a typical Veronese repast of hams and a magnificent rabbit stew with polenta.

My 4 p.m. flight back is delayed by an hour, and I eventually land at Gatwick at 6.30.

Verona is certainly a magnificent city, to be found along the Adige River at the foot of the Lessine Mountains, in an area that became part of the Kingdom of Italy in 1866.

Lake Garda
19–26 July 2002

19.7.02. A 5.30 a.m. cab takes Clare and me to Heathrow Terminal 1 for British Airways flight BA 572 to Milan, scheduled to depart at 7.40, but delayed in the event until 8.20. We are in seats 25A and B. We can be grateful the journey only takes 90 minutes, as the plane is full of shrieking schoolchildren. At Milan, we wait half an hour for our luggage, and then another half-hour for the Avis hire car, a Fiat Punto.

The route we must take is the A8 and A4 to Desenzano, at the southern end of Lake Garda, a 2½-hour drive. There, we check into the Park Hotel, where we are given suite 354, which has a view over the lake. Lake Garda is the largest of the Italian lakes, 48 km long and 16 km across at its widest point.

Going out for a preliminary stroll around the old town, we take in the Piazza Malvezzi and its sixteenth-century church, and then stop for a beer in the old port area. The weather is superb, with the temperature around 25°C. Life centres on the busy port, where the cafés are presided over by the statue of Saint Angela, foundress of the Ursuline order.

Another drive takes us to the port of Rivoltella, just along the coast, where we drink a ∈1 glass of Garda Trebbiano, a dry white with quite high acidity and an earthy finish.

At 8, we arrive at the Esplanade Restaurant at 10 via Lario, which has one Michelin star. It enjoys the most sumptuous setting of any European restaurant I have ever been to. Tables are set in the garden looking over the lake towards Sirmione. Proceedings begin with a complimentary glass of local Prosecco, a dry and well-balanced sparkler, before we are launched into the *menu degustazione*, at ∈60. Gamberini croccanti in salsa agrodolce are huge fresh prawns in an excellent sweet-and-sour sauce, and are followed by pressata di verdure con formaggi tenero di capra alle erbe e olive nere (pressed green vegetables and goats' cheese with herbs and black olives), ravioli di formaggi di pecora profumati al limone con salsa di ossibuchi in gremolata (ravioli of sheep's cheese seasoned with lemon in gremolata), filetto di tonno al lardo di colonnata con ceci profumati al rosmarino (fillet of tuna with rosemary-scented chickpeas), agnello al forno alle erbe aromatiche con patate, cipolle e funghi porcini (roast lamb with aromatic herbs, served with potatoes, onions and porcini mushrooms), white chocolate ice cream encased inside coffee ice cream, finishing with tiramisu, and then piccola pasticceria (petits fours) served with coffee.

With this majestic spread, we drink Lugana Superiore, Cà Molin (dry and well-balanced, with an earthy finish), Comincioli Groppello (a light-bodied red, similar to Bardolino, but a little heavier), both local wines from the Garda district; and then a Grappa di Trebbiano di Garda, all of which perfectly matched the food. Concluding that the place clearly deserves two stars, we return thoroughly satisfied to our hotel at midnight.

20.7.02. We awake at 8.30 to find sun streaming in through the balcony windows, enhancing our magnificent view over the lake. After coffee and croissants, we check out, and drive from Desenzano, heading north up the western side of the lake through Padenghe, Manerba, Raffa and Felice de Benaco – all pretty lakeside villages but sadly infested with camping sites and traffic jams – to Salo, a large, attractive bustling town on the lake shore. From here, we press on through Portese and Barbarano to the very smart Gardone Riviera, and thence to Fasano di Garda, and the Villa di Sogno Hotel, a majestic five-star establishment set up in the hills, with the most breathtaking view of the lake. Room 4 is the best suite in the hotel, and has a huge balcony terrace with a view to die for.

We eat a lunch of salade Niçoise, accompanied by Crystal beer made in Rome, by the pool, and then drive back to Manerba and Moniga to view a couple of houses that are for sale, neither of which turns out to be suitable. Back at the hotel at 5, we have a much needed swim and another beer.

Later, we have drinks (Prosecco) on the hotel terrace, with its magical evening view of the lake. Dinner, at 8, is at the Villa

Fiordaliso, a superb one Michelin star property in Gardone Riviera. With six rooms and a single suite, it was once used by Mussolini to house his mistress, Clara Pettuchi. We have an excellent table right on the lake, quite stunning.

After a Prosecco aperitif, the first courses are mussels in pumpkin cream with Parmesan, and red prawns in bitter honey with asparagus wrapped in Parma ham fat (quite a small portion for ∈24, but delicious and very delicate), and then we move on to double veal chops with onion in ashes, with miniature specimens of tomato, broccoli and garlic (which is another dish of delicate finesse, but with a high meat-to-vegetable ratio). This main course must be ordered by a minimum of two persons, and comes at ∈50 a head. With the food, we drink a half-bottle of 2000 Terre di Franciacorta, Cà del Bosco, from Lombardia, at ∈20 (a very well-balanced Pinot Bianco with a good fruity finish) and 1998 Stelle Sfursas, a Valtellina of 14.5% alcohol, priced at ∈70 (a blend of Pinot Nero and Nebbiolo with superb depth, huge fruit and admirable balance).

I resist the cheese menu, which is comprised of eight tasting-sized portions of different local cheeses, and we repair to the hotel for a grappa on the terrace, accompanied by a live group playing Brazilian music... a perfect way to end the evening.

21.7.02. I awake to the most awe-inspiring view of the sun shining across the lake. We breakfast on our terrace on eggs and bacon, croissants and honey.

Afterwards, we walk into the centre of Fasano, and then on to Gardone Riviera. The properties along the lakeside all look very smart and expensive; they are each worth something in the region of ∈7m. We stop for lunch at the Grand Fasano Hotel, a monster of a place, built on the lakeside in the late nineteenth century, and affording superb views across the lake to Sirmione. Linguine with pesto is followed by grilled lake trout with a green salad, accompanied by a half-bottle of Prosecco and a full bottle of Le Chiusure chiaretto, Garda Classico, a well-balanced local rosé. What is amazing is that this highly rated five-star hotel, with the highest hotel accolades in Michelin, does not accept credit cards.

Later in the day, we have drinks on our magnificent terrace, which is like a Roman villa, open on three sides, two with windows and one open to the lake, with pillars and a roof. It must be about 30 feet by 20.

At 8.30, we go to dinner on the restaurant terrace overlooking the lake. A glass of dry, well-balanced Prosecco precedes a first course of mezzalune (corn ravioli stuffed with clams), followed by poached anglerfish. We partner these courses with 2001 Lugana Cà Manol, an earthy white with traces of CO_2, before proceeding to tournedos with vegetables, which goes well with the 1998 Groppello del Garda Riserva Recioto from Comincioli, a huge wine of 14.5% alcohol, opaque, tannic and deeply flavoured. There is only a very small production of it, sold on allocation.

We retire at 11.

22.7.02. Checking out with the greatest reluctance, we drive back to Padenghe to see Madame Zander, who sounds like a fortune-teller, but has two properties for sale, both awful and both priced at over ∈2m.

We drive on along the western fringe of the lake, through numerous tunnels, to Limone, which I suppose was once a small, delightful old port and fishing village, but is sadly now rampantly commercialised. Here, we check into the four-star (but by whose standards?) Hotel Ilma. Cottage 722 at least has a good view of the lake.

A little later, we drive back to Toscolano, stopping for an excellent lunch of grilled trout, accompanied by draught Crystal beer.

At 3, we arrive for a meeting with the local estate agents, Tecnocasa, to go and view more houses and villas on the market. The first is a badly designed, three-bedroomed place, but nicely remote. How they can advertise it as having a view of the lake, though, is beyond me (somebody has a very powerful imagination). By this stage, we are becoming a trifle depressed, as the prospect of buying somewhere on Lake Garda is receding into improbability.

The next property we view is up a very narrow and winding path high in the hills above Gaino at Monte Castello, an abandoned pizzeria that has been derelict for the past six years. It is on two levels, with sumptuous lake views from the terraces, and no neighbours at all, as it would appear. Suddenly, we know this has to be the place. Set in four acres, it will require a huge amount of conversion work in order to be rendered habitable.

Back in Limone, we have a table reserved in Dal Pacco, which has a knife-and-fork in the Michelin guide, only to discover when we arrive to claim it at 8 that it is now Da Mary, a very seedy pizzeria. We leave at once, and drive down to the old port of Limone, in search of somewhere suitable for dinner. This proves somewhat difficult, as most visitors are on half board in their two-star hotels, and the bars at the port sell only drinks and ice creams.

Eventually, however, we find one, and feast on crayfish, Parma ham, and spaghetti amatriciana (I make it better than theirs myself), washed down with a 2001 Bardolino chiaretto, a light, fresh rosé. As a digestif, we have a Limoncella, which is the fairly sweet and sickly lemon liqueur made in the celebrated lemon-growing region of Limone. Back at the hotel, we take its taste away with a grappa on the terrace.

23.7.02. After breakfasting at 8.30, we check out and drive back yet again through the numerous road tunnels to Toscolano, heading up to the property that has taken our fancy, the address of which is via Castello. We have another good look round and measure up. It is indeed in a sorry state, but undoubtedly has fantastic potential.

At 11, we have a meeting at the offices of Tecnocasa with the owner, and eventually agree a sale price. We sign all the papers, and then open a bank account next door. What a project lies before us! Completion is anticipated by the end of August.

Driving back again through the tunnels, we stop for a lunch of some lake fish and salad, and then drive through Limone to Riva del Garda, a windsurfer's paradise as the winds here blow very strong. It's a lovely old town, sadly again spoiled by a surfeit of two- and three-star hotels and pizzerias. Continuing our drive, we reach the top of the lake, where it turns down the eastern shore at Tombole (equally spoiled), and on to Malcesine, which is even worse. It has 35,000 inhabitants and 17,000 beds available in two- and three-star hotels. It was obviously very attractive at one time, but now the streets are lined with trifle-truffle shops and ice cream vendors.

The wind begins to drop, and the dreadful tourist eyesores diminish slightly, as we reach Torre di Benaco. We check into the theoretically four-star Hotel Galavini at 3. Our small room overlooks the lake and the main road that runs alongside it.

At 6, we take a walk down to the harbour, past hordes of tourists doing their best to enjoy themselves on the meagre gravel beaches. The harbour area turns out to be much nicer, with its older buildings and winding streets. We stop for a bottle of Prosecco at the lovely old Hotel Gardensa, which overlooks the port and lakeside. Sadly once more, the old cobbled side streets are full of pizzerias, and we walk back along the main road to a restaurant called Al Caval (two Michelin knives-and-forks), which also has rooms.

Dinner here begins with an appetiser of lavaret, a local white fish in lemon oil, and continues with truffle ravioli, smoked pike with shallots and onions in balsamic vinegar, rack of lamb with lentils, and rabbit pieces in a truffle sauce. We drink 1999 Primofiore, a Veneto vino da tavola from Quintarelli, a superb wine of great depth, similar to the super-Tuscans in style, €45, finishing with a Grappa di Bardolino.

24.7.02. After breakfasting at 8 a.m. on scrambled eggs, croissants and coffee, we check out of our room, paying a bill of €150. Driving to Garda, we park by the port, and buy a round-trip ticket to Riva del Garda by catamaran. This is the northernmost port on the lake, known for its high winds, and the boat stops at Salo, Gardone, Fasano, Maderno, Gargnano, Malcesine and Limone on the way.

We have lunch at La Rocca, which has two Michelin knives-and-forks – river perch and tortellini with mushrooms, accompanied by a Bardolino chiaretto, all for €60. Afterwards, we stroll around the old port for a while, finding it inevitably full of tourists, before taking the boat back, and arriving back in Garda at 4.30.

Conditions are now overcast and humid, and we have a much needed beer by the port. We then drive to our hotel, Tobago, which is really just a two-knife-and-fork restaurant with eight rooms. At 5.30, the rain starts, soon developing into something like a tropical thunderstorm, with lightning and very heavy rainfall, all quite dramatic.

Despite the weather, at 8 o'clock, we are able to sit outside under a roofed terrace when we go down to the restaurant for dinner. After a glass of Prosecco, we move on to 1999 Soave Capitel Croce from Anselmi, which is quite superb, dry, rich and ripe with fine balance and a good long finish. This accompanies risotto misto mare (mixed seafood risotto), tagliolini al granchio (with crab), grigliate crostacci (grilled lobster, scampi and king prawns), and grilled sea bream. We finish with a Grappa Uve Nere, made from the skins of Cabernet Sauvignon and Maschio, and aged in oak to achieve a very smooth texture. We also try Grappa Rocca Sueva, and an over-sweet Recioto di Soave.

25.7.02. After an 8.30 breakfast, we take the 9.30 ferry to Sirmione, which arrives at 10.15. This is a very old attractive town on a peninsula, jutting northward from the southern share of Lake Garda with early remains and grottos, but typically overfull of tourists and pizza places. Taking the boat back to Garda at 11.30, we eat a snack lunch in Riva, and then drive through Bardolino and Lazise, which are both chock-full of campsites and pizzerias, to Pescheria, where we check into the four-star Hotel Fortuna, before promptly checking out again as it turns out to be such an awful place; the rooms were dirty and full of cobwebs. The receptionist had not only lost our reservation, but was surly and even rude into the bargain. Moreover, the place is situated on a main road, and must suffer from constant traffic noise.

Instead, we drive towards Milan, and stay in the Hotel Pinella in Busto Arizio, a great bleak hulk of a place, a most peculiar complex of badly designed modern architecture, a conference centre and poorly furnished suites. We ask the receptionist for directions to the restaurant we wish to visit. She says it's miles away in the next town, and having duly driven out there, we find it turns out naturally to have been around the corner from the hotel, at 15 Campanile Busto Arizio – the Antica Osteria.

Dinner begins with an appetiser of raw salmon in aspic with

tuna mousse. After a couple of glasses of Prosecco, the first courses are scallops with courgette mousse and a sweet sauce, and lovely farfalle with porcini, and the mains are buffalo steak (from Australia), served à point with no vegetables, and turbot with asparagus. The food is adequate (maybe ★★ at most), while the service is extremely slow.

With the food, we drink 1999 Canua Sforzato from the province of Sondrio in Lombardia, a Nebbiolo red made by Conti Sertoli Salis under the Valtellina DOC, a deep, rich, well-balanced wine of 14.5% alcohol, but soft and quite ready to drink, with no tannin to speak of. We round the evening off with a Grappa di Brunello di Montalcino 1967, which is quite yellow in colour. Its alcohol level is 62%.

26.7.02. We fly home at noon, feeling very pleased with ourselves at our purchase, but full of trepidation as to the next stages of development. It will hopefully not be another Peter Mayle adventure – but who knows?

USA, Japan, Thailand
2002

USA, Japan and Thailand
30 May–19 June 2002

30.5.02. To Heathrow Terminal 3 at 11 a.m. for the United Airlines First Class flight UA 919 to Washington, a seven-hour journey departing at 13.00 – theoretically. United have two lounges, split between Business and First Classes, with separate entrances – for the snob value, presumably. The First Class lounge is serenely decorated with leather sofas. Butlers serve Moët et Chandon and smoked salmon sandwiches, and escort you to your seat on the aircraft after all other classes have been boarded.

The plane finally takes off at 2, whereupon unlimited Pol Roger Cuvée Winston Churchill 1990 is served, fully mature and in perfect condition. The new configuration of seating in First Class means that everyone has their own private compartment with desk, table, a full reclining bed and private video – very cosy, but a bit singular and remote. A perfectly warmed selection of nuts is served, followed by smoked salmon with sourdough rolls, a crisp salad and croutons, and then grilled pork and leek sausages with onion demi-glace, mashed potatoes and sautéed cabbage, which is very good. The food is partnered by the excellent Robert Mondavi Cabernet Sauvignon 1997, a full-bodied, classic Cabernet with balanced tannins. We finish with Cheddar cheese, and more of the Cuvée Winston Churchill 1990.

After lunch, I watch *K-Pax*, an entertaining film with Kevin Spacey and Jeff Bridges, and then sleep for a couple of hours. Upon waking, I am served with a chilled deli plate containing smoked salmon, ham, salami, cheese and egg.

We arrive at Washington Dulles Airport with only 45 minutes to spare before my connecting flight, UA 917, leaves for Atlanta. As I am First Class, there is a concierge waiting at the aircraft door, to escort me personally through Immigration. He has arranged for the plane awaiting my arrival to be held up for me, much to the chagrin of the other passengers, no doubt. The 17.00

departure actually takes off at 17.25.

After a couple of large bourbon and sodas, I sleep for most of the two-hour flight. There are only six seats in First Class, and no food service, thank goodness. We land in Atlanta at 7.15 p.m. (six hours behind UK time), and guess what? My luggage fails to appear. The United luggage department could hardly be more helpful (they even ply me with a sponge-bag full of goodies), but it appears that, because the timing of my connection was so tight, my bags have missed the plane. They will now arrive on the flight that gets into Atlanta at 2 a.m., and be conveyed to my hotel then.

I take a $35 taxi to the Marriott Hotel on Lennox Avenue, where I am given room 2004 on the 20th floor. It's a very nice room with a view of the city and the intersections, in a typical American-style chain hotel. I'm soon descending to the bar in the lobby for a large Wild Turkey 101 bourbon and soda. The live pianist is probably the worst and the loudest I have ever heard, perhaps because, according to me, it's 2 a.m.

Repairing to the Lennox Grille on the second floor, I find it the nearest to a restaurant graveyard I have been in for years. There are just three other people there, who leave at 8.50, and a backing of awful piped music. I order a hamburger with all the trimmings (which turns out to be like eating cardboard), and accompany it with a glass of St Francis Old Vines Zinfandel at $10, a full, tannic wine with good balance and a long finish.

I retire at 9.30, feeling no pain.

31.5.02. Having slept until 7.30 a.m., I arise and an hour later have an 'omelette Atlanta', filled with onions, bacon, tomato, chilli, herbs, etc., an excellent balance of flavours, orange juice (which isn't fresh) and coffee. I discover that, notwithstanding the panoply of electrical gadgets I carry, I have no adaptor that will fit my razor to the hotel sockets. At 10, though, the mall opens, and what with every conceivable kind of shop congregated under one roof, spread out over three storeys, I manage to buy one with no trouble.

I take a cab to Virginia Highland, a 15-minute ride to an area of shops, bars and restaurants, and walk the full, five-mile length of it, taking in along the way the Jimmy Carter Center, a museum to himself and his wife. Well, he was once Governor of Georgia, as well as having been President of the United States, but what a farce. Photographs depicting almost his entire life dominate this colossal complex, which also incorporates a presidential library and museum.

At Atkins Park, a bar at 794 North Highland Avenue, I stop for a glass of the local draught beer, Sweet Water 420, which is very good. I then make another stop at Moe's and Joe's Bar, established in 1947, at No. 103, where a glass of Pabst Blue Ribbon turns out to be much drier.

I lunch at Doc Chef's Noodle Hovel, at 1424 North Highland, for a large bowl of Singapore noodles and a Rolling Rock beer, $10. This is an excellent place to eat.

Taxiing back to the hotel, I register for the fourth International Cane Collectors' Conference, and meet a lot of the 68 fellow collectors, who have come from all over the US, as well as Italy, France, Greece, and four from the UK.

At 5, I have Wild Turkey 101 in the hotel bar, although the most popular drink is seemingly 'Jack Coke' – Jack Daniels and Coca-Cola. Later, I share a taxi with Dominic Strickland, the son-in-law of Michael and Patricia German, antique dealers of Kensington Church Street, London W8, to the home of Emory and Kathy Mulling, 70 Old Powers Place. He is the chairman of this year's conference. It is a large, imposing house set in the country area, boasting a sizeable swimming pool with a floral collage in the centre. A bar in the garden serves Chalone Chardonnay and Cabernet Sauvignon, both of which are drinking well, and twenty tables have been set out. There is a full barbecue, offering pork, chicken, refried beans, sourdough rolls, corn-on-the-cob, all typical Southern food, I am reliably informed, and quite delicious.

A guided tour of his Cane Room has been organised. This proves to be completely over the top, designed like a shrine, with purpose-built cabinets and display shelves showing a large range of beautiful canes, a very top-end, expensive collection.

I taxi back to the hotel at 11.

My first impressions of Atlanta are as follows. The city which is 80 per cent black is split into three or four districts, quite a distance from each other, with lots of shopping malls containing all the major stores, Restaurants, etc. Everybody drives everywhere; this is not a city for walking. It is an expanding city, but with a lot of property for sale, and a place in which everybody seemingly knows everybody else. When one customer waltzed into the hotel bar earlier, the larger-than-life barman greeted him by his first name, even though he hadn't been in here since 1992. In addition to this, the area around Atlanta has the world's largest production of the sweet and mild Vidalia onion variety.

1.6.02. After a buffet breakfast at 8.30, I begin the morning attending a couple of lectures: at 9, 'Ten Years of Cane Auctions in America', given by Henry (Hank) Taron of Tradewinds Antiques, and then at 10, 'Canes from the American Civil War' by George Meyer, attorney and author of *American Folk Art Canes*.

From 11 till 2, I undertake a guided tour of the CNN headquarters, which is one great shrine to Ted Turner, quite an amazing building, encompassing an Omni hotel, and innumerable floors of newsreaders, computers and cameras. During the course of the tour, we fit in a boxed sandwich lunch.

The afternoon's business is taken up first, from 2 p.m., by a session of the Cane Collectors' Forum (Claude Harkins on Historical Canes, Robert Pearson on Eclectic Canes, Barbara Sanders on Tiffany Canes and Larry Mattson on Gadget Canes), and then by an excellent lecture from Ernest Helides on 'The Working of 19th-Century Cane Materials'.

Cocktail hour is from 6 till 7, and I avail myself of a couple of Wild Turkey 101s with soda. The size of the hand-poured measures is historic, and I am virtually staggering even before I go in for dinner. I sit with Ernest Helides, who is a specialist on tortoiseshell and whalebone and a thoroughly fascinating man. We dine on lobster bisque, salad, and chicken stuffed with rice and herbs, accompanied by Clos du Bois Chardonnay 2000, a very well-balanced wine with a long finish, and Beringer Cabernet Sauvignon 1999, a light, soft, commercial red. During the course of dinner, we are treated to another lecture – 'Good Taste, Bad Taste' – by Michele Aquino.

I retire peacefully at 11.30.

2.6.02. I awake to my 6.30 alarm call, eat breakfast from the buffet at 7.30, and then at 8, attend the day's first panel discussion. I must say that, over the last two days, I have learned an enormous amount about canes, and met a lot of interesting people.

My laundry having finally turned up at 11.15, I check out 15 minutes later, and on looking over my bill, spot an item marked 'Telephone call. Duration: 1 second', charged at $3.43. Even the cashier is reduced to hysterics by this, and promptly cancels the charge. The room was $200 a night.

I share a taxi to the airport and then check in for the United Airlines First Class flight UA 557 to Denver, changing to UA 251 to San Diego. The person checking in ahead of me is going to Ethiopia with his wife and baby; the amount of luggage they have looks rather as though they are moving house, and inevitably takes forever to process. Eventually, and not before time, a second official steps in to check in the First Class passengers.

The Red Carpet Club lounge by gate T14 is a complete disgrace. Firstly, there is no receptionist; you are simply issued with a code number to punch into a keypad on the door. Then there are no alcoholic drinks or snacks, only Coke, Sprite, coffee and water. I take great delight in filling in the questionnaire on what I thought of the facilities.

The flight to Denver is at 14.50, and I'm in seat 2B. We are initially served with Veuve Amiot, a sparkling Saumur, and then a Reubens roast beef and cheese toasted sandwich. The accommodation is Business Class only, and quite cramped, but the film, *Monsters Inc*, is mildly diverting. We arrive at Denver at 16.15 local time (two hours back), and I connect to the San Diego flight, which departs at 17.05. This Red Carpet Club lounge does have alcohol, but you have to pay for it – $5 for a beer, an outrage. The lounge itself, at least, is a large, air-conditioned space, useful as the temperature outside is 90°F. Apparently, for an annual charge of $450, you can use the Red Carpet lounges without having to fly First or Business Class.

We take off at 5.10. I drink a couple of bourbons, but refuse the pasta dinner, and we land in San Diego at 6.30 local time. I am met by my daughter, Danielle, and son-in-law, Gareth, who live just outside San Diego. They drive me to my hotel, L'Auberge at Del Mar, overlooking the ocean. It's a lovely, very smart hotel, and room 336 (which is $400 a night) has a great view over the pool and the Pacific.

At 8, we meet up in the Durante Bar, named after Jimmy Durante, who was a resident of Del Mar, and a very frequent visitor to the hotel and, of course, the nearby racecourse. After a Wild Turkey 101 and soda, we go to dinner at Cibbicco opposite the hotel, where I am served an embarrassingly gargantuan pork chop with garlic mash, accompanied by 2000 Beringer Merlot, a rather forward, commercial-tasting wine.

I am in bed at 11.

3.6.02. I breakfast at 8 in a very pretentious restaurant in the hotel, called J R Taylor. The French staff are all in suits and ties. There is good fresh orange juice, and I eat two poached eggs on a mound of smoked chicken, wild mushrooms, onions and hash browns, a quantity of food that would comfortably have served four people.

It's a fine, sunny day, and I read by the pool until Danielle arrives at 11.30 to take me shopping in La Jolla. We lunch at P F Chang's, which serves excellent Chinese food. I have chicken ho fun and a draught Kirin beer.

In the evening, we meet for drinks at 7 in the Durante Bar, and then drive to La Jolla to a restaurant called George's at the Cove, a stunning 170-seater place on three levels, set on a peninsula in the ocean. There, we meet friends of Danielle and Gareth in the bar. A glass of R H Phillips Viognier 2000 is very fresh, and a good example of the grape variety. We are given a fabulous table by the window, and with our dinner, drink two bottles of Kuentz-Bas Pinot Blanc 1999 from Alsace, a delicious wine.

I pass on a starter, as I am still pretty full from the Chinese lunch, but opt for an impressive main course of rabbit, well presented and served with red potatoes. We make our way home at 10.30, having enjoyed a great evening.

4.6.02. I decide to pass on the hotel's pretentious restaurant and take breakfast at 8 in an open-air restaurant across the road, poached eggs with bacon on seven-grain toast. I have never been offered such a variety of different toast options in my life. Having consulted the spa staff at the hotel, I am talked into trying out their 'ultimate experience', and so from 9.15, I find myself undergoing 90 minutes of non-stop pampering, including a facial treatment with two masks, from which I emerge with skin like a baby's bottom. Later on, at 3.30, I have a superb massage, another 90 minutes of pain and pleasure all at the same time. The total bill for this is $300, and looking in the mirror, I have to ask myself whether it is all worthwhile.

In between, I spend the day by the pool with Danielle, relaxing in glorious weather. Lunch, which we eat right there, is a mediocre hamburger with onion rings, partnered by the light and fresh Clos du Bois Chardonnay.

At 6, I have drinks in the Durante Bar, and then Gareth collects me for a dinner at their house, chicken meatballs and rice, with 1999 Ravenswood Merlot, a sumptuously rich, soft and full-bodied wine. Back at the hotel at 10, I have a Wild Turkey 101 nightcap, and then turn in at 11.15.

5.6.02. As I enjoyed it so much yesterday, I elect to start the day again at the restaurant over the road, sitting outside and breakfasting on scrambled eggs and bacon, this time on multigrain toast, with very fresh orange juice and coffee. I then check out of the hotel. The bill for three nights plus extras comes to a staggering $1,800.

A cab to the airport is a further $50, and I arrive at 8.45, to check in for the United Airlines Express flight to Los Angeles at 10 a.m. My bags are sent straight through to Tokyo. We land in LA at 10.50, whereupon, after an extremely complicated interchange, I eventually arrive in the All Nippon Airways departure hall. Here, I check in for the First Class flight NH 005 to Tokyo, seat 3C. Flying time will be 10½ hours. The bureau de change at LA is a complete rip-off, offering 150 yen to the pound, when the average rate is more like 200.

I then have another complicated time of it trying to find the ANA Signet First Class lounge, which turns out to be small, packed and not serving champagne. At noon, I pour myself a large Bloody Mary, and we are called to board at 12.20. Our scheduled take-off is 12.55. The First Class cabin consists of 17 high-tech seats, arranged in pairs with at least six feet of legroom, with hot towels and slippers being provided on boarding. Tokyo is 16 hours ahead of LA, so it's currently 5 a.m. tomorrow there.

Lunch encompasses the following dishes: sakizuke (tender egg custard with sea urchin); sushi of miso-flavoured prawn, grilled duck, crabmeat dumpling, soft-simmered whelk in the shell, thick omelette and boiled broad beans; a poached clam dumpling with garniture in clear soup; Japanese soba (buckwheat) noodles; kobachi (soft-simmered octopus in soy-based sauce); and simmered freeze-dried beancurd in soy with an assortment of stewed vegetables. The hot dishes are: stewed sea bream in soy; sunomono (quick-sautéed abalone and surf clam in citron-vinegared soy); steamed rice; and miso soup with Japanese pickles. Then there are seasonal fruits, dessert and Japanese tea to finish.

The in-flight wine list is comprised as follows: Krug champagne; 2000 Pouilly-Fumé, Les Trappes; 1999 Puligny-Montrachet 1er cru, Chalumeux, Drouhin; 1999 Chablis 1er cru Fourchaume, La Chablisienne; 1999 Chalone Chardonnay; 1995 Château Malescot St-Exupéry; 1997 Château Latour-à-Pomerol; 1998 Morey St-Denis 1er cru, Jadot; 1998 Heitz Cabernet Sauvignon.

It is all quite a treat when one finds one's glass being continually replenished with Krug. The film is *Oceans 11*, after which I sleep for around four hours, and awake to be regaled with apple juice, coffee and smoked salmon sandwiches, the film *A Beautiful Mind*, and more Krug.

6.6.02. We land in Tokyo at 4.30 p.m. local time. First Class luggage comes out first, and we are dealt with first at Immigration. I purchase a bus ticket for ¥3000 (the airport is 60 km out of Tokyo), for travel to the Hotel Washington. This takes an hour and a half in sticky traffic.

I try to check in at the hotel's main entrance, only to find that I have been booked into the annexe, not having realised that I have arrived in the middle of the football World Cup. Tired and weary, I wheel my suitcase outside to the back to the hotel, and check into room 979. All the jokes about small hotel rooms in Japan are certainly borne out in this one. (I closed the door and the doorknob got in bed with me – and I liked it. I had a headache and the guy next door took the aspirin. I put the key in the door and it smashed the window. I turned the key in the door and it rearranged the furniture, and so forth.) I have to bring the suitcase in sideways, and the bathroom is barely more than a plastic shower tray with a chemical loo, as though one were on board a boat. The air-conditioning only works when you insert the door key, which means that when you go out, it switches off. And this is £100 a night per person.

Trying to find the information desk, I eventually track it down to the main building, as it seems that reception is located on the second and third floors here, I book two city tours, for 7.45 on Friday (tomorrow) and the same time on Saturday.

As it's a lovely, balmy evening, I stroll over to the Hyatt Park Hotel for a drink on the 43rd floor (their reception is strangely located on the 41st). A Japanese whiskey and soda with compulsory service and tax is £13. I then go down to the 40th floor for dinner in the Konzu Restaurant. A 33cl draught beer is £12, and each course is a minimum £25, although the views of the city are pleasant. Slow-cooked pork (three cubes, including the fat) in a sweet sauce is very good, and accompanied by four green beans, and then some noodles arrive, at £20 for about two mouthfuls, with a single piece of tuna and what can only be described as flattened anchovy, wasabi and sliced leeks. The dish is cold, and served on a lotus leaf. With overall portions as small as this, no wonder the Japanese are so thin and slight. The four-course, gourmet speciality menu is £500. Dinner concludes with green tea.

An interesting fact is that I am the only European in the dining room. Bearing in mind that this is a Hyatt, the Europeans probably eat in the European restaurants in cheaper establishments. My total bill comes to ¥6,352 (about £50).

At 9.30, I go up to the 52nd floor Steak and Blues Bar at the hotel for a Nikka Hokkaido 12-year-old pure malt, at ¥3,500, about £25. A very accomplished Black American singer and pianist performs.

I turn in at 10.

My first impressions of Tokyo are very confusing. With a population of 27 million, very few people (and why should they, after all?) speak English, even in the international hotels such as the Hyatt. Notwithstanding that, all the staff are very polite, almost to the point of embarrassment. I realise I need a comprehensive crash course education in the food and etiquette of Japan. The rich guests, for example, appear to treat the waiters with disdain, offering neither a 'thank you' nor even any acknowledgement of their presence, even while the staff bow and back away in a ridiculously servile manner.

7.6.02. Although I awake at 4.30 a.m., it slips my mind that I was supposed to have gone to the Tsukiji Fish Market to see the tuna auctions. I put it down to being so jet-lagged.

At 7, I have a breakfast in the hotel coffee shop, consisting of tinned orange juice, a ham sandwich and coffee for £13.

My full-day tour of 'Dynamic Tokyo' begins at 7.45 at the Tokyo Tower, which stands 320 m high, and is the highest self-supporting iron tower in the world. Built in 1958, it is an oversized replica of the Eiffel Tower, and from its 25th floor (250 m up), we are afforded a fine view of the whole city.

Next stop is a tea ceremony at Happoen, an impressive garden with an astonishing range of bonsai trees, some of which are up to 300 years old. The tea ceremony, or *sado*, which takes place in the Old Muan teahouse in the gardens, is performed by a tea master, who brews a powdered green tea, whisked to a froth, which is then served in bowls that have to be turned twice clockwise before drinking, according to ancient ritual. It tastes like a bitter broth.

We then take a look around the Imperial Palace Plaza. When Tokyo was called Edo, the Tokugawa shoguns built themselves the world's largest castle, 16 km around and guarded by a maze of moats and walls which date back 400 years; sadly, the palace itself isn't open to the public.

Caption: tea ceremony, Japan

Lunch is at Chinzan-so, a *mokushondo* Restaurant set in the gardens. It's a kind of barbecue, with the food cooked on red-hot stones from Mount Fuji. There are pork, chicken, beef, vegetables and rice, served with two different dips, one of soy, the other of honey and mustard. We accompany this spread with Asahi dry lager, which is greatly appreciated, as the temperature is now well into the 80s. A wander around the gardens after lunch takes in the pagoda, stone statues of Rakan, a sixteenth-century figure, and pools full of large fish. The whole complex is situated next to the Four Seasons Hotel (which charges £500 a night).

A drive past the Diet building (government offices) brings us to the port on the Sumida River, from where we embark on a 40-minute boat cruise under the fourteen bridges to Asakusa, well worth the voyage as each of the bridges is built to a different design.

The Sensoji temple in the old downtown district of Asakusa, enshrining a tiny image of the Buddhist goddess of mercy, Kannon, which again is not open to non-Buddhists, is very large and full of people. For ¥100, you shake a tin of sticks until one of them pops out, giving a number that then opens a drawer to reveal your fortune. If it's bad news, you tie the paper on a rack of strings nearby. Guess what I choose!

A walk through the Nakamise shopping street can only be described as the world's largest trifle-truffle street, lined with numerous tiny shops selling souvenirs and toys (a load of utter junk). The bus back leaves at 5, and arrives at my hotel at 6.30.

I then make a dogged attempt to communicate with the girl who is supposed to be the concierge, but who speaks no English, regarding booking my bus to the airport on Sunday 9th. It takes fully half an hour to get through to her, with the aid of drawings and hand signs; and £30 later, I have my ticket for the 3 p.m. bus. Foolhardily enough, I then try to get her to make a booking for me at a restaurant in Roppongi, but there isn't a chance of her understanding this request, so I give up.

After a brief sojourn in my box of a room for a very necessary whisky, I take a taxi to the Roppongi district, which is the Covent Garden or Soho of Tokyo, full of trendy bars and restaurants, and thousands of people, the bars all full of young things watching the World Cup.

I spend some time searching for the Shabu Zen Restaurant in Minato-ku, pacing numerous streets milling with restaurant touts holding out menus and screaming in Japanese. There are endless clip joints and massage parlours, and finally I find the place I'm looking for. It specialises in shabu shabu, thin slices of beef that are cooked in a boiling broth at your table, and served with dipping sauces. I sit at a long, long table, order a draught Kirin, and speak to the manager, who has reasonable English (in fact, I am the only European in the restaurant, which is somewhat off the beaten track). I opt to follow his set-menu recommendations.

These begin with a salad of lobster shavings in a sweet vinegar sauce (8/10), which is followed by fried shrimps on eggplant (9/10), translucent raw lobster on a bed of ice with soy and wasabi (10/10), and the famed shabu shabu, a huge plate of thinly sliced beef, like Parma ham, with a cauldron of broth on a gas ring and a bowl of raw vegetables (tofu, mushroom, lettuce, seaweed, spring onions and translucent noodles, 9/10). You can eat as much meat as you wish – what a feast! As soon as you finish it, more meat arrives. Then there is miso soup with half a lobster in the shell (10/10), and noodles with the cooking broth, which contains an unidentified white object that tastes of stick dough, and is probably tofu (8/10). Dessert is a yoghurt-type cream, and there is Japanese tea to finish. The bill comes to about £75.

I leave at 10, and taxi back to the hotel for £14, totally exhausted but having had a great day.

8.6.02. I awake at 7, and wander down to the local coffee shop on the street corner for fresh orange juice and coffee, £6. The temperature is a staggering 85°F.

Planning my own itinerary, I decide to spend an all-walking day. At 10, I go up to the observatory floor of the metropolitan government offices (45 storeys up), which affords fantastic views of the surreal skyscrapers of Shinjuku. The panorama embraces the parks, the Meiji shrine, Mount Fuji, the Imperial Palace and Ginza.

My next port of call is Shinjuku railway station, which is a sight to be seen at rush hour. It's a state of organised chaos, with over two million commuters a day passing through. In the days of the shogunate, Shinjuku was still a day's march from the old capital of Edo (now Tokyo), but with the coming of the railways, it became a major junction. As late as 1970, it was known mainly for its station, as well as its red-light district and the sewage farm, the last since banished. Recent investment has led to the area's development, with many smart hotels appearing, and the upgrading of what is now a distinctly superior red-light district, safe and clean, in the area to the east of Seibu Shinjuku Station, around the Koma Stadium.

Behind the station is an area called Camera Village, which is an interconnected warren of shops large and small, dealing only in cameras, videos and computers. It would easily take a day to look through all the outlets.

Meanwhile, the red-light district by Seibu Shinjuku is already buzzing with activity at 1 p.m. I have lunch at a sushi bar with a *kaiten* (revolving conveyor belt), on which dishes are price-coded by the colour/design of the plate – ¥100, 130 or 300. Six plates and two Sapporo beers later, I emerge having paid a bill of just £10. The food is all superb and very fresh, comprising prawns on rice, rice wrapped in an omelette, tuna on rice, grilled eel on rice, and a couple of strange-looking items about which I was unable to get an explanation, but which may well have been sea urchin and abalone.

After lunch, I stroll around the red light district, which reminds me of Soho in the Sixties, but cleaner and less menacing. I then attempt to walk back to the hotel but, having asked at least three policemen, I find an hour later that I am heading in the opposite direction. Reluctantly, I call a cab to the hotel, for £10.

To relieve my aching limbs, I arrange some spa treatment by pushing a button marked 'Massage' on the hotel phone. I make a booking for 6.15, not knowing who or what would arrive. After showering and donning the hotel kimono, I answer the door to a five-foot grandmother carrying a plastic bag. She speaks no English, but proceeds to inflict excruciating pain on me, throughout my whole body and head, by application of a muslin cloth through the kimono (no flesh is touched). Well, there is always a first time for everything.

Forty minutes and ¥5,000 (£15) later, I feel ready to go out. I go to the 25th floor bar of the hotel for drinks, Ballantine's whisky and soda, ¥1,500. The hotel wine list's 'Wine of the Month' is a FIFA World Cup official licensed product called Mercien Festival, which comes in red or white at ¥3,800. There's also Grass Mountain Chardonnay (for Glass Mountain in the USA) and Frezer (otherwise known as Fetzer) Ber Arber Merlot. Cocktail of the Month is 'Charie Chaplin'. Among the menu offerings are 'humburg and chips', 'beef stamina steak', 'steamed shortneck clam of olive oil with grilled ox's tongues – cube cut size and stick salad'.

I call a cab to a restaurant called Nishi Azabu Manzara, at 1–4–33 Nishi Azabu, Minato-ku, which I have booked for 8.30. It's a ¥2,500 cab ride away in a trendy suburb of Tokyo. Even the cab driver has to ask directions. It's a tiny place, but with a lower floor and roof garden, and single seating for eight people around a bar facing the chef, who cooks to order. The other seven stools are taken by seven single women. The menu is in Japanese, but fortunately the girl next to me speaks English and asks the chef, who is just thirty and from Kyoto, and who opened here a year ago, to prepare a menu for me.

First up is hasu plant with ginger in a cold, glutinous liquid made with rice vinegar. This is followed by a kind of bento box with six compartments, containing ingen (green beans) with susani (peanut) pasty, pumpkin konuyaku (with gelatine potatoes), eggplant, togan (white winter cucumber) with ginger, spinach with dried tuna, swordfish and sea-urchin, all beautifully presented and first class. Grilled codfish with sweet miso paste is worth 10/10, although the fresh tofu from Kyoto, which is like a solid yoghurt, has very little natural taste, but can be dipped in soy, shredded chives, ginger and shredded dried tuna. The tofu is presented in a little bamboo dish with a small slotted scoop. Beef with sweet soy has been slow-cooked for 48 hours, and is served on very thinly sliced spring onions (9/10), and there is also tempura of elva pepper, which is something like okra, with wasabi and ginger and a light stock dip containing turnip. A further dish of beef and vegetables in rice comes wrapped in seaweed (10/10), but four rolls of this last finally defeat me. Finishing with a serving of quince jelly, I conclude that the food here is indeed excellent, and well worth the detour. I leave at 10.15, having paid a total bill of ¥7,300 (about £60).

Taxiing to the Kabuki-cho red light district, I find it very crowded, bustling with young and old alike, full of slot machine arcades, strip clubs, cafés and bars, Restaurants, prostitutes and S&M clubs. A girl who can't be more than about sixteen years old approaches me: 'I will show you my fanny for 600 yen.'

'What for?' I reply. 'Once you've seen one, you've seen them all.' Another cab gets me back to the hotel at 11.30.

9.6.02. Arising at 6.30 a.m., I take a cup of green tea and then go by cab to Yebiso Garden Place, which was the original site of the Sapporo Brewery, established in 1887, before pollution regulations constrained them to move. Its extensive acres now encompass gardens, museums, restaurants and theatres. The Sapporo Beer Museum has slides and videos, as well as original labels and equipment dating back to the inception of the brewery. In the tasting room, they sell you four tasting samples for ¥400, and you vote for the one you like best. The Edelpils, in my view, shows the best balance (I give it 9/10), while the Kolsch (6/10) is too sweet, the Weizen (6/10) too light, and the Mild-type Ale (5/10) too malty.

Also housed within the complex is a shopping mall, which has a brilliant food and wine section in the basement, a fantastic place teeming with fresh meat and fish, freshly cooked foods, three noodle restaurants and fruit and cookie stands – all very impressive.

I take the lift to the Yebiso Garden Palace Tower on the 25th floor to select a restaurant for lunch. Of the eleven, I choose Chibo, which specialises in okonomiyaki, a kind of Japanese omelette/pizza, as well as teppanyaki, which latter is what I opt for: noodles with chicken, pork, beef and mushrooms. You take your shoes off and sit at the counter, watching the chef prepare the various dishes on a large griddle, while you sip a cold Sapporo and take in the views over the city, with Mount Fuji in the distance. It is, all in all, a superb meal, and well worth £10.

After a little more exploratory wandering around the complex and gardens, I take a taxi back to the hotel, and get ready to check out. The airport bus arrives at Tokyo Airport at 16.15, rather early for my 19.10 flight. I check in for Thai Airways First Class flight TG 773 to Bangkok. Their First Class lounge is shared with other airlines, and is only of comparatively poor quality. I drink a large Bloody Mary, and we eventually board at 19.15.

On board, there is a choice of Dom Pérignon 1995 or Duval-Leroy Cuvée des Roys 1991. I diligently sample both, and go for the DP. The First Class cabin is quite shabby, compared to those on, say, Emirates or United, and the plane itself is a fairly old 747–400, with no personal videos, for example. More DP is served, with Japanese beans. We take off at 8 p.m. on a 6½-hour flight. We are served with a poor attempt at a selection of sushi and Thai delicacies, and then a main course choice of beef in soy, green Thai chicken curry, or prawns in a cream sauce. I go for the curry, which turns out to be bland and tasteless, served with rice, followed by a piece of dried-up Cheddar, with 1999 Château Larmande, a young, tannic St Emilion with good depth of fruit.

Nursing a Johnnie Walker Gold Label, I watch the film, *Time Machine*, and we eventually land in Bangkok at 1.30 a.m. local time, two hours behind Japan. A limousine service takes me to the Amari Boulevard Hotel, 2 Sois, Sukhumvit Road, arriving at 2.30, where I am welcomed by the general manager, Jacques Warner.

I sleep until 6.30 a.m.

10.6.02. I take breakfast at 8 a.m. from an excellent buffet – scrambled eggs, bacon, passion fruit juice and coffee. Arranging my flights to Phuket and Hua Hin turns out to be extremely complicated, as there is no direct flight between them. In addition, I had arranged to meet a friend in the hotel lobby at 11, and on calling his mobile at 11.45, I am told that he has business to attend to and will call me later.

The weather is overcast and very humid, and I have a couple of Singha beers in the lobby bar. Instead, I book a tour for myself of the Royal Grand Palace at 12.30. By this time, the temperature has climbed to 34°C, and the humidity is at 95%. The tour includes a look at the Nat Phra Kaew temple, the most sacred in all Thailand, with its Emerald Buddha (actually made of green jade), and the Golden Cheri, which is the pantheon of the Chakri kings.

Temple in Thailand

The Palace itself and the surrounding temples are set in two acres, and are in superb condition, the gold-leaf statues and the temple furniture being quite magnificent. Shoes must be removed to enter. The whole experience is like visiting a royal estate, with its chambers full of firearms and swords. The main palace was built for Rama V, who was educated by an English governess and who travelled Europe, eventually building this palace in the style of an English country house.

Back at the hotel at 5, I have a massage in my room for 800 baht. During the course of it, I am asked whether I would like 'a willy oil' for an additional 1000 baht, and smartly reply that whatever that involves, the answer is 'No!'

I make a reservation for dinner at Sala Rim Naan at one of the best hotels in Bangkok, the Oriental, which is an hour's drive away through very bad traffic jams. Part of the problem is that the city has no subways, being only two metres above sea level. The Oriental is an awe-inspiring place, right on the river. To reach the restaurant, you are taken by an ancient launch across the river to what must be the most fantastic setting for any restaurant anywhere. Shoes are removed at the door, and the seating is low but comfortable. There is music and a Thai cabaret, and the place is full. After a couple of Singha beers, I realise I am very hungry (I have, after all, had no lunch).

The fixed menu I choose consists of: pra thad lom, deep-fried prawn rolls with crispy vegetables and noodles in a honey and lime dip (8/10); yaam won sen, spiced salad of glass noodles (8/10); tom yaam ghoong, spicy soup of Blue River prawns (a delicate but quite spicy version, 6/10); gaeng khiew waan gai, very spicy green chicken curry (8/10); pla priaw naam pla waan, fairly spicy deep-fried fish with sweet and salty tamarind sauce (7/10); phad paag, stir-fried vegetables with oyster sauce (7/10); khow hommali, steamed jasmine rice (6/10); polamai gub khanom thai, very ornate carved fresh fruits with Thai sweets (7/10); finishing with cha (tea). Despite some of the higher marks, I find the food generally a little indifferent, but the floorshow is superb, the dancers arrayed in outstanding costumes. The only sour note is struck by a large group of noisy Americans. My bill comes to 2,070 baht (about £35).

A limousine taxi back to the hotel at 11.30 is 600 baht.

11.6.02. Following an 8 a.m. breakfast of omelette, bacon, papaya juice and coffee, I go shopping at 10.30. Walking the streets of shopping parades, I find it very humid once again. The hotel staff have recommended to me an outlet called 'Versacce' [sic] for Thai silk, and I buy 12 metres in turquoise and red for Clare, and choose a stone-coloured linen material for myself, to be made up into a jacket. (I'm measured up at 10.45, have my fitting at 11.30, and the jacket is ready at 6.)

The city is full of massage parlours, offering every conceivable type of treatment, including one called 'Sandwich', the explanation for which is that you are rubbed in oil and massaged between two girls – bizarre!

At 12.30, I take a bus to the harbour, as I shall spend the rest of the afternoon on a boat tour. A welcome breeze now leavens the humidity as we drift through winding canals, observing the more rural side of Bangkok life. All drinks on board are free. We make a stop at the Wat Chaloem Phra Kiat temple, built by King Rama III 180 years ago; its shrine is decorated with porcelain, and there are still separate quarters for the monks. We then transfer to an old rice barge and sail back to the harbour.

Back at the hotel at 4.30, I go for a very refreshing swim in the pool on the fourth floor, which is an open level.

A complimentary Thai whiskey in the hotel bar at 6 is welcome, if lacking some depth of flavour, and then I meet with Sonu Shivdasani, owner of the Six Senses group, which encompasses the Evason and Soneva resorts in Thailand and the Maldives, and the Ana Mandara Resorts in Vietnam. His office is on the 12th floor at 1 Plaza Arcade, two high-rise office blocks opposite my hotel that are connected by a highly exclusive central club/restaurant for members only, designed along the lines of a St James's gentlemen's club.

A range of Thai food is served: soft-shell crabs, red chicken curry, roast fish (cod, I think) and jasmine rice, offering a very appealing blend of flavours. With the food, we drink the over-oaked 2000 Joseph Phelps Chardonnay and a 1999 Hugel Gewürztraminer, which is excellent, well-balanced and mature.

Back at the hotel, I have another Thai whiskey and soda, and retire at 10.30.

12.6.02. I awake to a 5.15 a.m. alarm call, and have coffee and croissants in the hotel lobby before checking out and taking a limousine to the domestic airport. There, I take the 8.00 Thai Airways flight TG 921 to Phuket. I'm in Economy Class, but in seat 49K, which is in the bulkhead, with nobody next to me. The 90-minute flight travels along the Thai coastline, and offers fantastic views, particularly on the approach to Phuket, where small, uninhabited peaks poke up from the sea.

On arrival, I am collected by a car from the Evason Resort, and taken the hour's drive straight through the centre of the island to Rawai beach on the southern tip. The hotel, which was originally a two-star package holiday venue, has undergone an impressive refit, having been comprehensively renovated by a team of no fewer than 700 builders during a seven-month closure, elevating it into the five-star-plus category, so that it is now one of the finest hotels on the island. Set in 64 acres, it has 260 rooms overlooking the Andaman Sea, and encompasses a private island housing a bar and restaurant in addition to the two in the hotel itself, one of which is Western, the other East-meets-West. As the grounds are so extensive, there is a constant tram service that takes you around and drops you off all day, until 1 a.m.

I have lunch with the general manager, Giorgio, and the food and beverage manager, Christophe. We eat stir-fried noodles with chicken and vegetables, barbecue prawns, fish and octopus, with Singha beer. Between 4 and 5, I enjoy a Thai massage. Conditions are overcast and humid.

In the evening, I have drinks by the pool in the downstairs bar underneath the restaurant. Occupancy is naturally low at the moment as it's the quiet rainy season, together with which there is still a lot of renovation and construction going on. As I sip at a rum with lime and soda, I reflect that the bars still need upgrading, to incorporate more display area.

Dinner on Wednesdays is a superb Thai buffet with music and very good traditional Thai dancing. The quality of the cooking, and the range of choice, are flawless, although the glass of Hanwood Chardonnay 2000 from Australia that I drink with it is over-oaked. Afterwards, I have a Jim Beam and soda in the main lobby bar, and eventually turn in, exceedingly tired, at 10.

13.6.02. I eat breakfast at 8 a.m. in the restaurant overlooking the sea. A superb buffet of Eastern and Western food is on offer, with eggs of your own choice, Thai noodles, rice and stir-fried dishes spread across three groaning tables, together with fresh orange juice and coffee.

At 10, I take staff training. These are very raw and new staff members, who have absolutely no knowledge whatever about wine (and why should they, after all?). I give a two-hour lecture on viticulture, vinification and sparkling wines, and reflect that I shall be pleased if only 10% of it has got through to them.

Breaking at 12.15, I drink a much needed Singha beer. The weather is still humid and overcast, but at least it isn't raining. I meet up with Christophe for lunch, and dine on squid-ink pasta with chicken and mushrooms in tomato sauce, which is very good and goes well with another Singha beer (with its alcohol level of 6%).

A foot massage at 1.30 provides an hour of sheer bliss, and then at 3, I take a second session of staff training. The subject-matter is the same as this morning, but for another 15 staff.

At 6, I have a full oil Thai massage and a shower, and then at 7, repair to the bar for a rum, lime and soda. Appetite thus primed, I take the tram to the fusion restaurant overlooking the sea. What a glorious setting! The Bouchard-Finlayson Chardonnay 2000 from South Africa that I choose is a heavyweight wine that's even slightly unbalanced, but accompanies excellent chopped gravadlax with two types of caviare, while an equally impressive main course of barbecue roast duck with flat noodles is well served by a good Pinotage from the Backsberg Winery. I end the evening with a Jim Beam and soda in the upstairs bar.

14.6.02. The day dawns sunny and warm (32°C), and I breakfast at 8 on scrambled eggs and bacon, orange juice and coffee. My first training session lasts from 10 until 12, and then Christophe and I take the hotel speedboat to the outlying Bon island, owned by the hotel and equipped with private water sports facilities, restaurant and bar, as well as a wonderful beach.

For lunch, we have shrimp soup, seafood salad, stir-fried

chicken, and rice with pork, all quite delicious. I go for a massage at 1.45, and then take another training session from 3 till 5.

In the evening, I have a full meeting and dinner with all seven of the management staff. We rendezvous at 6.30 on the sea view terrace of the fusion bar. Léon Beyer's 1999 Pinot Blanc is a perfect aperitif for such a beautiful, balmy evening. Our first course is crispy octopus with Thai salad and barbecued pork, and is successfully partnered with the full and fruity L A Cetto Chardonnay Reserva from Mexico. Grilled red snapper on a bed of Thai noodles finds a good tablemate in the 2000 Alto Agrelo Malbec from Argentina, which is light and fresh and is served slightly chilled. The dessert, a chocolate soufflé, is accompanied by Quady's Elysium Black Muscat from California, which is well received by everyone, and makes a great end to a wonderful evening.

I conclude with a Jim Beam and soda in the lobby bar, and retire at 11.

15.6.02. I breakfast at 8 on fruit and coffee at the start of what looks like another very hot, sunny day. After packing, I read for a while by the Infinity Pool, so called because it seems to just disappear into the sea. A Singha beer at 11.30 makes a good aperitif to a midday lunch of Thai salads, and pasta with chicken and mushrooms.

I check out at 1, and receive a farewell send-off from all the staff and the general manager. A car then takes me on the one-hour drive to the airport, where I check in at 2 for Bangkok Airways flight PG 254 to Koh Samui, connecting to PG 422 to Hua Hin. The twin-propeller plane takes 40 minutes to get from Phuket to Koh Samui. At the connection, I transfer to another thatched building that houses the check-in desks for the scheduled 17.50 flight to Hua Hin, a 90-minute journey. By the end of the journey, I have travelled 6½ hours, having been the only passenger on the flight.

Once arrived, I am collected by the hotel car for the 40 km drive to the Evason resort at Hua Hin, a 200-room resort and spa spread over 25 acres on the shoreline. Many of the cottages have their own private swimming pools, and my room, 336, has a large balcony overlooking the garden.

I meet up with the food and beverage manager, Thomas Barguil, and the assistant general manager, Trent Mundy, for drinks in the bar by the sea. Los Boldos Cabernet Sauvignon from Chile accompanies a fusion buffet dinner in the main restaurant (to which I couldn't award more than 3/10).

After a nightcap, I'm in bed at 11.

16.6.02. A breakfast of scrambled eggs, bacon and baked beans, with juice and coffee, by the sea is an idyllic way to start the day. I spend the morning reviewing the new wine list, and then take a 12.30 lunch of chicken and cashew nuts with rice.

My first training session for the major food and beverage staff runs from 3 till 5, and at 6.30 there is a wine tasting for guests in the cellar. Eight guests sit around four built-in spittoons, a very professional cellar layout. We taste: 2000 Tuatara Bay Sauvignon Blanc from New Zealand, a youthful wine with a green appearance, a superbly grassy Sauvignon nose, and a good balance of fruit and acidity; 1999 L A Cetto Chardonnay Reserva from Mexico, which is mid-straw in colour, with a good, buttery, oaky Chardonnay nose and full-bodied attack in the centre, but which is slightly short on the finish; 1999 Alsace Pinot Blanc, Léon Beyer, mid-straw, with a full apricot/peach nose and good length; 2000 Fleurie, Domaine de la Presle, a Beaujolais with good deep colour, the classic strawberry Gamay nose, and full, rich structure on the palate, a very fine example; 1999 Echeverria Reserve Merlot from Chile, very deep and rich, with a sumptuous plum nose, and great softness and fullness; and 1999 Gamla Cabernet Sauvignon from Israel, an opaque red, earthy, roasted and ripe on the nose, and with a superbly rich finish.

Everybody seems to enjoy themselves, and I reward myself with a large J&B Scotch in the bar afterwards. I eat dinner alone in the fusion restaurant, sitting outside in an amazing setting among the lily ponds and small pontoons, listening to two wonderful Thai musicians. On the menu is pork with Thai noodles and vegetables, which isn't spicy enough for me, partnering it with the young, fruity and fresh 2000 Château du Galoupet rosé, Côtes de Provence.

I retire at 11.

17.6.02. I awake at 6.30 after a fitful night. I have developed a slight cough, which I think is a result of the air conditioning, plus being in a cold cellar for last night's tasting and then coming out into 34°C outside. A couple of hours later, I eat a breakfast of omelette and bacon, with orange juice and coffee, and then take a training session from 10 till 12.

A draught Singha beer precedes a lunch of chicken curry with rice, following which, at 1.30, I go for an excellent hour-long Thai massage. Between 3 and 5, I have my second training session, followed by a 30-minute pedicure, and then an hour of absolutely fantastic foot massage. I notice that my left ankle has swollen badly, presumably from some sort of bite.

At 7.30, there's a dinner with the general manager and guests. Echeverria Sauvignon Blanc 2000 is the crisp and fruity aperitif that precedes a tortilla of spicy seafood, with which we drink the full-bodied L A Cetto Mexican Chenin Blanc 1999, a superlative partner. Lamb chops masala are accompanied by the 1998 Gamla Merlot from Israel, a well-balanced classic Merlot, and we round things off by teaming the 2000 Essencia California Muscat with jasmine tea ice cream and tropical fruits, a perfect combination, and well liked by all. The whole evening seems to have been enjoyed by all the staff and guests.

I am in bed by 11.

18.6.02. Breakfast at 8 consists of fried eggs on toast with bacon, tropical fruit juice and coffee. The 10-till-12 staff training session concentrates on wine tasting (Geoff Merrill Sauvignon Blanc 2000 and Duboeuf Beaujolais-Villages 1999) and an introduction to the new wine list.

After a lunch of chicken and vegetable spring rolls with draught Singha beer, I go for a 1 o'clock facial, 75 minutes of blissful satisfaction, before afternoon staff training, running from 3 till 5.

For the evening, Geoffrey Bennun, the general manager, has arranged a wine tasting and dinner with five general managers of other hotels – the Chiva Som, the Hilton, the Marriott, the Sofitel and the Ayapura – for 6.30. The wines on show are: 2000 Tuatara

Bay Sauvignon Blanc from New Zealand (clean and crisp, with grapefruit flavours); 2000 Alsace Riesling, Léon Beyer (rich and ripe, with very good balance and a dry finish); 2000 Alto Agrelo Malbec from Argentina (soft and full, with good tannin and fruit); and 2000 Essencia Muscat from California (crisp and clean, sweet without being cloying).

For dinner, we each receive an individual dish divided into five sections, comprising chicken in pastry, prawns in a pancake roll, satay of pork, a vegetable samosa and grilled lobster in a Thai marinade, served with rice. We finish with coconut ice cream and fruit. After numerous bottles of wine, the evening finally breaks up at 11.30.

19.6.02. Arising to an alarm call at 6 a.m., I travel by the hotel car to Bangkok Airport, a 3½ hour drive north through many interesting villages, across the Mekong with its floating market, through the traffic and along the expressway to the airport. Arriving there at 10.15, I check in for the Thai Airways First Class flight TG 916 to London. The TA First Class service assigns a dedicated courier to whisk you through Customs and Passport Control like a VIP and into the First Class lounge, which is only for full paying first-class passengers (there are three other lounges, for either Business Class or upgraded passengers).

The lounge is quite small and sophisticated, with innumerable waitresses and bar staff serving hot and cold canapés and a full range of drinks. Two glasses of Moët et Chandon later, I am personally escorted directly to my seat on the aircraft, 2A. There are only two other passengers in First Class, and I am welcomed with a perfectly chilled glass of Dom Pérignon 1995.

We take off at 1 p.m., 50 minutes later, and more DP 95 is served. A selection of hot savouries opens the meal service, consisting of a prune wrapped in bacon (3/10), a Chinese prawn roll (8/10), and sui mai (shrimp and seaweed, 10/10). The next course combines caviare and goose foie gras, and then there is a main-course choice of salmon in red curry 'chu-chee', baked chicken in Provençal mustard sauce, or roast rack of lamb with tamarind, chilli and onion sauce. These are served with vegetables and steamed white and brown hommali rice. To finish, there are cheese, dried and fresh fruits, assorted sorbets, or bread-and-butter pudding, followed by tea or coffee. I opt for the cheeses (Roquefort, Cheddar and Emmenthal), with starfruit, dried strawberries and rose pear (or, as it can be called, rose apple), a rather odd, crisp but tasteless, specimen.

The wine list comprises: 1991 Duval-Leroy Cuvée des Roys; 1995 Dom Pérignon; 1998 Chablis Vieilles Vignes, 1999 Château Tour-Vachon, St Emilion grand cru (which is hard and tannic, 6/10); 1998 Morey-St-Denis, Clos des Ormes, Georges Lignier (served far too cold, a typically light, soft, berry-fruited burgundy, 5/10); and 1997 Gewürztraminer Altenberg, Vendange Tardive, Keinzheim-Kaysberg (a fine, well-made wine, full and long with ripe fruit, 9/10).

After a Chivas Regal Royal Salute 21-year-old, and the aid of a small pill, I sleep for four hours. Upon waking, I get through two films, *Crossroads* and *Time Machine*, and we are served with a selection of open sandwiches – smoked ham and melon, and marinated zucchini – and Danish pastries. Later on still, dinner consists of more canapés, smoked salmon, gaeng liang (Thai prawn and vegetable soup), and kiew wan (beef curry) with vegetables and rice. I drink more of the 1995 DP. We arrive at 6.45 p.m. local time (or 12.45 a.m., according to me).

What a marathon trip this has been – utterly exhausting but quite fascinating. I could entitle it 'Around the World in Eighteen Days (on Eleven Airplanes)', as follows: 1. London to Washington. 2. Washington to Atlanta. 3. Atlanta to Denver. 4. Denver to San Diego. 5. San Diego to Los Angeles. 6. Los Angeles to Tokyo. 7. Tokyo to Bangkok. 8. Bangkok to Phuket. 9. Phuket to Koh Samui. 10. Koh Samui to Hua Hin. 11. Bangkok to London.

Far East
2003

Vietnam and Thailand
9 March–4 April 2003

9.3.03. Clare kindly drives me to Heathrow Terminal 3, getting us there at 9 a.m. for the Thai Airways flight TG 911 Business Class to Bangkok, due to arrive at 6 a.m. on Monday 10th. From there, I shall travel on to Ho Chi Minh City on an 8 a.m. flight, TG 680, arriving at 10.20. As Thai Airways is operated by Air Canada at Terminal 3, I am escorted to their Maple Leaf lounge, which is quite spacious. There is coffee, but no champagne on offer!

I am undertaking this trip in my capacity as wine consultant to the Six Senses Hotel group, which has opened a five-star resort, the Ana Mandara, in Nha Trang, Vietnam. I am to select one of three wine suppliers, choose the wines, write the list and train the staff, devising a staff training programme into the bargain. Two of the suppliers are in Ho Chi Minh City (Saigon), and the other is in Hanoi. In Bangkok, I shall do the same for the group's two Evason resorts in Phuket and Hua Hin, choosing from five main Bangkok wine suppliers.

My flight, scheduled to depart at 11.50, takes off at 12.15. I'm in seat 12A. No champagne is served prior to take-off (I have been informed that it is only allowed in First Class). Luckily, there is nobody in the seat next to me. A glass of Charles Lafitte champagne (★★) is served before lunch, and is followed by Château Peychaud 2000 (★+), a Côtes du Rhône-Villages 2000 (x), an Hautes-Côtes-de-Beaune 2000 (★★) and a Gewürztraminer Altenberg 2000 (★★+). These accompany a fried Thai curry fish mousse cake (★★★), chicken and apricot terrine (★★), tiger prawn in dill vinaigrette (★★+), mixed green salad (x), stir-fried chicken in black pepper sauce (★+), choi sum, and steamed Thai rice (★★), then cheeses (x), and wild berry cheesecake with a passion fruit coulis (x).

After this rather indifferent lunch, I watch a movie, *Road to Redemption* with Tom Hanks, which I find equally mediocre. I then take a short sleep before clingfilm-wrapped sandwiches, which taste as though they have come straight from the deep freeze, are served. The latest James Bond film, *Die Another Day*, is shown. I refuse the offer of a cooked breakfast, and order a Jack Daniels and soda instead.

10.3.03. We land in Bangkok at 6 a.m. local time, whereupon I embark on the 20-minute walk to the transfer desk. The Vietnam flight is due to take off at 8.50, and I've been allocated seat 12K in Business Class. I eat a few curled-up sandwiches and sausage rolls in the dull lounge, and settle for a can of apple juice while I wait the two hours for my flight to be called.

The flight will take one hour and 15 minutes. The locals now prefer to refer to Ho Chi Minh City as Saigon once again, basically because it is easier to say. With a population of around five million, it is the largest city in the country, and is actually more of a province, covering as it does over 2,000 sq km, stretching from the South China Sea almost to the Cambodian border. We arrive at 10.30, and I find a brand new Mercedes waiting to collect me.

I am taken to the five-star Saigon Prince Hotel, where I am assigned room 924 on the top floor. Once installed, I sleep for two hours and, upon awaking, go for a walk down to the Riverside area in 90° heat. When I get back to the hotel, I find my return plane tickets to Hanoi have been delivered. It turns out, though, that the return flight will arrive in Saigon too late for me to catch my connection to Bangkok on the 19th. The flight I have requested is evidently full, but the excellent concierge knows my timetable and is working on the problem – with eventual success.

At 4, I go down to the health club on the second floor for a 90-minute massage. I am stripped and eased into a pair of cotton shorts suitable for someone with a 45-inch waist, with correspondingly large leg-holes. I am then wrapped in a waist-length kimono, and led into a semi-dark room that can only be described as being reminiscent of a mediaeval torture chamber, with brass hooks and chains hanging from the ceiling. A Vietnamese girl enters. She is about twenty years old, and well under five feet tall. She silently takes my kimono, and places me face down on a bed, before proceeding to suspend herself from the hooks while pummelling my back with her feet. The pain is excruciating, but strangely wonderful. She manages to crack each vertebra of my spine with her toes. After 90 minutes of mingled torture and bliss, I am released feeling superb. It has certainly been one of the best massages I have ever had, and is also available 24 hours a day. The total cost is US$24.

At 7, I shower and change in preparation for my meeting with Andrew Nguyen, sales director of Fortune Wines (one of the suppliers), which will involve drinks, followed by a tasting and dinner. I start with a dark rum, lime and soda in the ground-floor bar of the hotel, and Andrew arrives at 7.15. We then walk to the Temple Club, which is at 29 Ton That Thiep Street, for drinks. This is a very smart new trendy venue in a beautifully restored old building. There, we meet Vichai Saetia and his brother, proprietors of Fortune Wines. They are young, and have both been educated and trained in the UK and USA.

At 8.30, we take a cab to the Caravelle Hotel at 19 Lam Son Square, where I meet Brad Turley, the head chef of their Asian Reflections Restaurant, who is from San Francisco, and has prepared a special menu to accompany the wines that have been brought in. The menu is as follows:

Micronesian crispy shrimp baton with Malaysian melon salsa, served with Bisol Crede Prosecco (good, ★★); south-east Asian mixed ceviches, and Chi Pan-style pot stickers with miso chilli sauce, served with 1998 Kendal Jackson Chardonnay from California (dried out, x), 2002 Springfield Estate Fire Finch Sauvignon Blanc from South Africa (very good, ★★★), 2001 Catena Chardonnay from Argentina (excellent, ★★★★), and 2002 Jackson Estate Sauvignon Blanc from New Zealand (OK, ★★); blackened spiced rare-seared tuna with soy mustard sauce, garlic oil seared sea bass with roasted caper vinaigrette, tempura-crisped soft-shell crab with raspberry-sesame-vanilla vinaigrette, 'Flush and Flesh' peppered duck breast with black bean-chilli-mustard glaze, grilled veal chop with pickled beef vinaigrette, tenderloin of beef with green peppercorns and a mixed mushroom vinaigrette, and rack of lamb with spicy eggplant and a star-anise Cabernet reduction, served with 1997 Sella e Musca Villamarina Cannonau from Italy (very good, ★★★★), 2000 Fairview Prima Pinotage from

South Africa (very good, ★★★★), 1999 Concha y Toro Marques de Casa Concha from Chile (good, ★★), 2000 Catena Malbec from Argentina (corked), and 2000 Château Parenchère, Cuvée Raphael, Bordeaux Supérieur (corked); and tropical fruit spring rolls.

After this most superb dinner, we go for a Wild Turkey bourbon and soda in the trendy Q Bar opposite, and I eventually get to bed at midnight.

11.3.03. Having slept through until 7.30 a.m., I eat a buffet breakfast in the hotel, consisting of apple juice, freshly cooked omelette, bacon, mushrooms, tomatoes, hash browns and baked beans, with superb Vietnamese coffee.

Afterwards, I take the 15-minute walk down Dong Khoi Street, where there are many shops and stalls selling food, and on to the Metropolitan Building for a meeting with Youri Korsakoff, managing director of Ample Ltd, a wine wholesaler. They have also just opened a wine warehouse at 178 Pasteur District 1, which is managed by a young Spanish girl. Apparently, things are changing in Saigon, but this is still a communist-controlled country, with no alcohol advertising allowed.

We go to lunch in the French Restaurant at the five-star Sofitel Hotel – pea soup with prawns (★★+), and baked sea bream (★+), accompanied by Château Calon 2000, a light lunch-style claret from St-Emilion (★+).

Back at the hotel, I meet up again with Andrew, who conducts me on an excellent walking tour including the Ben Thanh market, stopping off at an amazing coffee bar, La Fenêtre Soleil, on the second floor of 135 Le Thanh Street. You walk up two flights of stairs, in what seems initially to be a derelict house, to the recently converted coffee house, which has a great view over the city. I try an authentic Vietnamese coffee, which takes ten minutes to drip through a single-cup metal filter on to condensed milk. It is then poured over ice cubes, the final brew being both very strong and highly refreshing.

We pay a quick visit to the soon-to-be-opened Sheraton Hotel, which will clearly be a great place, and then proceed to the Oasis bar at the top of the Caravelle Hotel for a 333 (local beer).

Back at my hotel at 5, I go for a 45-minute foot massage, and then meet up again with Andrew at 7. We go off to a most authentic Vietnamese Restaurant, Quan an Ngn, which turns out to be full of locals, and where we are joined by three lady friends of Andrew's, one Vietnamese, one American and one German, who all live in Saigon. The food here is cooked along the aisles in the open, and is similar to the dim sum style of service, in that they bring you lots of different dishes until you ask them to stop. There is pho (pronounced 'fur', a delicious noodle soup with beef), chicken noodle soup, lightly battered prawns, sausage meat that you wrap in thin rice paper rolls with lettuce, minced prawn wrapped around bamboo sticks, and so forth. It's all superb, and washed down with good Saigon beer.

Leaving at 9, we go on to Carmen, a South American bar in a grotto, frequented only by locals. The entrance door is three feet high and the place is packed. We drink Margaritas to live Latin music, enjoying the vibrant atmosphere. Then we go on to the Q Bar for Wild Turkey bourbon and soda, sitting outside in a lovely, freshening breeze. I'm back at the hotel at midnight.

Saigon really is a fascinating city, now thriving on tourism, which can only continue to increase. It is filled with thousands of mopeds, which criss-cross the streets like swarms of wasps. Crossing the roads, you take your life in your hands as you dodge precariously between them. The riders all wear coloured bandanas around their faces against pollution, which gives them the air of members of some secret sect. There are apparently around a hundred accidents a week involving mopeds.

12.3.03. After passing a very fitful night, I breakfast at 8 a.m. on scrambled eggs and bacon, apple juice and coffee. Checking out at 9.30, I take the hotel car to the airport's domestic terminal for Vietnam Airways flight VN 218 Economy Class to Hanoi, departing at 11.30. I find myself squashed between two Vietnamese, leaving me with no elbow room at all. The stewardess's safety announcements include the advice not to lie on the floor. It's a two-hour flight, during which lunch is served – quite a good dish of chicken with noodles and carrots, although it is difficult to eat in the exceedingly cramped conditions.

We arrive at 1.30 and I take a $10 taxi ride to the luxurious five-star Daewoo Hotel, which is just outside the centre of town. I'm in room 711. I immediately place a call to Sylvain Bournigault of Celliers d'Asie, the largest local wine wholesaler. We arrange to meet at 3.30.

The Vietnamese capital has a population of 3.5 million, and is a city of lakes, shaded boulevards and parks, more attractive than Saigon. They call it the Paris of the Orient. The climate is cooler here, with more rain, but it is far less Westernised than Saigon, the old quarter crammed with tiny shops and street markets, and the whole place again full of mopeds,, irascibly hooting each other all the time.

After a short tour of the company cellars, we go for a walk around the old quarter down to the bay, and then I am taken to an event in town at Bobby Chin's Restaurant and Bar, to promote Nebraska beef and Washington State wines, a great occasion complete with a local jazz band. Following this, we go to dinner with the general manager of the Sofitel Metropole Hotel, another top-drawer five-star hotel, where we are served a selection of Vietnamese dishes (pork rolls, beef tenderloin, etc.), accompanied by indifferent South African Chardonnay and Pinot Noir.

After dinner, we descend to their basement bar, where we drink a bottle of Bordeaux Supérieur 1998 (★+), and then pitch up at the Press Club next door, where we meet with the American executive chef, Donald Berger, plus a crowd who have spilled over from the previous party. Donald proceeds to open a magnum of Solace, a 100% Sangiovese from California, which is an Antinori venture (★★★★), a Pinot Noir from Santa Rosa (★★+), Montes Special Syrah from Chile (★★★), Guigal's 1998 Hermitage (★★), and his 1999 Châteauneuf-du-Pape (★+).

I take a cab back to the hotel at 2 a.m.

13.3.03. I start the day with a 9 a.m. breakfast of omelette with onions and peppers, baked ham, tomatoes, Cajun potatoes, watermelon juice and coffee. At 10.45, I meet up with Sylvain and Didier, the Sofitel Metropole's chef, for a guided tour of the local market. This proves to be an absolutely fascinating excursion, as

Didier buys all his produce from here, and this is just one of his daily visits. The large covered market is crammed full of small stalls selling every conceivable kind of vegetable, herb, fruit, fish and meat (including dog, frog, bat and rat). Many of the vegetables are grown locally and are totally unfamiliar to me.

At 1, it starts to rain, just as it did yesterday. At a place next to the market, we stop for a Hanoi beer, and then catch a cab back to the Sofitel, where I am treated to a full tour of the kitchens, which are in the process of preparing lunch. The hotel also runs a daily cooking school at $45 a day, which includes lunch and a tour of the market.

Later, Sylvain takes me on the back of his moped to a small back street, where we stop for lunch at a typical pho café, an extremely primitive place that is basically no more than a hole in the wall with three tables. It only serves pho, the noodle soup of beef and vegetables, their version of which turns out to be absolutely delicious. I certainly would never have ventured into such a place on my own, but will await the final verdict of my stomach later on.

Back at the hotel, I have a massage, an hour and a half of sheer bliss, and then at 7, go to the 18th-floor bar for a whisky and soda and a great view over the city. Dinner is in the hotel's Chinese Restaurant, Silk Road, where we are regaled with a *menu dégustation*, a fantastic spread accompanied by endless Tiger beers. The starter dishes are barbecued pork with honey sauce, marinated pork tongue, marinated spicy beef, jellyfish with onion oil sauce, shredded potato in fah plen sauce, and pork stomach with beansprout salad. These are followed by double-boiled pork stomach soup with pepper, and then fried prawns with onion, and steamed snake head with black bean sauce. For the main courses, there are braised pork intestine with pork blood, braised ox stomach soup with white turnip, sautéed shredded eel with chilli and fah plen, sautéed pork kidney with chilli sauce, and deep-fried pork intestine with chilli and fah plen, accompanied by Korean-style noodles with black bean sauce, noodles with shredded pork and local vegetables, and fried rice with curried minced beef. We finish with a sweetmeat of double-boiled snow fungus and lily seeds.

Street market, Hanoi

Street market, Hanoi

At 10, I round off the day with a large bourbon and soda in the ground-floor bar, and am in bed by 10.45.

14.3.03. I am awoken by an alarm call at 4 a.m., pack and check out. A $10 cab ride gets me to the airport, where I check in at 6.40 for the Vietnam Airways flight to Nha Trang, which is on the East coast, south of Hanoi. Flying time is one hour and forty minutes. Once there, I am collected by the resort bus and taken the 15-minute journey to Ana Mandara, a luxurious resort and spa right on the beach, with thatched cottages dotted around. My villa, 222, boasts a great view over the South China Sea. The rain of earlier on has now cleared to brilliant sunshine, giving a magical feel to the whole resort.

Nha Trang is the capital of Khanh Hua province. It has a population of 320,000, and one of the best beaches in all Vietnam. The dry season lasts from June until September, with the wettest months being October and November. When it does rain, it usually does so at night or in the morning, before the day gives way to beautiful sunshine.

I drink a draught San Miguel on the beach, prior to setting about a personal barbecue grill with fish, beef and chicken satay, which you cook at your leisure.

At 3, I have a 50-minute back, head and foot massage, during which I reluctantly fall asleep. The rest of the day proceeds with the diving school drinks party at 5.30, a magnificent buffet dinner at 8, and then bed at 11.

15.3.03. I awake at 9 a.m., and go to breakfast at the most sumptuous and varied buffet I have ever seen, covering seemingly all known countries and regions. You begin at the juice bar, where a drink from any combination of fresh fruits is made for you, and then move on to a choice from Japanese, Chinese, Vietnamese, Italian, French, German and English counters, all offering a staggering array of dishes. I settle for two poached eggs on toast, with a multi-vitamin fruit drink and the lovely, almost chocolate-flavoured Vietnamese coffee.

A demonstration of coffee roasting is fascinating, after which I set to preparing my notes for the training sessions. Lunch is a 333 beer and a bowl of beef pho.

Following a refreshing swim, I take my first training session at 2. Fourteen staff hear me talk on wine, from vine growing to winemaking. At 5, I repair to the spa for an hour and a half, undergoing the joys of pedicure, manicure, a facial and head massage, after which I can truly say I feel ten years younger. (Pity about the looks, though.)

In the evening, I have drinks with the chef, Christian Fogliano, who is Italian by birth but was brought up in Australia. He is young and prodigiously talented. His dinner is a buffet of seafood and a Vietnamese barbecue of quail, pork balls, minced prawn and pork on bamboo sticks, squid, fish, chicken wings, marinated beef, chicken sausages, and a range of Japanese delicacies, plus a salad and fruit bar. A choice of six white wines and six reds by the glass is offered. You help yourself to as much as you want for $14. Having tasted all of them, I opt for a 2001 Yalumba Chardonnay from Australia (★★) and Terrazas Argentinian Cabernet Sauvignon (★★+), the others being either thin and fruitless, or else out of condition.

At 10, I drink a large Jim Beam bourbon and soda in the beach bar, listening to the waves roll in. The weather today has been perfect, with clear blue skies and sunshine complementing the lovely rolling surf of the South China Sea. The waves make swimming difficult, but fun to try. With the slight sea breeze, one has to be very careful not to get sunburned. I was only out for a short while with the sun cream, and felt that my shoulders had had enough.

16.3.03. An 8.30 breakfast consists of a very wide choice of superb dim sum, croissants with jams of dragon-fruit, tamarind and ginger, blended multi-vitamin fruit juice and Vietnamese coffee.

I spend the morning continuing with my work in compiling the hotel's new wine list, and then break at 12.30 for a lunch of Vietnamese spring rolls and beef pho with 333 beer. At 2, I take a staff training session, and then repair to the spa at 4 for a spot of reflexology. My feet now feel they can really do the tango!

Christian, the chef, and I begin the evening with drinks – dark rum, lime and soda – in the courtyard beside the main bar, listening to two Vietnamese girls play very haunting indigenous music on zither-like instruments. Dinner is a buffet in the main restaurant by the pool, a seafood barbecue with a range of Vietnamese, Chinese and Japanese delicacies, plus a whole roast suckling pig. As usual, I eat far too much of everything, as it's all so delicious, washing it all down with Terrazas Argentinian Chardonnay. I end the evening with a large Jim Beam and soda by the sea, retiring at 11.

17.3.03. Waking early at 7 a.m., I go for a walk along the beach, followed by a swim in the newly built pool. Breakfast is fresh orange and vitamin juice, with four types of dim sum and Vietnamese coffee.

At 10.45, I take a training session for the bar staff on spirits, and then break for what has become my habitual lunch of beef pho and 333 beer. More staff training is scheduled for 2.15. The team is really responding well, and absorbing a substantial amount of information.

At 6.30, I give a tutored wine tasting to twelve selected guests of the hotel. We sample 2001 Santa Digna Sauvignon Blanc from Chile, well-balanced with good acidity (**), 2001 Yalumba Chardonnay from Australia, oaky and buttery, but with good ripe fruit (**), 1997 Wantz Réserve Alsace Gewurztraminer, rich and fully mature (***), 1997 Mondavi Pinot Noir from California, fully mature with good ripe Pinot fruit (**), 2000 Terrazas Cabernet Sauvignon from Argentina, deep, tannic and very well-made (***), and 1999 Yalumba Shiraz, very deep, ripe, rich and full-bodied (**+).

Afterwards, I dine with two of the guests, film-makers from Vienna, on stuffed ricepaper spring rolls, and stir-fried chicken and rice, accompanied by another bottle of the 1997 Gewürztraminer. A large bourbon and soda makes a suitable nightcap, and I retire at 11.

18.3.03. I am awoken rudely at 6 a.m. by the noise of endless heavy aircraft on manoeuvres. I turn on the TV and hear the news that Saddam Hussein has been given 48 hours to leave Iraq or there will be war. After that dose of gloom, I decide to go for a large breakfast. Eight different dim sum with soy and chilli sauces, Vietnamese coffee and watermelon juice make a fitting repast. The weather is superbly warm at 31°C, with clear blue skies and unbroken sunshine.

I swim before lunch, which as before consists of a delicious bowl of pho with the local 333 beer. There is staff training at 2.15, and then at 4, I go for a one-hour aromatherapy massage, followed by a glass of delicious fresh mango juice.

A drinks party has been laid on at 6.30 in the beach bar by the pool, to celebrate the new moon, an astonishing sight. Under a full moon in a clear sky, I meet up with Andrew from Fortune Wines for a Vietnamese buffet dinner by the pool, and then go into town to an amazing bar called Crazy Kim's. The owner, Kim, is a woman in her late forties with a larger-than-life personality. In years past, she was an escapee, one of the Vietnamese boat people. When the boat she was in was about to be turned away from Canada, she jumped overboard with no belongings and swam two miles to the shore. She has since returned to Vietnam and opened this very popular bar in Nha Trang. She has also become a pioneer in saving young boys from prostitution, feeding, clothing and schooling them at her own expense. After much Jack Daniels, we stop for a local beef pho, a rather spicy version, returning to the hotel at midnight.

I am not sure whether my Western stomach is accustomed yet to the very local food.

19.3.03. After waking to a 7 a.m. alarm call, I pack and get ready to check out. I'm taking Vietnam Airways flight VN 415 from Nha Trang to Saigon, a one-hour journey, and then connecting to Thai Airways Business Class flight TG 681 to Bangkok at 12.30, seat 12K. Leaving Vietnam, one has to pay a $12 departure tax.

I arrive in Bangkok at 2 p.m. in temperatures of 38°C and soaring humidity. The taxi to the D'Ama Hotel costs 250 baht (commercial rates of exchange are 43 baht to the euro, 40 to the US dollar and 63 to the pound). The hotel is at Nakorn Luang Plaza, New Petchburi Road. It is one of the efficiently run Six Senses Pavilion Business Hotels. I'm put in room 2306 on the 23rd floor, which is very clean and agreeable. A massage in my room costs 300 baht (about £5).

After showering and changing, I go to Happy Hour in the foyer bar for the 'buy-one-get-one-free' offer. There is a promotion on Jim Beam bourbon (what luck!). I avail myself of a couple of these, and then a car arrives at 7.30 to take me to the Mango Tree Restaurant, 37 Soi Tantawan, Surawongse Road. The traffic is the worst in any city I have ever encountered, including Bombay. I eventually arrive at 8.30 for what turns out, on the return journey, to have been a trip of about eight minutes. The restaurant is located in a tiny back street in a lively district with night markets, and massage parlours offering every conceivable service. There is an open courtyard with musicians and Thai dancing, and also a first-floor open balcony, which evidently has to be booked in advance.

I am given a table by the fountain, the noise of which is louder than the music. A large (65cl) bottle of Singha beer, correctly chilled, accompanies five shrimp cakes, freshly fried and deliciously served with a spicy honey sauce. I decline the satay, which is grilled to order on an open barbecue, and turned occasionally by the security guard, and instead go for a very good chilli chicken stir-fry, with a noodle dish to follow, containing sweetcorn, green beans and tomatoes.

I am back at the hotel at 11.

20.3.03. Having spent a fitful night (I think my stomach needs a couple of days' rest from chilli), I start the morning at 8, on the day that the war against Iraq is launched, with a breakfast meeting with Alain Ruffier, food and beverage manager of the Evason Hotel in Phuket. He has kindly arranged a series of tastings with five local wine suppliers, in order for me to select one or two to supply all the Six Senses resorts in Thailand. The depth of the stock carried by the top local wine merchants is unbelievable. I'm convinced it's a carry-over from the 1990s boom in sales of claret, which has now collapsed, leaving them all with sizeable residues of stock. One merchant, for example, has at least ten vintages of all the First and Second Growths back to the mid-1970s, as well as Cheval Blanc, Le Pin, Pétrus, etc.

We eat a buffet lunch of dim sum at the D'Ama, and then I have further meetings during the afternoon.

In the evening, I take a cab to Ban Klang Nam, 288 Soi 14 Rama 111 Road, a very traditional Thai restaurant right on the river. It seats over 500 people and the food is superb. My menu takes in: seafood hot pot soup with lemon grass, squid, mushrooms and vegetables; kale in oyster sauce; huge prawns with a spicy marinade dip of fish sauce, garlic, lemon grass and chilli (which takes 24 hours to prepare); papaya salad; steamed rice; a whole sea bass; sticky rice and coconut; fresh mango; and coconut flesh cakes. Also on the menu are fresh worm tails from Den Hoy Lord, duck tongue stew, 'amazing squid', deep-fried serpent head, crispy pig ear, baked goose web, stir-fried emu, serpent head gibler, and such variant spellings as 'chickhen', 'stir-fired', 'mashrooms' and 'vetgetable'.

After a nightcap at the excellent Regent Hotel, I retire at 11.

21.3.03. I breakfast at 7.30 a.m. on scrambled eggs and bacon, orange juice and coffee, and then the morning is taken up with meetings with two other wine wholesalers.

We take lunch at Girarosta l'Opera, the oldest Italian Restaurant in Bangkok – a mixed salad, pasta with lobster, and grilled yellowtail with tomato and capers, with a bottle of a light, thin Sangiovese that is shipped by the owner, and sells at $4 a glass. I then have a meeting with Ambrose Wines, biggest supplier to the off-premise trade in Thailand, the result of a management buyout from Seagrams.

Afterwards, I go back to the hotel to pack, and return to the bar for Happy Hour and that Jim Beam promotion again. Dinner is at Lemongrass, 5/1 Sukhumvit 24, where I have a table in the quiet garden. It's quite humid sitting out here, but the tranquillity is shattered by the people at the next table, a family unable to control their small daughter, who screams continually, and is only occasionally pacified by the monotonous recitation of nursery rhymes. Dinner is minced chicken balls wrapped in deep-fried vermicelli (quite dry, and reminiscent of small balls of knitting wool) served with a honey, nut and chilli sauce, followed by sliced grilled pork with steamed rice in a piquant sauce of soy, chilli and garlic, accompanied by two large Singha beers. Overall, this is a disappointing meal, with some evidence of rather clumsy cooking.

I cab back to the hotel at 11.

22.3.03. Checking out at 9 a.m., I take a taxi with my luggage to the Peninsular Hotel, a most stunning 37-storey place overlooking the river. Sadly, conditions are overcast, with possible rain in the offing and very high humidity. I'm assigned a Superior room, 3508 on the 35th floor, with breathtaking views over the city and the river.

At 3.45, I collect Clare from Bangkok Airport in a chauffeured Mercedes provided by the hotel. On our return, we drink champagne on the terrace, and then at 6 p.m., embark on a long private boat trip along the winding canals, a very interesting and thoroughly worthwhile excursion. We reach the Ban Klang Nam Restaurant by boat too as the place is situated right on the river – undoubtedly the best way to arrive. Our table is right by the water's edge, and is plentifully supplied with 60cl bottles of Singha beer, which seem to appear from nowhere in rapid succession. We dine on a clear soup with cuttlefish, prawns and vegetables cooked in a metal pot, grilled langoustines with a spicy sauce, stir-fried kale in oyster sauce, and a mango and sticky rice dessert.

A cab returns us to the hotel at 10.30.

23.3.03. For breakfast in the Terrace Restaurant by the river, we are offered a buffet of every country, and plump for dim sum, eggs, ham and baked beans, and papaya juice. We then take a shuttle boat across to the River City shopping complex, which turns out to be very disappointing.

At 11, a journey by tuk tuk taxi takes us to Jim Thompson's house and museum for a guided tour. This is a collection of seven old Thai houses fashioned into one dwelling which belonged to the man who helped restore the Thai silk industry after World War Two, and proves to have been well worth a visit. There is also very good shopping here. Afterwards, we walk to the Dusit Than Hotel for a less than inspiring buffet lunch on their 22nd floor. The range is extensive but the cooking doesn't impress, and the bill with two beers comes to around £50.

We take the Sky Train to N8 Chatuchak, a covered market of 9000 stalls, which only opens on Saturdays and Sundays. As we are wandering around this rabbit warren of a place, the heavens open, and torrential rain sends us back in a cab to the hotel at 4.30.

The downpour eventually stops at around 7, and gives way to clear skies once more. We take drinks in the hotel bar to the accompaniment of a very good jazz trio, and then cab to the Mango Tree. Dinner encompasses shrimp cakes, feather fish cakes, pad thai noodles with shrimps, stir-fried morning glory, and jelly noodles with pork and various fungi – all excellent. With these dishes, we drink a 2001 Australian Chardonnay/Semillon.

We return to the hotel for a Jim Beam and soda, and get to bed at 10.30.

24.3.03. Awakening to a 5.30 a.m. alarm call, we take a light breakfast and then cab to the airport for Thai Airways flight TG 917 Bangkok to Phuket, which will take 90 minutes. We take off at 8 and arrive at 9.30, to be collected by chauffeured car and taken to the Evason Resort Hotel at Raiwa Beach, which is on the southern tip of the 30 x 15-mile island (two hours distant from the airport, which is on the northern side). Room K130 overlooks the sea. It is a truly immaculate setting, with a vista of uninhabited islands dotted about. We have a lunch of Chinese snacks and Singha beers in the open restaurant.

At 6, I go for a massage, and later we have dinner in the Thai Restaurant right on the beach – various Thai appetisers followed by pork noodles, partnered with 2000 Château du Galoupet rosé. We retire early.

25.3.03. I arrange the rest of the week's staff training programme, which will include a 2.30–4 p.m. session each day, plus a wine tasting for the guests on Friday at 6.

A taxi takes us into Phuket town, where there are some strikingly grand Sino-Portuguese mansions built by tin barons, plus a lively market and numerous tailors' shops, offering such deals as three suits and three shirts, all ready-made within 24 hours, for a total of US$199. The weather is hot and humid, and the sky is turning overcast.

We eat a snack lunch of filled rice rolls and Singha beer by the pool, and then the rain starts. Staff training from 2.30 until 4 is for the heads of staff, and is succeeded by an hour of sheer bliss in the form of shiatsu in the spa.

The evening's buffet dinner is comprised of Indian food and matching wines, five reds and five whites, as much as you can drink. We settle for Santa Anna Sauvignon Blanc and Cabernet Sauvignon from Chile. We are in bed at 11.

26.3.03. Today's conditions are humid and overcast, with slight rain. After a dim sum breakfast, we take the Thai traditional longboat over to Bon island, a 15-minute ride. It boasts a lovely beach with thatched restaurant and bar, and just the one honeymoon cottage to rent at $1,000 a day. On the return journey, heavy rain sets in.

Lunch is Thai fishcakes and Singha beer, after which I take staff training between 2.30 and 4. Afterwards, I go for another superb treatment in the spa, from 5 till 6.30.

Dinner is in the Evason Restaurant, a fantastic menu that comprises Thai omelette roulade, confit of duck in nam prik sauce, and chilli rice, accompanied by a quite good 2000 McGuigan Cabernet Sauvignon from Australia.

The weather continues unsettled and intensely humid.

27.3.03. After an 8.30 breakfast of freshly cooked scrambled eggs and bacon, we take the 9.30 longboat to Bon island. Clouds begin to form in the sky, and then right on cue, the rain starts, but not too heavily. We have lunch at the beach restaurant – grilled red snapper with stir-fried vegetables, accompanied by Phuket lager. The weather begins to improve, and a little sun even appears.

We take the boat back at 1, and my afternoon continues in the prescribed fashion with staff training from 2.30 until 4, and then off to the spa between 5 and 6.30, for a treatment called Harmony, which entails various oils being applied to the back, neck and head.

A table is booked for us at the Boathouse Restaurant on Kata Beach at 8 p.m. After drinks in the hotel bar, a cab collects us at 7.45. The restaurant is situated in the centre of a three-star resort full of cheap tailors' shops, and is something of an oasis in the surroundings. It's a fine, smart place positioned right on the beach with a stunning menu and award-winning wine list written by Serena Sutcliffe MW. We begin with a Siam mixed platter, various Thai delicacies all beautifully presented, crabs, prawns and chicken satay with various dips. Fried grouper fish is the whole fish, filleted and then reassembled together with the head, while a trio of lobster dishes is each cooked in a different sauce and served in the shell. With the food, we drink a 1998 Argentinian Torrontes, which is quite rich and spicy.

Suddenly, the heavens split open and we are engulfed by a tropical storm of violent thunder and lightning. A cab takes us back to the hotel at 10.30.

28.3.03. The sensational storm continues all through the night, with constant flashing lightning, torrential rain and gale force winds. By 8.30 a.m., it's calm and cloudy, with just a slight gentle rain, and by the time we have eaten a dim sum breakfast, the skies have cleared altogether, and it's a very hot and sunny day.

We have lunch in the pool bar: tempura snapper and Singha beer. At 3, I go for a shiatsu massage, 90 minutes of agony and bliss in equal measure, and then at 6, I take a tutored wine tasting for the senior management.

Dinner is in the fusion restaurant, a perfect setting for a balmy evening. We eat Szechuan chicken with chilli vegetables, accompanying it with 2000 Tyrrells Cabernet/Merlot from Australia, a very good wine.

29.3.03. The day dawns overcast again, with a little rain. I eat a very good breakfast at 8.30 of poached eggs, ham and tomatoes, apple and lime juice and coffee.

Despite the mixture of sun and slight rain during the morning, it continues very hot. At 12.30, we have Bloody Marys, prior to a nam prik lunch that includes a very spicy paste of crushed dried shrimps as a dip for raw vegetables and rice. I also sample a selection of herbs that have been steeped in Thai whiskey – interesting! Later, I receive a 50-minute foot massage.

In the evening, we have an Asian buffet dinner, accompanied by the very good 2000 Saint Clair Merlot from New Zealand.

30.3.03. Breakfast at 9 a.m. is dim sum, and I later have a satay lunch with Alain Ruffier at 12.30.

At 1.30, a car takes us the one-hour journey to Phuket airport for the Bangkok Airways flight PG 422 to Kho Samui, with its thatched airport. We sit in the transit lounge here for an hour, before proceeding on to Hua Hin, where we are collected in a car on behalf of the Evason. A half-hour drive brings us to the hotel, which is situated on the beach in a magnificent setting. We are given room 424, the Garden Villa.

After a quick shower and change, we go to a cocktail party with all the Six Senses directors, who happen to be in the resort for a week-long conference. A superb buffet dinner, with food ranging from all the eastern countries, is served. Successive bottles of Beau Rivage Sauvignon Blanc are all corked, but the Rioja Crianza proves to be quite good.

We retire at 11.30.

31.3.03. After an omelette and bacon breakfast at 8.30, the day proceeds briskly with staff training from 12 till 1, and then a massage from 2 till 3. I am to give a tutored tasting with dinner for all the directors at 7.

The aperitif is 2002 Babich Sauvignon Blanc from New Zealand, which seems to lack zip. Léon Beyer's 2000 Alsace Riesling is mature, with good depth of fruit, while the 1998 Yarden Cabernet Sauvignon from Israel is superbly rich, deep and classic. The dinner menu consists of shrimp and crab roulade mixed with celeriac, tomato and spicy shrimp soup, lamb crusted with herbs and spices, and various mousses and ice creams. We finish with 2000 Essencia Orange Muscat from California.

1.4.03. The weather today is excellent, with 33 degrees of sunny heat. I start the day at 8.30 with an enormous cooked breakfast. The morning is taken up with meetings and staff training, and then at 1.15 I have a lunch of Singapore noodles with chicken and prawn, accompanied by Singha beers.

The afternoon passes restfully before rain moves in at 5.30. I am to conduct a tutored wine tasting for guests in the wine cellar from 6.30 till 8. I have arranged a varietal tasting of Chardonnays from Chile (2002), Australia (2000) and Mexico (1998), and Cabernet Sauvignons from France (1998), Chile (2000) and Australia (2002). This is followed by a seafood buffet dinner, which seems to be comprised of every conceivable dish, and which we accompany with a 2000 Enate Spanish rosado.

2.4.03. We awake to 35°C on another glorious sunny day. A light breakfast suffices, during which I sample a range of home-made jams – starfruit, mango and papaya – with a selection of equally good home-baked croissants. Later, I am pampered at the spa with a foot-soothing pedicure, and Clare attends a Thai cookery course in the hotel kitchens.

From 12 until 1, I take staff training on basic viticulture, vinification, etc. They are responding well, despite the communication problems thrown up by the language barrier. A lunch of pad thai noodles and Singha beer at the bar is followed by a further visit to the spa to experience the benefits of neck and scalp therapy for one hour (sheer bliss!), and then a large dark rum, lime and soda.

My tutored wine dinner for tonight has been cancelled, which is fortunate in a way as all the directors from Bangkok and the general managers from the resorts have gathered at Hua Hin for their quarterly meeting, and Gregg, the larger-than-life chef, has organised a street market buffet on the beach. This turns out to be brilliant, with various stalls cooking an amazing array of Thai delicacies, accompanied by 2000 Rivallana Blanco from Bodegas Ondarre in Rioja. Fire balloons are then set off, rising picturesquely into a star-filled clear night.

3.4.03. I have learned a word of Thai – *sawadee* means 'hello'.

It's another wonderful day, with bright sun and clear skies, and for breakfast, I have a Japanese rice dish. The resort is hosting the finalists for Miss Sweden, who are all aged between 18 and 23, and look very beautiful being photographed in their bikinis. I sit by the pool during the day, drinking in the scenery and sipping Singha beers.

Dinner is a *menu dégustation* they call the 'grazing menu'. The first courses are salmon and seasonal vegetable terrine with sesame soya quark, deep-fried oyster Thai style, minced pork tenderloin salad, sautéed chicken liver in Cantonese herb sauce with fettucine, pan-fried crêpes with crabmeat and peppercorn cumin cream sauce, and steamed beancurd boat filled with vegetables in a sweet-and-sour sauce. The array of second courses comprises curry cream soup with pranburi seafood, beef consommé with winter melon and shiitake mushrooms, and Filipino gazpacho soup. Following these are steamed sole fillets topped with curried capsicum sauce on wild rice, fried lamb cutlets with banana mint sauce on creamed barley, roast duck medallion in honey mustard sauce on Asian vegetables, sautéed ostrich pad khu phao and jasmine rice, wasabi risotto with squid and prawns, grilled beef tenderloin with capsicum and coriander sauce, and sweetcorn galettes. The dessert offerings are pandan parfait with orange sauce, lemon grass crème brûlée with caramel, moonberry tart with yoghurt and kiwi sauce, banana chocolate strudel and cinnamon sauce, kaffir lime mousse with strawberry black pepper sauce, and crème caramel and mint ice creams.

With this spread, we drink the very good 1999 Alto Agrelo Malbec from Argentina.

4.4.03. An alarm call wakes us at 6 a.m., and we are taken by car at 6.30 to Bangkok Airport, 3½-hour drive. We check in for Thai Airways flight TG916 Business Class to London (me in seat 12K), scheduled to take off at 12.10, but delayed until 12.40.

On board, Duval-Leroy Fleur champagne is served, followed by chicken curry. We get through numerous films during the course of the twelve-hour flight to Heathrow Terminal 3.

Australia
(via Singapore and Hong Kong)
1992

27 March–8 April 1992

27.3.92. I arrive at Heathrow Terminal 3 at 9.30 a.m. My flight schedule is Qantas flight QF 02 to Bangkok, changing to flight QF 062 to Singapore. My seat allocations are 50C and 54B. The estimated flying time to Bangkok is 11 hours.

The 747–400 is full to capacity, with a preponderance of screaming children. Service is appalling, the civility of Qantas staff leaving a lot to be desired. The food – prawn cocktail followed by steak – is inedible, wines are sparkling wine masquerading as champagne and oxidised red wine in screw-top bottles, and to put the tin lid on matters, the film, *Man in the Moon*, is diabolical.

28.3.92. We arrive at Bangkok at 6.30 a.m. local time after 11½ hours. We change planes and wait another hour, and then the Singapore flight departs at 8.15. This is a 2½-hour flight, and the time zone is another hour ahead, so we arrive around midday local time.

Feeling very tired indeed, I am met at the airport and escorted to an upgraded suite at the Hyatt. It is a superb hotel with a swimming pool and health club, and I book a massage for 7 p.m. I go for lunch in the Picnic Park at 1, an amazing gathering of food hawkers offering a full range of Indian, Chinese, Nonya, Thai and Malaysian food, and I enjoy some excellent satay beef, chicken and other specialities including deep fried scorpion on prawn toast.

At 2, I embark on a guided coach tour of the now sanitised city created by Sir Stamford Raffles in 1819 as a halfway house between Britain's empire in India and its expanding trade marked with China, now with its high-rise hotels covering some 625 square kilometres 136 km north of the equator and a population of more than three million people, of whom over 75% are Chinese. We started at the Indian quarter strolling through the streets with the shops full of bangles, jasmine and joss sticks, and even a psychic parrot who tells your fortune; then to Chinatown, covering two square kilometres (where the most enormous rat I have ever seen scuttles nonchalantly by me), walking along the rows of traditional shophouses, and visiting Thian Hock Kheng, the temple of heavenly happiness built in 1841 without a single nail and decorated with tiles from Holland, railings from Glasgow and trimmings from China. Then I go to the Menilon pewter factory and the stunning Orchid Gardens, arriving back at the hotel at 6. I write some postcards and book a table for dinner at Siamese Fins, which was recommended by our tour guide.

My massage is very invigorating, a full hour of having my back walked on and so forth by a tiny Singaporean girl, after which I take a cab to Raffles Hotel. Originally the home of Captain Dare it became the Raffles Girls' boarding school, though the Captain continued to serve curry tiffin in its converted billiards room. In 1886 the Sarkies brothers purchased the house, and Raffles Hotel opened its doors on December 1, 1887.

This great institution reopened on September 16, 1991 after a two-year major restoration, and is quite superb, sporting over 700 oriental carpets. I drink a couple of Singapore Slings in the Long Bar; it's $19 per drink, and you get to keep the glass. This famous drink was created at Raffles in 1915 and is a combination of gin, cherry brandy, fruit juice, liqueurs and bitters. Big bowls of peanuts are provided free of charge. You throw the shells on the floor, which is covered. Beer is served in a mini-yard glass mounted on a wooden frame.

At 9, I leave for dinner, arriving at Siamese Fins about 15 minutes later. The address is 45 Craig Road, Tanjong Pagar, well off the beaten track, and the clientele seems exclusively composed of locals. Having had a chat with the head chef, Teeravat Pornsethakoon, I order Thai goose web in brown sauce, fried crab with Thai chilli, sauté pork with ginkgo nuts, superior black mushrooms and the house special fried rice. There is an appetiser of raw vegetables and fruit with two different spicy dips, followed by shark's fin soup served in a clay pot. I drink Tiger beer. The crab was outstanding, the best I have ever tasted, quite overshadowing the excellent pork, but the goose web, sadly, failed to appear.

Back at the hotel, I take a bourbon-and-soda nightcap in the Canopy Bar and am in bed at 11, completely shattered.

29.3.92. I awake at 6 a.m. after a good night's sleep, but start the day feeling awful. I take some aspirin, and eat a complimentary breakfast of fruit, cereal and coffee on the 13th floor.

A cab takes me to the cable car terminal at Mount Faber and I go on a ride 65 metres above the city, past the World Trade Centre to Sentosa Island, 'a pleasure centre'. A monorail trip takes me around the island, and then I visit the Underwater World and the lovely beaches, which I can imagine will be very crowded in the season. I have my palm read – all good news, of course.

Back at the hotel I pack up but leave the luggage, and take a taxi to lunch at the Nonya and Baba restaurant, River Valley Road, which specialises in the local Peranakam cuisine. Here I eat otak otak, fish cooked with coconut milk, chilli paste, yellow ginger and lasak leaves, which is made fresh daily and barbecued; buak keluak (which means 'black nut') from Jakarta, prepared by being soaked for three days and then chipped to extract the paste, which is mixed with minced meat and prawns and then stuffed back into the nut, cooked with fresh chicken, lemon grass, chilli paste and assam juice (superb); babi ponteh, pork in a sauce with bamboo shoot, mushrooms, fresh green chillies and brown soya bean paste; sambal lady's fingers, okra with chilli paste and prawns; all served with boiled rice and draught Tiger beer. I finish with kueh pisang, which is only served at weekends, bananas covered with a floury pink paste like blancmange, wrapped in a banana leaf and served cold. All in all, a thoroughly memorable meal.

Once I am safely back at the hotel, a storm brews up and the humidity goes off the scale. I drink coffee and write more postcards, and at 2.30, go for a session of reflexology. This turns out to be extremely painful, but beneficial. Afterwards, I relax with a mixed fruit juice and then sleep for one hour.

At 6, I take a taxi to Changi airport. It is the cleanest and finest airport I have ever seen, and boasts the largest duty-free shopping area in the world. I board the 8 p.m. Qantas flight QF 10 to Melbourne, seat 37H. The food is once again dreadful (duck, I think, but it's hard to be sure; even the stewardess was unsure), and I have no success at sleeping.

30.3.92. We arrive at Melbourne at 5.15 a.m. local time, and I am met by the Brown Brothers Winery export director, Greg Quinn. This is one of the oldest wineries in Australia founded in Milawa, Victoria, by John Francis Brown in 1885. I am now running a temperature and have a very bad dry cough. He takes me on a visit to the winery, which is a superb state-of-the-art operation including the Kindergarten Winery, built in 1989. This has all the equipment of the main winery but in miniaturised form, so as to be able to experiment with new grape varieties and crossings such as Tarrango (which consists mainly of Touriga Nacional, and which smells and tastes just like a cru Beaujolais) and Orange Muscat and Flora, a superb dessert wine blended from those two grape varieties. The nursery set-up is like something straight out of *Gulliver's Travels*.

We have a meeting over sandwiches with sales and marketing director Ross Brown. I then meet John Brown Snr and the present chief executive John Brown Jnr, and then viticulturalist Peter Brown for a tour of the vineyards. It really is a family-run concern. I ask how they have managed to stay independent when most of their competitors have been taken over and absorbed by the big conglomerates. John Brown responds, 'It's very simple. We have no bank borrowings.'

I am installed at the Gateway Hotel in the nearby local village of Wangaratta, which consists of one main road, a large veterinary surgery, a few small shops, and a couple of restaurants and bars. Back at the hotel at 5, I realise I am feeling ghastly, and start on the course of flu pills I have been given. I meet Greg at the hotel bar at 6.30. Its name is Ray's Bar, and its eponymous manager is built like a barrel. We go to an appalling local establishment for spaghetti Bolognese, after which – back at the hotel at 8.30 – I am very sick.

My temperature is rising, and I pass a horrendous night sweating and shivering, racked with a fearful cough.

31.3.92. I make a feeble attempt to get up, feeling absolutely dreadful. When I eventually succeed, Greg collects me at 8.30 and takes me to a local doctor. I am diagnosed with a viral chest infection, and am prescribed a course of antibiotics. Not being a doctor, I thought it best not to question his diagnosis, even though I disagreed. The fever increases to 103°F, and I spend all day in bed with no food.

1.4.92. I awake feeling slightly better. Greg collects me at 9, and although I start wilting pretty fast, by mustering all my resources, I manage to get through a tasting of 30 dry white and dessert wines and a full range of fortified wines. After a quick sandwich, I go back to bed, sweating copiously, and sleep through until 5 p.m.

When I awake, the bed is soaked but I feel much better, confident enough in fact to arrange to meet Peter and John Brown at 7.15 for dinner. We go to Peter's 47 Cellar Restaurant, quite near the hotel, and I note that I am beginning to feel distinctly better at last. We eat Moreton Bay bug tails, a local scampi-like seafood, and then steak. Although I order mine medium-rare and without sauces, it arrives very well done, accompanied by a sauce of cheese, bacon and mushrooms. There is lots of good Brown Brothers wine, which we have brought ourselves, but I only drink modestly, which is quite unlike me. I get back to the hotel at 11, and start to feel very ill again. This time, my stomach is badly affected. The whole thing is becoming quite unreal.

2.4.92. After another night of fitful sleep, accompanied by endless sweating and now diarrhoea, I can barely believe my bad luck. What the hell is the matter with me?

I meet Greg at 9, engage in various meetings, and then take tea with Mr and Mrs Brown Snr, a charming couple. At lunch with Public Relations manager Mark McKenzie, I just about manage a small sandwich, but it still feels as though there is a volcano in my stomach about to erupt. Nonetheless, at 2, I amazingly make it through a full tasting of 25 red wines making copious tasting notes, I haven't the slightest idea how.

Back at the hotel at 4 with a raging temperature, I try to sleep but am suffering from bad stomach pains. I get up at 5.30, make some phone calls and pack. After a shower, my temperature seems to moderate somewhat, but my stomach is still churning like a washing machine. Greg comes back to meet me for supper at the hotel. I'm not quite sure how I manage to get through three unmemorable courses. Clare always says I have a strong constitution, perhaps because it seems to be tested to the extreme limits.

3.4.92. The day begins with a breakfast meeting at 8 a.m. with Greg and product manager Glenn Phelps, and I am pleased to find that I am feeling much better at last. Just as well, as I now have to check out of the hotel for the drive to Melbourne. We go via their offices, for a sandwich lunch, leaving at 1.30. Also en route, we visit their Whitlands Vineyard high in the Alps, and eventually make Melbourne by 6.

I'm staying at the Rialto on Menzies, Collins Street, a superb hotel now owned by the Meridien, in room 714. An old Australian friend of mine, Dick Fyffe, arrives from his office around the corner for a drink, and then we go to his house, meeting up with his wife Caroline, and their neighbours, Charles and Lucy. From there, we go to Vince and Juliet Wong's. They have just opened a restaurant, Café Provence, 2, Wellington Parade, Williamstown. He is a fine chef who used to work in London. Juliet originally hails from Melbourne. They haven't changed a bit. The food is very good, with some great Australian wines from small cult growers, and somehow I end up paying the total bill.

I'm back at the hotel at 11.30, feeling much better. The only sour note comes in the form of an idiotic fax from my office, insisting that I have to be in Bordeaux on Monday. Notwithstanding that, I sleep well.

4.4.92. I awake at 8 a.m., feeling better still. I weigh myself and find that I'm down to 75kg. That will never do. I breakfast on scrambled eggs, bacon, hash browns, guava juice and coffee, and then take a walk out into the city.

My return to Melbourne has reminded me that it is quite a boring city, and the people often uncouth. In the Queen Victoria market, I overhear a pair of hard-nosed Australian stallholders being hassled by a middle-aged woman giving them some heavy number about heaven. The riposte she received from one of them was, 'Lady, there ain't nothing up there but bloody skippies.' The market is fascinating though, selling everything from clothing to live animals, including parrots. I buy a bushman's hat for Toby, and a koala bear bag and purse for Holly, together with two boomerangs, and then repair to the hotel for a beer.

I book myself on a city tour at 2, which turns out to be very good. We visit Captain Cook's cottage, located in the beautiful Fitzroy Gardens, the Shrine of Remembrance war memorial, where on Armistice Day each year, a ray of light hits a stone illuminating the word 'Love', and the spectacular Botanic Gardens. Then we go over Westgate Bridge for panoramic views over Port Philip Bay.

Back at the hotel, I shower and then go for a drink in the Edinburgh Bar, before taxiing to Lygon Street in the Carlton district. This is an attractive quarter featuring lots of cafés with pavement tables (I have a whisky at one of them). I go to dinner at the Lemon Grass Thai Restaurant, 189 Lygon Street, which gets a good notice in the Melbourne *Good Food Guide*. The menu is: goong son klin, a cold dish of minced prawn salad served in small lettuce balls seasoned with chilli, herbs and lime juice; puo moo goong gai, sliced pork with prawns, onions, peppers and lots of chillies in a tasty sauce; gaeng keow wahn, green curry in coconut soup; rice; and Singha beer. I also try the award-winning cocktail 'Lemon Grass Lover', consisting of vodka, peach liqueur, Midori, pineapple juice, lime and soda.

I leave at 9.30 and go to the Limerick Arms Hotel on Park and Clarendon Streets for some jazz, and am back at my own hotel at 11.

5.4.92. Arising at 8, I have breakfast in my room, and then pack. I taxi to the airport, where I find I have been upgraded to Business Class, seat 12C (this turns out to be the non-viewing seat for the film screen, and opposite the loo, but I'm not complaining!). The service is Cathay Pacific flight CX 102 to Hong Kong, due to leave at 1.15, but delayed until 2.45. I relax in the VIP lounge.

The flight takes nine hours, owing to an air traffic strike and a diversion over Indonesia. We arrive in Hong Kong at 11 p.m. local time, having gone backwards two hours. The upgrade, however, means superb food and service, and a car is awaiting me at the airport to take me to the excellent Hyatt Regency Hotel in Kowloon. There, I am met by Paul Turner, the night manager, who personally escorts me to my room. I have been upgraded to Gold Passport room 1534 – delightful!

6.4.92. I awake at 7 a.m. to find it pouring with rain. After phoning a recommended tailor named Jack Mann, I go for a walk, and then call on him at 9. I order trousers and shirts, to be collected on Wednesday at noon. He also takes me to buy a suitcase, video camera and fake ladies' Rolex, a great chap.

Back at the hotel, I book a tour of Kowloon and the New Territories, and it continues to rain all the while. I take lunch at the Golden Bull, a Vietnamese Restaurant in the New World Centre, ordering pork and prawn spring roll, beef noodle soup, barbecue pork balls and Tsing Tao beer.

The tour begins at 1.50. We take in Lok Ma Chau, an old rural village situated on a hilltop overlooking the Shenzhen River in the north-western New Territories with a view of mainland China, the very old and smelly Luen Wo market, with traditional stalls selling dried salt fish and 1,000-year-old eggs, and the Wong Tai Sin temple with its bright yellow roof tiles named after Hong Kong's most popular deity. The tour concludes with a fascinating visit to a working gemstone factory. Despite having bought an umbrella, I get soaked.

Returning to the hotel, I confirm my lunch with Mr and Mrs Mok (friends of a colleague in London) at the China Club on the mainland. I arrange my tour of the island for tomorrow, and then take myself off to the Peninsular for a whisky and soda. It is a grand old hotel with a very imposing lobby, but I am driven mad by an American – Phil from Philadelphia – who is wearing gloves and continually buys me drinks. The drinks bill comes to $99.

Back at the hotel, I have another drink in the Chinese bar and Restaurant, which has a fine view of Nathan Road – Hong Kong's golden mile. Thank God it has stopped raining at last. My next drink to arrive – horror of horrors! – is a whisky with of all things *lemonade*, which was promptly returned. I eat a light supper in the restaurant, consisting of a combination of mixed roast meats (suckling pig, soya chicken, roast goose and barbecue pork), accompanied by soft noodles with mushrooms, and Tsing Tao beer.

7.4.92. After breakfasting in my room at 7 a.m., we rendezvous at 7.30 for the tour of Hong Kong Island. We start in Stanley Market, a lively spot on the south side of the island with narrow winding lanes which are packed with shops and stalls selling everything from designer clothes to curios and jewellery, I buy birth-sign gemstones, we are then driven through the Repulse Bay area, where the beach is gorgeous. A 30-minute sampan ride around the waters is a delight.

I then take a cab into the city for the arranged meeting with Frances Mok and other friends for lunch at the China Club. This is situated on the 13th floor of the old Bank of China building, refurbished in the original style. It's a superb location, very exclusive and full of poseurs. Lunch is good though: dim sum, roast goose, chicken and pork, noodles with green beans and minced pork, custard tart, a couple of gin and tonics, and tea.

Afterwards, I take the Peak Tram from the Garden Road terminus to climb the 397 metres to the Peak Tower. The journey takes about five minutes and from the top, there is a spectacular 360° view of Hong Kong Island, Kowloon, the New Territories and the islands of the South China Sea. On the journey up to the Peak, we pass some very smart residences. We return across the harbour on the White Star ferry, $1.20 (about 8p) which is probably the cheapest first-class trip in the world – an eight-minute journey between Hong Kong Island and Tsim Sha Tsui, Kowloon. The distinctive green-and-white ferries have been plying the harbour waters since 1898.

In the hotel bar, I book myself a trip to Macau for tomorrow. I watch a film on TV, *The Terminators*, and then return to the bar at 8 for the first of three bourbon and sodas. Kowloon is full of tourists, camera shops and neon signs. Hong Kong Island is for the business and smart set, with far too many very tall buildings too close to each other. It's full of poseurs on mobile phones and life is very fast, with no time to breathe or relax. I make the acquaintance of a commercial traveller from Newcastle, selling printing equipment. He tells me he travels seven months of the year, nearly beating my record.

At 9.30, I go to the Wu Kong Shanghai Restaurant for steamed dumplings (which are not on the menu), a boring pork and veg dish, plain rice and Chinese beer. It's a shame that all the interesting dishes appear only on the Chinese version of the menu.

8.4.92. I check my baggage out at 7.30 a.m., take a bus to the Island and then book the one-hour hydrofoil journey to Macau, which is the oldest European settlement in the East, dating back to 1557. It was once also the richest, the fulcrum of Portugal's trade with the region. The tour bus brings me to the temple of Kun Iam, goddess of mercy. Here is the table where the first treaty was signed between the USA and China in 1844. I visit the border gate with China, and admire the towering façade of the ruins of St Paul's Cathedral which was burnt down in 1835. My next stop is the summer residence of the Bishop of Macau on Penha Hill and the historic Monte Fortress, which defended the city against the Dutch in the seventeenth century. The organised lunch at Poerto Nouve is awful commercial food, and then we have a look at one of the six casinos. Our choice is an amazingly large place full of Chinese, gambling at three in the afternoon. As gambling is illegal on the mainland, the gambling-mad Chinese go to Macau. I lose $20 on the slot machines in as much time as it takes to blink an eye.

We return on the ferry to Hong Kong, and then to the hotel. I go to collect my clothes from Jack Mann, the tailor, and then a car takes me to the airport. I am put on standby for an upgrade, but denied entry to the Business Class lounge. Fortunately I receive an upgrade for the journey home, which is excellent, all thanks to the superb food, wine and service of Cathay Pacific.

I am pleased to say my weight has returned to normal.

Europe
1977–2003

Bulgaria
April 1977

My first trip to Bulgaria took place when the country was still a member of the old Soviet bloc. 'You are invited to Bulgaria for a week,' the letter tersely said, and I found myself thinking, Bulgaria! A country steeped in mystery, magic, Balkan gypsy violins, sour cream, plum brandy... Information on the Bulgarian gastronomic scene not being readily forthcoming, I had nothing to rely on but my imagination...

I arrive at Heathrow, as instructed, at 11 a.m. sharp, there being only one Balkan Airways flight per day, only to be told on check-in that there is an indefinite delay. The information desk is unable to give any reason, but estimates five hours at least. No sooner have I settled down for a drink than the loudspeaker announces that my flight is now closing. Choking down my Bloody Mary, I rush through the gate and am escorted on to the plane.

There are five passengers, including myself, with seat reservations apparently unnecessary. Our flight time to Sofia will be seven hours, as we shall be stopping at Brussels, Belgrade, Bucharest, etc., to pick up other passengers. Over Belgium, it is announced that there are no passengers waiting there, so we are spared the Brussels stop, and indeed this turns out to be the case at every other one of the scheduled stops, meaning that we make Sofia in just four hours.

During the flight, lunch is served, hunks of delicious chargrilled meats with gherkins, and two litre bottles of wine each. The white is a 1976 Dimiat, fresh and clean but very high in acidity, while the red is a Cabernet Sauvignon of the same vintage, a wine of 14% alcohol, which cuts through the spicy meats very well.

Unexpected delays greet our arrival at Sofia. Since I am a guest of the Bulgarian Government, I need no visa, but this hasn't been relayed to the immigration officers who were about to detain me.

Eventually, my guide appears, and I am whisked through the formalities in minutes, after assuring Customs that I was bringing in neither foreign currency nor coffee.

Once in the car, my guide (who, having lived in Leeds for two years, speaks perfect northern-accented English) informs me that I shall be staying just outside the capital. We proceed to Gorna Bania, some fifteen miles out of Sofia, which I am told is the site of a famous spa, and indeed there are public fountains everywhere, gushing forth a warm liquid reputedly good for kidney and rheumatic ailments.

Having been allowed precisely five minutes to unpack and change, I am then driven back to Sofia for dinner at the Russian Club.

Two aspects of the local gastronomy strike me at once. One is the enormous quantities of alcohol everybody gets through (the spirits are served in measures of 100ml), and the second is the pronounced Turkish influence on the cuisine. Dinner is a salad of tomatoes, cucumber and spring onions covered with strongly flavoured sheep's cheese, accompanied by voluminous quantities of a local schnapps flavoured with rose petals, and then for the main course, a kind of steak formed of heavily spiced minced meat, served with both potatoes and rice. My host orders a 1976 Cabernet of 14.5% alcohol, which is tough, but well balanced and very fruity. I decline a dessert, but am prevailed upon to try the black tea and pliska (the local brandy), both of which prove excellent.

On returning to the hotel, I am told that, the following day being Sunday, a day of relaxation has been arranged. I am to be in the lobby by 8 a.m., all set to go skiing.

The local ski resorts are half an hour's drive out of Gorna Bania, and this being the end of April, the season is just drawing to a close. The temperature is in fact in the 90s, and there is only one ski run open. At the hire shop I am offered a pair of lace-up boots and a pair mismatched skis, and I ask, as unfacetiously as I can, whether it might be possible to have two the same length.

In the evening, I am taken to eat at a local bistro near the hotel, dining on kebabs, rice, and what turns out to be the ubiquitous salad, accompanied by a bottle of Mavrud, an indigenous red varietal, which is excellent, not unlike a half-decent claret. The currency is the leva, of which there are 1.46 to the pound. This repast costs about £1.50.

On my return to the hotel, I discover a note instructing me to be ready in the lobby at 8 a.m. sharp next day.

The wine and spirit industry in Bulgaria is owned and controlled by the state company Viniprom, whose export division is called Vinimprex. It is to their offices that I am now taken. I am greeted by the overseas director and UK manager, who promptly takes me up to their tasting room to begin what turns out to be a very arduous three days of tasting.

More red than white wine is produced. Whites include Dimiat, Misket and Tamianka, while reds encompass the likes of Cabernet Sauvignon, Mavrud, Melnik, Gamza and Dadarka. There is also some sparkling wine, both red and white, mainly quite sweet, as well as dessert wines in both colours. One of the latter was a memorable red Tirnovo 1975, which was exactly like concentrated raisin juice, with barely a hint of alcohol detectable on the palate. As it was, it was 18% – the local equivalent of port.

In the evening, I am taken to the Park Hotel for dinner. The Park is Bulgaria's attempt at a Hilton, and has somewhat missed the mark. Drinks in the 'American Bar' are followed by a meal that begins with a single slice of ham with cucumber, served with a 1976 Dimiat (slightly reminiscent of a Touraine white), and then a very tough piece of either veal or pork (no one knows which), which has been grilled for who knows how long. The saving grace is a bottle of 1974 Melnik at 13.5%, which has some of the characteristics of a good Châteauneuf-du-Pape.

As it is becoming clear that Bulgarian haute cuisine leaves something to be desired, I ask my guide if, in future, we could perhaps eat in local restaurants and avoid the tourist hotels. He looks shocked but acquiesces, nonetheless insisting that tomorrow we must eat at The Crystal, in his opinion Sofia's best restaurant.

After three hours of further tasting in the morning, we head off for The Crystal. I am exceptionally hungry, but elect to leave the menu to him. To my amazement, the first course is the unavoidable salad, followed by a spin on veal chasseur (for which the very sharp knife is a godsend), served with tepid chips, rice, and a cold purée of tomatoes with chopped spring onions. The wine was a 1974 Misket, full, fresh and well balanced, with an understated flavour gently reminiscent of Muscat. My guide then insists I try a traditional dessert dish, which turns out to be plain pancakes with a scoop of strawberry ice cream in the middle. This is washed down with an excellent 1967 Tamianka dessert white, which is full and rich, with a lingering, vaguely Muscatty finish.

It is then suggested that I see some of the sights. Bulgaria has a population of only eight million people, mostly concentrated around the capital. Sofia itself is a very attractive city, full of parks and tree-lined streets, many monuments and statues. Especially memorable is the Georgi Dimitrou house museum, which is guarded by soldiers in brightly coloured uniforms, crowned by extravagantly plumed hats. The national art gallery, housed in the sumptuous palace of the former King Boris, has a splendid collection of works.

The next day, we visit one of the state vineyards at Plovdiv, some 200 miles south-east of Sofia. Each vineyard has its own bottling line, and bottles only its own production. Plovdiv is pretty much state-of-the-art, with recently modernised equipment and extensive new planting to cope with the ever-increasing demand.

At the present, Bulgaria is the world's premier exporter of bottled wines, with 80% being exported to the Soviet Union, followed by West Germany and Japan. For the time being, very little is exported to the UK, and what does arrive is nearly all shipped in bulk and bottled under various labels in Britain. It is hoped this will soon change. The country can trace its viticultural lineage back to classical times, when, as Pliny records, the first vineyards were established by the Thracian farmer, Eumolpius.

Once my guide has got the message, all our further meals are in the local equivalent of bistros. I enjoy many different types of kebab, ranging from pork to liver, with side-dishes of chargrilled meatballs and a local skinless sausage, all served with the delicious cold tomato and onion purée. The food is always tepid, but I am assured this is normal.

The drinking habits are an unending source of fascination. Red wine is customarily mixed with orange or bitter lemon, with the same treatment applied to the local beer. The quantities of spirits consumed – vodka, schnapps, etc. – make my jaw drop. When I enquire delicately whether there is a high rate of alcoholism, the answer is an emphatic 'No!' but when I persist, pointing out that the streets are full of reeling men from six o'clock every evening, I am then told that it is legal for anyone to grow vines in their gardens and take the grapes to the local distillery, to be converted into schnapps at an equivalent cost of about 4p a litre.

Further sightseeing reveals much beautiful countryside, dotted with small villages, with tables outside the cafés. Sadly, I have no time to visit the Black Sea area, which is reportedly the perfect holiday resort – golden sands, a warm sea, good hotels – and is now very popular. Tourism is basically the Black Sea and skiing. The two main central hotels in the capital are the Grand Hotel Sofia and the older Grand Balkan Hotel.

We spend the last night in a local taverna, being entertained by a dancer performing to eastern harem-type music. The various kebabs arrive en masse. I enquire which is which, but as usual nobody knows. The food is accompanied by endless supplies of slinova (plum brandy) and Cabernet Sauvignon. After dinner, I reluctantly accept an invitation to join in the dancing, but return very quickly to my chair with bruised ankles.

Upon my return to the hotel, I find a message informing me that a driver will be collecting me at 2.30 p.m. tomorrow to take me to the airport. This is strange, as my flight is due off at 8.55 a.m. Trying to explain this to the night porter, who hasn't a word of English, is no easy task, but eventually, by means of a mixture of French, German and sign language, the matter is resolved.

To my great surprise, the return trip to London passes without incident.

Bulgaria
25–30 April 1995

In 1995, I was invited for a second time to Bulgaria to visit and offer advice to various wineries as to the viability of exporting their wines independently to the UK using their own resources, as distinct from the previous regime, when they were strictly under government control.

25.4.95. The trip begins with British Airways flight 2580 from Gatwick North to Sofia at 10.15 a.m. There is a one-hour delay, and I have to pay £48 to obtain a visa. We arrive at 3 p.m. local time, which is two hours ahead. At the airport, I am collected by Boris (Bob) Kurnov in a chauffeur-driven Mercedes, to be taken to the four-star Novotel Europa Hotel, 131 Maria Louisa Boulevard, Sofia. I am put in room 1407, which is quite small, but adequate for one night.

I go for a walk in the centre of the city, taking in Vitosha Boulevard, which looks on to the Vitosha Mountains and Borisova Gradina Park. The shops are reasonably well stocked with goods these days, and there are many bars and restaurants. I spend an hour walking through the local market, and buy a packet of 'cep powder', which is used in the local cuisine, for £1. After stopping off for a beer in a local bar, I return to the hotel at 7.

At 7.30, I am collected by Bob, and we walk the 20 minutes back into the city centre, passing along the way the former headquarters of the Communist Party, which once had a huge red star on top, now removed. Dinner is at a restaurant called Arizona, up a small side street, and down some steps. It turns out to be fairly empty. I taste a range of vodka and schnapps, including Slivenska Perla (flavoured with plum) and Pomoriska Muskatova (grape). These accompany a very typical salad of sheep's cheese with cucumber and tomato, called Shopska Salata.

We are then joined by Bob's partner, Daniella, who speaks just as good English as he does. The main course is kavarma, which is an omelette filled with minced pork, fried onions, mushrooms and tomatoes, together with a kebache, which is minced meat with seasonings, rolled into a sausage and grilled. The food is all quite salty.

A taxi takes me back to the hotel at around 11, and I go to its casino, the Las Vegas, for a spot of gambling. Here, US dollars are the only currency accepted. Having done well on the roulette wheel, I am in bed at 12.

26.4.95. I awake at 7.30. Breakfast is served in the Grill, and offers a large range of meat and sausages, salami, eggs and spaghetti. I drink a fruit juice of unknown origin, and some coffee that tastes of leather. I ask instead for a large espresso, which tastes exactly the same.

At 8.30, I am collected for the five-hour drive north through open countryside, passing through the towns of Botevgrad, Lukovit, Telis, Pleven and Byala, to Rousse on the Romanian border, the largest Bulgarian city on the Danube. The Viniprom Winery here, one of the largest in the country, is still government-owned, its vineyards located along the Yantra Valley, overlooking the Danube.

After another cup of identical-tasting coffee, we have a short meeting, and then lunch in the works canteen. There is salad of course, and soup (a meaty tomato broth), and very dry barbecued chicken, to start, and then a veal escalope with chips. I drink schnapps, a 1994 Sauvignon Blanc and a wood-aged 1991 Cabernet Sauvignon, which is full and robust in structure and altogether very good.

After lunch, we embark on a two-hour tasting of the full range of their wines, during the course of which an etiquette problem arises. I am naturally spitting out the wines as I taste, but the winemaker becomes quite agitated. When I enquire through the interpreter what seems to be the matter, he replies, 'Why do you not like my wines, that you have spat them all out?'

I explain that this is the technique used in my country, and indeed internationally, whereupon he shrugs his shoulders and stalks off in a huff. On completion, I make a point of complimenting him on his well-made wines, and this apparently seems to heal the rift.

Another three hours' driving brings us to Lovech, a small town with a lovely, well-preserved old sector in a surrounding wall, with a large statue up on a hill. I snatch a quick schnapps. The accommodation that has been provided here leaves nothing to the imagination. It's a seventeenth-century cottage up a small cobbled street, which sounds ideal, but turns out to be absolutely filthy, with neither water nor sanitation. There is a truckle bed with a single blanket, which I have to make up myself. The shower, for such it is styled, looks like a home-made pot still, ending in a blue plastic bucket.

I go into the town square in search of dinner, and fetch up at Osamska Prouhlada, where I order a Pleven lager, and then feast on baked sheep's cheese, and slow-cooked lamb with chips (all tepid). Outside, it starts to rain, and I can feel a severe sore throat coming on (or has the dreaded psychosomatic condition reappeared?).

Back at the hotel, I pass a most uncomfortable night. I'll look back with amusement at this, I'm quite sure, one day.

27.4.95. After a very fitful night, I awake at 7 a.m. There is no water, so I must brush my teeth in soda water. The sore throat persists, and I take some more aspirin.

We make the hour-long drive to the Suhindol Winery, only to find that my appointment has been cancelled. Another hour's drive brings us to the small independent Rossina Winery in Pavlikeni, where they are not ready for us. We sit and drink coffee in a very old-fashioned boardroom. I phone London to try to rearrange my flight to go home on Friday instead of Sunday, but it transpires that BA do not fly on Fridays or Saturdays. This news plunges me into depression, as I feel truly awful.

After a long wait, the female winemaker arrives, and we taste back to 1978 – Gamza, Cabernet-Merlot, Reserve Merlot and Reserve Cabernet Sauvignon. All the wines share the common fault of having spent too long in old oak.

We drive back to Suhindol and have lunch at a fairly good workers' café, the usual salad, followed by a kebache and chips. There is rhakia and local schnapps to start, both reminiscent of what I can imagine the original Red Indian firewater must have tasted like, and then a much more pleasing 1988 Suhindol Reserve Cabernet. The weather has now taken a particularly miserable turn, with thunder and lightning, accompanied by heavy rain. Our four-hour drive back to Sofia is a nightmare.

Arriving back at the Novotel, I am assigned room 1512, and go straight to the bar for a gin and tonic. I then amble over to the Sheraton, where the prices are outrageous compared to everywhere else. (A gin and tonic in the Novotel, for example, is about £1.10; here it's £5. The average salary is only £60 a month.) I have another, now purely for medicinal purposes, in a local bar called Dani, and then eat a rather good dinner in a nearby business club: stuffed vine leaves, and a pork stew with onions and rice, accompanied by another bottle of the 1988 Suhindol Reserve Cabernet, which is showing some volatility.

I am in bed by 11.30.

28.4.95. Having passed another fitful night with a bad cough and a blocked nose, I start the day with a coffee at 9 and a short meeting with Bob Kurnov. Then I have a breakfast of ham and eggs with bread.

I book a city tour at 11, which consists of a very interesting two-hour walk around the capital led by a young guide. We visit the Alexander Nevski Memorial Church, which was built between 1904 and 1912, and commemorates the liberation of Bulgaria from the Ottomans, then the church of Saint Sofia (dating back to the sixth century), the fourth-century rotunda of St George, with its beautiful frescoes, and then the main synagogue, which was built between 1905 and 1909 in the Moorish style, plus many other interesting historic buildings and museums.

At 1, we stop for a lunch of kebache and rice with local beer, and then I return to the hotel and change into my jacket and tie in preparation for a meeting with the vice-minister of agriculture. He is very optimistic about the future of private enterprise and export among the wineries. The meeting lasts until 6, after which I book a table at the 33 Chairs Restaurant for dinner at 8.30.

Leaving the hotel at 7.15, I walk to the Dani bar and have a large gin and tonic, after which I try to find the restaurant. It seems to be near the French embassy, but manages to elude me, and so I stop at the Hotel Rila and buy a 20p street map, only to discover that it's a cab ride. I find a cab, but the driver also has no idea where the restaurant is, but following my street map, we eventually get there. Bob and Daniella are waiting outside.

It's a very nice restaurant, supposedly the best the city has to offer, located at 14 Assen Zlaratov Street. We drink three bottles of 1989 Château de St. Biald, an excellent Bulgarian wine that resembles a cross between a second-growth claret and an Australian Cabernet. This accompanies corn off the cob, and then a very traditional stew called kapama, which is comprised of goose and various other meats cooked in a clay pot and decanted on to the plate, served with mashed vegetables. For Bulgaria, it's quite superb.

I return to the hotel partly on foot and partly by cab, and am in bed at midnight.

29.4.95. I breakfast on ham and eggs at 9.30.

Later we walk to Rimskata Steha for lunch at a local Restaurant called Gostilnica. Stuffed vine leaves with cabbage and carrot salad, veal roasted in stock with vinegar, and local beers accompany lots of garlic and parsley, served with chopped sauté potatoes.

Back at the hotel at 3.30, I sleep for two hours, and curiously find that I am starting to feel a little better. I celebrate by losing $20 in the hotel casino, and then have a number of gin and tonics in the lobby bar. Bob collects us at 8.30, and we take a cab to the Sofia Grand hotel, 5 Narodno Sabranie Square, which turns out to be quite impressive. Dinner has been booked in the rooftop restaurant, and Daniella once again joins us.

The meal begins with hors d'oeuvres – smoked salmon, olives, ham stuffed with cream cheese, aubergines and courgettes – and proceeds to a delicious stew of pork and mixed vegetables in a clay pot, with which we drink a deep, soft, well-balanced non-vintage Cabernet Sauvignon, and a Dimiat Varna, which is a light, commercial, slightly sweet white of 12.5% alcohol.

Afterwards, we repair to the nightclub in the hotel basement, which features a very good cabaret, and then go back to the

Novotel at 3.30 a.m. During the course of a quick flutter in the casino, I win $50.

I finally make it to bed at 4 a.m. It's been a very enjoyable evening.

30.4.95. Awakening at 9, I pack and check out of the hotel. After a few beers in the bar at 11.30, I take a cab to Kitai, a Chinese Restaurant at 6 Shipka Street, only to find that it has changed hands and become a Bulgarian Restaurant, and is about to play host to a huge wedding. Instead, I have an appalling plate of noodles in some unknown sauce at a place just around the corner.

I cab back to the hotel, and then get a lift to the airport for 3 p.m. with Bob and the driver in the Mercedes. I'm booked on BA flight 2891 at 4.05, seat 6C. I have a gin and tonic in the bar, which is crawling with cockroaches. The four-hour flight to Gatwick arrives at 6.30 local time.

It's been a very interesting trip, I think.

Useful words for next time: *blagordaria* (thank you).

Hungary
13–16 November 1997

13.11.97. I arrive at Heathrow Terminal 2 at 6.40 a.m. for the 7.35
Malev Airlines flight MA 617 to Budapest, and am upgraded to
Business Class, seat 2C. I sit for a while in the Business Lounge
and drink an awful attempt at an espresso coffee made from the
contents of a sachet. A 15-minute delay is announced, but we take
off at 7.45.

Their so-called Business Class turns out to be something of a
disgrace: normal seats, with limited legroom and no champagne.
Breakfast is a quiche with mushrooms and spinach, all dried out,
tepid and horrid. The flight time is 2½ hours, and we arrive in
Budapest at 11.05 local time. Nobody is here to meet me. I wait
half an hour and then start to get desperate, even contemplating
an immediate return flight to London. I recall that the last time I
was in Budapest was in 1973, and timekeeping was no better then.

At last, Istvan Putzai arrives. It is his job to try to introduce
new Hungarian wines to the UK market. We drive due south
through delightful countryside, arriving at a place called
Kiskunsag, near the town of Bosca on the Croatian border. Here
we visit Weinhaus, a medium-sized winery established in 1994.
The managing director, Joska, meets us, and takes us to lunch in a
nearby restaurant owned by the husband of Weinhaus's lady
winemaker. He is also the chef, and the food is good. After a pork
soup with noodles and fresh paprika, we go on to a delicious main
course comprising tongue, turkey, gnocchi and onions in a
paprika cream sauce, accompanied by Warsteiner and Budvar
beers.

At 3.15, we proceed to a full tasting, including tank samples of
eight whites (including Chardonnay, Olaszrizling and Ranjai
Rizling) and ten reds (including Kadarka, Zweigelt, Cabernet
Sauvignon, Merlot and Kékfrankos) from the 1997 vintage, none
of which has yet undergone its malolactic fermentation. The
vintage shows some promise, particularly for the Merlot. After a

further meeting to discuss modern-style labels, we go off to a local hotel. My room is the size of a cardboard box. As the great comedian Henny Youngman would say, à propos small hotel rooms, 'Even the mice were hunchbacked.'

I meet the others for drinks, large Ballantine's and sodas at 7.30, including Joska's wife, who looks like a wartime prison guard, complete with wide leather belt, from which dangles a very large bunch of keys. They take me to dinner at a restaurant called Vendiofa Etterem at Kiskorov, a small village 20 km from the hotel. It's a dark and gloomy place, with dark wood panelling and dark red tablecloths. We drink apricot brandy and eat confit of goose with potatoes and the obligatory salad, followed by two crêpes, one with jam and one with cottage cheese. With the food, we drink a great range of wines, including a 1993 Merlot, which turns out to be surprisingly good, with lots of fruit and a substantial finish.

I am in bed at 11.30, quite exhausted. At least the weather has been fine, the temperature holding up at 51°F.

14.11.97. I pass a fitful night. The room is airless and there is no way to open the window without a hammer. Breakfast at 8 is two fried eggs with ham, bread, orange juice and two strong coffees. It seems to be pouring with rain, but mild.

At 9, I arrive back at the Weinhaus Winery, and undergo a four-hour session of blending red and white wines, eventually selecting three whites and two reds, one of which is a very good Merlot, which I consider has a reasonable chance of success in the retail export market.

Lunch at 1.30 is at Szakal Vendeglo in Soltivadkert, a small village 50 km from the Serbian border. The food is superb: orjaleves (pork shoulder soup with noodles and fresh paprika), followed by vadkerti pinceporkolt (diced beef leg in red wine with marrow, rich paprika sauce and bread). We get through two litres of Kaiser Bier. This is a fine, very authentic restaurant, which offers the following dishes to those who book in advance: pig's spine soup with marrowbone and grated horseradish; bean soup with smoked hoofmeat; lamb's spine with garlic and stewed spinach; Transylvanian brown bear's paw with pickles.

After lunch, we make our way back to Budapest. On the way, we stop at a farm that is normally open to the public, but is currently closed for the off-season. Nevertheless, we drive through and have a look around. It is stocked with what I am told are original breeds of Hungarian farm animals, such as pigs with what looks like sheep's wool, grey cows with ox horns, and sheep that look as though they have been crossed with goats. All quite fascinating and weird, if a little reminiscent of some sci-fi film.

Another two hours on the road brings us back to Budapest at 5.30, during which time I read some background history, discovering that the city only came into being when the three towns of Pest, Buda and Obuda, together with Margaret Island, were united in 1873 to form one large capital. We take a mini-tour on the west side of the Danube to Pest, which was laid out largely in the nineteenth century on the Paris pattern of grand boulevards and straight avenues. This is the real downtown of the capital, full of shops. Vaci Utca is one of the main shopping streets, and enjoys a view across the Danube towards Buda Castle. We then proceed across the chain bridge to Buda, looking leftwards at the other bridges, each as interesting as the last.

I check into the Hotel Mercure, room 517. Since the break up of the Soviet bloc, Western customs and clothes have started to infiltrate the city, and I notice a female fashion for micro miniskirts worn with white leather boots.

At 6.30, I take drinks in the bar, a couple of Johnnie Walker Red Labels with soda. Istvan comes to collect me at 7.20, and we walk through freezing cold rain to one of the city's oldest restaurants, Marvanymenya Szony. Istvan's doctor wife has organised a dinner here for one hundred people who have been attending an oncology conference. I sit next to a pair of plastic surgeons, who take a professional interest in my nose. A traditional Hungarian gypsy band plays (two violins, bass, zither and clarinet), and I am invited to join in the cabaret. This entails drinking a full glass of wine in one go while blindfolded, as well as dancing precariously between arrangements of bottles set out on the floor.

Dancing between bottles, Budapest, Hungary

The food has a rather mass-produced air: veal and pork with tomatoes and peppers, goulash soup, and pancakes filled with tinned fruit. We drink schnapps and some oxidised wines, and I am back at the hotel by 11.30.

15.11.97. I breakfast at 8.15 on scrambled eggs and bacon, apple juice that tastes of nothing, and coffee of a similar nature. A sightseeing tour has been organised for me at 9.30. The weather is sunny, but very cold (zero, in fact).

The bus tour takes in numerous cathedrals and castles around Buda, with its craggy hills topped by medieval ramparts, cobbled alleyways and the superb Royal Palace, situated on a hill, occupying a commanding position overlooking the river. The main sights can comfortably be taken in during the course of a morning's tour, unless you want to spend time exploring the 200 museums and galleries. The Hilton Hotel sits high up next to the main cathedral, an amalgam of a building that incorporates part of the old cathedral, as well as a more modern addition. The oldest part has a modern dome on top, which doubles as the casino for the Hilton!

The tour concludes at 1, and I go to the Hyatt Hotel for a couple of Dreher beers (about £2 each) and to wait for Mrs Puztai and her son, who will take me to lunch at the best authentic Hungarian restaurant in the capital – Fatal, at 67 Vaci Utca. We make it there by 2.30, and begin with bableves (a bean soup served in a saucepan, which could be a meal in itself), followed by toltott kaposzta (meat and rice wrapped up in cabbage, also served in a pan with sauerkraut and vegetables in stock). I drink two 50cl bottles of Stella. All in all, a very filling lunch.

At 5, I return to the Hotel Mercure, sleep for half an hour, and then go for a sauna and massage at 6. At 8, I go to the bar and have a very large Johnnie Walker Red Label and soda. I'm still not really hungry, and can't quite decide where to go. Finally, having reached a decision, I take a 1,500-florint cab ride to Kehli Restaurant Vendeglo at 22 Mokus Utca.

Dinner begins with a dish called lecso, steamed tomatoes with paprika and onions, a clumsy dish that arrives instantaneously.

The main course should be fried goose breast with stewed cabbage and boiled potatoes, but what actually arrives is deep-fried goose liver (like McNuggets) with mash, so I send it back.

Then the obligatory gypsy group arrives, playing 'Viva España', 'Roll Out The Barrel' and the theme from *The Flintstones*. This place is quite beyond belief. When my goose breast with chopped boiled potatoes and choucroute finally arrives, it is 10.20. The food has clearly been rather over-acquainted with the microwave. With it, I drink a bottle of well-balanced 1995 Egri Cabernet Sauvignon from Thummerer. The bill comes to FL1,980. Opposite to where I am sitting, across a long corridor, is an anteroom where a party of about fifty are all taking it in turns to make extremely loud speeches.

A FL1,200 cab journey brings me back to the hotel, and I get to bed at midnight, but only to spend a fitful night.

16.11.97. After breakfasting at 7.30 on orange juice that is as vapid as yesterday's apple juice, with a roll and coffee, I take an 8 a.m. minibus to the airport. The weather is lovely today, sunny and not as cold as before. I am upgraded to Business Class.

In the Duna Lounge, I have a large, strong black coffee. I'm on the 10.05 Malev flight MA 610 to Heathrow, and again, the Business Class seats are identical to those in Economy, with no additional legroom. I set my watch back one hour and order a large gin and tonic. Lunch is disgracefully poor, no better than the worst sort of Economy food: some sort of tasteless fish pâté with the inevitable shredded cabbage, and a plastic dish containing – lurking under its tinfoil cover – a species of veal stew with rice. The wine is a thin and watery Weinhaus Cabernet Sauvignon 1994.

I arrive at Heathrow at noon, to be collected by my wife and children.

Cyprus
13–17 December 1999

13.12.99. A taxi arrives at 7.30 a.m. to take me to Heathrow Terminal 1. At 8.50, I check in for Air Cyprus Economy Class flight CY 0327 to Larnaca, seat 22C. The plane is half-full, and we take off at 10.15, half an hour late. As usual, there is very little legroom. I begin proceedings with a gin and tonic, and we are served an indifferent meal of pork and rice, with cheeses and the light and fruity Othello red wine.

I read up a little about Cyprus and its wines. Mainly known for its 'sherry', it has one of the oldest wine-growing traditions in the world. The Troödos Mountains, which attract rain, are what make viticulture possible in what would otherwise be too dry a climate. The vineyards are planted where the rain falls, in idyllic green valleys, at nearly 900 metres up in the hills.

After a 4½-hour flight, we arrive in Larnaca at 4.30 (two hours ahead). I am collected from the airport by Andreas Giorgiou, a Cyprus Airways pilot who has formed the Wine and Dine Circle, for which he has asked me to conduct a course on wine appreciation. We drive the half-hour journey into Nicosia, where I shall be staying at the four-star Holiday Inn, room 414.

We rendezvous at 7 p.m. in the bar, to the strains of a hideous automatic piano. Andreas shows up at 7.20, and offers me a coffee, which I decline politely. We then drive to a deserted wine bar in the residential district, and find it closed. He spends the whole time on his mobile phone while driving a new BMW 525. The next place we try is also closed.

Eventually, we arrive at a restaurant and wine bar that seems to be open, Domus, at 5 Korai Street. We are the only customers in there. A bottle of Ayios Andronicos white from the Monte Royia Winery is ordered. Made from the Xynisteri grape, it's aromatic but very thin and hollow, with high acidity. George, who is head of flight control at Larnaca Airport, arrives, and we eat a few pre-dinner tapas items, cheeses, salads and bread, served with a range of flavoured butters.

We then go on to a most superb local taverna, the Plaka Tavern, which is packed solid. There is no menu, but numerous dishes are served, including fish, meats and snails, which arrive in dizzying profusion. We drink 1994 Afames from the Sodap Winery, a light, thin, burnt, tannic red with slight volatility; 1990 Cornaro from Etko, a well-made Carignan with good depth, balanced fruit and tannin, and 1995 Semeli, also from the Etko Winery, which is soft but with some tannin, slightly hollow and young, with a roasted finish. Zivania is a local spirit decanted and served in 5cl Famous Grouse miniatures straight from the freezer.

I'm back at the hotel at midnight.

14.12.99. I wake at 8 after a good night's sleep and go for a walk to the border, as Nicosia is divided. It's two-thirds Turkish, and the no-go zone is guarded by UN troops, with many bullet-damaged buildings in evidence.

Returning for breakfast at 8.45, I eat some croissants and drink some coffee and orange juice, before the day's first meeting at 9.30, for which Andy arrives at 9.45. The sun is shining and it's a lovely morning, but I take a sweater just in case.

We drive to the Aes Ambelis Winery, which is on the road to the Troödos Mountains. It's a new winery, still under construction. The winemaker is Savvos Fakoukakis, and on the strength of the tank samples I taste, the best one can say is that he still has a lot to learn. There is a thin Xynisteri white and a couple of not-bad Cabernet and Mavron reds. It starts to rain.

After the visit, we collect a friend of Andy's and go for lunch at a 'kitchen', the local name for a very small, family-run café. We eat rabbit and pasta with liver, and drink Keo beer.

Back at the hotel, I book a conference room for my wine appreciation lectures, which will run from 4 till 6, and from 7 till 9. There are fifteen people at the first one, and twice that at the second, although the room has curiously been laid out for sixty. The 4 o'clock is attended by an all-male group. With the aid of videos I cover viticulture and vinification, and the making of champagne and sparkling wines, and it goes reasonably well. They are a very attentive group, and ask many questions.

The second session starts at 7.15, is again all-male and is much more relaxed. I meet the food and beverage manager of the five-star Elias Beach Hotel in Limassol, rated the best hotel on Cyprus, according to him.

Later, we go to dinner with Andy and friends, Chris, Bambos and Savvos, to Graikos, a classic Byzantine Restaurant. We have ouzo, and then a full range of meze, including a huge rib of beef. The food is all superb, and I round off the evening with a nightcap back at the hotel at midnight.

15.12.99. I wake at 8.30 after a sound night's sleep, to find the sun shining again. I eat a full breakfast of scrambled eggs, bacon, ham, mushrooms and tomatoes (all strangely cold), with apple juice and coffee.

At 10, I rendezvous with Andy and Bambos, and we drive up to the Kykko monastery in the Troödos Mountains in Bambos's 4.6-litre Range Rover. We meet some of the monks, visit the winery and speak to the winemaker, who is quite out of touch with modern methods. I am given a bottle of white wine, which, I am assured, is produced from only free-run juice, and taste a new 50/50 blend of Cabernet Sauvignon and Cabernet Franc from the 1995 vintage, which isn't bad at all. Lunch is at a restaurant called Kamnos in a village near the monastery, an excellent full meze board.

I am back at the Holiday Inn at 3.30 to prepare for my two lectures, the first of which – from 4.30 to 6.30 – attracts twelve people to hear about Burgundy and the Rhône and taste six wines. After a beer in the bar, I take the second, from 7.30 till 9, which is attended by twenty-eight people.

We then take a 30-minute drive to Larnaca and have dinner at Sivaris Restaurant, a buffet with meat dishes and rice, accompanied by a good white wine and an awful red, both of which are served in jugs. Strangely for me, I find I am not very hungry. Andy's wife is there, together with Bambos and his wife, and a number of his friends. After a J&B whisky, I am driven back by Bambos, and get to bed at 1 a.m.

16.12.99. I awake at 8.45, and breakfast at 9.15 on croissants with honey, orange juice and coffee. Afterwards, I read and drink some Keo draught beer.

At 1.30, I meet Andy and the owner of the Holiday Inn for an indifferent buffet lunch, accompanied by more Keo bottled beer.

My first session, from 4 till 6, attracts eight people to hear about Bordeaux, while the second, from 7 till 9.30, brings in twenty-three. They are a great crowd for the final night.

Afterwards, we drive to just outside Larnaca for dinner at TABEPNA KOYTEONIKONIAE, which is located in the barn of an old farm at Kano-Xodio Napnakae, and run by a young and very talented chef. Including people who have joined us from the lecture course, there are twenty of us. The menu takes in roasted goat and a whole barbecued suckling pig, ampelo povai (buntings), goat's testicles, grouda (semolina with toast), snails and much, much more – a very interesting spread – accompanied by plenty of Aes Ambelis wine.

Later, we go to a very seedy nightclub, at which the extremely amateur entertainment includes topless girls and dancers. Oddly, all the hostesses and dancers are from Russia and Romania. We are all served with whisky and water. We return to Nicosia at 2 a.m.

17.12.99. After breakfasting at 9.30, I go for a walk around the medieval city, taking in the old Venetian walls. Nicosia became the capital of Cyprus around 965 AD and, during the period of Lusignan rule over the island, became one of the twelve Lusignan provinces. It was then called Nicossie. A visit to the Cyprus Museum is well worthwhile, as is St John's Cathedral, the seat of the Orthodox church on Cyprus.

Following a lunch with Andy, I return to the airport to take the 6 p.m. flight to Heathrow, which will take four-and-a-half hours.

I wish the Larnaca Wine and Dine Circle great success.

Cyprus
31 October–4 November 2003

31.10.03. I check in at 8.30 a.m. for the Cyprus Airways Business Class flight CY 327 to Larnaca. They have a strange system at check-in, in that although there is a separate Business Class desk, everybody is entitled to use it, so one ends up queuing with the Economy Class customers. I have coffee in the British Midland Business lounge, which they share with Cyprus Airways.

We are due to depart at 9.45, and take off half an hour late in the event. I'm in seat 3G on an Airbus A330, a modern and comfortable plane. Flying time should be just over four hours, and Cyprus is two hours ahead of UK time.

Oddly, only orange juice is offered prior to take-off. The Apollo Executive Class menu comprises three canapés (a prawn on toast, salmon and egg), and then a choice of smoked salmon salad, fillet of sole stuffed with prawns in a lobster sauce, grilled chicken in mushroom sauce, or penne pasta with ham in a white wine cream sauce (which I choose), cheese and fruit. The pasta is a complete disgrace; it comes in a plastic dish with a tinfoil cover still in tact, and is quite dried out. 'Hunt-the-ham' is the name of the game. The choice of cheese is very poor – Cheddar and Emmenthal – all dried out, and served with an unripe kiwi. For a ticket in excess of £1,000, I feel this deserves a letter to Cyprus Airways.

To drink, there is Moët & Chandon (drinking well), Nefeli Etco from Limassol (an earthy, dull white with high acidity), and Domaine d'Ahera from the Keo Winery (a light, unbalanced red). After having watched the film, *Bruce Almighty* with Jim Carrey, I am served an extremely large Johnnie Walker Black Label and soda, which promptly puts me to sleep.

We arrive at Larnaca at 4.15 local time. I am collected by Marc Aeberhard, who is to be the general manager of a brand new five-star grand hotel resort, the Thalassa, of 60 suites, right by the sea on the peninsula of Paphos beach. A two-hour drive through the traffic of Limassol takes us to its sister hotel, the Coral Beach Resort, which has 400 rooms and is 50 metres away from where the new resort is being built. My well-appointed, split-level suite 2206 overlooks the sea.

In the evening, we have drinks outside in the hotel bar, but it starts to rain. A buffet dinner in the hotel restaurant is under par, all the meat, chicken and so forth being severely overcooked. We drink what are ostensibly the 1990 and 1992 vintages of Othello, but I wonder whether the wines really are from these years, as they appear much younger, and very similar to each other in colour, aroma and taste. It's a medium-bodied red, with an overcooked, roasted, earthy nose, and a burnt-earth finish showing sharp acidity and some tannin.

I retire at 11.30.

1.11.03. The day dawns warm and sunny, with 27° of heat. I breakfast at 9 from the buffet on the fourth-floor terrace, an area reserved exclusively for the guests in suites. There is a full assortment of fresh juices, cereals, fruit, eggs, bacon, sausages, etc., and very good coffee. After breakfast, I wander around the hotel for a while to get my bearings. It has three swimming pools, four restaurants, two bars, and a gymnasium and spa.

At 11, I take my first staff wine-training session. Curiously, the staff for the new resort includes a high proportion of young, bright South Africans. I eat a delicious buffet lunch at 1, a Cypriot-style beef dish with rice and a Keo beer, and then go for a quick swim.

In the afternoon, at 3.30, we meet up for an excursion to the Chrysorroyiatissa monastery some 40 km north of Paphos in the mountains, which has been beautifully restored after having been devastated by fire in the 1960s. When we arrive, they are in the middle of prayers, which are being loudly amplified through numerous speakers. The monastery also own vineyard land and produces a small selection of wines under the Monte Royia label, all in serial-numbered bottles. Ayios Andronicos is a dry white, very young and fresh, slightly unclean, with extremely high acidity and some evidence of SO_2. The 2002 Riesling, which bears a neck-label stating that it is a 'Gold Metal Winner', is pale and earthy, but again with searing acidity and an unclean finish.

I get back to the hotel at 6, having been treated to a superb sunset across the mountains on the journey back, and go to the spa at 7 for a 50-minute body massage, which is conducted by an amazon of a Russian woman, built like an Olympic weightlifter, who attacks me with the vigour of a rugby prop forward. In response to my screams of agony, she barks the word 'Good!' to which I can only yelp out, 'Not good!' prompting her to insist, 'Yes, good!' leaving me with the distinct expression that that is the entire extent of her English vocabulary. Having endured this 50 minutes of KGB torture, I repair to my room for a hot shower, and thence to the bar at 8.30 for a medicinally restorative large whisky and soda. Sitting outside overlooking the sea in perfect climatic conditions, all is well once more.

At 9, we have dinner in the hotel's Limani Taverna by the beach. The fish meze are very good, and include inkfish, sardines, octopus and squid, plus a full range of delicious cold dishes. With this, we drink 2002 Semillon from the Fikardos Winery (semi-oxidised, with an earthy, unclean flavour), 2001 Thisbe white from Keo (dank, earthy, roasted and unpleasant), and 2002 Danae white from the Sodap Winery (semi-oxidised, with bitter flavours).

I am in bed at 11.30.

2.11.03. It's another glorious day, 27°C and sunny. Going to breakfast at 8.30, I confine myself to fruit, cereal and coffee, as I ate so much last night.

A second session of staff training including videos takes place between 11 and 1, and rapidly proves that the team for the new resort is going to be excellent, as they are very keen and absorb most of the information fired at them.

After a lunch of roast beef and roast potatoes, with Keo beer, I spend the afternoon working on the wine list for the new resort. At 7, I go for some spa treatment, an hour of absolute bliss, including a full facial – not that I am vain, of course.

Marc and I meet up for drinks at 8.30. The centrally located large bar area is situated in the hotel lobby, and arranged around a grand piano played by a woman of indeterminate age. There is an air about her of 1920s vaudeville, which her repertoire reinforces. She has a stride piano style, a cross between Winifred Atwell and James P Johnson, with one in every five notes wrong, but hammered out with style and panache regardless. She is dressed in what can only be described as a clown's outfit, with frizzy hair piled high on her head, and announces in a deadpan voice 'I play requests only when I am asked.'

Dinner in the buffet restaurant involves taramasalata and houmous to start, followed by grilled chicken with sautéed potatoes in a wine sauce. With it, we drink the monastery's Monte Royia red wine, which is tannic, with high acidity and an earthy finish.

I retire at 11.30.

3.11.03. The weather today is hot and sunny again, 29°C. I eat an early breakfast at 7.15 of apple juice, fresh green figs and black coffee, followed by scrambled eggs, bacon and sausages. I do wish these breakfast buffets were not so tempting.

At 9, I have a massage session with Vladimir Borisov. Actually, it's more than just a massage, as he has trained for the last five years under the great master of medicine, Tao Ye, at the Hei Lun Zhan Scientific Research Institute in Harbin. Tao Ye's father treated Mao Zedong. He practises what is called energetic balance, the theory behind which is that the disruption of the body's natural balance can lead to diseases and illness. The principal method of recovering the disrupted balance of vital energy is a type of Chinese massage called *an'mo*, which reinforces the protective functions of the body's organs against infection, as well as decelerating the rate of ageing. The masseur's hands generate vibration and heat in the areas of your body where there is pain.

As a dyed in the wool sceptic, I go for an hour's treatment, tongue firmly in cheek, only to be amazed by this man's ability. I have never experienced such a phenomenon; it is truly astonishing. All the back and neck pain that has been plaguing me for years seems to vanish. I shall definitely return tomorrow.

Feeling 20 years younger in mind and step, I conduct the staff training session with renewed vigour. Today, we are tasting Greek and Cypriot wines. The Greek whites include Ambelon 2002 from Domaine Hatzimichias, which is deep straw in colour, smells earthy and unclean, with very high SO_2, and is demi-sec in style on the palate, with an unclean finish; and Capinias 2000 from the same producer, mid-straw, with a cinnamon-scented oaky nose, and a clean, fruity, demi-sec style. Among the Cypriot reds are a 1999 Cabernet Sauvignon at 13% ABV, deep, oaky and tannic, but quite hollow, with a short finish; and a 2001 Shiraz, also 13%, which has a very deep, good leathery nose, and is young and tannic but well made.

After the session, at 1, I take a buffet lunch of chicken and rice, accompanied by Keo lager, and then spend a restful afternoon.

At 7.30, we meet for drinks in the bar, and I have a Dewar's (not one of my favourite blends) whisky and soda. Dinner at 8.30 is at the Vasidas Taverna in Tala, 10 km north of Paphos, a superb old taverna in the middle of nowhere. A bottle of 2001 Aracas red, which is reminiscent of Doctor Collis Brown's cough mixture in smell and taste, accompanies a magnificent spread of halloumi, taramasalata and salads, with tahini, brawn, lamb and pork sausages, chitterlings, lard bacon lunza, rice and vegetables, liver, deep-fried new potatoes with coriander seeds, pork intestines, wild mushrooms, pig's trotters, pork, sheep and goat sausages with herbs wrapped in caul, pork kebab, pork belly with coriander seed, souvla chicken kebab, local guava, apples and grapes. A Restaurant to be recommended.

I am back at the hotel at 11.30.

4.11.03. I sleep only fitfully, probably as a consequence of eating far too much meze last night. At 8 a.m., I have another session with Vladimir, who continues his agonising treatment on my back. As a result of his attentions, though, I eat a healthy breakfast at 9 of green figs, yoghurt and coffee.

A journey into Pegeia village just outside Paphos is undertaken, to sample with the locals a superb sweet style of Cypriot coffee called *glyko*, and then I return for a tour of the site where the Thalassa resort will be opening next June. The setting is stunning, right on the peninsula of Coral Bay, overlooking the sea on three sides.

At 1, I have a buffet lunch of chicken and rice, with Keo beer, and then at 2.30, a taxi collects me for the journey to Larnaca Airport. There, I check in for the Cyprus Airways Business Class flight CY 326, seat 4B, to London Heathrow Terminal 1. As the flight isn't until 17.45, I go for a restorative drink in the executive lounge – restorative in that I can feel the preverbal cold and sore throat coming on.

The flight takes off at 18.15, and we are served with Moët et Chandon, which is still drinking well. The food, however, is again absolutely appalling, with dried-up canapés, an inedible smoked fish starter, and tasteless ravioli, which has been overcooked in the microwave, and is brought forth with the tinfoil still covering the plastic dish.

Back at home, I take to bed at 11 with an aspirin.

Dubai, India, Maldives
2002

Dubai/India/Maldives
9 February–4 March 2002

Prior to the age of oil, Dubai was a minuscule trading post on the western shore of the Persian Gulf. It only began appearing on maps in the early years of the nineteenth century. The dynasty that presently rules it was founded in 1833 by Sheikh Maktoum bin-Buti, whose rule initiated a prosperous city state, and whose descendant, Crown Prince Mohammed bin-Rashid al-Maktoum, is the state's current ruler.

In the 1950s, after India imposed controls on its gold market, Dubai capitalised by cornering a large part of the Arab-Indian jewellery market, and has grown rich on both oil and the export of wedding jewellery to India. Now part of the United Arab Emirates, Dubai has been transformed into a major financial centre and luxury travel destination, boasting the world's largest port, tallest hotel and richest horse race. The aim is to attract 15 million visitors annually by the year 2010.

9.2.02. The chauffeur, provided courtesy of Emirates Airlines, arrives at 5 p.m. to take me to Heathrow Terminal 3. It's a nightmare journey, taking an hour and a half just to get from Balham to Hammersmith. We eventually arrive at around 7, and I check in for the First Class Emirates flight to Dubai with Clare and Toby, seats 2A, 2B and 2E.

There's just time for a little shopping and then a round of Moët et Chandon in half-bottles in the First Class lounge, before boarding at 7.50. The champagne served before takeoff is the delicious Lanson Noble Cuvée 1988. We depart at 8.40, after which the aperitif appears – Dom Pérignon 1993 in perfect condition. Emirates' first-class accommodation is truly superb, for both service and comfort. The appetisers alone are delicious: minced lamb kebab, chicken puff and onion bhaji. The first course is meze with prawns, garnished with caviare, and is followed by a choice of Moroccan chicken with rice, fish, pasta or rack of lamb, all beautifully presented and served from the trolley. Then there is a range of puddings, and cheeses served with Taylors 1985 port. I somehow manage to drink far too much Dom Pérignon, and sleep for two hours.

We arrive in Dubai at 6.30 a.m.

10.2.02. Another courtesy chauffeur collects us on arrival and transfers us to the superb Royal Mirage Hotel, which is situated right on the beach. We have rooms 507 and 508 overlooking the ocean.

I breakfast at 8.30 on the Celebrity Restaurant terrace (an omelette and bacon, with delicious coffee), and then spend the morning exploring the hotel and its various restaurants and bars, taking in a couple of beers and a Bloody Mary at 12 noon along the way.

At 1.30, we go to lunch in the Olives Restaurant, which consists of an excellent buffet, including smoked salmon, beef carpaccio, chicken curry, and fish with onions, served with a perfectly chilled bottle of Caves de Plaimont blanc. This is the prelude to a relaxing afternoon, during which I catch up on some sleep.

Dinner is booked for 8 p.m. in the Tagine Restaurant. Prior to that, I take a couple of refreshing large rum and sodas, one in the lobby bar on the terrace, the other in the courtyard outside the Tagine. The ambience there is Moroccan, with hubble-bubble pipes much in evidence, and the music provided by a guitar-drum combination playing the same continuous hypnotic drone. That influence is clearly discernible in the cooking too, and we dine on a puff pastry pastilla filled with meat, rice and seafood, another filled with pigeon seasoned with cinnamon and sugar, couscous royale containing lamb, chicken, vegetables, chickpeas and raisins, marinated chicken tagine, and chicken kebabs. To accompany it all, we drink Domaine Riad Jamib 1997, an acceptable Moroccan red.

I am in bed at 11.

11.2.02. I sleep in until 9.30, and then take a late breakfast on the terrace of the Olives Restaurant. It's another superb buffet of both hot and cold items, with eggs in whatever style one cares for.

There is turkey, pork, bacon, chicken, sausages, baked beans, etc., juices of carrot or watermelon, and lovely coffee.

I take a bus to the souks, an amazing warren of side streets in the old town, with each section selling different products. There is gold by the ton, pots and pans, clothes, shoes, spices, frankincense and myrrh, and rock salt (for use as a deodorant). After this, I take a taxi to the city centre, which is very modern, with a two-acre, three-storey shopping mall containing virtually every designer store known to man. It's all meticulously clean too. Having looked round, I cab back to the hotel for a well-deserved draught lager. It's getting on, and so I decide to skip lunch as we have a booking at the beachfront seafood restaurant for dinner at 8.

We arrive at 7.30 for drinks by the ocean. The setting is astonishing, and especially now that the wind has dropped, it's a beautiful evening. I order an aperitif of dark rum with lime juice and soda. First course is a prawn kebab sizzler threaded on sugar cane with a Vietnamese-style dip, served in three very large portions. While Clare has lobster tails, and Toby opts for rack of lamb, I order the cataplana with a side dish of rice. This event comprises chorizo sausage, clams, crab, mussels, scallops, tomatoes and onions, which is all very tasty, but not quite as good as the version I had in Portugal. With it, we drink a well-balanced 1998 Cuvée Henri Fabre, a rosé from Provence.

Later, we repair to the Tagine's courtyard bar for more drinks and shisha (the hubble-bubble pipes). We are assured they contain no tobacco (I wonder), but are charged with apple and mint, mango, bananas, etc. – great fun.

12.2.02. I eat an unnecessarily large late breakfast at 10 a.m., before taking myself off to the gold souk in search of Clare's 50th birthday present. I finally settle on a very attractive eternity ring set with a ruby and diamonds, and get the price halved – through some remarkably energetic haggling. As I walk around the amazing souks, the weather gradually becomes very hot, and I finally give in and taxi back to the hotel for a couple of thoroughly well-earned beers at the poolside bar, followed at 2 p.m. by an excellent massage.

At 6, I cab to the Burj al Arab Hotel, possibly the most amazing feat of architecture ever conceived, built in the shape of a windsurfer 27 floors high. There's no reception, as it's all suites, each with its own butler who checks you in and out, and is generally at your beck and call 24 hours a day. There is a breathtaking bar and restaurant on the top floor. We take drinks on the mezzanine with a full view of the gold-leaf atrium, prior to dinner in the seafood restaurant, which is below the level of the hotel and is accessed by a model submarine, which bumps its way to the bottom of the supposed ocean operated by a uniformed sailor. It's an experience, to say the least. At the centre of the dining room is an enormous tank full of tropical fish of all sizes, including sharks, completing the illusion of being below the ocean.

Dinner begins with langoustine with white truffles and nut rice, which is followed by lobster Singapore with noodles. The wines are Penby Estate Chardonnay 1999, an over-oaked Australian, and the same producer's Verdelho, which has very high acidity, together with Marilyn (Monroe) Merlot from the Napa Valley, a good wine but something of a travesty of the woman. The food is all superb, but works out very expensively at over £200 a head.

Dubai is very expensive altogether, with five-star hotel rooms costing between £300 and £500 a night for a basic double. Beers are £5 each, while an average hotel meal will set you back about £50 a head.

13.2.02. After waking at 7.30 a.m., I have an interesting meeting with a local wine importer, who informs me that although alcohol is taboo in this Muslim state, there are a few liquor stores, which have to have blanked-out windows, but the demand from all walks life is thriving. Back at the hotel, I have a light breakfast of eggs, bacon, baked beans, tomatoes and toast, with carrot juice and coffee. The rest of the morning is taken up with swimming and the odd beer, before a light salad lunch at 1.

At 3, a car arrives to take us on a desert trip. Toby goes dune-bashing, which consists of being strapped into a four-wheel drive and being driven at high speed by a young maniac driver across the desert dunes. Having tried this white-knuckle experience on a previous visit, I decide that once is enough. Meanwhile, Clare and I rest in the desert camp. At 5, we go for a camel ride, followed by drinks and an early dinner of barbecued chicken and lamb with rice, accompanied by whiskies and beers. Entertainment is provided by a glamorous belly-dancer. We return to the hotel at 9.30, and have drinks in the shisha courtyard.

Interesting note: the assistant in the hotel postcard shop is either deaf, thick, or permanently high on unknown eastern substances. All requests are met with the same unvarying response, an uncomprehending 'Eh?' in the manner of *Fawlty Towers'* Manuel.

14.2.02. The day begins with an 8.30 breakfast of poached eggs and bacon, with the excellent coffee. The temperature is 23°C, just right for a lazy morning, though one could have done without the tedium of trying to buy a Valentine's card from 'Manuel' in the shop. After ten minutes of trying to explain the significance of the date, I give up.

We take lunch at the Beach Restaurant, which has ravishing views. Arabian meze, red snapper and salad are accompanied by a bottle of Cuvée Henri Favre Provence rosé, after which I go for a full 'Earth, Sun and Moon' massage lasting an hour and 50 minutes. I am given to understand that after one of these, one never sees life in quite the same way. We shall have to wait and see.

After this holistic experience, we cab to the Jumerai Beach Hotel, which is next to the Burj al Arab, and is yet another amazing architectural achievement. This one is built to resemble a roller coaster. Small golf carts drive you around the various bars and restaurants outside. We stop for drinks at one of the bars, located on what can only be described as a pier. Then it's up to the 24th floor for more rum and soda, after which we cab back to the hotel for a buffet dinner in Olives. There is lobster, smoked salmon, lamb, veal, etc., and a bottle of 1998 Norton Merlot from California.

15.2.02. I have a large breakfast at 8.30 once again, as the buffet is so tempting. I must have put on at least half a stone so far this week. At 10, we go for a speedboat ride, although the sea is quite choppy. We follow the extensive line of the beaches, and notice the staggering amount of development taking place. There are hotels cropping up seemingly everywhere. Later, I receive a phone call from Bombay. the *Indian Times* wants to run a profile of me, and will arrange an interview for when I arrive tomorrow.

At 2.30, we take a late lunch – Arabian kebabs at the Beach Restaurant, accompanied by a very good bottle of Comte Anthony Provence rosé 2000.

After lunch, Toby goes off paragliding, and I spend an entertaining hour struggling to receive a fax from the UK. I eventually get through to the girl in charge of faxes, who tells me, somewhat to my incredulity, that she will connect me to the Golf Club, who will be able to give me further information. Needless to say, it never does reach me.

Later, I meet Ian Senior, head of the local hospitality training college for all hotel staff, over drinks in the bar. We go to dinner in the Bierkeller at the Jumerai Beach: liver with rösti, with plenty of German beer. The evening is rounded off with drinks in the hotel nightclub.

In summary, I can say that Dubai has a great future for tourism. It's very clean, has some top hotels, and a range of different ethnic foods, but it is terribly expensive. A beer can cost £6–8, wine is £30+++ a bottle, while a two-course dinner can easily come in at £60+ a head. Our hotel bill for two rooms over six nights, including food and drink for three persons, came to £5,000.

16.2.02. We breakfast at 9 a.m. There's a little wind and some slight cloud, but the temperature is still 24°C. Clare and Toby are returning to London today on the Emirates flight at 2.45 p.m.

At 11.30, I check out, and am chauffeured to the airport for my Emirates flight EK 502 to Bombay. I'm in First Class, seat 2B, and have a beer in the First Class lounge before boarding.

Once on the plane, we are given Lanson Black Label prior to takeoff. When we are in the air, we are served with a delicious

Duval-Leroy Cuvée du Roy 1991, and then a choice of marinated lamb, stir-fried chicken, chilli and rice. The flight time is 2½ hours, and we arrive in Bombay at 5 p.m. local time.

I am met by the foreign wine imports manager of the Indage Group, who takes me to drinks at the chairman's wonderful house. We drink Chivas Regal on the large terrace overlooking the ocean.

Afterwards, I check in at the Taj President Hotel, room 1715 on the top floor. It's a good room with a superb view over the city. I have a couple of drinks in the Library Bar, and then go for a late dinner at 10.15 in the hotel's Thai Pavilion Restaurant. A huge portion of indifferent pad thai noodles with chicken (the noodles, oddly, are totally encased in an omelette, rather than mixed with the eggs) is accompanied by Kingfisher beer.

My God, I love India! It doesn't seem to have changed much in all the years I have been visiting. The evocative smell of poverty and spices as you leave the airport is reminiscent of a Wellsian trip back in time. As the song goes, 'The rich get rich and the poor get poorer'. There is, however, the distinct evidence of an aspirant middle class forming, whose higher-toned lifestyle might be indicated by the choice of a glass of Chardonnay where once it would have been Kingfisher beer.

It is quite fantastic to see the explosion of Western-style restaurants and clubs. There are Italian, French, Thai and Chinese places that serve no Indian food at all. Conran-type restaurants and brasseries pop up, there are wine bars, cocktail lounges, cigar bars, even a Calvados bar. Everywhere, one sees the British- or American-educated second- and third-generation wealthy in their Ferraris and Armani suits.

Vikrant Chougule, the chairman's son, has brought another dimension to clubbing in Bombay (or Mumbai, as one should now call it) with the opening of Athena, all smoked glass and chrome, with a stepped membership scheme divided into Silver, Gold and Platinum, allowing access to private lounges. Membership fees range from $500 to $10,000, with waiting lists at all levels.

Still, though, the poverty prevails, with hordes sleeping in the streets and a certain number found dead every day. This is the unacceptable side of it all. A further expansion of the shanty towns, an inadequate birth registration system, poor education and a failing health programme all play their parts. Even so, it all adds up, perversely enough, to a hypnotic country with a magnetism that draws you back, still inexplicable after all these years. I very much doubt the underlying culture will ever change. How can you change a country of a billion people from all cultures, religions and levels of education?

17.2.02. I decide to have a late breakfast in my room. At 10 a.m., I telephone room service, and am greeted with 'Good morning, Mr Benson, what would you like?' I order an omelette and black coffee, and what arrives is – an iron and ironing-board! I call again, and am greeted as before, followed now by 'What more can I send you?' As I have a perverse sense of humour, I reply that my breakfast of an iron and ironing-board having now been delivered, I would like a knife and fork. The response is, 'I will send them to you straight away.' A classic!

This is Day 1 of the Indage Wine Festival at the Roof Garden on top of the Taj President Hotel, lasting from 2 p.m. to 2 a.m. The temperature is 35°C, with humidity of 92%. In the opening session, from two till four in the afternoon, I meet a whole succession of hotel food and beverage managers and restaurateurs. There are interviews with TV and the national press. A seemingly endless finger buffet of Thai and Indian food is served. Forty wines from France, Australia, Chile, Argentina, South Africa, Spain and Italy are on show, as well as a good range of Indian wines.

The evening session turns into what is effectively a party for the trendy Mumbai set (over a thousand people); there is grape-treading, as well as live music and dancing until 2 a.m. The whole event is a huge success. I slip away to the bar at about 10 for a large whisky, and then to bed. I'm far too ancient to keep up with this lot.

18.2.02. The day begins with an excellent breakfast of scrambled eggs on toast with bacon, sweet lime juice and coffee – not in my room, I may add.

Head chef, Taj President Hotel, Bombay

I decide to go for a walk along the ocean front, after which I have a light lunch in the indifferent Italian trattoria restaurant at the hotel. Afterwards, wandering around the hotel lobby shops, I buy ten postcards and request twenty stamps for UK airmail, only to be told that the shop that sells the postcards does not sell stamps. Stamps are available next door, at a tiny kiosk that sells nothing but stamps. Apparently nobody told the shopkeeper they were adhesive, and he insists on taking the postcards and spreading them out on the counter. Then he produces a plastic board, and spends 28 minutes gluing each one on to the postcard. I don't have the heart to tell him he could just have moistened the back. There was glue everywhere, much of it all over the counter, as well as his hands. The stamps evidently kept sticking to him instead of the postcards. All in all, another classic episode.

I take a local taxi to the shopping centre. The car, like most in Mumbai, is a very old Ambassador, seemingly only held together with string and glue. There are no lights on it at all, except inside, where there is a two-foot-long neon light (the sort of thing that could only happen in India). Shopping is very cheap at a rate of about 75 rupees to the pound. A pair of trousers is about £10, shirts £3 each.

Back at the hotel, I have a large J&B whisky and soda, before dinner at 8.30 at the Konkan Restaurant, which specialises in classic south-west Indian cuisine. The meal is specially prepared for me by Solomon, previously head chef of the Hotel Ananda: two types of poppadums, with dried chilli and cumin; two dips, one of red chilli and coconut, the other of coconut and mint; a superb soup of crabmeat, vegetables and stock; and wonderful king prawn miri, with garlic and black pepper. All the dishes are decanted into a large serving dish lined with a palm leaf. A glass of draught Kingfisher is slightly flat, so I order a pint bottle (65cl), on the label of which is written a motto, 'The King of Good Times'.

The food continues with: lobster malai, a very mild, creamy dish, delicately flavoured with cumin, coconut cream and fish sauce, served with basmati rice; a rice pancake with a difference; and Mangalore fish curry, another very mild dish made with Goan vinegar and coconut. The fish in the last is pomfret, which has an interesting flavour, but one needs to be aware of the bones. I discover later that the chef thought I would prefer non-spicy food. How wrong could he be? I wonder. It all comes to a total of 2,822 rupees – about £40.

19.2.02. I breakfast at 9 a.m. on a superb omelette accompanied by sweet lime juice.

Trying on the trousers I bought yesterday, I discover that the Indian 36-inch waist is more like a 34 (or have I put on weight?), and so I take a taxi to the pantaloon shop past the Seaview Hotel. This is a sight to behold, a run-down shack in the centre of the slums overlooking a rubbish tip. That's style for you. It turns out the trouser shop has no more of the larger size in the colour I want, but a slightly different colour attracts a price increase of some 200 rupees. 'Why?' I ask, but the question is met only with blank expressions and heads nodding from side to side, so I pay with a good grace. The taxi back to the hotel is half the price of the journey there. Why?

I have a wine tasting and presentation at 1 p.m. at Indigo, a very small but trendy French restaurant. I arrive promptly, only to be told it has been inexplicably postponed until tomorrow. I have their typical lunch of duck confit with pasta, accompanied by lethal sangria containing wine, port, vermouth, tequila and many other ingredients.

At 4, I am at the Taj Mahal Hotel for a full presentation to all the food and beverage staff and the general manager, Manek Patel. The tasting and talk last until 7, after which I repair to the Athena Club for a tasting and dinner with various hotel managers and their food and beverage staff, twenty in all. I leave at around 1 a.m.

I can't resist these extracts from the local daily newspaper:

'Lose 8 kg in a month, 5' to 15' in one hour. Safe, guaranteed, stay young and slim forever. Dr Damani: Slim N Slender 3012376.'

'Lose/gain weight, breast enhancement/firming, hair problem, complexion, pimple, wrinkles, black circles, eye shades, scars, frackles treatment at your house. For orders/details – 9821118845.'

'TELESCOPES BINOCULAR Behold the ring of mighty Saturn. The ancient craters of the moon. Read the newspaper one km away. Astra Sales. 6372260.'

'Ladies/gents feeling lonely? Make life happy and enjoyable!!! Meet new friends daily (females free membership) (100% confidential) Sweety/Dolly/Reshmi/Pinky 6707868/6716644/6710495/6718973.'

'EXCLUSIVE CLUBS Have a ball anytime!! Exotic international concepts at your doorstep. Call now @ 95250–349272. Admissions restricted for polished erudites only.'

I could go on forever.

20.2.02. The day kicks off with a 10.30 meeting with the Indage Group, after which I go to the postponed tasting at the Indigo Restaurant. A fashionable pan-Pacific menu has been devised, consisting of smoked salmon, followed by chicken with balsamic sauce, mashed olive potatoes and glazed carrots, and the wines served are Hardy's Semillon-Chardonnay and Shiraz-Cabernet 2000, Louis Latour Chardonnay de l'Ardèche 1999, their 1998 Chablis and the 1er cru Chablis of the same vintage, 2000 Santa Carolina Merlot, a 1997 Beaune 1er cru and 1996 Château Reynella Shiraz.

Back at the hotel, there is a message. Manek Patel has invited me for dinner at 8.30. Prior to that, he takes me on a tour of the hotel, which is one of the bastions of old Bombay. The old part has been restored magnificently. We have a look at the Chambers, a very exclusive members-only section with the air of a Pall Mall or St James's club.

Dinner is in the hotel's new French restaurant, Zodiac, which has the style of a top Michelin-starred establishment. A couple of large Glenmorangies precede prawn feuilleté, Brie soufflé and Arabian lobster, which are accompanied by Léon Beyer's 1998 Pinot Gris. The digestif is Hennessy XO. The food is typically French, well presented but lacking in finesse. I shudder to think what the bill for the two of us must come to.

21.2.02. Breakfast at 9 a.m. is overcooked poached eggs on toast with bacon and coffee, after which I spend a quiet morning working in my room.

I take lunch in the Thai Pavilion restaurant at the hotel: stir-fried chicken in oyster sauce with soft noodles, and a large Kingfisher beer. Between 4 and 5, I have a massage from a bruiser of a man who nearly cripples me.

At 7 p.m. I am at the theatre, the Homi Bhabha Auditorium, to see a production of Medea, a Scottish adaptation of Euripides' text. The whole scenario is bizarre, a modern auditorium similar to the National Theatre built plumb in the middle of the most squalid Mumbai slums. The Scottish actors are speaking in the thickest accents imaginable. Even I have immense difficulty understanding them, so I can only guess how the Indian audience must be reacting. (Also, there is a fair amount of foul language.) Still, it's an hour and a half of fine acting, and the theatre is 90% full.

I take a taxi back to the hotel, and have a J&B and soda in the Library Bar, prior to dinner at the hotel's Konkan Indian Café. With a large Kingfisher on hand, I start with chicken pepper fry with onions, a medium-hot and very well-balanced dish containing huge slices of garlic. There are also poppadums with two dips, one of red chilli and one of green chilli, both made with dried chillies and both excellent. Rawas is Indian salmon fillet, deep-fried and dry (a little like British fried fish), while the sauce from the mutton masala ends up all over my shirt and trousers, and will provide a challenge for the hotel laundry. A small, very dry, chapati-style naan adds to the impression of a rather clumsy and commercial approach. The bill comes to 1,126 rupees (about £16).

22.2.02. Breakfast today is complimentary on account of my checking out tomorrow for the Indage Group weekend wine festival at the Narayangaon Winery, three hours east of Pune.

Later, I go to the Jewel of India for a buffet lunch consisting of chicken in a masala sauce, fried fish, and mutton in a delicious dark gravy, served with a large draught Kingfisher.

In the evening, at 9.30, I host a Laurent-Perrier dinner for thirteen people at the Athena Club. We drink the NV Brut with a prawn starter, and then the Rosé with both the soup and a chicken main course, finishing with the stunning 1990 Grand Siècle with a strawberry dessert. I am seated next to the charming vice-president of Oberoi Hotels. Dinner only finishes at around 1.30 a.m.

I am taken back to the hotel in a white Rolls-Royce, registration number 007.

23.2.02. My alarm call comes at 6 a.m. After picking up some visiting journalists from the U.K., we embark on the six-hour drive to the winery, taking the old road for reasons best known to the driver, armed with provisions and drinks. It's incredibly hot, 35°C+.

We make it to the winery by 2 p.m. and are regaled with the sight of a full procession with ox carts and local musicians, as well as a lovely lunch buffet – chicken, fish, lamb and rice. The *Indian Times* interviews me for a full profile with photographs. This whole festival is again reminiscent of an Ascot garden party, except that it's happening in the middle of the Sahydri mountains. Later, there is grape-stomping to live music, which attracts around 300 people.

At 6 p.m. we leave, and set out on the three-hour drive to Pune. There, we check into the Meridien Hotel, which is very agreeable. I have been assigned the very spacious room 837. I go straight to the rooftop terrace poolside bar for the first of many large pre-dinner drinks. Dinner on the terrace comprises mixed kebabs of lamb, fish, prawns and chicken, accompanied by Kingfisher, and I am able to retire painlessly at 1 a.m.

24.2.02. I breakfast at 8.30, asking once again why it seems impossible to get one's scrambled eggs served on toast. I give up.

At 10, we head off for a tour of Pune. Our first stop is the Tribal Museum, where we are given a fascinating talk for over an hour by a renowned expert on tribes and tribal life in India. He has written over twenty books on the subject, and has lived with many of the tribes in question, of whom there are more than sixty left, with their own lands and culture.

After this, we are taken to the Agha Khan Palace, where Gandhi was once interned. We are given a full guided tour, ending with an affecting performance by a wonderful lady who sings two unaccompanied songs. Then we stop by at the synagogue, but have to be content with photos only as it's closed.

Lunch is at the home of Karen, who is rated as one of the finest cooks in India. She also does cookery writing and appears on television. Her apartment has its own kitchen garden. The whole scenario is like being in Spain or Portugal or some similar European country. Her buffet comprises smoked salmon, ham, and Goan hotpot, which contains a sort of chorizo cooked with potatoes, onions, etc., all served with beers and wine.

Afterwards, we take the three-hour drive back to Mumbai, where I collect my suitcase from the hotel and proceed to the airport, arriving at 12.30 a.m....

25.2.02. I check in to the Air Lanka flight to Colombo for Male, business class. One is only allowed one free drink in the Business Class lounge, a Scotch and soda, after which the second must be bought. The flight is scheduled for 3.45 a.m. Who should I meet in the lounge but the cast of the Scottish production of *Medea* on their way back to Heathrow...

We board at 3.30 and take off on time. It's a 2½ hour flight. I'm in seat 3C, despite having had my preferred seat 2C reserved for me in the UK. I eat an omelette and drink some Lanson Black Label champagne before sleeping. We arrive in Colombo at 6.30 a.m. local time, which is 30 minutes ahead of Mumbai.

I have coffee and croissants in the Business Class lounge before joining Air Lanka flight UL 545 to Male. We take off at

8.40, and more Black Label is served, along with croissants, fruit and coffee. The flight takes 90 minutes, arriving in Male at 11.30 local time, another hour ahead.

A speedboat takes me on the 15-minute crossing to the Soneva Gili resort. After a swim, I lunch with the genial general manager and his wife, both Swiss, and meet with the food and beverage manager to arrange the week's staff wine training programme. In the afternoon, I go for a massage, during which I promptly fall asleep.

Later, I shower and change, and walk across the sands on duckboards to the most spectacular circular glass-bottomed bar. The temperature is 32°C, tempered by a gentle breeze. Everybody is presented with a large tricycle for getting around on, but one ride turns out to be enough. I think I'd rather walk. I drink a couple of Pusser's dark rums with lime and soda, gazing out on to the most idyllic view imaginable. Then I wander over to the sand-floored restaurant area. It's all open and quite wonderful to sit outside, hearing nothing but the waves lapping around you. I dine on a superb piece of beef served with a red wine reduction sauce and al dente vegetables, and accompany it with a glass of 1999 L A Cetto Cabernet from Mexico, which is drinking very well. Back at the bar, I round things off with a nightcap, and collapse into bed at 11.

26.2.02. I awake to a gorgeous sunrise over the ocean. The bedrooms are windowed on three sides. What a view to start the day with! Breakfast at 9 begins with passion-fruit juice squeezed while you wait, followed by omelette '*à sa moment*', and toast with honey, which is collected from a huge honeycomb.

Between 10 and 12, we start the staff training programme from scratch. It is something of a challenge to explain viticulture and vinification to a team of young Maldivians who have never seen anything other than these sandy islands that are barely above sea level. However, being young and enthusiastic, they learn fast, for all that their religion precludes the drinking of alcohol. Then, from 12.30 to 1.30, I have a gentle massage while listening to the waves lapping the beach. Lunch is yellowtail fish with vegetables and noodles, accompanied by a delicious bottle of 2000 Château du Galoupet rosé. The second set of staff lectures occupies the period between 4 and 5.30.

Soneva Gili resort, February 2002

As the resort is still in the process of being completed, they are bringing in a vast number of 20ft-plus palm trees, which are being planted by hand. The process is thoroughly intriguing, and a joy to see.

At 8, I go to the bar for drinks – Pusser's rum with fresh lime juice and soda, a very good drink in hot climates. For dinner, there are giant prawns, kingfish and al dente vegetables (carrots, corn, potatoes, mini-asparagus spears and broccoli). I drink the 1999 Hamilton Russell South African Chardonnay, and then follow it up with a large bourbon nightcap, before retiring peacefully at midnight.

27.2.02. It is unusual to say the least actually to look forward to waking up, but the view that awaits you is a pleasure. Especially when one then eats a healthy breakfast, with fruit and cereal and freshly squeezed fruit juice of your choice.

I have staff training from 10.30 to 12.30. The topic is vinification, which is quite difficult for the staff to understand, considering they have never seen a vineyard, let alone a fermentation tank. Lunch to follow is a Thai green chicken curry with rice and Tiger beer. The weather is closing in dramatically, with dark clouds gathering, followed by torrential rain. I take further staff training classes from 4 till 6.

At 6.45, I host a tutored tasting and food pairing for eight guests, young CEOs from the USA and UK. There is an exclusive club called the YPO (Young Presidents' Organisation), of which they are all members. The wines shown are: Léon Beyer Pinot Blanc 1999; Bouchard Aîné Rully 1998; Rockfield Semillon/Sauvignon 2000 from Australia; and Schloss Halbturn Beerenauslese 1995 from Austria. They are paired, respectively, with an Indian chicken (murgh) dish; lobster; tuna carpaccio; and Gorgonzola. It's all very interesting, and great fun.

I then have dinner with the general manager and his wife: a green salad in a superb balsamic dressing, and chicken in a lightly curried coconut sauce. We drink Don David Chardonnay 1999, from Michel Torino of Argentina. I am in bed at midnight.

28.2.02. Awakening at 8 a.m., I find it's still very overcast. For breakfast, I have a Sri Lankan pancake filled with ham and mushrooms, something like a galette.

Today's staff briefing includes a wine nosing, but no tasting because of their religious precepts. It's quite amusing to hold a tasting by colour and nose only. Notwithstanding this, there are some very commendable observations about the various fruits associated with each grape variety. The Gamay reminds them of strawberries, the Chardonnay of peach, the Sauvignon of apple and the Australian Semillon of mango. One needs to bear in mind that this is the first time they have ever smelt wine. Budding Masters of Wine, surely!

The massage I opt for is listed as 'Coma', concentrating on the head and neck only. It turns out to be a wholly apt description as I eventually wander out to lunch not knowing or caring what day or time it is. I shall, however, remember the excellent grilled reef fish, similar to mullet, which goes perfectly with a Sancerre rosé, Domaine la Moussière.

The afternoon then seems to drift carelessly by, until I am brought back to my senses by a swim in the ocean, followed by a power shower.

6.45 p.m. is cocktail training time. This is great fun as the bar staff have had some prior training, but need guidance on the presentation and ingredients of certain drinks. I must say we did manage to produce a delicious piña colada and a wickedly dry Martini (without the stuffed olive), plus my own recipe for Rum Blood Cooler, which contains a large measure of Pusser's dark rum with ice, fresh lime juice and soda, a delightfully cooling concoction – hic!

Dinner consists of chicken and noodle soup, which is a bit heavy on the coconut but delicious nonetheless, followed by grilled salmon with paprika noodles. With this, I drink a (slightly unclean) 1999 Clifford Bay Sauvignon from New Zealand. I retire to bed at 11.

1.3.02. I get up at 7, and sit outside watching a magical sunrise in clear skies over the Indian Ocean. After an 8 o'clock breakfast of omelette, toast and honey, I have staff training on spirits and liqueurs from 9 till 11. The weather is once again very sunny and hot.

After the session, at 12.30, I go for another hour-long head and neck massage. Lunch is chicken satay and noodles, with Tiger beer followed by Provence rosé.

At 4 p.m. a cyclone hits the resort, cutting off all the electricity. There is torrential rain and very high winds, which cause the ocean to erupt into my open sitting-room area – quite a dramatic sight! By 6, though, all is calm again, with blue skies and just a gentle breeze.

Another tasting and food-pairing session has been scheduled for 6.30, with eight guests. We serve the Rully 1998, the Pinot Blanc 1999, the Don David Chardonnay 2000, and also Rockfield Shiraz-Cabernet 2000, a 1998 Chinon, and Michel Torino Malbec 2000. Afterwards, I have dinner with the general manager of the other resort, Soneva Fushi, and his wife, as well as the executive chef. The Michel Torino Malbec makes a reappearance, perfectly partnering fillet of beef.

I am in bed at midnight.

2.3.02. It evidently rained heavily during the night, with strong winds, which is most unusual for this time of the year. At 9, I have a breakfast of scrambled eggs and ham, with orange juice and coffee.

At 10.15, I take the speedboat to Male Airport, where I check into Business Class (no First on this flight), seat 3F on the four-hour flight EK 810 to Dubai. It's a dry lounge, so one must be content with water. We take off at 11.30 local time.

Duval-Leroy Fleur de Champagne is served, before a soggy salad of prawns and a scallop, followed by excellent chicken biryani. The film is *The Mummy Returns*, which I fall asleep halfway through. We arrive in Dubai at 3 p.m. local time (back one hour).

My next flight is EK 005 to Heathrow Terminal 3, and I'm in seat 2B. We are delayed by half an hour to 5.40. The Emirates

First Class lounge in Dubai is huge and extremely luxurious, with leather armchairs and sofas, a running hot and cold buffet 24 hours a day, and a full bar, which is however oddly lacking in champagne. The young Arab man at the reception desk asks me whether I will take a large envelope to London for him. Naturally, I decline.

We take off at 6, and are served with Dom Pérignon 1993 and caviare, followed by Moroccan lamb and rice. I sleep for three hours, and we eventually arrive at Heathrow at 9.30 p.m. local time (3.30 a.m., according to my internal clock).

This has been another exhausting and fascinating trip. At the conclusion of the last few years travelling I, my liver and constitution feel just about ready for an extended holiday in a health farm.

2160433R00219

Printed in Great Britain
by Amazon.co.uk, Ltd.,
Marston Gate.